# Nietzsche's Philosophy
# of the Eternal Recurrence
# of the Same

# Nietzsche's Philosophy of the Eternal Recurrence of the Same

## Karl Löwith

Translated by J. Harvey Lomax

Foreword by Bernd Magnus

UNIVERSITY OF CALIFORNIA PRESS

*Berkeley / Los Angeles / London*

This book is a print-on-demand volume. It is manufactured using toner in place of ink. Type and images may be less sharp than the same material seen in traditionally printed University of California editions.

University of California Press
Berkeley and Los Angeles, California

University of California Press
London, England

**Library of Congress Cataloging-in-Publication Data**
Löwith, Karl, 1897–1973.
[Nietzsches Philosophie der ewigen Wiederkehr des Gleichen. English]
Nietzsche's philosophy of the eternal recurrence of the same / Karl Löwith; translated by J. Harvey Lomax; foreword by Bernd Magnus.
    p.   cm.
Includes bibliographical references and index.
ISBN 0-520-06519-0 (cloth: alk. paper)
1. Nietzsche, Friedrich Wilhelm, 1844–1900. 2. Eternal return. 3. Resemblance (Philosophy) I. Title.
B3318.E88L63   1996
193—dc20                             96–19802
                                                 CIP

Printed in the United States of America

The paper used in this publication meets the minimum requirements of ANSI/NISO Z39.48 ( R 1997 ) ( Permanence of paper )

# Contents

ACKNOWLEDGMENTS     ix

FOREWORD TO THE ENGLISH
     TRANSLATION     xi

TRANSLATOR'S INTRODUCTION     xix

NIETZSCHE'S PHILOSOPHY
OF THE ETERNAL RECURRENCE
OF THE SAME

Foreword to the First Edition     3

Foreword to the Second Edition     7

1
Nietzsche's Philosophy: A System in Aphorisms     11

2
The Division of Nietzsche's Writings into Periods     21

3
The Unifying Fundamental Idea in Nietzsche's Philosophy     27

     The Liberation from "Thou Shalt" to
     "I Will"     27

     The Liberation from the "I Will" to
     the "I Am" of the Child of the World     36

The Death of God and the Prophecy
of Nihilism                                                    36

"Noon and Eternity," or the
Prophecy of the Eternal Recurrence                            55

    The Reversal of the Will to the Nothing
    into the Willing of the Eternal Recurrence    56

    The Eternal Recurrence in the Parable of
    *Zarathustra*                                 60

    The Double Equation for the Allegory of
    the Eternal Recurrence                        82

    The Problematic Unity in the Discord of
    the Double Equation                           94

4
The Anti-Christian Repetition of Antiquity on the
Peak of Modernity                                            108

5
"How One Becomes What One Is" in the Idea of the
Eternal Recurrence                                           122

6
The Problematic Connection between the Existence
of Man and the Being of the World in the History of
Modern Philosophy                                            137

7
The Eternal Recurrence of the Same and the Repetition
of the Selfsame                                              156

8
The Critical Yardstick for Nietzsche's Experiment           174

APPENDIX: ON THE HISTORY OF THE
INTERPRETATION OF NIETZSCHE
(1894–1954)                                                  195

REFERENCES                                                   231

AUTHOR'S NOTES                                               233

TRANSLATOR'S NOTES                                           259

INDEX OF NAMES                                               273

# Acknowledgments

The preparation of this volume was made possible by a grant from the Translations Program of the National Endowment for the Humanities, an independent Federal agency, and by grants from the Earhart Foundation and the University of Memphis. The Bradley Foundation munificently provided support for the Translator's Introduction, and Hillel Fradkin merits special thanks.

Robin Cackett made literally thousands of helpful suggestions and translated all the French passages. Werner Dannhauser generously contributed in many ways, both to inspire the project and to improve the final product. Not only in general, but especially for this translation, the boundless friendship and unstinting support of David N. Cox, William R. Marty, and James D. King in Memphis, of Hans-Georg Gadamer, Käte Gadamer-Lekebusch, and Rüdiger Völkel in Heidelberg, and of Heinrich and Wiebke Meier in Munich proved indispensable. The translator's debt to Joseph Cropsey can hardly be overestimated, and George Anastaplo, Lawrence Berns, and Ralph A. Rossum also deserve acknowledgment for their important assistance. Sharon Beasley and Laura Ebke kindly typed and proofread manuscripts. Ed Dimendberg of the University of California Press earned a special place in heaven for his superhuman patience, without which the present book would not exist.

# Foreword to the
# English Translation

The best of all places to hide, typically, is in plain sight.
Heidegger once called this "the inconspicuousness of the obvious."
I call attention to this provocative suggestion because for many decades I have been at a loss to explain why there has been no English
translation of Karl Löwith's magisterial Nietzsche study, *Nietzsches
Philosophie der ewigen Wiederkehr des Gleichen*,[1] while during these
same decades the ruminations of virtually every European Nietzsche-
scribbler—from the insightful to the laughable—have been translated
and discussed. In the meantime, Löwith's Nietzsche remained shrouded
in silence. The reason now seems both obvious and inconspicuous to
me. It is entirely political. Löwith was a Jew, in early self-imposed exile
from Nazi Germany (thanks to the Rockefeller Foundation); he was
strikingly clearheaded about National Socialism at the very beginning
of its hegemony in Germany; and he was an apostate student of Martin
Heidegger who saw in Heidegger's unpublished Nietzsche studies as
well as in his other writings an *intrinsic* affinity to Nazism.[2] It has taken
Anglophone scholarship more than half a century to recapture Löwith's
insight.

1. *Wiederkunft* in the 1935 edition, *Wiederkehr* in the 1956 and subsequent editions.
2. This may also help to explain why some of Löwith's other books were translated
into English or first published in English and were well received—e.g., *Meaning in History* (Chicago: University of Chicago Press, 1949); *Nature, History, and Existentialism*
(Evanston, Ill.: Northwestern University Press, 1966); *From Hegel to Nietzsche* (New York:
Holt, Rinehart and Winston, 1964)—while his incisive 1953 Heidegger study (*Heidegger: Denker in dürftiger Zeit* [Frankfurt am Main: S. Fischer Verlag]) was not translated until 1995 ("Heidegger: Thinker in a Destitute Time," in the volume of selections

As J. Harvey Lomax points out in his Introduction to this volume, it took considerable courage for Gerhard Bahlsen, owner of the press "Die Runde," to publish Löwith's *Nietzsches Philosophie der ewigen Wiederkunft des Gleichen* (*Nietzsche's Philosophy of the Eternal Recurrence of the Same*) in 1935, in the capital of Hitler's Germany. By 1935 several other German presses and journals had already begun to refuse to publish Löwith's work, including *Kantstudien*. Indeed, the entire Appendix to *Nietzsches Philosophie der ewigen Wiederkunft des Gleichen* could not be published in the 1935 edition, primarily because it consisted of twelve book reviews, each one of which incisively critiqued the author under review, including Alfred Baeumler, a Nazi Party hack and third-rate scholar whose 1931 publication *Nietzsche: Der Philosoph und Politiker* ("Nietzsche: The Philosopher and Politician") had become a staple of the Party's propaganda machine and made Baeumler, in effect, the "official" interpreter of Nietzsche for the Nazis. To appreciate the fully noxious aroma in Germany when Löwith's classic work was written, it should also be recalled that Nietzsche's sister, Elisabeth Förster-Nietzsche, was still alive at the time that Löwith submitted his manuscript to Bahlsen from Rome. There were very few Germans who rivaled Elisabeth in her admiration for Hitler and the Party, and none who worked as diligently as did she to accommodate Nietzsche's writings to Nazi ideology.

To be sure, while much of this may help to explain the initial lack of influence of Löwith's book in Germany, none of this explains why the English-speaking community should have ignored Löwith's Nietzsche book for so long. Indeed, should not his status as a virtual persona non grata in Nazi Germany have recommended him to us instead?

There are many possible and competing explanations for this incongruity. The most obvious one is that Löwith's book does not rise to the stature of other already-translated Nietzsche studies—for example, Karl Jaspers's *Nietzsche und das Christentum* (1938, translated as *Nietzsche and Christianity*, 1961), his *Nietzsche* (1936, translated 1965), Georg Simmel's *Schopenhauer und Nietzsche* (1907, translated as *Schopenhauer and Nietzsche*, 1986), or Hans Vaihinger's *Die Philosophie des Als Ob* (1911, translated as *The Philosophy of "As If,"* 1924), to mention only some of the better-known translated works that deal with Nietzsche. There is no a priori way to settle such an important

from Löwith published as *Martin Heidegger and European Nihilism,* ed. Richard Wolin, trans. Gary Steiner [New York: Columbia University Press]).

question. The reader must study each author's translated Nietzsche commentary, compare it with this Löwith volume, and then decide.

My own hunch is strikingly different. Just as his Jewish ancestry functioned as a defeating condition, in Germany, for serious study of *Nietzsche's Philosophy of the Eternal Recurrence of the Same,* his well-known differences with Heidegger and especially their differences about Nietzsche played a similar role in the United States. Heidegger's influence among English-speaking professors of philosophy who are (mistakenly) characterized as "Continental philosophers"[3] has been nothing short of extraordinary from the 1960s until today. It is no exaggeration to say that Heidegger is widely regarded among SPEPies[4] as the most important philosopher of our times. For those of us who have witnessed the recent revival of an old controversy concerning Heidegger's relationship to the Nazis, the zealousness and idolatry of American Heideggerians is difficult to overestimate. Given this milieu, Löwith's Nietzsche study drew limited—and often unsympathetic—attention.

What, then, recommends *Nietzsche's Philosophy of the Eternal Recurrence of the Same?* Until the 1930s, Nietzsche was almost universally regarded—in Germany and beyond its borders—primarily as a literary phenomenon. He had been elevated to the status of a prophet by Stefan George and his circle of poets, and was considered a critic of culture by others. His initial, most lasting, and most prominent appropriation, however, was literary: André Gide in France; Gottfried Benn, Robert Musil, and Hermann Hesse in Germany; the Russian symbolists Vyacheslav Ivanov, Andrei Belyi, and Valeri Bryusov; William Butler Yeats and George Bernard Shaw (whose *Man and Superman* debuted on the London stage in 1903) in England; and August Strindberg in

3. There is a double mistake made in speaking of Anglophones as "Continental philosophers." The first is that virtually all are teachers, who happen to make their living teaching philosophy courses. It is no more obvious that the approximately ten thousand persons who teach philosophy courses for a living in the United States deserve to be called "philosophers" than would be the case if we started to call thirty thousand professors of English "writers." The second mistake is that Anglophone "Continental philosophers" are not Continental either. They are persons who typically earn their keep by teaching the works of those who *are* Continental philosophers. If there is any confusion about this, I know of no Anglophone "Continental philosopher" who is taught on the Continent. It would be just as misleading to call an Anglophone philosopher who taught Chinese philosophy—but was not Chinese—a "Chinese philosopher."

4. I refer to members of the Society for Phenomenology and Existential Philosophy (of which I, too, am a member), numbering approximately eleven hundred—10 percent of all teachers of philosophy in these United States.

Sweden. There were other appropriations of Nietzsche as well, of course, from Georg Brandes and Gabriele D'Annunzio to the musical tributes of Gustav Mahler, Frederick Delius, and Richard Strauss.

To the extent that Nietzsche figured at all specifically as a *philosopher*, however, he was lumped together with Georg Simmel, Ludwig Klages, and Henri Bergson during the early part of this century; or else he was dismissed by his contemporaries altogether—by Wilhelm Dilthey, for example. With the exception of Martin Heidegger's Nietzsche lectures delivered from 1936 to 1940—and published in 1961— no one other than Jaspers and Löwith was able to argue successfully that Nietzsche was, first and foremost, a philosopher.

Jaspers stressed Nietzsche's writings as a sort of philosophical activity rather than a congealed body of theses or doctrines, an existential demonstration that all alleged certainties could be hurled into a vortex of endless reflection, a vortex from which no fixed doctrine, teaching, or thesis could survive unchallenged. In stark contrast, Heidegger argued the by now familiar thesis that Nietzsche was the last metaphysician of the West, an inverse Platonist in whose writings the last logical consequences of Platonism are exhausted, all of which are a consequence of the forgetfulness of Being (*Sein*) and the transformation of "truth," through Plato—from the self-disclosure of beings in their Being, to the correspondence of beliefs to states of affairs. Within Heidegger's metahistory of philosophy, Nietzsche's "will to power" became the essence (*essentia*) of beings whose existence (*existentia*) took the form of "the eternal recurrence of the same." In an earlier, Kantian vocabulary, "will to power" could be regarded as noumenal reality, as the thing in itself, and "eternal recurrence" could be regarded as mere appearances (phenomena).

Karl Löwith's *Nietzsche's Philosophy of the Eternal Recurrence of the Same* shares with Jaspers and Heidegger the impulse and achievement of situating Nietzsche squarely in the philosophical rather than the literary tradition. That is where the similarities end, however. Löwith's extraordinary book wears its thesis on its sleeve, on its title: Nietzsche is a philosopher and, specifically, he is the philosopher of "the eternal recurrence of the same." Moreover, Löwith situates the genre of Nietzsche's philosophy in the title and the subtitle of his first chapter, "Nietzsche's Philosophy: A System in Aphorisms." By privileging the doctrine (*Lehre*: teaching) of eternal recurrence as the central organizing concept of Nietzsche's "system in aphorisms," Löwith departs markedly and brilliantly from Heidegger's attempts to make the doctrines of the will to power and eternal recurrence compatible; and he departs as well from Jaspers's tendency to eschew the very possibility that a coherent philosophical position lurks beneath Nietzsche's aphorisms.

As the reader will see, Löwith surfaces with enormous clarity the paradox he believes he finds latent within Nietzsche's doctrine of eternal recurrence itself. On the one hand, argues Löwith, eternal recurrence is a cosmological theory replete with a history he traces back at least to Heraclitus. In all of its formulations, however, it suggests that, roughly, a finite number of states of the world is destined to unfold in time—which is infinite, not finite. Hence, given the finite number of possible states of the world and the infinity of time, any single state of the world must recur. More than that, it must recur eternally: the eternal recurrence of the same. At the same time, however, Nietzsche's aphorisms also exhort an imperative, namely the injunction to live in such a way that you would gladly will the eternal recurrence of your life—without change or emendation—over and over again.

The cosmological version, which Löwith sometimes characterizes as "a physical metaphysics," would on the surface seem to be incompatible with the ethical imperative to choose to live each moment in such a way that you could will its eternal recurrence. How could one will a state of affairs which—given the cosmological account—will have to occur no matter what one wills? Is there not a fatalism implicit in the doctrine of the eternal recurrence of the same which renders any imperative impotent? Even the decision to live in such a way that you would gladly will the eternal recurrence of each and every moment of your life would seem to be predestined, as would its rejection or indifference. How can one *will* what must happen in any case?

Löwith argues that this paradox breaks Nietzsche's central and unifying doctrine of eternal recurrence into "incommensurable shards." For Löwith this was an inevitable consequence of Nietzsche's attempt to tether a "physical metaphysics" to an "atheistic religion." This tension that Löwith diagnoses in Nietzsche is best captured in a note Nietzsche himself later discarded rather than publish: "The task is to live in such a way that you must wish to live again—you will anyway!" ("So leben dass du wünschen musst wieder zu leben ist die Aufgabe—du wirst es jedenfalls!"). The task given us would appear to be undermined by the final interjection "you will anyway!" since it seems to deprive this task of any choice of outcomes—including accepting or rejecting the very task itself.

I encountered Löwith for the first time as an undergraduate, when I read his *Meaning in History*. It was not until the early 1960s, while I was thinking about possibly writing a doctoral dissertation on Heidegger and Nietzsche, that I stumbled across Löwith's *Nietzsche's Philosophy of the Eternal Recurrence of the Same*. I read it with interest and enthusiasm, although I rejected its major theses as well as much of its argument. It would therefore have been highly misleading to suggest that it had a great deal of influence on me.

Or so I thought.

It is not until recently, three decades later, that I have come to realize that virtually all of my writings on Nietzsche—whether books or articles—have been in unconscious and unwitting conversation with Löwith's book. My first book on Nietzsche, for example, which treated the doctrine of eternal recurrence as an "existential imperative," clearly moves within the framework established by Löwith. Why else would I have singled out the doctrine of eternal recurrence as the unifying notion that motivates all of Nietzsche's writings (apart from the textual evidence, of course)? This is especially obvious—with 20/20 hindsight—in my early and sustained attempts to debunk the doctrine of eternal recurrence as a cosmological hypothesis. Granted that the cosmological construal of eternal recurrence was still much in vogue when I first began to write *Nietzsche's Existential Imperative,* I can no longer believe that this alone, or even primarily, explains why I spent so much time and energy trying to show that Nietzsche's published and unpublished writings render moot his commitment to the doctrine of eternal recurrence in its cosmological form. And why would I have spent so much intellectual and analytical energy showing the conceptual impossibility of a coherent version of eternal recurrence as a physical theory? Surely Löwith's shadow, deeply repressed, was cast over the pages I wrote. In innumerable ways—I now realize—I am still in dialogue with Löwith. Perhaps all that has been done is to update the vocabulary of the fundamental distinctions Löwith introduced into the Nietzsche debate.

This belated recognition and confession does not, of course, say very much about the stature I have claimed for *Nietzsche's Philosophy of the Eternal Recurrence of the Same* as a classic work of Nietzsche scholarship. All it shows is my unacknowledged (and unconscious) indebtedness. It does seem to me, however, that those of us who have been emancipated from Heidegger's Nietzsche[5] and have nonetheless continued to grapple with the doctrine of eternal recurrence, as well as with its connection to other themes in Nietzsche's philosophical arsenal—Arthur C. Danto, Maudemarie Clark, Tracy B. Strong, Richard Schacht, Alexander Nehamas, Kathleen M. Higgins, Gary Shapiro, and many others—owe Löwith a debt of gratitude, whether we are aware of it or not. In many, many ways, Löwith's Nietzsche established the framework within which much Anglophone Nietzsche scholarship has moved in the past three decades and is likely to continue to move at the onset of the new millennium.

Like the literary figure "misprision," which Harold Bloom has employed to such good affect in his *The Anxiety of Influence,* it is time to recognize the shoulders upon which we have been standing, even as our eyes are turned in different directions.

Bernd Magnus
Big Bear Lake, California
4 February 1996

5. I don't intend to demean Heidegger's influential *Nietzsche.* Far from it. It is one of the most suggestive Nietzsche studies in any language. What is wrong with it as Nietzsche commentary, however, is the same thing that is wrong with his work on Kant—for example, his *Kant and the Problem of Metaphysics.* Many decades after its publication, after all of its deficiencies had been discussed to death, Heidegger told a friend of mine: "It may not be good Kant, but it is awfully good Heidegger." I feel the same thing can be said of Heidegger's Nietzsche studies: They may not be good Nietzsche, but they are first-rate Heidegger.

# Translator's Introduction

*The identity of philosopher and king . . . is a noble lie, but it is not a lie of the city.*
—Seth Benardete, *Socrates' Second Sailing*

In 1935 Karl Löwith,[1] a gifted, well-educated German scholar of Jewish descent, first published in Berlin this classic of the Nietzsche literature. By then he had already emigrated to Italy after having endured, as a university docent in Marburg, over a year of National Socialism. Not accidentally, Nietzsche had served as the focal point of Löwith's final courses in Marburg: "I wanted to make clear to the students that Nietzsche prepares the way for, and at the same time represents the severest rejection of, the present situation in Germany. Nietzsche is a 'National Socialist' and a 'cultural Bolshevik'—depending on how one maneuvers him. In opposition to this usage that is

---

1. For a very thoughtful and sensitive portrait of Löwith by the man who brought him to Heidelberg after the war, see Hans-Georg Gadamer, *Philosophische Lehrjahre* (Frankfurt am Main: Vittorio Klostermann, 1977), pp. 231–239; translated as *Philosophical Apprenticeships* (Cambridge, Mass.: MIT Press, 1985), pp. 169–175. Arnold Levison provides a useful introduction to Löwith for English-speaking readers in his opening, editorial essay entitled "Nature and Existence" in Karl Löwith, *Nature, History, and Existentialism and Other Essays in the Philosophy of History,* ed. Levison (Evanston, Ill.: Northwestern University Press, 1966), pp. xv–xl. For those who cannot read German that collection of essays, together with *From Hegel to Nietzsche: The Revolution in Nineteenth-Century Thought* (New York: Holt, Rinehart and Winston, 1964) and *Meaning in History*

suited or perhaps unsuited to the times, I tried to establish the idea of eternity as the center of his philosophy."[2]

Löwith took advantage of the first year of a crucial Rockefeller Foundation Fellowship held during the years 1934–1936 to perfect his studies on Nietzsche in Rome.[3] The 1935 decision by Gerhard Bahlsen, proprietor of the press "Die Runde," to publish *Nietzsches Philosophie der ewigen Wiederkunft des Gleichen* ("Nietzsche's Philosophy of the Eternal Return of the Same") in the capital of Hitler's Germany must have required both courage and some appreciation of the quality of Löwith's scholarship. By contrast, the journal *Kantstudien* declined in 1935 to publish Löwith's article on the relationship of Marx's to Kierkegaard's stance on Hegel—despite the editor's having formally accepted the piece a year earlier—for "technical reasons." As Löwith dryly observes in his memoir, the "technical reasons were that Marx was taboo in Germany and the author was not Aryan."[4]

Nietzsche, of course, was by no means taboo in Germany in the 1930s. The Nazi Party went to some length to legitimate itself in the cloak of his authority, and Nietzsche's anti-Jewish sister, Elisabeth Förster-Nietzsche, proved only too willing to lend support to that unworthy purpose. Alfred Baeumler's crude depiction of Nietzsche as the philosopher of the "will *as* power," already published in 1931, served Party propaganda well and became more or less the official interpretation.[5] In that context the political significance and daring of Löwith's pathbreaking work emerges unmistakably, for Löwith demonstrates here that the Nietzschean doctrine of the will to power is unintelligible apart from what Baeumler dismisses, the eternal recurrence of the same. Löwith did not shrink from making a harsh attack on Baeumler by name in section 7 of the Appendix,[6] but for that very reason the entire Appendix had to be expunged before publication of the book could pro-

---

(Chicago: University of Chicago Press, 1949), offers the principal access to Löwith's work and thought. See also note 8 below.

2. Karl Löwith, *Mein Leben in Deutschland vor und nach 1933: Ein Bericht* (Stuttgart: J. B. Metzlersche Verlagsbuchhandlung, 1986), pp. 79, 137, 5–6. Hereafter cited as *Leben.*

3. Ibid., pp. 81, 104.

4. Ibid., p. 106. In 1936 Löwith could not find any German press for his book on Burckhardt, which was published in Switzerland by B. Schwabe.

5. *Nietzsche: Der Philosoph und Politiker* (Leipzig: Reclam Verlag, 1931). Baeumler was the official editor of Nietzsche's works during the Third Reich.

6. The Appendix can be found at pp. 195–229 below, with specific discussions of Baeumler and Heidegger at pp. 210–214 and 225–229.

ceed. All twelve book reviews in the Appendix could only be circulated separately until 1956, when the revised and expanded second edition appeared in Stuttgart under the imprint of the W. Kohlhammer Verlag as *Nietzsches Philosophie der ewigen Wiederkehr des Gleichen* ("Nietzsche's Philosophy of the Eternal Recurrence of the Same").[7]

More serious than Baeumler by many orders of magnitude, but like him entangled with the Nazis nonetheless, Löwith's own teacher Martin Heidegger provides another target of severe and not altogether dispassionate criticism in the concluding section of the Appendix. Of course the critique included in this volume does not encompass Löwith's full assessment of Heidegger or even of his interpretation of Nietzsche.[8] Heidegger's two-volume, 1,150-page tome entitled *Nietzsche* did not appear until 1961,[9] whereupon Löwith published an extended, scorching review.[10] The later review develops more fully and in a broader context the trenchant criticisms and probing questions raised at the end of the present book. At all events, the decisive influence on Löwith of Heidegger's mentorship remained indelible, as did the student's disapprobation of the master's cooperation with the National Socialists. Löwith regarded Heidegger's collaboration as a consequence not just of his political naïveté or personality flaws but of his *thought*. Speaking of Heidegger's intellectual intensity and his concentration on "the one thing needful," Löwith asserts that this one thing was "a nothing, a pure resoluteness" that lies concealed beneath

7. The present translation is based on the authoritative third edition published by Felix Meiner Verlag in Hamburg in 1978. That edition incorporates corrections made in accordance with the author's handwritten manuscript. In 1986 the Meiner press issued a fourth edition that duplicates the third. Vol. 6 of the *Sämtliche Schriften*, entitled *Nietzsche* (Stuttgart: Metzlersche Verlagsbuchhandlung, 1987), collects all Löwith's publications on Nietzsche and includes a summary of his doctoral dissertation as well as a letter from Karl Schlechta in response to Löwith's reviews; the text of *Nietzsches Philosophie* in that volume follows the Meiner edition, albeit with occasional transcriptional errors.

8. The first edition of Löwith's *Heidegger: Denker in dürftiger Zeit* ("Heidegger: Thinker in a Destitute Time") reached the public in 1953 (Frankfurt am Main: S. Fischer Verlag), and release of the second, expanded edition occurred in 1960 (Göttingen: Vandenhoeck & Ruprecht). The work has recently been made available in English translation, forming part of the volume of selections from Löwith published as *Martin Heidegger and European Nihilism*, ed. Richard Wolin, trans. Gary Steiner (New York: Columbia University Press, 1995). Vol. 8 of *Sämtliche Schriften* collects Löwith's public statements on Heidegger, including *Denker*.

9. Pfullingen: Verlag Günther Neske, 1961. David F. Krell's fine, four-volume English translation was published by Harper and Row (San Francisco, 1979–1986).

10. *Merkur* 16, no. 1 (1962): 72–83. Reprinted in Karl Löwith, *Aufsätze und Vorträge, 1930–1970* (Stuttgart: Verlag W. Kohlhammer, 1971), pp. 84–99, and in *Sämtliche Schriften*, vol. 8 (Stuttgart: Metzler, 1984), pp. 242–257.

Heidegger's quasi-theological approach.[11] Man's "facticity" and mortal-
ity replace the immortality of the soul, and immanent, historically determined Being substitutes for the transcendent, eternal God Almighty,
in this inverted, atheistic theology. Although Heidegger characterized
his own struggle with the question of Being as an attempt "to develop
fully what Nietzsche brought about,"[12] Löwith contrasts the emptiness of Heideggerian resoluteness with Nietzsche's love of wisdom in
persistently focusing on the whole of *nature,* on the eternal that always
recurs because it remains the same in all alteration and change of the
things that are.

Heidegger could have rejoined that he is more genuinely Nietzschean
than is Nietzsche himself. Does not Heidegger, in eradicating every
trace of eternity from his world, remain truest to the earth and least
susceptible to the attractions of metaphysical "backworlds"? Does not
Nietzsche, in proclaiming the affirmation of the *eternal* recurrence to
be the peak of human existence and the secret for weaving the accident "man" back into the whole of Being, succumb to that very spirit
of revenge (against the *transient* world of the senses) he warns against?
And if the ontic status of the eternal recurrence depends on human affirmation or willing, does not precisely that teaching require a non-
transcendental analysis of the emphatically transitory existence of the
human being in his historicity? In other words, *contra* Löwith, does not
Nietzsche's philosophy make Heidegger's necessary?—On the other
hand, one can ask whether Heidegger accepts too uncritically what he
considers to be Nietzsche's most fundamental parameters. The foundation of atheist theology is atheism, and Heidegger goes so far as
to call faith the mortal enemy of philosophy.[13] Does Heidegger ever

11. *Leben,* p. 29 and generally pp. 29–42; *Sämtliche Schriften* 8:61–68 and 297.
Löwith's account of Heidegger's 1936 trip to Rome to present a lecture on Hölderlin
deserves particular note: "I declared to Heidegger that . . . in my opinion his advocacy of
National Socialism derives from the essence of his philosophy. Heidegger agreed with
me without reservation and elaborated by telling me that his concept of 'historicity' is
the foundation for his political commitment" (*Leben,* p. 57). Cf. Löwith's "Zu Heidegger's Seinsfrage: Die Natur des Menschen und die Welt der Natur," in *Aufsätze und
Vorträge, 1930–1970,* pp. 189–203. Löwith found it hard to speak of his stance toward
Heidegger's philosophical project "without including [my] personal relationship" to
Heidegger (ibid., p. 192).
12. *Einführung in die Metaphysik,* 4th ed. (Tübingen: Max Niemeyer Verlag, 1976),
p. 28.
13. "Phänomenologie und Theologie," in *Gesamtausgabe,* vol. 9, *Wegmarken* (Frankfurt am Main: Verlag Vittorio Klostermann, 1976), p. 66. See Heinrich Meier, *Die Lehre*

demonstrate that the life of faith is based on an error, or does his phi-losophizing itself not rather rest on faith? Heidegger makes no secret of his higher esteem for the pre-Socratics than for Plato's Socrates, and on crucial matters Heidegger like the pre-Socratics not infrequently shows a dangerous, un-Socratic preference for issuing pronouncements from on high rather than elaborating intricate, rational arguments.[14] The danger that attaches to Heidegger's failure to follow the Socratic turn by first of all challenging and then justifying with cogent argu-ments the philosophic way of life lies not so much in atheistic theol-ogy per se as in a self-destruction of philosophy, an ultimately unphil-osophic "philosophy" based on faith. Thus Löwith's clarion call, in Nietzsche's name, for a return to nature from History can be said to have the most profound warrant after all.

Löwith composed the main text of *Nietzsches Philosophie* "*sine ira et studio,* without sentimentality or vagueness, and with competence and a natural grace."[15] Unlike Heidegger and Jaspers,[16] who without regard for finer sensibilities do not hesitate to intrude themselves "cre-atively" into their portrayals of Nietzsche, Löwith loyally strives to

*Carl Schmitts: Vier Kapitel zur Unterscheidung politischer Theologie und politischer Phi-losophie* (Stuttgart: Verlag J. B. Metzler, 1994), p. 136 note 48, and in general pp. 13–186.

14. Admittedly, circumstances that warrant writing between the lines—persecution, for example, or certain pedagogical requirements—can sometimes fully excuse a writer's failure to make explicit the rigorous arguments that lead to his conclusions, to say noth-ing of the ultimate conclusions themselves. See, for example, Löwith's "Skepticism and Faith," in *Nature, History, and Existentialism,* pp. 120–121: "Sextus Empiricus . . . say[s] that the skeptic, for reasons of benevolence, tries to cure the dogmatists by way of persuasion. However, just as physicians administer medicines of different strengths, according to the seriousness of the ailment, the skeptic's arguments, too, have to be lighter or stronger depending on how superficial or deep-rooted the dogmatist's folly is. For this reason the skeptic, intentionally, does not refrain from using weak arguments occasionally." See also Leo Strauss, *Persecution and the Art of Writing* (New York: The Free Press, 1952), pp. 7–37. But as Löwith recognizes, these considerations have no vindicatory bearing on Heidegger, for in spite of the enormous difficulties involved in coming to grips with his corpus, he may well be the least ironic, least esoteric of all the great thinkers in the philosophic tradition.

15. Leo Strauss, *What Is Political Philosophy? and Other Studies* (Glencoe, Ill.: The Free Press, 1959), p. 268.

16. Karl Jaspers, *Nietzsche: Einführung in das Verständnis seines Philosophierens,* 3d ed. (Berlin: Walter de Gruyter, 1950). Translated as *Nietzsche: An Introduction to the Under-standing of His Philosophical Activity,* trans. Charles F. Wallcraft and Frederick J. Schmitz (Tucson: University of Arizona Press, 1965).

interpret Nietzsche's oeuvre authentically from within and as a whole.[17] Accordingly, he takes full cognizance of the aphoristic, seemingly fragmented character of many major writings of Nietzsche and of Nietzsche's disdain for the will to systematize as betokening a lack of integrity,[18] while simultaneously treating seriously Nietzsche's claim to have a single concern and a whole teaching and vision.[19] As Löwith persuasively argues, "Nietzsche's philosophy is neither a unified, closed system nor a variety of disintegrating aphorisms, but a system in aphorisms."[20] To be sure, in important respects Nietzsche's understanding changed and above all deepened; but Löwith shows that the earlier phases, Nietzsche's romanticism and positivism, were not so much supplanted as completed by the mature phase of the eternal recurrence.[21]

Loyalty to the text does not at all hinder Löwith from taking a critical view of the Nietzschean accomplishment, however. True, he masterfully articulates the connections between most main themes in Nietzsche—nihilism, the superman, courage, the will to power, the revaluation of all values, *amor fati*, death, the last man, the death of God—and the overarching motif of the eternal recurrence.[22] Nevertheless, the central thesis of the present work is that that very overarching conception or red thread which provides the key to grasping Nietzsche's system qua system contains a discord that ultimately causes the entire fabric to unravel tragically beyond repair. Löwith makes clear that the ostensibly unified allegory of eternal recurrence splits into two irreconcilable parts, one cosmological and the other anthropological—one portraying the goalless revolution of the universe, the other, a superhuman act of the human will that consummates the self-overcoming of nihilism. In its cosmological mode the eternal recurrence represents a natural-scientific "fact" consisting of the goalless, self-contained existence of the world of forces. In its anthropomorphic mode the recurrence signifies an ethical gravity that gives goalless human existence a goal again. (In particular, the teaching of recurrence is meant to re-

17. Hence Löwith includes what is probably a far greater number of direct quotations of Nietzsche, especially of quite lengthy ones, than can be found in any other commentary. The present translation often relies, with occasional emendations, on the generally superb renditions of Nietzsche's writing by Walter Kaufmann.

18. *Twilight of the Idols*, "Maxims and Arrows," aph. 26.

19. See, e.g., *On the Genealogy of Morals*, preface, aphs. 1–2; notes 29–33 to chap. 1 below.

20. P. 11, and more generally pp. 11–20, below.

21. Pp. 21–26 and pp. 27–107 below.

22. Pp. 27–136 and 174–192 below.

constitute and elevate humanity by means of the new categorical imperative: live in every moment so that you *could* will that moment back again over and over endlessly.) So on the one hand the recurrence as unwilled, physical fact replaces ancient cosmology with modern physics; but on the other hand the recurrence as the willing of an ideal replaces Christian faith in the afterlife with the will to self-eternalization and a new way of life. "This double explicability as an *atheistic religion* and as a *physical metaphysics* shows that in its totality the teaching is the *unity of a conflict* between the *nihilistic* existence of the man who has rid himself of God and the *positivistic* presence of physical energy."[23] Löwith leaves little doubt that the doctrine of eternal recurrence shatters into incommensurable shards, for one need not will a fact, and the knowledge that one wills a fiction necessarily undermines the believability of what one wills. The huge structure of Nietzschean metaphysics crashes so resoundingly and so hopelessly under Löwith's powerful assault that one might wonder in the aftermath: Did Nietzsche completely overlook this fundamental flaw in his teaching of eternal recurrence? Or could that flaw point to a deeper, far less manifest teaching? In *Thus Spoke Zarathustra* II, "On Redemption," Zarathustra instructs his disciples about how to bring about redemption from the past and from the spirit of revenge against the past, namely by creatively willing the past as one's own creation. This memorable speech obviously makes a preliminary announcement of *amor fati,* of the necessity of willing the eternal recurrence. As Löwith does notice, an astute hunchback objects here that Zarathustra speaks differently both to hunchbacks and to himself than he does to his pupils. Zarathustra's discourse about the eternal recurrence is evidently exoteric-esoteric. Löwith appears to take no notice of the fact that of all human beings an astute hunchback is least likely to be hoodwinked by implausible tales of the redemptive will.

Löwith supplements, not to say embellishes, his interpretation proper with a series of learned reconstructions that locate Nietzsche within the history of thought, principally in the modern period. Of the various ancients who spoke of an eternal cycle of things—Heraclitus and Empedocles, Plato and Aristotle, Eudemus and the Stoics—Heraclitus's philosophy wins the laurels as the primary antique model for Nietzsche's eternal recurrence. Nietzsche sees in Heraclitus the highest form of pride, and justice prevails as the supreme law of necessity in

23. P. 83 and more generally pp. 82–107 below.

Heraclitus's eternal process of becoming. Christianity, of course, comprises Nietzsche's antipode, signaling a momentous revaluation of values by the victorious slave morality of the antiaristocratic, vulgar multitude. In Löwith's view Nietzsche never truly overcomes Christianity, however, but remains trapped in an antinatural, Christian–anti-Christian perspective directed at redemption in the future. As for the "modern historical consciousness," in Löwith's cast of characters Nietzsche is "the first" to take his bearings by the eternal. The grave difficulty confronted by all moderns concerns the problematic relationship between human existence and the Being of the world. Especially with a view to the development of the "historical consciousness," one might reasonably describe that difficulty as the problem of how to establish a basis for human freedom and morality in a world of ineluctable, universal, mechanistic causation that in principle allows no room for a distinct, human empire within an empire. Spinoza seems to escape Löwith's attention, however, perhaps because Descartes serves as a substitute. (In the spirit of Aristotle and with a bow to Husserl, Löwith could have pointed out that whereas the thesis of universal mechanism—though of great utility for centuries of progress in modern natural science and technology—allows of no apodictic proof, on the level of consciousness the thesis of human freedom that is so vital to morality can be directly verified through immediate, personal experience by the human being who persistently *deliberates* over choices.) In any case Descartes's insistence on clarity as the criterion of truth and his consequent mathematization of the world does much to liberate humanity and philosophy from ecclesiastical authority. But Descartes's ostensible quest for irrefragable certainty leads him to distinguish between man the thinking being who has certainty about his own existence, and the corporeal world that finally remains uncertain. Ever since, man has tried to construct a bridge between the human ego and the world. Although Nietzsche regards Descartes's faith in reason and in immediate certainty as naive and superficial, in Löwith's historical interpretation the discord in Nietzsche's eternal recurrence emanates from the duality of Cartesian subjectivism. Kant only deepens the bifurcation begun by Descartes. Fichte tries to bind the ego and the eternal natural world by means of faith in a divine will and divine providence—for Nietzsche a nonsolution after the death of God. Löwith calls Schelling, who affected Nietzsche only indirectly through Schopenhauer and von Hartmann, the only thinker within German idealism with a positive relationship to Nietzsche's eternal return. For Schelling the comprehensive, primeval being of nature develops purely out of itself through its own drive and desire, remains present always, and outlasts everything that once was. This primal nature continues in constant, rotating motion that neither begins nor ends, and seeks only itself. But Schelling, too, posits divine will as the source of human freedom. In Hegel's thought, nature has no original, independent meaning. In his quarrel with Kant, Fichte, and Schelling, Hegel tries to restore the lost unity of man and world in a philosophy of absolute spirit. Löwith maintains that absolute spirit takes the place of God, and that the philosophy of absolute spirit only makes man's separation from the world more visible. The reader may regret the lack of a fuller treatment of Nietzsche's relationship to Rousseau by way of Goethe on the one hand and Kant and Hegel on the other, but Löwith does address this theme more extensively in *From Hegel to Nietzsche*. Considering the space devoted to Stirner, Marx, Weininger, and Kierkegaard,[24] however, the astonishing neglect of the most towering philosopher of antiquity and pivotal figure of Nietzsche's thought is all the more striking.

Löwith's imposing scholarship, a treasure trove of sober reflection and elegant expression, will likely remain in the forefront of commentaries for many generations. No serious student of Nietzsche can afford to ignore the achievement of this book. Nevertheless, one must consider that the author uncharacteristically and conspicuously disregards a central Nietzschean theme of the greatest consequence: Nietzsche's relationship to Socrates.[25] Disconcertingly, Löwith refers to Plato fewer than a half-dozen times and, even more strangely, to Socrates only once—only to subordinate him completely to Heraclitus. By contrast, Nietzsche's own writings, including the literary remains, are replete with discussions of both Plato and Socrates. In 1875 Nietzsche says, "Socrates, just to confess it, stands so close to me that I almost always fight a battle with him."[26] From *The Birth of Tragedy,* where Socrates as the antihero gets the blame for the destruction of Greek

24. Pp. 150–173 below.

25. See Kurt Hildebrandt, *Nietzsches Wettkampf mit Sokrates und Plato* (Dresden: Sibyllen Verlag, 1922); Werner Dannhauser, *Nietzsche's View of Socrates* (Ithaca, N.Y.: Cornell University Press, 1974); and Lawrence Lampert, *Nietzsche's Teaching: An Interpretation of Thus Spoke Zarathustra* (New Haven: Yale University Press, 1986), esp. p. 168.

26. *Kritische Studienausgabe,* vol. 8 (Munich: Deutscher Taschenbuch Verlag, 1980), p. 97. Does Nietzsche, by calling the whole, ossified philosophic tradition into question and thus making possible and pursuing a fresh, truly philosophic confrontation with the most fundamental issues, earn the title of Socratic philosopher?

tragedy, to *Twilight of the Idols,* where in the chapter entitled "The Problem of Socrates" he continues to play a key role, Nietzsche struggles with his chosen companion and antagonist, whom he calls the vortex of world history. It is true that *Thus Spoke Zarathustra* never explicitly mentions either Plato or Socrates. But the same does not hold for Nietzsche's two elaborations of *Zarathustra,* namely, *Beyond Good and Evil* and *On the Genealogy of Morals.* Moreover, the last three aphorisms (340–342) of Part IV of *The Gay Science* suggest significant ligatures between Socrates, the eternal recurrence of the same, and Zarathustra. Also, in aphorism 340 Nietzsche describes Socrates as the wisest chatterbox there ever was, and then adds that he was just as great in his silence. Löwith's seeming indifference notwithstanding, one has to call Nietzsche's characterization of Socrates extraordinary, and one has to move him to front and center stage. Undeniably, Löwith—by being as faithful to Nietzsche as he is—pioneers a path to the only vista where Nietzsche's kaleidoscope of lovely fragments suddenly comes to view as a breathtaking, intelligible work of art. But in the end he fails to disclose the full meaning and beauty of that artistic masterpiece and riddle, because he does not see it in the transfiguring light of the Platonic Socrates.

Heidelberg
Summer 1995

# Nietzsche's Philosophy
# of the Eternal Recurrence
# of the Same

# Foreword to the
# First Edition

*My work has* time—*and I do not want to be mistaken
at all for what this present age has to solve as* its *problem.
Fifty years hence a few . . . will perhaps become aware of*
what has been done through me. *At the moment, however, it is not only difficult but (according to the laws of
[historical] perspective) altogether impossible to speak of
me publicly without* lagging *boundlessly behind the truth.*

Venice, 1884[T1]

In the last chapter of his writings, Nietzsche explained to
the world why he is a "destiny"—his own, loneliest destiny, likewise
the public and common destiny of us all.

The good fortune of my existence, its uniqueness perhaps, lies in the calamity
of my existence; to express it in the form of a riddle: as my father, I have already died; as my mother, I still live and grow old. This double descent, as it
were both from the highest and from the lowest rung on the ladder of life, at
the same time a decadent and a beginning—this explains, if anything does, that
neutrality, that freedom from partiality in relation to the total problem of life,
which perhaps distinguishes me. I have a keener scent for the signs of ascent
and decline than ever a man has had; for these I am the teacher par excellence—I am familiar with both, I am both.[1]

Thus "placed between today and tomorrow" and "clamped into
the contradiction between today and tomorrow," he knew himself as
a premature birth of the coming century and of a still unproved[T2]

future. Accordingly, he left open in *Zarathustra* the question of what he really is: a promiser or a fulfiller, a conqueror or an heir, an autumn or a plowshare, a physician or a man who has convalesced, a poet or a man of truth, a liberator or a tamer—because he knew that he was neither the one nor the other, but both in one.[T3]

Nietzsche's philosophy, being a twofold "prophecy" of *nihilism* and of the *eternal recurrence of the same,* is as *ambiguous* as Nietzsche himself. This teaching was consciously his "destiny," because his will to the nothing (being a "double will") wanted to get back to the Being of eternity. Many have not understood this movement of the "new Columbus" toward the setting of the sun of Being at the edge of the nothing, only to emerge anew at the edge of Being. It has been said of Nietzsche that he teaches the boundless freedom of the individual who is left to his own devices, or else a new legislation and order of rank; that he teaches a "heroic realism," or else a philosophy of the "orgiastic"; to say nothing of interpretations that have an even more limited grasp of Nietzsche's thought. Zarathustra's remark is still valid: "They all talk of me . . . but no one thinks—of me! This is the new silence I learned; their noise about me spreads a cloak over my ideas."[T4]

In contrast with these obscurations of Nietzsche's thought, the present interpretation is an attempt to comprehend Nietzsche's aphorisms within the hidden whole of their peculiar set of problems, according to their philosophical outline. In accordance with my intention to provide a methodical summary, I have forgone the extended riches of a total presentation of Nietzsche.

The real problem in Nietzsche's philosophy is, however, at bottom none other than what it always was: What meaning does human existence have in the whole of Being? In order to discover a "new land of the soul," Nietzsche ventured upon the "open sea," and as a last disciple of the god Dionysus, the "highest type of Being," he finally found himself crucified in insanity. It would be naive or presumptuous to suppose that we stragglers behind his pioneering already had an answer to his burning question, as if *we* had already discovered the "new possibilities of life" for the sake of which Nietzsche, with his last "plan of a new way to live," repeated a most ancient view of the world. But as far as the *judgment* of this experiment is concerned, the following passage from a letter can serve as a guide:

If you should ever get around to writing something about me (you doubtless lack *time* for that, worthy friend!!), have the good sense, which unfortunately no one yet has had, to *characterize* me, to "describe" me—but *not* to "depreciate" me. This approach does confer an agreeable neutrality: it seems to me that one is permitted here to leave one's pathos aside and all the more gets one's hands on the *finer* spirituality. I have not ever been characterized—neither as a *psychologist* nor as an *author* ("poet" included) nor as the inventor of a *new* kind of pessimism (a Dionysian pessimism, born out of *strength,* which takes its *delight* in seizing the problem of existence by the horns) nor as an *immoralist* (—the highest form of "intellectual integrity" so far attained, which *may* treat morals as illusion once "intellectual integrity" itself has become *instinct* and *inevitability*—). It is *not* at all necessary, not even *desired,* that one thereby take sides for me; on the contrary, a dose of inquisitiveness, as if before a strange plant, with an ironic resistance would seem to me to be an incomparably *more intelligent* stance toward me.[2]

Rome, June 1934

# Foreword to the
# Second Edition

After the publication of *Zarathustra*, Nietzsche lived with the certitude of one possessed by a task—in the self-assurance that his work had time. He predicted in 1884 that not until a half-century later would it be disclosed to a few what had been done through him.[1] Meanwhile the time has also run out on Nietzsche's "Prelude to a Philosophy of the Future," and the "war of desperation" to which Nietzsche wanted to provoke the Germans by means of an anti-German league[2] already lies behind us, half-forgotten. Thus Nietzsche today appears to us otherwise than he did fifty years ago, when his fame and efficacy were on the ascent. He still stands close to us, and he is already distant. Some of his prophecies about the future of Europe have, although in unforeseen ways, been fulfilled, and statements that in Nietzsche's time were unheard-of have become commonplaces within which all present thought moves. He not only called "European nihilism" by name for the first time, but also helped it come into existence, and through his reflection he created a mental atmosphere in which the "will to power" could be practiced without reflection. Now one has blasted with "dynamite" and obediently followed the maxim "live dangerously" long enough for such principles to lose their seductive appeal. The age of destruction has done its work so thoroughly that one prefers to get on with the reconstruction on nonexistent foundations.

When one bears in mind the change of meaning that Nietzsche's image and work have undergone, a displacement of gravity in the

7

judgment and appraisal of Nietzsche becomes evident. It began with recognition of the brilliant moralist and psychologist; it came to a peak in the veneration of Zarathustra by the young generation of the First World War; it boiled over in the caricature of Nietzsche by the Third Reich, which did indeed philosophize "with a hammer"; it ends with the thesis of the end of history, namely that in Nietzsche the total metaphysics of the West logically completes itself.—It ought to have "sung," this new soul, it was said in 1908 in a poem by Stefan George; the world will convalesce in "the essence of Zarathustra,"[T5] announced the Nazified Nietzsche Archive in 1938; "Who Is Nietzsche's Zarathustra?" is asked in 1953 by a thinker who has no misgivings about elevating Nietzsche into the ranks of the greatest European metaphysicians and just by that means incorporating him into the history of the "forgetfulness of Being."[3]

But is Nietzsche really a great thinker, or is he a would-be poet? Measured against Aristotle and Hegel, he is an impassioned dilettante, who as a "physician of culture" wanted to work against his age in favor of a coming age, and finally came to the conviction that he held the future of Europe in his hands. Measured against Sophocles and Hölderlin, Nietzsche's poems and parables are, with a few precious exceptions, the artificial clothing for "experiences of thought." Nietzsche is (judging by what stands in the foreground and receives extensive treatment) a philosophic author, just as Kierkegaard was a religious author; but the former lacks the latter's schooling in abstract thinking. Nietzsche's teacher was not Hegel but Schopenhauer. But in the depths and in the background, Nietzsche is nevertheless a true lover of wisdom, who as such sought the everlasting or eternal, and therefore wanted to overcome his time and temporality altogether. Nietzsche experienced the fullness of time, when to him the world became "perfect," in an ecstatic moment to which he gave the name "noon and eternity." An eternity at noon does not negate time, as if that eternity were the timeless eternity of God before the creation of the world; rather, it means the eternity of time itself in the world: the eternally recurring cycle of coming into being and passing away that is always the same, a cycle in which the permanence of "Being" and the change of "becoming" are one and the same. What is "always" is not timeless; what always remains "the same" is not temporal. In this eternity so understood, without beginning and end or origin and goal, what otherwise would be temporally scattered into the dimensions of time is perfectly gathered together. Nietzsche's teaching of the overcoming of the temporality of time in favor of the eternity of the eternal recurrence of the same is thus neither a mere flight out of time nor a mere praise of transitoriness. The proclamation of this "new eternity"—new only in relation to the old eternity of timelessness—became Nietzsche's most authentic teaching, and accordingly *Zarathustra* is his real work and "testament." The teaching of the eternal recurrence of the same also is the central and conclusive idea that lies at the bottom of the uncompleted *Will to Power,* which is an "Attempt at a Revaluation of All Values." The overturning of the truth of nihilism (that is, of the devaluation of all higher values) into the truth of the eternal recurrence is the general principle for all particular revaluations, too. The essential difference between the notes on the teaching of the return in *The Will to Power* and the proclamation of that teaching in *Zarathustra* is, however, that the latter compresses into a parable what the former examines speculatively, though one must add that the poetically composed parable disintegrates into its unequal components.—The question is whether and what we can learn, nevertheless, from Nietzsche's teaching. Whoever came close to that teaching and took seriously Nietzsche's unmistakable testimony to its decisive meaning could not help trying to give himself an account of its sense or nonsense—even if that were by way of taking it as mystical or dismissing it as a symptom of incipient insanity.

The following interpretation of Nietzsche's whole philosophy as a teaching of the eternal recurrence of the same is the revision and completion of a work with the same title published in 1935.[4] This book does not impose an interpretation from without but rather extracts it from the Nietzschean texts. It also takes a critical stance for the interpretation of the texts (herein set off typographically) only out of the texts themselves, by showing how these texts are inconsistent internally or with one another. The present work is intended to display the fundamental contradiction that is based on Nietzsche's desire to perceive the physical truth of the necessary cycle of the natural world as a "turn of necessity";[T6] so that already in *Zarathustra* the *will to power* becomes, under the title "Of Self-Overcoming," an essential component of the "vision" of the eternal return—but without itself fitting in with the return. The teaching of the eternal recurrence of the same is in itself as discordant and ambiguous as its temporal symbol, the "noon." As "noon and eternity," noon signifies the highest time of a standstill and of a perfection; but it also and above all signifies the highest time of a most extreme distress and danger and as such a critical "center" in which a decision is at issue. On this contradiction the astonishing unity and logical consistency of Nietzsche's train of thought breaks asunder. To be sure, discrepancies and contradictions may appear unimportant if one presumes oneself capable of dispensing with the logic of the principle of contradiction as unphilosophic and supposes that contradictions and ambiguities are, as such, already signs of a deeper insight. The contradiction that moves Nietzsche's thought, however, neither lies on the level of contradictory individual sentences nor belongs to those countless, polemically occasioned, contrary assertions that do indeed show up continually in Nietzsche's writings; for these inconsistencies dissolve when one takes into account in each case the intention with which, and in opposition to what, something is said. In contradistinction to such formal and apparent contradictions, the contradiction that moves Nietzsche's thought is *one* essential and comprehensive contradiction, which arises from a fundamental conflict in the relationship of man and world—where there is no God and no common order of creation. From beginning to end, the boundless exertion of Nietzsche's passionate thought (which is more a tentative experiment than a knowledgeable explanation) revolves around the solution to this conflict and the redemption from it. The ostensible solution occurs in the way that Nietzsche-Zarathustra projects the accident of his own existence, in need of redemption, into the whole of the natural world, and brings his own will to self-overcoming ecstatically into harmony with the self-willing of the heavenly world. His attempt to find his way out of the finite nothing of the self-willing ego back into the eternal whole of Being finally ends in his mistaking himself for God, around whom everything becomes world.[5, T7] Nietzsche's reflection ends in insanity. It is not easy to decide whether that insanity was a senseless, external accident, or a destiny that belonged to him inwardly, or a holy insanity at the onset of which the phenomenon of Dionysian frenzy (to which Nietzsche's first work was dedicated) was embodied in him like lightning, only to expire in idiocy.[6]—"And it is preferable to resemble a black, half-destroyed fortress sitting alone on its mountain, reflective and silent enough; so that even the birds are afraid of this silence."

Carona, October 1955

# 1

# Nietzsche's Philosophy:
# A System in Aphorisms

Nietzsche's philosophy is neither a unified, closed system nor a variety of disintegrating aphorisms, but rather a system in aphorisms. What is peculiar about the philosophic form of these aphorisms characterizes their content as well.[1] The systematic character of Nietzsche's philosophy results from the specific way in which Nietzsche sets about, persists in, and carries out his philosophical experiment; the aphoristic character results from the experimenting as such. The single meaning of Nietzsche's multiple metamorphoses must be understood in terms of the fundamentally experimental character of his philosophizing.

Nietzsche once characterized the whole modern age as an age of experiments. For him this characterization applies not only to future breeding experiments of a biological sort; rather, "whole sections of the earth" can "dedicate themselves to conscious experimenting."[2] Historically, he was speaking of the great discoverers and experimenters of the Renaissance, daring and at-tempting[T8] spirits like Leonardo da Vinci and Columbus, to whom he often compared himself (just as Kant compared himself to Copernicus). In the same sense Nietzsche named the new philosophers, too, "at-tempters," who test themselves to the point of uncertainty "in order to see how far one gets therewith. Like the skipper on an unknown sea."[3]

A new species of philosophers is coming up. I venture to baptize them with a name that is not free of danger. As I unriddle them . . . these philosophers of the future would claim a right—it might also be a wrong—to be characterized as at-tempters. This name itself is finally only an attempt and, if you will, a temptation.[4]

As an at-tempter, Nietzsche-Zarathustra is always in transit, a "wanderer" who attempts, and walks along, different paths in order to come to the truth.

On various paths and in various ways I came to my truth. . . . And only with reluctance did I ever ask about paths. . . . I preferred to question and at-tempt the paths themselves. All my walking was an at-tempting and questioning.[5]

By way of an attempt, Nietzsche's experimental philosophy anticipates the possibility of fundamental nihilism—in order to pass through to its opposite, to the eternal cycle of Being.[6]

The special meaning of Nietzsche's *criticism* and *skepticism*, too, is determined by the fundamentally experimental character of Nietzsche's philosophy: both serve the testing. His criticism is the "attempt" at a revaluation of all previous values, and his skepticism that of "audacious" manliness.

Supposing, then, that some trait in the image of the philosophers of the future poses the riddle whether they would not perhaps have to be . . . skeptics, this would still designate only one feature of them—and *not* them as a whole. With just as much right one could call them critics; and certainly they will be men of experiments. With the name with which I dared to baptize them I have already expressly emphasized their at-tempting and delight in at-tempting: did this occur because as critics in body and soul they like to employ experiments in a new, perhaps wider, perhaps more dangerous sense? . . . These men coming up will be least able to dispense with those serious and by no means unproblematic qualities that distinguish the critic from the skeptic; I mean the certainty of value standards, the conscious employment of a unity of method, a shrewd courage, the ability to stand alone and take responsibility for themselves; indeed, they admit to a certain pleasure in saying no and in taking things apart, and to a certain levelheaded cruelty that knows how to handle a knife surely and subtly. . . . They will be *harder* (and perhaps not always only against themselves) than humane people might wish; they will not get involved with the "truth" in order that it "please" them or "elevate" and "inspire" them.[7]

Nietzsche adhered to this experimental character of his philosophy from his first "years of attempts" to the teaching of the eternal recurrence. That teaching, too, is still a "last attempt with the truth," and *Dionysus philosophus* himself is an "at-tempter god."

If Nietzsche's philosophy were from the very beginning a carefully reasoned system, his critique of philosophic systems would not be intelligible; on the other hand, if his philosophy were a mere series of aphorisms, it would not be understandable how Nietzsche could insist from *The Birth of Tragedy* onward that "all is one and has but one will." The more recent view that Nietzsche is at bottom a systematic thinker is just as correct, and just as wrong, as the older view that he is an aphoristic literary author. For it is unmistakable that his writings consist of more- or less-developed aphorisms, and that he sketched out plans concerning the whole by means of which all fragments cohere. And they cohere exactly in what both the systematic interpretation and the renunciation thereof leave out of consideration, namely, the teaching of the eternal recurrence. Only in that teaching (as his last experiment) does the sequence of Nietzsche's attempts dovetail, with systematic consistency, into a "teaching."

Nietzsche does not combat the philosophic system for its unity of *method,* which unity a "basic will to knowledge" produces, but rather for the system's phony simulation of a dogmatically fixed and "stipulated" world. A lack of courage for the problem leads the systematic philosopher to close the open horizon of at-tempting examination and questioning. The correlate to the critique of the system is a philosophic will to the rediscovery of the world and to the open horizons of questioning. The unsystematic form of Nietzsche's thought originates, in a positive way, in his new position toward Being and toward truth. All earlier human beings, even the skeptics, *"had the truth,"* whereas the "novelty of our current position regarding philosophy" is a conviction *"that we do not have the truth."*[8] Because "nothing is true anymore" but "everything is permitted," Nietzsche makes a new attempt with the truth, and the probity of the attempt takes the place that the system (which has become untrue) held in those ages that still had the truth. Truth is no longer present in trust in the Being that is in the truth, but rather in mistrust of all truth that previously was thought to have existed.

Then do you want to be the teacher of mistrust of truth?—Pyrrhon: Of mistrust as it has never been in the world . . . , mistrust of all and of each thing. It is the only path to truth. The right eye is not permitted to trust the left eye, and for a while light will have to be called darkness: this is the path on which you must go. Do not believe that it leads you to fruit trees and beautiful pastures. Hard little kernels you will find on this path—those are the truths.[9]

The aphoristic "seed corn" of language corresponds to these little kernels of truth. Only in the superhuman language of *Zarathustra,* in the metaphysically substantiated parable, does Nietzsche himself claim to be in the whole of truth.[10] The at-tempting language of the experiment changes into the language of "inspiration," to be continued in plans for a systematic main work. Up to *Zarathustra,* however, Nietzsche held fast—in uncertainty—to his experimenting will to open horizons, a will that caused him always to overtake and overcome himself anew.

One observes in my earlier writings a good will to unlocked horizons, a certain sagacious caution before convictions, a mistrust of the enchantments and dupings of conscience that every strong faith brings with it. One may see therein in part the wariness of the child who has been burned. . . . More essential, it seems to me, is the Epicurean instinct of a friend of riddles who does not want to have the enigmatic character of things too easily taken away from him—most essentially, at last, an aesthetic aversion for the big, virtuous, unconditional words; a taste that defends itself against all crass, square antitheses, *desires* a good bit of uncertainty in things, and takes way the antitheses, as a friend of intermediary colors, shadows, afternoon lights, and endless seas.[11]

Nietzsche's critique of the closed world of the system, as well as the meaning of his "provisional" thought and speech in the aphoristic, little pieces of truth, must be understood in terms of this good will to open horizons. The will to a system is "now"—where everything is in flux once again and a mild breeze breaks the ice and the ice breaks all footbridges—a "lack of integrity."

*The provisional truths.*—It is . . . a kind of deception if a thinker now sets forth a whole of knowledge, a system; we have learned too much from experience not to bear in ourselves the deepest doubt of the *possibility* of such a whole. It is enough if we agree on a whole of *presuppositions of method*—on "provisional truths" according to the guidelines of which we want to work, just as the navigator of a ship on the ocean adheres to a certain direction.[12]

In a philosopher, the will to a system is, morally speaking, a more subtle corruption; immorally speaking, "his will to make himself stupider than he is—stupider, i.e.: stronger, simpler, more domineering, less educated, more imperious, more tyrannical." "I am not narrow-minded enough for a system—and not even for *my* system."[13] Inasmuch as the systematizers "want to complete" a system "and therefore make the horizon round, they have to try to present their weaker qualities in the style of their stronger ones—they want to present themselves as complete and uniformly strong natures"—that is their "play-acting."[14] The systematizer lives in a "house of knowledge, pieced together and firmly believed in";[15] he lets the truth escape in the play of the accident. His basic prejudice is that "*true Being*" is in itself uniform, ordered, and systematically secured, so that one can have trust in it.[16] What the systematizer wants is not truth in the sense of *discoveredness* but truth in the sense of *certainty*. Even the doubt of Descartes assures itself, on its path to truth, of certainty above all. The systematizers all still *believe* in the truth, but do not dare to live "on hypotheses," because it is easier to cling to a "dogmatic world" than "to an incomplete system with indeterminate prospects." All smaller spirits perish, however, on this test.[17]

And if one contradicts oneself a thousand times and goes on many paths and wears many masks and finds in oneself no end, no last horizon: is it probable that such a person learns less of the truth than does a virtuous Stoic who has set himself once and for all . . . in his place? But such prejudices sit on the threshold of all philosophies so far: and especially the prejudice that certainty is better than uncertainty and open seas.[18]

In spite of this honest will to sail off upon open seas, Nietzsche's experiment is, by the *direction* that it maintains, nevertheless systematically guided. It is a systematic attempt, but no untested system. The aphoristic tendency toward open horizons is automatically limited by an "innate relatedness" of concepts.

That individual philosophical concepts are not anything capricious or autonomously evolving, but grow up in connection and relationship with one another; that, however suddenly and arbitrarily they seem to appear in the history of thought, they nevertheless belong just as much to a system as all the members of the fauna of a continent: that is betrayed in the end also in how certainly the most diverse philosophers again and again fill in a definite fundamental scheme of *possible* philosophies. Under an invisible spell, they always revolve once more in the same orbit: however independent of one another they may feel themselves with their critical or systematic wills, something within them leads them, something impels them in a definite order, one after another—to wit, the innate systematic structure and relationship of their concepts. Their thought is, in fact, far less a discovery than a recognition, a remembering, a return and a homecoming to a remote, primordial, total household of the soul, out of which these concepts once grew. Philosophizing is to this extent a kind of atavism of the highest rank.[19]

Thus Nietzsche's newest experiment, too, moves within the compass of an oldest origin: his last attempt with the truth, directed at the overcoming of nihilism, recalls again the origins of Western philosophy. The same recollection also occurs in the emergence of a particular system out of "productive basic ideas."

A perfect analogy can be drawn between the simplification and condensing of countless experiences into general principles *and* the development of a sperm cell, which in abbreviated form carries in itself the whole past; and likewise, [an analogy can be made] between the artificial formation of a "system" out of creative basic ideas *and* the development of an organism as a thinking out and thinking forth, as a *recollection* of all life so far, its retrospective realization, its embodiment.[20]

The "convictions" of the philosophers result from such creative basic ideas, which are embodied in the system generated from those ideas. Learning changes us, to be sure, but

at the bottom of us, really "deep down," there is, it is true, something unteachable, some granite of spiritual *fatum*,[T9] of predetermined decision and answer to predetermined selected questions. Whenever a cardinal problem is at stake, there speaks an unchangeable "that's me"; e.g., about man and woman a thinker cannot relearn but only finish learning—only finish discovering ultimately how this is "settled" in him. At times we find certain solutions of problems that inspire *us* with strong faith; perhaps we call them henceforth our "convictions." Later—we see them only as steps to self-knowledge, signposts to the problem we *are*—more correctly, to the great stupidity we are, to our spiritual *fatum*, to what is *unteachable* very "deep down."[21]

What speaks then is a "sovereign drive," which is stronger than the human being.

There are probably many human beings in whom a drive has *not* become *sovereign*: in whom there are no convictions. This is accordingly the first character trait: every closed system of a philosopher proves that *one* drive is sovereign in him, that *a firm order of rank exists*. This then calls itself "truth."—The accompanying feeling is: with this truth I am on the summit "Human Being"; the other man is of a *lower type than I*, at least as a knower.[22]

Nietzsche, too, wanted to attain a last and "highest position toward existence" when at last he returned to the place from which he had started. As the teacher of the eternal recurrence, he remembered the problem of the birth of tragedy, and the end of his attempt combines systematically with its beginning in the highest kind of Dionysian Being.

But because according to this teaching the "lot of humanity" has already "*been there* eternally" and has long been decided, there is in human knowing, too, no capriciousness but only *fate*.[23] Already in Nietzsche's attempt to refrain from a system, there rules first and finally a necessity that compels him to develop as a system the idea of eternally recurring Being. And in the aphorism, which is seemingly the fleeting form of merely accidental ideas, Nietzsche wanted—in agreement with his philosophy—to mold not a transitory apothegm but a *"form of eternity."*

To create things on which time tests its teeth in vain; in form, *in substance,* to strive for a little immortality—I was never modest enough to demand less of myself. The aphorism, the apothegm, in which I am the first among the Germans to be a master, are the forms of "eternity."[24]

This form is "eternal" in the way that Nietzsche generally speaks of eternity: it has already existed once and also always recurs. And if, in an age in which philosophy lacked "wisdom,"[25] Nietzsche had no choice but to attempt the aphorism and the parable as his philosophic language, even here he rediscovered something that had already been, namely, the old wisdom of the philosophic proverb. His dissolution of the linguistic form of systematic philosophy (a form that had become arbitrary) is an attempt to reestablish linguistic necessity out of the plight of present thought. Whereas currently [in Nietzsche's time] the system gives a seeming necessity to the idea, a necessity that the idea does not truly have, the innermost compulsion drives Nietzsche to his new attempt with linguistic accident; and he does not have, consequently, a system (although he writes in aphorisms), but rather he makes another attempt with the *necessary ac-cident*[T10] of the proverbial wisdom. Thus an unwanted necessity manifests itself in the plight, of which he himself was conscious, of his aphoristic thought and writing. This necessity, however, is at home precisely in the accident of the idea and not in the system, which in excluding the accident also excludes the necessary.

Nietzsche's dissolution of the system (as a whole that is no longer possible) into a loose connection of aphorisms and parables ultimately drives to the fore a *teaching,* the linguistic form of which is as ambiguous as everything in the compass of modernity. The language of Zarathustra, which is a system of parables, does indeed seem at first to be a philosophic language only so to speak. But even in this new kind of language, what always has been, recurs, namely the age-old form of the philosophic didactic poem.[26] Only when measured by the yardstick of positive science must this language appear to be what at bottom it is

not: a mere mixture of "truth" and "poetry"; and only by this yardstick must Nietzsche appear to be what he is not, a mixer who is half
poet and half prophet. If one measures his attempt with Nietzsche's
own standard, however, then Nietzsche is no "poet-philosopher" but
the modern restorer of a most ancient philosophic language. This intention emerges indirectly in Nietzsche's denial, precisely in *Zarathustra*, that either the "scholars" or the "poets" have Being in the truth,
because the former only knit the "stockings of the spirit," and the latter "did not think into the depths enough," so that their "sentiment"
did not sink to the "foundations."[27] In the battle between "wisdom
and science,"[28] Nietzsche remembered again the original unity of truth
and poetry in the didactic language of the philosophic proverb of wisdom. His modernity achieved this unity, however, only in the ambiguous form of a system of contrived metaphors in which artful wordplay
and ingenious wit mingle with the seriousness and pathos of the whole.
Whereas the philosophic didactic poem from Parmenides to Lucretius
expounds a pondered idea in an instructive way, the speeches of Zarathustra imitate the language of the Gospels in order to proclaim an
anti-Christian message. The philosophic content of this anti-Christian
message is more veiled than apparent in the parables of Zarathustra.

Nietzsche himself stressed the *unity* of his aphoristic production.
The concern in his writings is "the long logic of a very specific philosophic sensibility" and "not a mishmash of a hundred arbitrary para-
doxes and heterodoxies."[29] "The continuous, unconscious, unwanted
concurrence and fellowship of ideas in the colorfully layered heap of
my more recent books has aroused my amazement: one cannot get
free from oneself; therefore, one should dare to let oneself go to a great
extent."[30] In accordance with the unity of his creation, he wished
"that for once another man" might make "a kind of résumé of the results of my thought" and thereby compare him with previous thinkers.
Nietzsche owed this unity to the unity of his philosophic task. "Gradually something—what most turns inward, to be sure—disciplines one
back to unity; that *passion* (for which one long has no name) saves us
from all digressions and dispersions, that *task* whose involuntary mis-
sionary one is."[31] And the more his destiny is realized, the more certainly he knows himself "in synthetic insights," and the more capable
he is of formulating down to its last conclusions the philosophical sensitivity that distinguishes him.[32] Eventually he gains the "absolute conviction" that from *The Birth of Tragedy* onward, "everything is one
and wants one."[33] For we "philosophers have no right to *isolated* acts

of any kind: we may not make isolated errors or hit upon isolated truths. Rather do our ideas, our values, our yeas and nays and ifs and buts, grow out of us with the necessity with which a tree bears fruit—related and each with an affinity to each, and evidence of *one* will, *one* health, *one* soil, *one* sun."[34] A "*fundamental will* of knowledge," which spoke and commanded ever more decisively, demanded this unity from him.

In the knowledge of this unity, Nietzsche demanded of his reader an *interpretation* of his aphorisms; for it was his ambition "to say in ten sentences what others do not say in a book."[T11] "In aphoristic books like mine, between and behind short aphorisms stands nothing but forbidden lengthy matters and chains of ideas." In order to gain access to these lengthy matters, one requires above all slow, philological reading.

Such a book, such a problem is in no hurry; moreover, we are both friends of the *lento*,[T12] I just as well as my book. One has not been a philologist to no avail, perhaps one still is, that is to say, a teacher of slow reading:—at last one also writes slowly. It now belongs not only to my habits but also to my taste . . . to write nothing else that will not bring every kind of man who "is in a hurry" to despair. Philology, that is, is that honorable art which demands of its venerators one thing above all: to go aside, to allow oneself time, to become silent, to become slow—, as a goldsmith's art and goldsmith's expertise of the *word* that has to finish off nothing but fine, cautious work, and that achieves nothing if it does not achieve *lento*. But precisely for that reason, this art is more needed today than ever before; precisely thereby it draws us and charms us most strongly, amid an age of "work," that is to say: an age of haste, of indecent and sweating speediness, that wants "to get finished" with everything right away, with every old and new book, too;—the philologic art itself does not finish with anything so easily; it teaches one to read *well*, that is, to read slowly, looking with depth, consideration, and caution, with ulterior motives, with doors left open, with sensitive fingers and eyes. . . . My patient friends, this book wishes for only perfect readers and philologists: *learn* to read me well![35]

It is *Zarathustra* above all that demands this art of reading.[36] Not only *Beyond Good and Evil* and *On the Genealogy of Morals,* but all other writings that chronologically follow *Zarathustra* are to be understood as commentaries on it; for there is no idea in them that has not already been hinted at, with equal brevity and suggestiveness, in the allegorical talk of *Zarathustra*.[37] The difficulty of interpreting parables of *Zarathustra* is, however, not smaller than that of interpreting the aphoristic production: both mislead one into skimming over them, because they allow of much too easy access. With regard to the *Genealogy of Morals* it is said:

An aphorism, properly stamped and molded, has not been "deciphered" when it has simply been read; rather, one has then to begin its *interpretation,* for which is required an art of interpretation. I have offered in the third essay of the present book an example of what I regard as "interpretation" in such a case:—an aphorism is prefixed to this essay, the essay itself is a commentary on it. To be sure, one thing is necessary above all if one is to practice reading as an *art* in this way, something that has been unlearned most thoroughly nowadays—and therefore it will be some time before my writings are "readable"—, something for which one has almost to be a cow and in any case *not* a "modern man": *rumination.*[38]

Proverbs, says Zarathustra, should be peaks for those who have grown unusually tall, who with long legs can step from one peak to another. The question remains, however, whether aphorism, proverb, and parable summon forth what Nietzsche demanded: a considerate and cautious reading by one who lingers to interpret what has been said. No one recognized the seductive element in Nietzsche's aphoristic production more clearly than his friend Overbeck: through the "cosmetic force" of its brevity, the aphorism gives paradox an undeserved luster and stretches effect out of proportion at the expense of justification. The possibility of refuting everything that has been justified is only half as dangerous as the "congenital defect with which *everything that lacks justification* . . . has entered into the world"—where the defective newborn thus cannot last.[39] We will therefore attempt to make up for this [neglected] justification in a unified interpretation of Nietzsche's diffuse production, and therewith simultaneously to make possible a critical reflection.

# 2

## The Division of Nietzsche's Writings into Periods

Nietzsche's philosophy, along with Nietzsche himself, changed several times during the implementation of his experiment. These changes only seemingly contradict the hidden system in Nietzsche's writings. In the "Aftersong" to *Beyond Good and Evil* is the well-known saying "Only he who changes stays akin to me." But the question that precedes that remark is whether Nietzsche "became another man," alien to himself. Nietzsche repeatedly gave the apt answer to this question in the parable of the "shedding of skin." To be sure, he often enough lost his patience and jumped out of his skin, but only because he was an expert in the snake sagacity of *"changing one's skin."*[1] This self-interpretation—which implies that he remained the same amidst his becoming something else, because only what also remains the same can change—stems from the time of the "noon," when Nietzsche stood still in the middle of his life.[2] In this decisive noon of his life and thought, he looked ahead as well as back, in order to understand himself in the whole.[3] In looking ahead at the future task, he was for the first time capable of reading backward the "long sentence" of his life. "In reading forward, there is no doubt about it, at that time I read only 'words without meaning.'" And because the future of his task controlled him in advance—so much so that the meaning of even his first school essays becomes fully clear only in the light of his last teaching—he was later able to see his own past, too, as "explicating the future," and to survey his whole philosophic experiment as a transformation of something that is the same.[4] In this transformation he had not

21

become alien to himself but rather had become himself, and by deciding in favor of a "second nature," he gained possession of his first nature.[5] "Thus I regained the way to that bold pessimism which is the opposite of all romantic mendacity and also, as it appears to me today, the way to 'me' myself, to *my* task."[6] This task consisted in the development of the irresolute pessimism of the nineteenth century into a resolute nihilism and into the "self-overcoming" thereof.[7] He who has learned to read Nietzsche systematically will thus be astonished not at the motley riches of his alternating perspectives but at the continuity and even the monotony of his philosophic problem. "If one has character, one also has one's typical experience, which always returns."[T13]

Nietzsche's retrograde interpretation of himself in terms of the problem that lay before him manifests itself most clearly in the new prefaces of 1886 to his earlier writings. With *Human, All-Too-Human,* his own, lonely voyage of discovery begins, the voyage that finally leads him back in a circle to his point of departure. Two critical metamorphoses justify the differentiation of Nietzsche's writings into three periods: first, the transformation from the reverential disciple into the self-liberating spirit, and second, from the spirit that has been liberated into the teaching master. At first, as the eagerly admiring, younger friend of Richard Wagner, Nietzsche believed in the renewal of German culture.[8] Afterward, as a spirit who had painfully been liberated, he believed "in nothing at all," in order to seek his own path—until finally, in the willing of fate, he became the teacher of the eternal recurrence. The "ring" of the eternal recurrence is Nietzsche's reply to *The Ring of the Nibelung.*

The tie to Wagner, and the break with him, was the decisive event in Nietzsche's life, and he never got over it. The dedication of *The Birth of Tragedy* "Out of the Spirit of Music" marks the beginning of this relationship, and *Nietzsche contra Wagner* its end. It comes to a peak in Nietzsche's intention to give up his professorship in Basel in order to put himself into the service of "Bayreuth" as a literary propagandist. To Nietzsche, Wagner was *the* antipode, but he was also "the only one, or the first" who had given Nietzsche a feeling for what significance he himself had, while Cosima Wagner was the first and only woman whom Nietzsche revered as Ariadne, even into the time of his insanity. After *Zarathustra,* Nietzsche enjoyed the idea of taking over "the inheritance" of Wagner and thereby separating Wagner's "big enterprise" from his all-too-human shortcomings. Nietzsche and Wagner belong together still more and differently than Nietzsche himself was aware, and not least through the common theme of "redemption," which derived from Schopenhauer's metaphysics of the will.[9]

The first period comprises, of the writings published by Nietzsche himself, *The Birth of Tragedy* and the *Untimely Meditations*. The second includes the writings of the "plowshare": *Human, All-Too-Human*; *The Dawn of Day*; and the first four books of *The Gay Science*. The third period begins on the foundation of the idea of the eternal recurrence, with *Zarathustra*, and ends with *Ecce Homo*. This period alone contains Nietzsche's genuine philosophy. Corresponding to the break with the first period is a critical transitional step from the second period to the third which is subsequently expressed in aphorisms 341 and 342 as well as in the "Epilogue" to *The Gay Science*, but which already appears in *The Dawn*. The dedicatory verses of *The Gay Science* and the question mark at the end of *The Dawn* already refer to the motif of "*eternity*," which not only dominates *Zarathustra* and was to form the conclusion to *Ecce Homo* in the poetic figure of "fame and eternity," but also justifies philosophically the critique of [his] *time* in *The Will to Power*.

> The task for the years that were to follow was sketched out as clearly as possible. After the yes-saying part of my task had been solved, the turn had come for the no-saying, *no-doing* half: the revaluation of values so far, the great war—the conjuring up of a day of decision. . . .
>
> When one considers that this book followed *after Zarathustra*, one may perhaps also guess the dietetic regimen to which it owes its origin. The eye that had been spoiled by a tremendous coercion to see *far* . . . is here forced to focus on what lies nearest, the age, the *around-us*,[10]

says Nietzsche toward an explanation of *Beyond Good and Evil*, which as the "Prelude to a Philosophy of the Future" connects *Zarathustra* with *The Will to Power*.

This division into periods is no mere external schematization that one could, without damage to one's understanding of Nietzsche's system, replace with another, better scheme.[11] Rather, the periodic division is confirmed in its full significance by Nietzsche himself. Its methodological weight derives from the fact that it marks the essential stages on Nietzsche's "path to wisdom." That he twice lost this path was, both times, a crisis.

> *The path to wisdom.* Pointers toward the overcoming of morality.
> *The first passageway.* Venerate (and obey and *learn*) better than anyone. Gather into yourself all things venerable and have them struggle with one another. Carry everything heavy . . . the time of community . . .

*The second passageway.* Shatter the venerating heart when you are *most tightly bound.* The free spirit. Independence. The time of the desert. Critique of everything venerated (idealization of the unvenerated), attempt at reverse valuations.

*The third passageway.* The big decision whether one is suited for a positive stance, for affirmation. No more god, no more man *above* me! The instinct of the creator who knows where he sets his hand. The big responsibility and the innocence. (In order to have joy in anything, you must approve of *everything.*) Give yourself the right to act.

(Beyond good and evil. He espouses the mechanical view of the world and does not feel humiliated under destiny: he *is* destiny. He has the fateful lot of humanity in his hand.)

Only for the few: most will perish already in the second path.[12]

In the prefatory materials of 1886, Nietzsche himself grouped his writings in the corresponding way, and from the point of view of his last philosophy of the "noon," he understood the writings of the second period as a philosophy of the "dawn" and of the "morning."[13] They are for him the avenue to understanding that specimen of humanity in whom the liberated spirit frees itself once again *from* its most extreme freedom *toward amor fati.*[T14] In contrast, the *Untimely Meditations* signify for him mere "promises," and "perhaps there will yet come a human being who will discover that from *Human, All-Too-Human* onward, I have done nothing but fulfill my promises."

Disregarding *The Birth of Tragedy* (the philosophic interpretation of which occurred only in the new preface of 1886, in *Twilight of the Idols,* and in *Ecce Homo*), the chronologically first decisive step on Nietzsche's path to wisdom is the conscious "progress within *decadence*"— up to the critical edge of an extreme nihilism, in which *nothing is true any more,* but *everything is permitted.*[14] The further transitional step to the philosophy of the eternal recurrence is depicted in *Zarathustra* by means of a second crisis; it happens between the "most silent hour" and the "convalescence" in the transition from the second to the third Part. From *Zarathustra* on, everything further fits easily into a philosophy of the eternal recurrence as the self-overcoming of extreme nihilism. The critique of all values so far that is contained in *The Will to Power,* the No to modernity, presupposes the already gained Yes to the eternal cycle of things. And the "innocence of becoming" as a "guide to the redemption of morality" is itself guided by the redemption that *Zarathustra* contains. The last total plan for *The Will to Power,* written in 1888, corresponds to this division: In the first three books, under the names "Antichrist," "Free Spirit," and "Immoralist," this plan contains Nietzsche's negative philosophy of redemption, that is, *from* nihilism; and in the fourth and final book, it contains the positive philosophy of redemption *toward* the eternal recurrence of the same, under the name "Dionysus."

*Zarathustra* proves, in a conspicuous passage, how little our characterization of the metamorphoses of a *same* means reading something into the text; rather, we are following Nietzsche's own interpretation. The first speech at once deals with "three metamorphoses" of one and the same spirit. The man who has become a spirit of burden, who reveres the strange and bears what is most difficult to bear, becomes in the first crisis the courageous spirit who consumes the spirit of veneration and wills himself. "Here the spirit becomes a lion who wants to capture his freedom and be master in his own desert."[15] He transforms the alien "*Thou shalt*" of reverential faith into his own "*I will.*" But "to create new values—even the lion is not yet capable of that." He can only create for himself the freedom for new values to his No to "God" and to "duty," which say "Thou shalt." He who has become free must yet become the game-playing child of the world,[16] in order simply to exist in the cosmic innocence of continual becoming. This last metamorphosis from the "*I will*" to the "*I am*"[17] of the child of the world occurs in the second crisis of the most silent hour. Only with this metamorphosis does the spirit regain, out of the "desert of his freedom," the lost world as his own world—in a holy Yes to the eternally recurring Being of all that is.

This double turning of the path, on the *one* way to wisdom (from the "Thou shalt" of the faithful one to the "I will" of the spirit that has become free, and from the latter to the "I am" there and always recur), characterizes the philosophic system of Nietzsche as a whole. A first decision for the "I will" frees *from* all previous ties and *for* nihilism. The second decision—to shape oneself out of freedom—is the obverse of an inspiration received from the highest star of Being. A "double will," which liberates itself toward *amor fati* from its already attained freedom toward the nothing, turns the extreme nihilism (of an existence that has decided for the nothing) around into the necessary willing of the eternally necessary recurrence of the same.

Three allegorical figures characterize this path from the spirit that is liberated through negation to the teacher of the eternal recurrence. The *wanderer* accompanied by his shadow symbolizes the progress up to the edge of the nothing. The wanderer accompanies the superhuman *Zarathustra* (who also still wanders) as his shadow, and finally the *god Dionysus* takes Zarathustra's place. In the end, Nietzsche knew that he himself was, from the very beginning, the last disciple of Dionysus. A last and "highest" position toward existence is achieved in the Dionysian position, which once and for all says Yes to the whole of Being and of time.[18] This last position toward existence is beyond good and evil but not beyond good and bad. The correlate to this Dionysian interpretation of the world is the "highest kind of Being" in *Dionysus philosophus* himself. In the *amor fati* of Nietzsche's teaching, the self-affirmation of eternally recurring Being thus unites with an eternal Yes of one's own existence to the whole of Being.

> Shield of necessity!
> Highest star of Being!
> —Which no wish achieves,
> Which no No stains,
> Eternal Yes of Being
> Eternally I am your Yes: for I love you, O eternity![T15]

The division of Nietzsche's writings into periods according to a double metamorphosis (the first of the "three" metamorphoses is not characterized in further detail regarding its point of departure) would be incompletely conceived if one did not see at the same time that at the end of his path Nietzsche recurs to the starting point,[19] so that the whole of his movement comes to a retrograde conclusion in a circle and at the end catches up with the beginning. Only thereby does his philosophy become a "system" at all. "It only recurs, it comes home to me at last—my own self," it is said in *Zarathustra* at the conclusion of the wandering. In *Twilight of the Idols* ("What I Owe to the Ancients"), this recurrence to himself is expressly called a repetition of the problem of *The Birth of Tragedy*.

And herewith I again touch that point from which I once went forth: *The Birth of Tragedy* was my first revaluation of all values. Herewith I again stand on the ground out of which my willing, my *ability* grows—I, the last disciple of the philosopher Dionysus—I, the teacher of the eternal return.

The teaching of the eternal recurrence repeats *The Birth of Tragedy* and makes possible the "revaluation of all values" that follows, because this teaching pertains in its *principle* not to just any single value but to the now problematic "value of existence" as such and as a whole: the reversal of the will to the *nothing*, of nihilism, into the willing of the *Being* of the eternal recurrence of the same.

# 3

# The Unifying Fundamental
# Idea in Nietzsche's Philosophy

## The Liberation from "Thou Shalt"
## to "I Will"

The writings of the second period, in which Nietzsche for the first time liberated himself, have been generally understood as "positivist." But this understanding does not conceive these writings in their connection with the successive writings and from the standpoint of these. The works of the second period are positivistic only in the sense in which Nietzsche himself understood philosophically the scientific positivism of the nineteenth century, namely as a "disappointed romanticism" that is on the way to a resolute nihilism.[1] Nietzsche's own positivism is, as a still irresolute nihilism, a skepticism that is in a state of suspense, a first attempt in investigative traveling. Nietzsche decided on this "emigration" after the break with Wagner and his public, "the Germans of the nineteenth century." From then on he lived and thought "on his own credit," until insanity finally made him have faith in himself.

The new prefaces to *Human, All-Too-Human* exhaustively explain the philosophical meaning of Nietzsche's commencing these wanderings, which set him apart from the people around him in an obvious sense, too, through his resignation of his Basel professorship. The subtitle of *Human, All-Too-Human* is "A Book for Free Spirits."[2] The freedom that is tested for the first time in this book is at first negative: a freeing *from* . . . by the resolute separation from all traditionally received ties. *Human, All-Too-Human,* as a monument to a first crisis, is the document of a departure and of a setting out for new goals.[3] The separation does not result, as in the Enlightenment, in a struggle against the ecclesiastical authorities; rather, it only draws the conclusion from the dissolution of all previous ties that has already taken place.

. . . the modern free spirit is not born out of struggle like his forefathers, but rather out of the *peace of dissolution* in which he has seen all spiritual powers of the old world of ties and commitments decline. After this greatest revolution in history has occurred, his soul can be without envy and almost without need; he no longer strives for many things for himself, nor for plenty; that free, fearless hovering over human beings, manners and morals, laws, and the traditional evaluations of things satisfies him as the most desirable situation. He gladly communicates his joy over this situation; whoever wants more from him he directs, with a little mockery on his lips and a benevolent shaking of his head, to his brother, the free man of action, whose "freedom" is, to be sure, a story in itself. . . .[4]

As a spirit free of its ties, the free spirit is a "relative" concept.

They call a free spirit the man who thinks otherwise than one expects from him because of his descent, his environment, his social status and office, or because of the prevailing views of his time. He is the exception, spirits with ties are the rule; the latter reproach him on the ground that his free principles either have their origin in the inordinate passion to be conspicuous or even suggest free actions of the free spirit, i.e., actions that are irreconcilable with the morality of ties and commitments. Occasionally they also say that this or that *free principle derives from eccentricity* and extravagance in the mind of the free spirit; thus speaks only wickedness, which does not itself believe what it says but wants to harm thereby: because the testimony for the greater goodness and sharpness of his intellect is written in the face of the free spirit so legibly that the spirits with ties understand this testimony well enough. But the two other derivations of free-spiritedness are honestly meant; and in fact many free spirits originate in the one way or the other.[5]

The free spirit believes nothing out of habit, but rather asks for reasons in every case. "All states and orders of societies: the social classes, marriage, upbringing, law, all these have their power and duration solely in the faith in these institutions that the spirit with ties maintains—that is, in the absence of reasons or at least in guarding against the request for reasons." The free spirit is thus the opposite to all rooted spirits, but precisely as a rootlessly "hovering ambiguity,"[6] he has an investigating "spirit." The ten commandments of the free spirit read as follows:

Thou shalt neither love nor hate peoples.
Thou shalt practice no politics.
Thou shalt not be rich and also be no beggar.
Thou shalt avoid the famous and influential.
Thou shalt take thy woman from another people than thine own.
Thou shalt have thy children reared by thy friends.
Thou shalt submit to no ceremony of the church.
Thou shalt not repent of a sin, but do an extra good deed on that account.
Thou shalt prefer exile in order to be able to say the truth.
Thou shalt give the world full play against thyself and thyself full play against the world.[7]

The separation from the received ties occurs in two steps: it *removes* one, at first, from the customary world of traditional opinions and appraisals of value; and it makes possible, by reason of this removal from . . . , a new and authentic *nearness* to . . . the "things that are nearest."[8] Looking back on what happened to him then, Nietzsche understands the first step in his process of separation as a breakthrough of the "*will to the free will*."[9] In the first instance and for the most part, however, the human being does not want his own will but an alien will that he can obey instead of having to command himself. This first, preliminary will to the free will, which as master of itself then becomes master over things, too, already sketches out the later, superhuman idea of the "masters of the earth" who replace God because they are able to command themselves. Likewise, the "revaluation of all previous values," too, is already prefigured in the free spirit. He attempts to see how things look *if* one reverses them and gives preference to "what has been neglected"—the "sides of existence that hitherto have been denied." With this craving for the reversal of the generally valid, he isolates himself in relation to his contemporaries. From *The Wanderer* on, "loneliness" becomes a basic problem of self-willing existence.[10]

One may suppose that a spirit in whom the type "free spirit" should once become ripe and sweet to the point of perfection has had its decisive event in a *great separation,* and that he previously was all the more a spirit with ties and seemed to be chained forever to his corner and pillar. What ties most tightly? . . . Among men of a higher and select type, that will be duties: that veneration, as it befits youth, that shyness and sensitivity before everything venerable and worthy, that thankfulness for the ground out of which they grew, for the hand that led them, for the shrine where they learned to worship—their highest moments will themselves tie these men most tightly, bind them to duty the longest. The great separation comes suddenly for men so tied, like an earthquake: the young soul is all of a sudden shaken, torn away, torn out—he himself does not understand what is happening. An impulse and thronglike pressure rules and becomes master over him like a command; a will and wish awakens to go forth, anywhere, at any price; a violent, dangerous curiosity for an undiscovered world . . . throbs in all his senses. "Better to die than to live *here*"—thus rings the commanding voice and seduction: and this "here" and this "at home" is everything that he has loved until then! A sudden scare and mistrust of what he loves, a flash of disdain against what was called his "duty," a turbulent, arbitrary, volcanically thrusting desire for wandering, the alien, alienation.[11]

This first experimental self-liberation is, however, not yet the "mature freedom" of the spirit, which is just as much self*ishness* as self-*discipline* and allows the path to multiple and opposite ways of thinking. The liberated spirit has the right to live experimentally after he has succeeded with his first, trial experiment. He now lives voluntarily far from things and voluntarily close to them, because what concerns him, no longer troubles him; whereas what does not at all concern the spirits with ties, does trouble them. Because of his alienation, he draws near to life again, "as if only now his eyes opened up to the near things." He becomes master of his own virtues, too, and he recognizes the element of perspective in all things; he does so as the noble betrayer of all things that can be betrayed at all, and yet he does this without a feeling of guilt.

Like a physician who puts his patient into a completely alien environment so that he will be removed from his entire "until now," his cares, friends, letters, duties, stupidities, and torments of memory, and learn to stretch out his hands and senses toward a new nourishment, a new sun, a new future; just so did I force myself, as physician and patient in one person, to a reversed, untested *climate of the soul,* and in particular to retiring travels into alien parts, into *the* alien, to a curiosity for all kinds of strange things. . . . A long traveling about, searching, changing resulted from this, an aversion for all steadfastness, against every clumsy affirmation and denial . . . ; a minimum of life, an unchaining from all crude covetousness, an independence and every kind of external disfavor . . . , some cynicism, perhaps . . . , but just as certainly . . . much silence, light, more subtle folly, hidden revelry—all that finally yielded a great spiritual strengthening.[12]

Nietzsche not only had his own experience and destiny in this liberation of all ties, into a resolute nihilism, but he was at the same time sensible of the general experience of the European spirit.

Should my experience—the history of an illness and a convalescence, for it ended up in a convalescence—have been only my personal experience? And just merely *my* "human, all-too-human"? I should like to believe the reverse today; confidence returns to me again that my wander-books were not recorded only for me, as it has sometimes appeared.[T16]

And just as he later foresaw the coming up of resolute nihilists,[13] he also already saw the free spirits coming, those who are rid of and exempt from the old ties in order to be free—for what? For a new attempt with an oldest truth.[14]

He who has in this way come to the freedom of the spirit can only feel like a *wanderer.* A "wanderer"—the secular form of the Christian pilgrim—concludes (as the forerunner of the likewise wandering Zarathustra) the first Part of *Human, All-Too-Human*; then converses with his own shadow at the beginning and end of the second division of the second Part.

He who at least to a certain extent has come to the freedom of reason cannot feel otherwise on earth than as a wanderer—however, not as a traveler to a last goal: for the latter does not exist. But surely he wants to look on attentively and keep his eyes open for everything that really goes on in the world: therefore he may not fasten his heart too tightly to anything in particular; there must be within himself something wandering that takes its joy in change and transitoriness. Granted, ill nights will come to such a man when he will be tired, and he will find the gate to the city, which should offer him rest, locked. . . . But then will come, as compensation, the blissful mornings of other places and days wherein . . . afterward, when in the calm symmetry of the morning soul he quietly takes a stroll under trees, there will be thrown to him, out of the tree-tops and the hiding places of their foliage, nothing but good and bright things, the presents of all those free spirits who are at home on the mountain, in the forest, and in loneliness; and who, like him, in their now gay, now reflective way, are wanderers and philosophers. Born out of the secrets of the early hour, they meditate on how the day can have such a pure, illuminated, transfigured-serene look between the tenth and twelfth strokes of the clock:—they seek the *philosophy of the morning.*[15]

That is the philosophy before the "great noon," when Zarathustra teaches the eternal recurrence. The connection of the philosophy of the morning with that of the noon is repeatedly intimated in the two dialogues between the wanderer and his shadow. The very skepticism of the free spirit of the wanderer already has a hidden "will to wisdom."[16] And just as the "abyss" of extreme nihilism "speaks again" only when the opposite idea, that of the eternal recurrence, also wants to be spoken, so does the shadow, too, "speak" to the wanderer, as if "the latter" heard "himself speak." Light and shadow belong together like Yes and No or like the height and depth of the highest Being and the deepest nothing.[17] And at noon—and this "highest time" when the shadow is shortest because the sun of knowledge then stands directly over things—the free spirit of the wanderer already has a kind of "eternity" in view.

*At noon.*—For the man destined for an active and stormy morning of life, a curious longing for tranquillity overtakes his soul at the noon of life, a longing that can last for moons and years. It becomes still around him, the voices sound far and farther away; the sun shines straight down upon him. On a hidden forest glade he sees the great Pan sleeping; all things of nature have fallen asleep with him, an expression of eternity on their faces—so it seems to him. He wants nothing, he cares about nothing, his heart stands still, only his eye lives; it is a death with eyes awake. There man sees many a thing that he has not seen before, and as far as he sees, everything is woven into a net of light and, as it were, buried therein. He feels happy about this, but it is a heavy, heavy happiness.[18]

Yet also the happiness of Zarathustra, when he has convalesced from the nothing, is melancholy like an "evening sun over the last catastrophe." Zarathustra's teaching at "noon" completes what is, at the level of the first liberation (from "Thou shalt" to "I will"), only a first and transitory prefiguration of eternity.

At first, however, it appears as if the philosophy of the morning displays *only* the shadow and not *also* the light of everything that is. Primarily for that reason, the wanderer confers with *his* shadow in order to indicate at the end of the first dialogue that they have "agreed" about something. The wanderer, who supposes that in our views we have so far only perceived the shadow, is answered by the shadow with a question, "*More the shadow than the light? Is it possible?*" In truth both are as much a one as the prophecy of nihilism is one with the prophecy of the eternal recurrence of the same. They are not opponents; "they rather hold hands lovingly, and when the light disappears, the shadow slips away after it." Shadow and light go hand in hand, like the nothing of resolute nihilism and the Being of the eternal recurrence. Both together form the Heraclitean "double world" in which Hades, the lord of shadows, and Dionysus, the lord of eternal life, are one and the same Being of all that is.[19] During the final discussion between the wanderer and his shadow, it unexpectedly becomes evening, "the sun goes down,"[20] and together with the shadow, the wanderer, too, has disappeared.

This preliminary philosophy of the noon has its own high point in a "minimum" of faith. Nietzsche himself had become a shadow unto himself when he wrote *The Wanderer.*

In the thirty-sixth year of my life, I reached the lowest point of my vitality—I still lived, but without being able to see three steps ahead of me. Then—it was in 1879—I retired from my Basel professorship; spent the summer in

St. Moritz like a shadow; and spent the next winter, the poorest in sunshine in my life, in Naumburg *as* a shadow. This was my minimum; *The Wanderer and His Shadow* originated during this period. Doubtless at that time I was an expert in shadows.[21]

The philosophic expression for this highest minimum—and one such minimum is the "peak" of the eternal recurrence out of the "abyss" of nihilism—is, within the text of *The Wanderer,*[22] the dialogue between Pyrrhon and an old man.[T17] Out of Pyrrhon's laughing silence speaks the nihilism that still hangs in a state of suspense.

Later the liberated laughter of the transformed Zarathustra takes the place of the silence of Pyrrhon, who in a "last self-overcoming" and "indifference" is silent like a "Buddhist for Greece"[23] because he has nothing more to say. Zarathustra pronounces his own laughter holy after he has brought up the abyss. The most extreme skepticism of the wanderer Pyrrhon is a nihilism that for him is not yet resolute. And because of this irresoluteness, the last result of Nietzsche's first liberation—he calls it "logical world-denial,"[24] epistemologically speaking—is, in the context of his whole attempt, nevertheless only the penultimate expression of a penultimate will. As a human wanderer "without a goal," he lost the way to his own path to wisdom before, in the figure of Zarathustra, he climbed over himself to a goalless, recurring existence. On this path a "horrid" necessity precedes him,[25] a necessity that to Zarathustra changes into the "shield of necessity," the highest star of Being. "No more path! Abyss all around and the stillness of death! Thus you wanted it! Your will strayed from the path! Now, wanderer, it counts! Now look with a cold and clear eye. You are lost if you believe—in danger."[26] This pathlessness is portrayed in the presentiment of the way out that in fact became available.

I stand still, I am suddenly weary. Ahead, it seems, it goes downhill, fast as lightning, abyss all around—I do not like to look on. Behind me tower the mountains. Shaking, I grasp for a support. What? Has everything around me suddenly become rock and precipice? Here the bushes—they break to pieces in my hand, and yellowed leaves and scanty little roots crumble down. I shudder and I close my eye.—Where am I? I look into a purple night, it pulls me to itself and waves at me. But how am I? What happened to make your voice suddenly fail and to make you feel as if you were buried under a load of drunken and obscure feelings?[27]

The wanderer who has become pathless looks into the purple night of madness.

Not Nietzsche himself, only Zarathustra has found the superhuman way out by means of which one comes from the nothing "into the something."[28] Without any path, Zarathustra climbs over himself to his last greatness. Peak and abyss become one for him, and what hitherto was his last *danger* has become a *refuge* for him. This refuge unto the last danger already begins when Zarathustra rides to hell "like a shadow." The "highest time," when this occurs, is a noon between the shortest time in the fore-noon and the eternal moment at "noon and eternity."[29] The wanderer of the previous time accompanies Zarathustra only as a shadow,[30] and Zarathustra, like the wanderer earlier, is now called by his shadow, which seems to have longer legs than Zarathustra himself.

"Who are you?" Zarathustra asked violently. "What are you doing here? And why do you call yourself my shadow? I do not like you."

"Forgive me," answered the shadow, "that it is I; and if you do not like me, well then . . . for that I praise you and your good taste. I am a wanderer who has already walked a great deal at your heels: always on my way, but without a goal, also without a home. . . .

"What? Must I always be on my way? Whirled by every wind, restless, driven on? O earth, you become too round for me!

"I have already sat on every surface; like weary dust, I have gone to sleep on mirrors and windowpanes: everything takes away from me, nothing gives, I become thin—I am almost like a shadow.

"But after you . . . I flew and blew the longest; and even when I hid from you, I was still your best shadow: wherever you sat, I sat too.

"With you I haunted the remotest, coldest worlds like a ghost that runs voluntarily over wintry roofs and snow.

"With you I strove to penetrate everything that is forbidden, worst, remotest; and if there is anything in me that is virtue, it is that I had no fear of any prohibition.

"With you I broke apart whatever my heart revered; I overthrew all boundary stones and icons; I pursued the most dangerous wishes: verily, over every crime I have passed once.

"With you I unlearned faith in words and values and great names. . . .

" 'Nothing is true, all is permitted': thus I spoke to myself. . . .

. . . "Where has all that is good gone from me, and all shame, and all faith in those who are good?! Alas, where is that mendacious innocence which I once pursued, the innocence of the good and their noble lies?!

"Too often, truly, did I follow close on the heels of truth: so she kicked me in the face. Sometimes I thought I was lying, and behold! only then did I hit—the truth.

"Too much has become clear to me: now it no longer concerns me. . . .

"What is left to me now? A heart weary and impudent, a restless will . . . a broken backbone.

"This searching for *my* home . . . was *my* affliction; it consumes me. Where is—*my* home? I ask and search and have searched for it, but I have not found it. O eternal everywhere, O eternal nowhere, O eternal—in vain!"[31]

The wanderer of the previous time has survived himself in this shadow that accompanies the truth, but in such a way that he lives on as Zarathustra's shadow. And the shadow also finds "home" through him who knows that the nihilistic wisdom of the shadow is a part of his own wisdom—home, that is, to the "in vain" of the eternal recurrence of the same, in which the goallessness of the endless wandering changes into the entirely different goallessness of eternal revolving. This metamorphosis is no small danger for the free spirit:

> You have had a bad day: see to it that you do not have a still worse evening!
>
> To those who are as restless as you, even a prison will at last seem blissful. Have you ever seen how captured criminals sleep? They sleep calmly, enjoying their new security.
>
> Beware lest a narrow faith capture you in the end—some harsh and severe illusion! . . .
>
> You have lost your goal; alas, how will you jest over and digest this loss? Therewith—you have also lost your way.[T18]

The question remains whether Nietzsche himself has not become, with his transformation of the freedom unto the nothing into the love of fate, what he called the "apostate of the free spirit."[32] At last, is not the nihilistic truth of the shadow affirmative precisely because to love, everything is permitted (which was permitted to freedom only because to freedom nothing was true any more)?

In *Twilight of the Idols,* the free spirit is finally interpreted as the "most comprehensive" spirit, who can permit himself everything because he has the "tolerance of strength" that says its Yes to everything that is. There is for the free spirit nothing forbidden any more, save weakness. He who previously was the teacher of the most extreme mistrust now stands as a spirit who has become free, "with a joyful and trusting fatalism amidst the universe, in the faith that only the individual thing is damnable, that in the whole of Being, however, everything redeems and affirms itself—*he does not deny any more.*"—"But such a faith is the highest of all possible faiths: I have baptized it with the name of Dionysus." The concealed Yes was stronger than all negativity, and "if you must go to sea, you emigrants, then what compels you, too, to do so is—a *faith!*"[33] The traditional ideals have, to be sure, been frozen forever through the work of the first liberation—Zarathustra-Dionysus, too, no longer believes in the great terms: genius, saint, hero, poet, faith, conviction[34]—yet the truly liberated spirit also does not cling

to "the ideal of a complete lack of ideals" and "the belief in unbelief."
The truly liberated spirit transforms the last result of "logical world-
denial" into a metaphysics of eternally recurring world-affirmation.
And if *Human, All-Too-Human* is dedicated to [the atheist] Voltaire
whereas Nietzsche finally speaks in the name of the god Dionysus, this
seeming contradiction finds its explanation as follows: free-spiritedness
has from the outset, "against a deeper and more passionate current
at the bottom," and with a tough "will to wisdom," "kept the upper
hand."[35] On the other hand, however, Dionysus, too, is still an "at-
tempter god," and Zarathustra is a "skeptic" who, as a liberated spirit,
only avails himself of convictions without submitting to them.

   The positivistic appearance of Nietzsche's writings of the early period conceals the nihilism that underlies them, just as the nihilism conceals the reverse tendency toward a "classical" positivism. Radical skepticism is the precondition for resolute nihilism, just as nihilism is the
precondition for the resolute Yes to the eternal Being of all that is.

*Redeemed from skepticism.*—A: Others emerge ill-tempered and weak, gnawed
to pieces, worm-eaten, even half-corroded by a general moral skepticism—but
I emerge more courageous and healthy than ever, with regained instincts.
Where a biting wind blows, where the sea surges high and no little danger is to
be endured, I will be at ease. I have not become a worm, although I often have
had to work and dig like a worm.—B: You have plainly *ceased* to be a skeptic!
Because you *deny*!—A: And therewith I have learned *to say Yes* again.[36]

On the path to this redemptive reversal, Zarathustra succeeded in ward-
ing off the last danger of the liberated spirit and in not clinging to his
own unfettering,[37] whereas Nietzsche himself, bent "between two nothings," found redemption in insanity.[38]

# The Liberation from the "I Will"
# to the "I Am" of the Child of the World

## THE DEATH OF GOD AND THE
## PROPHECY OF NIHILISM

   Because all "Thou shalt" of the moral imperatives is finally measured against the Christian God who commanded man regarding what he should do, the death of *God* is at the same time the

*principle of the will* that wills itself in man. In the "desert of his freedom," man prefers to will the nothing rather than not will, for he *is*
"man"—without God—only insofar as he also "wills." The death of
God means the resurrection of the man who is abandoned to his own
responsibility and command, the man who finally has his most extreme
freedom in "freedom toward death." At the peak of this freedom,
however, the will to the nothing inverts itself into the willing of the
eternal recurrence of the same. The *dead Christian God,* the *man before the nothing,* and the *will to the eternal recurrence* characterize Nietzsche's system as a whole as a movement first from "Thou shalt" to the
birth of the "I will" and then to the rebirth of the "I am" as the "first
movement" of an eternally recurring existence amidst the naturelike
world of all that is.[39]

In order to understand what Nietzsche means by the "death of
God," we must recall what Hegel conceived by this term. Because
Hegel wanted to grasp what the ideas of faith mean for philosophic
thought, he included the absolute truth of the Christian religion in his
own completion of "Christian-Germanic" philosophy. Hegel's philosophy of spirit not only begins with studies of the spirit of Christianity,
but also is from the beginning to end a philosophical theology, and
does not just contain a particular philosophy of religion. Like a second
Proclus, Hegel—in a big reversal of the world and of the spirit—con-
cluded the history of the Christian *logos* philosophically.[40]

Whereas Hegel still reminiscently preserved, in Greek concepts, the
whole of the Western philosophy of the *logos* (in its Christian transformation), Feuerbach in 1840 proclaimed the "necessity of a change"
and postulated for the first time a "resolutely unchristian" philosophy.
For him Hegelian philosophy meant a last, magnificent attempt to restore the lost Christianity by means of philosophy, in the ambiguous
unity of theology and philosophy, of religion and atheism, of Christianity and paganism on the peak of metaphysics.[41] For Nietzsche, too,
Hegel's ambiguous conservation of Christianity signified "a last delay
of straightforward atheism" "in accordance with the grand attempt that
he made to persuade us of the divinity of existence—with the help, as a
last resort, of our sixth sense, the 'historical sense.' "[42] It was possible
for Nietzsche to see in Hegel the great delayer of a "straightforward"
atheism, however, only because he saw as his own, preliminary task
something that in its very principle went beyond the "pious atheism"
of Feuerbach, namely: to bring about a "crisis and highest decision" in
the problem of the already legitimated atheism.[43] And because he

knew himself to be a "turning point" within the post-history of Christianity, he was also able to understand again, in the problematical character of ambiguous modernity, the world-historical *unity* of antiquity and Christianity—but he understood this unity critically and not, like Hegel, in a conciliatory mode. Now, to be sure, looking back on the history of Christianity, one could well foresee "that one day Christianity *must* end." But in Christianity, antiquity too projects into our time, and if Christianity vanishes, the understanding of antiquity will likewise vanish. According to Nietzsche, now is the best time to know Christianity, because no prejudice leads us to favor Christianity. But we still understand it and in it antiquity, too, insofar as antiquity conforms to Christianity. Conversely, a critique of Hellenism means at the same time a critique of Christianity, for both had their foundation in a religious cult. Consequently, it is the task of the philosophic philologist "to characterize Hellenism as irretrievable and *therewith* also Christianity and the previous foundations of our society and politics." For Christianity has not overcome antiquity unilaterally, but has also let itself be overcome by antiquity[44] in order to be able to hold its own in the world. We moderns, however, suffer from the "witty mendacity" that ancient Christianity brought upon man when it produced a denatured man in its battle against the ancient, natural man. *Our* alleged culture has no permanence, because it is erected on "untenable conditions and opinions that have already almost disappeared": on the remains of the culture of the Greek city, which was based on myth, and of Roman Catholic society.[45]

Thus between Hegel and Nietzsche the will to a last preservation of tradition first developed into the revolutionary intention to "change" tradition[46] and then into the consciousness of its untenability. And there also corresponds to that development a characteristic transformation in the philosophic position toward Christianity. Hegel's absolute philosophy of spirit is itself still philosophy of religion; Feuerbach reduces the "essence" of Christian religion into the divine essence of man; and Nietzsche declares, "God is dead—now we will that the superman live." That is to say: *the death of God demands from the self-willing man an overcoming of man along with getting rid of God*: the "superman." But if God is really dead and if faith in him has expired, the distinction between still conceiving the death of God speculatively and conceiving it only anthropologically becomes minute. In the horizon of Nietzsche's "atheism," which recognizes for the first time that the "*death of God*" means for man "*freedom toward death*,"[47] Hegel and Feuerbach draw together as "church fathers," "half-priests," and "veil-makers."[48, T19]

Hegel, at the end of "Faith and Knowledge," transforms faith in the God who died in Christ into a "speculative Good Friday." To Hegel the death of God[49] is the abyss of the *nothing* into which all *Being* sinks, in order to emerge anew in the movement of becoming.

The pure concept, however, . . . as the abyss of the nothing into which all Being sinks, must characterize endless pain purely as an element, but also as not more than an element, of the highest idea. The endless pain was previously only in formation, historically, and existed as the feeling on which the religion of the new age is based—the feeling: God himself is dead (that which so to speak was expressed only empirically, in Pascal's terms: "la nature est telle qu'elle *marque* partout un *Dieu perdu* et dans l'homme et hors de l'homme"[T20]). And thus the pure concept must give a philosophic existence to what was, perhaps, either a moral imperative of sacrifice of the empirical essence or the concept of formal abstraction. And thus the concept gives to philosophy the idea of absolute freedom and therewith absolute suffering or the speculative Good Friday, which otherwise was historical. Therewith, too, the speculative Good Friday is restored in the whole truth and severity of its godlessness. Out of this severity alone . . . the highest totality, in its whole seriousness and out of its deepest ground (at once all-encompassing) and in the most cheerful freedom of its form, can and must rise from the dead.[50]

The correlate in Nietzsche's writings to this philosophic interpretation of the "empirical" thesis of Pascal is the judgment that Pascal is the "most instructive victim of Christianity."[51] These different stances toward Pascal reflect the opposed meanings that the "death of God" has for Hegel and Nietzsche: Hegel bases his *completion of Christian philosophy* on the *origin of Christian belief* out of the "whole truth" of "godlessness." Nietzsche bases his attempt to overcome the "mendacity of millennia"—by means of a *return to the beginnings of Greek philosophy*—on *Christianity that is drawing to its end*. For Hegel, God's becoming man in Christ signifies the reconciliation, achieved once and for all, of human and divine nature. For Nietzsche it signifies that man was crucified and broken in his true nature.[52] Hegel's philosophic critique of the Christian faith moves within that faith and limits itself to the distinction of various "forms" of the same absolute content. Nietzsche's critique refers to all forms of Christianity and ends with the sharpest opposition between Dionysus and the Crucified. Hegel's unification of philosophy and Christianity presupposes that the Christian God is "spirit" and is conceived only in spirit. Nietzsche says that what is divine is that there are many gods but not the one, Christian God.

He who said "God is a spirit"—he took the biggest step and jump toward dis-belief ever taken so far on earth: such a remark cannot easily be redressed on earth![53, T21]

unless it be through the rebirth of an incarnate god such as Dionysus was.

To Nietzsche's mind the spiritual God of Christianity (whose death Hegel philosophically conceived once more at the termination of Chris-tian belief) has "refuted itself historically" in the course of the historical decay of Christianity.[54] "Now Christianity is coming to an end." What is still to be seen of Christianity are waters receding after a tremendous flood.

All possibilities of the Christian life, the most serious and the most casual, the most harmless and thoughtless and the most considered, have been tested one after the other; it is time to invent something new, or one must again and again wind up in the old cycle; granted, it is difficult to emerge from the whirl after it has spun us around for a couple of millennia. Even mockery, cynicism, en-mity toward Christianity have run their course; one sees an expanse of ice in warmed-up weather; everywhere the ice is cracked, dirty, lusterless, covered with pools of water, dangerous. Only a considerate and altogether seemly ab-stinence seems to me to be in place there: through it I honor religion, even if it be one that is already dying out. Our business is to soothe and to calm, as among the seriously, hopelessly ill; only against the bad, thoughtless, quack physicians (who are mostly scholars) must one protest—Christianity will very soon be ripe for critical history, i.e., for autopsy.[55]

What is left of God is only his shadow. It is characteristically a "gay" science that, at the beginning of the third book of *The Gay Science,* proclaims the death of God for the first time—but also already pro-claims nihilism and the eternal recurrence.

After Buddha was dead, his shadow was still shown for centuries in a cave—a tremendous, gruesome shadow. God is dead; but given the way of men, there may still be caves for thousands of years in which his shadow will be shown.— And we . . . still have to vanquish his shadow, too![56]

In this struggle against the shadowy afterlife of a dead God and an antiquated morality, Nietzsche only stirred the godlessness of mod-ern man back to life and consciousness again out of the satisfaction of atheism. Nietzsche has a "madman," who prematurely states the deed of the "ugliest" man, announce the great event.

Have you not heard of that madman who lit a lantern in the bright morning hours, ran to the marketplace, and cried incessantly: "I seek God! I seek God!"—Because many of those who did not believe in God were standing around just then, he provoked much laughter. "Has he got lost?" asked one. "Did he lose his way like a child?" asked another. "Or is he hiding?" "Is he afraid of us?" "Has he gone to sea? emigrated?"—Thus they yelled and laughed all at once. The madman jumped into their midst. . . . "Where has God gone?" he cried. "I will tell you. *We have killed him*—you and I! All of us are his murderers! But how did we do this? How could we drink up the sea? Who gave us the sponge to wipe away the entire horizon? What were we doing when we unchained this earth from its sun? Where is it moving to now? Where are we moving to? Away from all suns? Are we not plunging continuously? Backward, sideways, forward, in all directions? Is there still any up or down? Are we not straying as through an infinite nothing? Do we not feel the breath of empty space? Has it not become colder? Is not night and more night continually closing in on us? Do we not need to light lanterns in the morning? Do we hear nothing as yet of the noise of the gravediggers who are burying God? Do we smell nothing as yet of the divine decomposition?—Gods, too, decompose! God is dead! God remains dead! And we have killed him! . . . What was holiest and mightiest of all that the world has yet owned has bled to death under our knives. . . . With what water can we cleanse ourselves? What festivals of atonement, what sacred games shall we have to invent? Is not the greatness of this deed too great for us? Must we ourselves not become gods simply to appear worthy of it? There has never been a greater deed; and whoever is born after us—for the sake of this deed he will belong to a higher history than all history hitherto!" Here the madman fell silent and looked again at his listeners; and they, too, were silent and stared at him in wonder. At last he threw his lantern upon the ground, and it broke into pieces and went out. "I have come too early," he said then; "my time has not yet come. This tremendous event is still on its way, still wandering—it has not yet reached the ears of men. Lightning and thunder require time; the light of the stars requires time; deeds, though done, yet require time to be seen and heard. This deed is still more distant from them than the most distant stars—*and yet they have done it themselves!*"—It has been related further that on the same day the madman forced his way into several churches and there struck up his *requiem aeternam deo*. Led out and called to account, he is said always to have replied nothing but: "What after all are these churches now if they are not the tombs and tombstones of God?"[57]

Thus the big event is that with the death of God the "sea" and the "sun"—that is, what is highest and most comprehensive, and therewith the whole "horizon"—have disappeared. But Zarathustra's soul (and the world of the eternal recurrence that corresponds to it) is also a new "sea" in which the nihilism of the prophet is supposed to "drown." In one of the literary remains, written at the same time [as the foregoing excerpt from *The Gay Science*], the nihilistic character of this event is expressly emphasized:

The greatest events reach men's sentiments with the most difficulty: for example, the fact that the Christian God "is dead," that *no* heavenly grace and up-bringing, *no* divine justice, *no* immanent morality whatever express themselves in our experiences any more. That is a terrible novelty that requires another couple of centuries to reach the *sentiments* of the Europeans; and then for a while it will seem as if all gravity has departed from things.[58]

And because the *new* "gravity" in existence (which has now become transitory) is the idea of the eternal recurrence, a clear connection arises between the death of God, nihilism, and the eternal recurrence of the same.

Exactly qua origin of nihilism, however, the death of God is also an inducement to philosophic cheerfulness. For in spite of the darkening that at first follows the death of God, one can be relieved at the news that no more "Thou shalt" sets a burden on man's will after God's death has unburdened man as such from the duty of existence. It is again a *first* aphorism that treats this theme, in the fifth book ("We Fearless Ones") of *The Gay Science*.

The greatest recent event—that "God is dead," that the belief in the Christian God has become unbelievable—is already beginning to cast its first shadows over Europe. For the few, at least, whose eyes—the *suspicion* in whose eyes is strong and subtle enough for this spectacle, some sun seems to have set and some ancient and profound trust seems to have been turned into doubt; to them our old world must appear daily more like evening, more mistrustful, stranger, "older." But in the main one may say: the event itself is far too great, too distant, too remote from the multitude's capacity for comprehension even for the tidings of it to be thought of as having *arrived* as yet. Much less may one suppose that many people know already what has really come to pass with this event—and how much must collapse (now that this faith has been under-mined) because it was built upon this faith, propped up by it, grown into it; for example, the whole of our European morality. This long plenitude and se-quence of breakdown, destruction, ruin, and cataclysm that is now impend-ing—who could guess enough of it today to be compelled to play the teacher and advance proclaimer of this monstrous logic of terror, the prophet of a gloom and an eclipse of the sun whose like has probably never yet occurred on earth? . . . Even we born guessers of riddles who are, as it were, waiting on the mountains, placed between today and tomorrow, clamped into the contradic-tion between today and tomorrow, we firstlings and premature births of the coming century, to whom the shadows that must soon envelop Europe really already *should* have appeared by now—why is it that even we look forward to the approaching gloom without any real sense of involvement and above all without any worry and fear for *ourselves?* Are we perhaps still too much under the influence of the *initial consequences* of this event[?]—and these initial consequences, the consequences for *ourselves,* are the opposite of what one might perhaps expect: they are not at all sad and gloomy, but rather like a new and scarcely describable kind of light, happiness, relief, exhilaration, encouragement, dawn. . . . Indeed, we philosophers and "free spirits" feel, when we hear the news that "the old God is dead," as if a new dawn shone on us; our hearts overflow with gratitude, amazement, premonitions, expectation.—At long last the horizon appears free to us again, even if it should not be bright; at long last our ships may venture out again, venture out to face any danger; all the daring of the man of knowledge is permitted again; the sea, *our* sea, lies open again; perhaps there has never yet been such an "open sea."

On land the correlate to the departure onto an open sea is the allegory of the wanderer, whose shadow accompanies even Zarathustra. Zarathustra is "the godless" par excellence, and he makes his appearance at the same time as the death of God, because the superhuman man who has climbed over himself cannot live until the Christian God-in-man[59] is already dead. Zarathustra enters at the time of the great noon,

when man stands in the middle of his road between beast and superman and celebrates his path to the evening as his highest hope: for this path is the path to a new morning,

which *The Dawn* already announces during the fore-noon.

Then the one who goes under will bless himself that he is one who passes away, and the sun of his knowledge will stand at noon for him,

after it has already temporarily stood, for the wanderer, at the noon of the fore-noon. But not only the God of Christian morality is dead; rather, *all* gods are dead, although it remains an open question whether gods who have died do not also resurrect.

All gods are dead: now we want the superman to live: let this be, one day at the great noon, our last will![60]

This last will to overcome man at first lures Zarathustra away from "God and gods." A superhuman will of the man of the future, a will that creates itself and the world as its own, takes the place of God, who creates Being out of nothing. The great noon in which Zarathustra (at one with the superman) teaches the eternal recurrence is, however, also a "dangerous mean" between two opposed possibilities. Man stands before a possible ascent or else a decline, down to the "last man" or up to the "superman." Self-overcoming and self-satisfaction are the two connected possibilities of man who has become godless.[T22] In general the destiny of man now moves within these two intrahuman possibilities. For if God is dead, man loses his previous position as an intermediate being between divinity and animality. Left to his own devices, it is as if he were on a rope that stretches over the abyss of the nothing, and were put into the void.[61] His existence, like the life of the rope-dancer of the Prologue to *Zarathustra*, is essentially in danger, and danger is his profession. The "courageous spirit" to live dangerously, now seen in retrospect, turns into "the whole prehistory of man"—now, that is, in view of the "high-spiritedness" in the *amor fati* of the superman. What results from the disappearance of the fear of God is, at first and for the most part, the possibility of the last, irreverent man who no longer asks at all what is the meaning of his existence, but wants to have a middling happiness.

Alas! The time is coming when man will no longer shoot the arrow of his longing beyond man, and the string of his bow will have forgotten how to whir!

. . . The time of the most despicable man is coming, he who is no longer able to despise himself.

Behold, I show you the *last man*.

"What is love? What is creation? What is longing? What is a star?"—thus asks the last man, and he blinks.

The earth has become small, and on it hops the last man, who makes everything small. His race is as ineradicable as the flea beetle; the last man lives longest.

"We have invented happiness"—say the last men, and they blink.

They have left the regions where it was hard to live, for one needs warmth. One still loves one's neighbor and rubs against him, for one needs warmth.

Becoming sick and harboring suspicion are sinful to them: one proceeds carefully. A fool, who still stumbles over stones or human beings!

A little poison now and then: that makes for agreeable dreams. And much poison in the end, for an agreeable death.

One still works, for work is an entertainment. But one is careful lest the entertainment be too exhausting.

One no longer becomes rich or poor: both require too much exertion. Who still wants to rule? Who to obey? Both require too much exertion.

No shepherd and one herd! Everybody wants the same, everybody is the same: whoever feels different goes voluntarily into a madhouse.

"Formerly, all the world was mad"—say the most refined, and they blink.

One is sagacious and knows everything that has ever happened: so there is no end to mockery.

One still quarrels, but one is soon reconciled—else it might spoil the digestion.

One has one's little pleasure for the day and one's little pleasure for the night: but one pays tribute to health.

"We have invented happiness"—say the last men, and they blink.[T23]

But in the whole of existence that has become godless, the type "last man" is just as necessary as the ruling caste and the single super-man over this caste. The superman, whom Nietzsche created "at the same time" as the last man, is the "antipode" to the average man.

The *one* movement is necessarily: the leveling of humanity, big antheaps, etc.

The *other* movement, my movement: is on the contrary the intensification of all oppositions and chasms, the elimination of equality, the creation of the super-powerful man.

*The former* movement produces the last man; *mine,* the superman. It is *not at all* my goal to conceive the latter as the masters of the former; rather, two types should exist next to each other—separated as much as possible—the one type, *like the Epicurean gods, not caring about the other.*[62]

In contrast with the self-sufficient last man, the precondition for the man who has grown beyond himself is the "cry of distress" in the "*higher*" man; because the will to overcome previous humanity demands at first the higher man's despair over the humanitarian man of the present.

The "*ugliest*" man is one such deeply desperate and self-despising, but precisely for that reason not despicable, man. He is a higher man because he can still despise himself.[63] He is the murderer of God. Thus, through the higher man of ugliness, the death of God points upward and downward to the two possibilities that have newly arisen, that of the superman and that of the despicable, last man whose humaneness is the break with being human.

The Prologue to *Zarathustra* reports how Zarathustra, in his solitude, meets another solitary, a Christian saint who has not yet heard that God has died. Later Zarathustra meets an old man who already knows that God is dead. This latter old man reveals himself to Zarathustra as the "last pope," who is "retired" because his Lord has died. He associates with Zarathustra as one who has also given blessings. Zarathustra asks the last pope, who in what pertains to God is more enlightened than Zarathustra himself:

Is what they say true, that pity strangled him, that he saw how *man* hung on the cross and that he could not bear it, that the love of man became his hell, and in the end his death?—

The old pope, however, did not answer but looked aside shyly. . . .

"Let him go," said Zarathustra after prolonged reflection. . . .

"Let him go. He is gone. And although it does you credit that you say only good things about him who is now dead, you know as well as I *who* he was, and that his ways were queer."[T24]

Zarathustra questions whether God died only from the weakness of age, as the pope explains it to Zarathustra, and was not also murdered by man. At the close of the conversation, the pope once again returns to what he had remarked upon at the beginning, namely that Zarathustra is "the most pious of all those who do not believe in God." Some god must, no doubt, have converted him to his godlessness.

"Is it not your piety itself that no longer lets you believe in a god? And your overgreat probity will yet lead you beyond good and evil, too.

"Behold, what remains to you? You have eyes and hands and mouth, predestined for blessing from all eternity. One does not bless with the hand alone.

"Near you, although you want to be the most godless, I scent a secret, sacred, pleasant odor of long blessings: it gives me gladness and grief.

"Let me be your guest, O Zarathustra, for one single night!

"Nowhere on earth shall I feel better now than with you!"

"Amen! So be it!" said Zarathustra in great astonishment. "Up there goes the way, there lies Zarathustra's cave.

"I should indeed like to accompany you there myself, you venerable one, for I love all pious men. But now a cry of distress urgently calls me away from you."[T25]

The cry of distress rings out from the ugliest man in a province of death. Only green, ugly snakes live in this valley of death. The shepherds call it Valley of Snake Death.

Zarathustra, however, sank into a black reminiscence, for it seemed to him as if he had stood in this valley once before. And much that was grave weighed on his mind, so that he walked slowly, and still more slowly, and finally stood still.[T26]

That is: in the cry of distress of the ugliest man, whose riddle Zarathustra is the only one to know, Zarathustra encounters himself. The rattling "something" that this man is, is as "inexpressible" and hard to bring into "speech" as is "Being" generally, and the "abyss" of the nothing.[64] His "riddle," that he is the murderer of God, refers back to Zarathustra's "vision" of the eternal recurrence in the "riddle" of the shepherd and the deadly snake, because Zarathustra's liberation of this other "shepherd" from another "snake" is the overcoming of the sickness unto death that issues from the death of God. The motivation for the ugliest man's crime that delivers him from God—namely, "revenge" on God's existence—also refers back to Zarathustra's self-redemption; for the latter occurs by means of a will that no longer disgustedly takes "revenge" on human existence.

Had the ugliest man not become the murderer of God, he would have had to destroy himself, like Dostoyevsky's Kiriloff.[65] With the guilt that he has taken upon himself, the ugliest man returns innocence to existence. In doing away with God, he does away with the "biggest objection to existence," because the man who listens obediently to God's "Thou shalt" does not want to command himself.

"He—*had* to die: he saw with eyes that saw *everything*—he saw man's depths and grounds, all his concealed disgrace and ugliness.

"His pity knew no shame: he crawled into my dirtiest nooks. This most curious, overobtrusive, overpitying one had to die.

"He always saw *me*; on such a witness I wanted to have revenge—or not live myself.

"The God who saw everything, saw *man, too*: this God had to die! Man cannot *bear* it that such a witness should live."[66]

This deed gives honor to the ugliest man as a higher man; it spares man shame from now on.[67] Man can respect himself again. He no longer needs to despise himself in an ambiguous "love of the neighbor."

"How poor man is after all . . . how full of hidden shame!

"They tell me that man loves himself: oh, how great this love of himself must be! How much contempt stands against it!

"This fellow, too, loved himself, even as he despised himself—to me he is a great lover and a great despiser.

"None have I found who despised himself more deeply: *that*, too, is a kind of height.

"Alas, was *he* perhaps the higher man whose cry I heard?

"I love the great despisers. Man, however, is something that must be overcome."[T27]

This overcoming of being human ultimately occurs in the willing of the eternal recurrence. In the always recurring whole of Being that has always existed, the biggest objection against existence *as such*, against the accident of naked being-there, is removed. What the death of God liberates man's existence *for*, is, however, at first not already the *Yes* to the eternal recurrence of the same, but nihilism, which in man is first a sickness and then a freedom unto death.

This connection between nihilism and the death of God is divided into several stages, which together comprise the preliminary stage to

the *reversal of the truth of the nothing into the truth of Being*. The historical decline of the faith in God and in the morality sanctioned by God
leads logically to the "interim condition" of European nihilism. The
romantic pessimism and scientific positivism of the nineteenth century
are irresolute expressions of this nihilism. The nothing itself temporarily becomes God. Radically consummated nihilism veers over into the
"classical" positivism of the Dionysian philosophy of the eternal recurrence of the same.

On the basis of the position gained in *Zarathustra*, Nietzsche looks
back critically, in the preface to *The Will to Power*, on the dawning of
European nihilism.

What I relate is the history of the next two centuries. I describe what is coming,
what can no longer come differently: *the advent of nihilism*. This history can
already be related now; for necessity itself is at work here. This future already
speaks in a hundred signs, this destiny announces itself everywhere. . . . For
a long time now, our whole European culture has been moving as toward a
catastrophe, with a torturing tension that is growing from decade to decade:
restlessly, violently, headstrong, like a river that wants *to reach the end*, that no
longer reflects, that is afraid to reflect. He that speaks here, conversely, has done
nothing so far but *reflect*: a philosopher and solitary by instinct, who has
found his advantage in standing aside and outside, in patience, in procrastina-
tion, in staying behind; as a spirit of daring and at-tempting who has already
gone astray once into every labyrinth of the future; as a prophet-bird spirit
who *looks back* when relating what will come; as the first perfect nihilist of Europe who, however, has already lived through to the end the whole of nihilism
in himself—and who leaves it behind, beneath, and outside himself.

Looking back on the advent of nihilism, Nietzsche discerns the lost
faith in the divinely sanctioned values of Christian morality to be the
final motif of nihilism. These values determine the whole system of
our interpretation and evaluation of existence. Out of the emptiness of
the traditional, gradually degenerated, but still retained values ensues the
conclusion of a "revaluation of all previous values" (as opposed to the
nihilism that has actually occurred and that implies that now everything is "valueless" and "meaningless"—measured, that is, by the standard of the previous highest values). A fundamentally different type of
evaluation—in relation to existence as such and as a whole—becomes
possible with the questioning of the "value of these values." But at first,
all gravity seems to have departed from existence if man is no longer
duty-bound to anything through the weight of an authoritative value
that tells him what he should do. What must necessarily arise after the
decline of the Christian interpretation of existence is *the problem of the*

*value of existence as such.* For what is the purpose of being-there if no more purpose is available and the will of existence is goalless?[68] This problem of the value of existence generally characterizes modern "pessimism" as it has been expressed philosophically by Dühring,[69] Eduard von Hartmann, and Schopenhauer, but also by Bahnsen and Mainländer. The relation of this pessimism to Hellenism[70] was the first theme of that reflection which Nietzsche later develops in *The Will to Power.*

The event *after* which this problem was to be expected for certain—an astronomer of the soul could have calculated the very day and hour for it—the decline of the faith in the Christian God, the triumph of scientific atheism, is a generally European event in which all races should have their share of credit and honor. Conversely, one might charge precisely the Germans—those Germans who were Schopenhauer's contemporaries—with *delaying* this triumph of atheism most dangerously for the longest time. Hegel in particular was its delayer par excellence. . . . As a philosopher, Schopenhauer was the *first* admitted and uncompromising atheist whom we Germans have had: this was the background of his enmity toward Hegel. The ungodliness of existence was for him something given, . . . indisputable. . . . This is the locus of his whole integrity; unconditional, honest atheism is simply the *presupposition* of the way he poses his problem, being a triumph achieved finally and with great difficulty by the European conscience, being the most fateful act of two thousand years of discipline for the [ pursuit of ] truth, which in the end forbids itself the *lie* of faith in God. . . . Looking at nature as if it were proof of the goodness and governance of a God; interpreting history in honor of some divine reason . . . interpreting one's own experiences as pious people have long enough interpreted theirs, as if everything were . . . designed and ordained for the sake of the salvation of the soul—that is *all over* now, that has man's conscience *against* it, that is considered indecent and dishonest by every more refined conscience, as mendacity, feminism, weakness, and cowardice.—It is in this severity, if anywhere, that we are *good* Europeans and heirs of Europe's longest and most courageous self-overcoming. As we thus reject the Christian interpretation and condemn its "meaning" like a counterfeit . . . the question immediately . . . comes to us: *Does existence have any meaning at all?* It will require a few centuries before this question can even be heard completely and in its full depth.[71]

What "was left over" after the decay of the Christian faith (which commanded man what he "should do") was only an "I will."[72] Man who has become godless[T28] must give himself his own will.

I am Zarathustra the godless: where shall I find my equals? And all those are my equals who give themselves their own will and reject all resignation.[T29]

Yet this seeming *residue* of faith is at bottom its *core.*[73] The will is actually the "principle" of faith, because the man of faith does *not* will himself. To be sure, European nihilism—its problem being "whether it can will"—did arise with the fading away of the Christian faith, but the Christian faith itself had arisen in late antiquity when the will became ill. Whoever does not endure in his own ruling and willing seeks aid and support in the strange faith that another will is already there that can tell him what he should do.

Faith is always coveted most and needed most urgently where will is lacking; for will, as the affect of command, is the decisive sign of high-handedness and strength. In other words, the less one knows how to command, the more urgently one covets someone who commands, who commands severely—a god, prince, class, physician, father confessor, dogma, or party conscience. From this one might perhaps gather that the two world religions, Buddhism and Christianity, may have owed their origin and above all their sudden spread to a tremendous *disease of the will.* And that is what happened in truth: both religions encountered a situation in which the will had become ill, giving rise to a craving that towered into nonsense, that became utterly desperate for some "Thou shalt"; both religions were teachers of fanaticism in ages in which the will had become exhausted, and thus they offered innumerable people some support, a new possibility of willing, a delight in willing. For fanaticism is the only "strength of the will" that even the weak and insecure can be brought to attain. . . . Once a human being reaches the fundamental conviction that he *must* be commanded, he becomes a "believer"; conversely, one could conceive of such a pleasure and power of self-determination, such a *freedom* of the will that the spirit would take leave of all faith and every wish for certainty, being practiced in maintaining itself on insubstantial ropes and possibilities and dancing even at the edge of abysses. Such a spirit would be the *free spirit* par excellence,[74]

but free also to the willing of the nothing, to the "deed of nihilism" that the Christian faith cannot will.[75] "Instead of this faith," which itself was originally a "counterweight" against a weakened will to existence, "we put a strong *will* over ourselves, a will that holds on to a provisional series of basic evaluations as a heuristic principle, in order to see *how far* one can get thereby. . . . In truth, all that 'faith' was nothing else."[76]

But as long as the will that has become free toward itself does not know whether it wants to acknowledge its own will, man finds himself in a problematic *"interim state,"* and nihilism can mean two things: it can mean a symptom of the enervation of the will of an emptied existence, but on the other hand, it can be a first sign of the strengthening of the will and of a willed destruction—a nihilism of passive weakness or of active strength, like all symptoms of decadence.[77] The ambiguity of this still irresolute nihilism characterizes romantic "pessimism" and scientific "positivism," which are both preliminary forms of "radical" nihilism. In relation to romantic pessimism, scientific positivism is already an advance along the way to dis-illusionment,[T30] with a view onto the nothing.[78] For lack of a new faith, he believes in disbelief for the time being. As a backlash against romanticism, positivism is a reaction, but still not an action of its own.

The symbol for the ambiguity of nihilism is *the gentle wind that comes with thawing weather,* the wind that breaks the ice on which we are now still able to walk. "Ice, however—*breaks bridges*! . . . Is not everything *in flux* now? Have not all railings and bridges fallen into the water? Who would still *cling*[T31] to 'good' and 'evil'? Woe to us! Hail to us! The thawing wind blows!"[T32] And Zarathustra himself is a "railing by the torrent: let those who can, grasp me! Your crutch, however, I am not."[T33]

It is necessary to make a deliberate resolution, one way or another, of this ambiguity of "hail" and "woe," the ambiguity that is the double meaning of our disintegrating present.

> Oh, that you would reject all *halfhearted* willing and would become resolute in sloth as in action!
> Oh, that you would understand my word, "Do what you will, then, but first be such as are *able to will*!"[79]

A naked, pure "resoluteness," to this as to that and to all as to nothing, characterizes the capacity to will *as such* in the interim state of nihilism, which indeed already wills, but does not yet know what it wills.

By dint of resoluteness, nihilism progresses on the indicated path to the revaluation of all previous values. At first this revaluation concerns "morality," which no longer binds man's existence because morality itself has no sanction any more and hence ends in nihilism.[80] The decline of the moral interpretation of the world is, after the decay of the Christian dogma into a bourgeois morality, the "big spectacle" that is reserved for "the next two centuries"—the most questionable spectacle and perhaps also the one richest in hopes, because only a completed nihilism also makes "new values" necessary on the basis of a new evaluation of human existence as a whole. Through a movement that is more than a mere reaction, the resolute nihilism concludes the interim state of European pessimism and positivism. The "revaluation of values" expresses a "countermovement" "that in some future time will supersede that *perfect* nihilism, but that *presupposes it* . . . , and that certainly can arise only *after* perfect nihilism and *out of* it."[81] But what does this resolute nihilism will, this nihilism that is hopeful because it wills again at all? Does it actually will something, or is that "something" the *nothing*?

As long as the *Christian* gravity prevailed,[82] man was held firmly in existence. One thought one knew why one is there at all, for the sake of what goals. The suffering of being-there[T34] was interpreted; the monstrous emptiness, the "*horror vacui*" seemed to be filled; "the door to all suicidal nihilism was closed." All that signifies, it is true, an aversion to natural existence and to the first preconditions of life, but the Christian gravity nevertheless is and remains a *will*, for "man would rather will *the nothing* than *not* will." "*The will itself was saved*" precisely through the "ascetic ideal"; the "Thou shalt" of the ascetic ideal did not release the "I will." This ideal was up to now "the only meaning" that gave a significant answer to the question, "What is man for, anyhow?"[83] But what happens if this Christian gravity on the existence of man completely disappears from him, and man in the world as a whole is only a fleeting, meaningless *accident*? Did one not at long last have to sacrifice God himself and *all* faith and out of cruelty against oneself "worship gravity, fate, the nothing"?—or the fate of the meaningless eternal recurrence?[84] "To sacrifice God for the nothing—this paradoxical mystery of the final cruelty was reserved for the generation that is now coming up: all of us already know something of this," namely we whose existence is bounded and held by nothing any more, we who are thrown without any foothold into the endless expanse of the world. That endless expanse is at the same time the emptiness of existence, for "since Copernicus, man rolls from the center into an x."[85]

We are allowed, as no other men have ever been, glances on all sides; everywhere there is no end to be seen. We therefore have the advantage of a feeling of tremendous expanse—but also of tremendous *emptiness*; and in our century the ingenuity of all higher men consists in their getting over this terrible *feeling of desolation*. The opposite of this feeling is *intoxication*. . . . This age, then, is the most inventive in the invention of intoxicants. We are all familiar with intoxication, as music, as blind, self-blinding enthusiasm and worship before individual men and events; we know the intoxication of the tragic, that is, cruelty while viewing rack and ruin, especially when what is most noble perishes; we know the more modest types of intoxication, unreflective work, self-sacrifice as a tool of a science or of a political or moneymaking party; any stupid little fanaticism, any unavoidable rotation in the smallest circle already has an intoxicating power. There is also a certain modesty that becomes eccentric, a modesty that causes the feeling of emptiness itself to be felt lustfully; indeed, an enjoyment of the eternal emptiness of all things, a mysticism of faith in the nothing and a self-sacrifice for this faith. . . . How we record and as it were bookkeep regarding our *little* pleasures as if we could attain with the *sum* of the many little pleasures a counterweight to that emptiness, a filling of that emptiness—: how we deceive ourselves with this guile of addition![86]

And then it can seem as if one had already filled the emptiness of existence with this "mysticism of the nothing" in self-intoxication through destiny, work, and politics.[87] *Instead of believing in God, one temporarily believes in the nothing.*

Before the nothing of nihilism, everything becomes a matter of indifference. Nietzsche as little succumbed to the aforementioned divine semblance of nihilism[88] as did Kierkegaard. To be sure, both did put themselves into the temporal nothing. Yet they did so willing the Being of eternity or what is always, through which time is overcome. The teaching of the eternal recurrence, too, is thought of as the most extreme form of nihilism and of the self-overcoming of nihilism. Only with this teaching does Nietzsche draw the final conclusion from the knowledge that God is dead and that man is in freedom unto death. Consequently, nihilism has a systematic interim position in the whole, owing to its origin and its future, that is, the death of God and the rebirth of a Dionysian view of the world. Because of this double meaning, deriving from the decline of every "Thou shalt" and the ascent of a new will, nihilism summarizes the problem of "modernity," which "does not know which way to turn." The teaching of the symptoms of decadence, that teaching in which Nietzsche is a psychological master, distinguishes the modes of appearance of modernity immediately according to the standard of ascending or declining "life." But life itself is understood as the universal "will" to power, and thus Nietzsche's fundamental distinction of the phenomena of life according to strength and weakness refers to the strength and weakness of the will based in life. The will's possibilities are still undecided in the interim state of nihilism, but they press for a prompt decision.

In accordance with this systematic position of nihilism, the proclamation that *God is dead* already refers to the wholly different proclamation that *everything recurs.* In *Zarathustra* the connection of godlessness with the willing of the eternal recurrence is intimated several times; and one of the plans for a (never executed) continuation of *Zarathustra* begins with a festival of thanks and commemoration for the dead God and closes with the teaching of the eternal recurrence. After man has been freed from the obtrusive eye of the Christian God, the abyss of light, the pure eye of heaven—which is an eternity that always recurs in the same way—looks in through the smashed ceilings of the churches into the graves of God.

To sacrifice God for the nothing is, it is true, the paradoxical mystery of the new generation coming up. But he who has long striven to think the pessimism of the nineteenth century beyond good and evil into the depths of nihilism and thus to "redeem" pessimism from the "half-Christian, half-German narrowness and simplicity"—he has perhaps

just thereby, without really meaning to do so, opened his eyes to the opposite ideal: the ideal of the most high-spirited, alive, and world-affirming human being, who has not only come to terms and learned to get along with whatever was and is, but who wants to have it repeated *just as it was and is,* into all eternity, shouting insatiably *da capo*[T35]—not only to himself but also to the whole play and spectacle, and not only to a spectacle but at bottom to him who needs precisely this spectacle—and who makes it necessary because again and again he needs himself—and makes himself necessary.——What? And this would not be—*circulus vitiosus deus*?[89, T36]

But the philosophizing god Dionysus makes the spectacle necessary. Nietzsche believes that he knows how to act the role of Dionysus when the circle of Nietzsche's willing and thinking closed. "Zarathustra himself is, to be sure, merely an old atheist; he believes neither in old nor in new gods. Zarathustra says, he *would*—; but Zarathustra *will not.* . . . One should understand him correctly,"[90] namely to the effect that only the epiphany of Dionysus teaches faith to the disbelief of Zarathustra. To Nietzsche himself, "in whom the religious, that is, *god-forming* instinct was inopportunely alive from time to time," the divine revealed itself

in those timeless moments that fall into life as if from the moon, when one simply no longer knows how old one is already and how young one will yet be. . . . I would not doubt that there are many kinds of gods.[91]

In the "ass festival" of *Zarathustra,* it is finally said that the murderer of God is to blame not only for the death of God but also for his resurrection again in a new form. For among gods death is only a "prejudice"; they molt but do not die, and it can never be settled "how many gods are still possible," even though two millennia have elapsed— "and not a single new god!" The retired pope worships the newly arisen god Dionysus in the form of an ass.[92] In his concealed, Dionysian wisdom, this ass never says No but always Yea-Yuh. The ugliest man gives the ass wine to drink, for Dionysus is a winegrower god, and all figures out of *Zarathustra* gather festively around the divine ass, which since antiquity has been a symbol of potency and lust. The wanderer, the shadow, and the prophet of nihilism, and all higher men worship the ass, which gives its blessings; for in the Yes-saying ass, their higher will to the nothing is redeemed for the highest kind of self-willing Being. As the "*most pious* of the godless," Zarathustra becomes Zarathustra-*Dionysus,* in whose name Nietzsche accomplishes the last metamorphosis, from the heroic principle of "I will" into the godlike principle of "I am." This latter principle is like the gods because through it what was previously heavy and difficult becomes light and easy.T37 "The 'gods who live light and easy': that is the highest adornment that is granted to the world, however emotionally heavy and difficult life may be."93

## "NOON AND ETERNITY," OR THE PROPHECY OF THE ETERNAL RECURRENCE

Nietzsche characterizes himself as the teacher of the eternal recurrence, and he knew this—his authentic—"teaching" as his "destiny." For answering the question of the philosophic meaning of this teaching, the context in which one places the teaching is decisive. To the extent that any serious attempt to interpret this teaching has been made, that attempt has occurred in connection with the "*superman*" or with the "*will to power*"—whether the interpreter wanted to prove the reconcilability or irreconcilability of the eternal recurrence with the one or the other.94 The teaching of the superman is the precondition for the teaching of the eternal recurrence, because only the man who has overcome himself can also will the eternal recurrence of all that is; and the plans for *The Will to Power* presuppose on their part the teaching of *Zarathustra.* Precisely the final plans for *The Will to Power*95 show that for this work, too, the teaching of the eternal recurrence would have remained the definitive answer—that is, to the question of nihilism, which for its part arises out of the death of God. The overcoming of nihilism by means of the man who overcomes himself is the precondition for the prophecy of the eternal recurrence, and Nietzsche's philosophy does not, in principle, go beyond this prophecy. The will to the superman and to the eternal recurrence is Nietzsche's "last will" and his "last idea," in which the whole of his experiment is systematically summarized.

As a result of this essential connection of the eternal recurrence and nihilism, Nietzsche's teaching has a double aspect: it is the "self-overcoming of nihilism," in which "he who overcomes" and "what is overcome" are one.[96] Zarathustra overcomes "himself" (that is, the will to the nothing that has become free and the nausea over man so far) and achieves the willing of an eternally recurring existence in the whole of all that is.

The "prophecy" of the eternal recurrence is one with the wholly different prophecy of nihilism, that is, just like the "double will" of *Zarathustra*, the Dionysian "double look" into the world and the Dionysian "double world" itself are *one* will, *one* look, and *one* world.[97]

As a *movement*, however, the will to the eternal recurrence is two-fold, because it reverses its advance toward the nothing into a retrogression to eternally recurring Being. The will accomplishes this reversal by repeating the ancient view of the world on the peak of anti-*Christian* modernity.

## The Reversal of the Will to the Nothing into the Willing of the Eternal Recurrence

*The world now laughs, rent are the drapes of fright,*
*The wedding is at hand of dark and light.*[T38]

Nietzsche characterizes his teaching as the "most extreme form of nihilism" and at the same time as the "self-overcoming" of nihilism, because his teaching is intended to recognize precisely the meaninglessness of an existence that recurs without any goal. "Let us think this idea in its most terrible form: existence just as it is, without any meaning or goal, but inexorably recurring, without a finale into the nothing: '*the eternal recurrence.*' That is the most extreme form of nihilism: the nothing (the 'meaningless') as eternal!"[98] As the *most extreme* form of nihilism, the eternal recurrence is, however, also the "crisis" of nihilism, and at the peak of its com-pletion,[T39] nihilism veers into the reverse teaching of the eternal recurrence.[99] The "reverse men" teach the eternal recurrence.[100] The belief in it gives man's existence "the new gravity" after man has lost the old gravity that he had in the Christian faith. Like the Christian faith, the belief in the eternal recurrence is a "counterweight" against the will to the nothing. The "redeeming man of the future" is therefore not only the conqueror of God but also the conqueror of the nothing, for this nothing is itself the logical expression for the success of godlessness.

This man of the future, who will redeem us not only from the hitherto reigning ideal but also from *what was bound to grow out of it,* from the great nausea, from the will to the nothing, from nihilism; this bell stroke of noon and of the great decision that liberates the will again and restores its goal to the earth and his hope to man; this Antichrist and antinihilist, this conqueror of God and the nothing—*he must come one day.*[101]

The "goal" of the earth, however, is "the goallessness as such" of its revolving, just as the goal of the last metamorphosis is freedom from all goals and purposes, from every for-the-sake-of.[T40] The first aphorism of *The Gay Science* already refers to this element of Nietzsche's thought, and at the end of Book IV, Nietzsche indicates his teaching for the first time under the title "The Greatest Gravity."

What if some day or night a demon were to steal after you into your loneliest loneliness and say to you: "This life as you now live it and have lived it, you will have to live once more and innumerable times more; and there will be nothing new in it, but every pain and every joy and every idea and sigh and everything unutterably small or great in your life will have to return to you, all in the same succession and sequence—and even this spider and this moonlight between the trees, and even this moment and I myself. The eternal hourglass of existence is turned upside down again and again—and you with it, speck of dust!"—Would you not throw yourself down and gnash your teeth and curse the demon who spoke thus? Or have you once experienced a tremendous moment when you would have answered him: "You are a god and never have I heard anything more divine!" If this thought gained dominion over you, it would change you as you are and perhaps crush you. The question in each and every thing, "Do you desire this once more and innumerable times more?" would lie upon your actions as the greatest gravity. Or how well disposed would you have to become to yourself and to life to *demand* nothing *more fervently* than this ultimate confirmation and seal?

The heading to the aphorism that immediately follows is "*Incipit tragoedia*"[T41] and refers to Zarathustra. In *Ecce Homo* the reversal is likewise characterized as the "psychological" problem that lies at the bottom of the type Zarathustra: the bringing forth of a most extreme *Yes* out of a most extreme *No* and of a highest *levity* out of a deepest *melancholy.*[102] Through the Dionysian Yes-saying, everything that was previously heavy becomes light, because the Yes-saying liberates from the burden of being-there, which has fallen to man like an accident.[T42] For this reversal, however, further development of the various kinds of the widespread "pessimism" is at first necessary: the craving for "being *different,* for the half *No* and for the sheer *nothing.*"[103] In contrast with the foregoing, *the radical nihilist*[104] attempts "to want to have nothing different" from what it is, already was, and also will be again.

Step by step, Zarathustra becomes unhappier *and* happier, and he attains his highest happiness only when the greatest *need* reaches him, too. This highest happiness is that *flexibility* vis-à-vis need which is at the same time *necessity*.[T43] Zarathustra learns in the end "to love his abyss." "Peak and abyss" become one for him. For: "Where do the highest mountains come from? Thus I once inquired. Then I learned that they come out of the sea. The evidence is written into their rocks and into the walls of their peaks. It is out of the deepest depth that the highest must come to its height."[105] Zarathustra walks on this path to the last greatness. All ladders to this path are missing, and it can be walked upon only in such a way that man as such climbs over himself. And as he at last brings up his "most abysmal" idea and changes from a No-sayer to the advocate of revolving life, Zarathustra says, "My abyss speaks." That is, the nihilism in existence speaks at one with the advocacy of life. With that, Zarathustra has "turned his last depth up-side down into the light,"[106] which implies in turn: nihilism and eternal recurrence are preconditions for each other like Yes and No or like light and darkness. Before he begins his last journey to the final loneliness, Zarathustra climbs down again "further down than he had ever climbed," down into the "darkest flood tide" where his "last danger" becomes a "last refuge" for him.[107]

Just as the eternal recurrence in the parable of *Zarathustra* is a reversed nihilism, so in Nietzsche's own existence, too, the search for self-*eternalization* is in a perverse way at one with the temptation to self-*destruction*. The will to eternalization is itself ambiguous, therefore: it can stem from gratitude for existence, but on the other hand it can be the tyrannical and vengeful will of one who despairs over existence.

The will to *eternalization* requires . . . a dual interpretation. It can be prompted, first, by gratitude and love:—art with this origin will always be an art of apotheoses, perhaps dithyrambic like Rubens, or blissfully mocking like Hafiz, or bright and gracious like Goethe, spreading a Homeric light and glory over all things. But it can also be the tyrannic will of one who suffers deeply, who struggles, is tormented, and would like even to turn what is most personal, singular, and narrow, the real idiosyncrasy of his suffering, into a binding law and compulsion; one who, as it were, takes his revenge on all things by stamping them with *his* image, the image of *his* torture, forcing that image on all things, branding them with it. This last version is *romantic pessimism* in its most expressive form, whether it be Schopenhauer's philosophy of will or Wagner's music—romantic pessimism, the last *great* event in the destiny of our culture. (That there still *could* be an altogether different kind of pessimism, a classical pessimism—this premonition and vision belongs to me as something inseparable from me, as my *proprium* and *ipsissimum*;[T44] . . . I call this pessimism of the future . . . *Dionysian* pessimism.)[108]

With this "invention" Nietzsche-Zarathustra—in the decisive chapter "On the Vision and the Riddle"—slays not only "suffering" and "pity" and "dizziness at abysses"[109] but also death itself. In his discouraged ill-humor over the burden of existence (which he has carried high), he plucks up courage and says "*to death*," after his convalescence from the sickness unto death: "Was that life? Well then, once again!" and again and again.[110] The will to the eternal recurrence of all existence is thus a "self-overcoming of nihilism," because by means of this will man overcomes the idea of the final: self-destruction, "the crime of nihilism." This abyss and this depth make the eternal recurrence the "most abysmal idea," through which Zarathustra conquers the will to the nothing once and forever. And because he has already turned his last depth upside down into the light,[111] he can now bring light to the underworld, too.[112] For Nietzsche himself, however, Zarathustra's downgoing signifies—in "the language of man"—no ascent to a new morning, but an "evening sun over the last catastrophe"[113] and a "Medusa's head" by means of which all features of the world become stiff in a "frozen agony of death."[114]

As a result of this connection, the death of God (from which nihilism stems) is, it is true, "the greatest danger" and the "most terrible event" for the prophet of nihilism, but for Zarathustra's own prophecy it is the event that is "richest in hopes" and the "cause of the greatest courage." For in courage toward the nothing, nihilism finally completes and overcomes itself to the point of the excess courage[T45] of the superman, which Nietzsche draws upon to teach the eternal recurrence.[115] In *The Will to Power* this reversal is expressly characterized as the authentic movement in Nietzsche's philosophizing.

Such an *experimental philosophy* as I live anticipates experimentally even the possibilities of fundamental nihilism; but this does not mean that it halts at a negation, a No, a will to the No. Rather, it wants to get through to the reverse—to a *Dionysian Yes-saying* to the world as it is, without subtraction, exception, or selection—it wants the eternal cycle: the same things, the same logic and illogic of entanglements. The highest state a philosopher can attain: to stand in a Dionysian relationship to existence—my formula for this is *amor fati*.[116]

With this formula for the will to the eternal recurrence, Nietzsche simultaneously describes the principle of his "revaluation of all values";

those values, for their part, derive from that first revaluation which Christianity accomplished vis-à-vis antiquity when antiquity's will to existence became ill. Nietzsche sets the teaching of the eternal recurrence against the "paralyzing feeling of universal dissolution." For "extreme positions" such as European nihilism, which has been thought to the end, "will not be superseded by moderate positions but once again by extreme positions—but of the *opposite* extreme."

The essential connection between nihilism and recurrence is a problem that is to be developed in detail through *Zarathustra* (pp. 60–82 below). Then (pp. 82–94 below) it must be shown that the will to the eternal recurrence, which arises out of the will to the nothing, poetically unifies what falls apart. For on the one hand the idea of the eternal recurrence teaches a new purpose of human existence beyond human existence, a will to self-eternalization; but it also teaches the exact opposite: a revolving of the natural world in itself, a revolving that is just as selfless as it is goalless, and that includes human life. The cosmic meaning clashes with the anthropological meaning, so that the one contradicts the other.

### The Eternal Recurrence in the Parable *of* Zarathustra

*Zarathustra* occupies a special place, both literally and philosophically, within Nietzsche's complete works; not, however, because *Zarathustra* does not fit into the other works, but because it contains Nietzsche's whole philosophy in the form of a thoroughly pondered system of parables.[117] Even the sketches toward a "revaluation of all values," which were left behind in the literary remains and published under the title *The Will to Power,* contain nothing new in principle. The fundamental idea of *Zarathustra*—the eternal recurrence of the same—*is* already the principle of the revaluation of all values, because it reverses nihilism. *Zarathustra* is the only "work," which in its way is complete (each of its Parts is a "ten-day work"), and at the same time it is the unavoidable "vestibule" to the incomplete revaluation of all values. The first Part of this revaluation is *The Antichrist,* in which the "old and new tablets" of *Zarathustra,* those broken to pieces and those only half-written, are expounded without parables. *Zarathustra* is, according to Nietzsche's own testimony, the justification of everything he lived, worked, and suffered through, his "testament," which contains in the sharpest focus an image of his essence—"as it is as soon as I have once thrown off my whole burden."[118] Nietzsche considered it possible that someday "specific academic chairs" could be established for the interpretation of *Zarathustra*.

Now I shall relate the history of *Zarathustra*. The fundamental conception of this work, *the idea of the eternal recurrence*, this highest formula of affirmation that is at all attainable—belongs in August 1881: it was penned on a page with the notation underneath, "6,000 feet beyond man and time." That day I was walking through the woods along the lake at Silvaplana; at a massive, towering, pyramidal rock not far from Surlei I stopped. It was then that this idea came to me.[119]

It accords with this history that a first plan for *Zarathustra* had "Noon and Eternity" as a general title. Then, according to later plans, this title was to be reserved for the third or fourth Part of *Zarathustra*. Finally, this title made its way into the last plans for *The Will to Power*.[120] For the most part, the subtitle of "Noon and Eternity" reads: "Plan of a New Way to Live." By means of this "plan"—that is, out of modern "thrownness"[T46]—Nietzsche found himself "reborn" from the sickness unto death to a life that wills itself anew eternally and to a "new way of dying."[121] "The sun of knowledge once again stands at noon; and the snake of eternity, curled up in rings, lies in the light of this sun." "With this book I have entered a new 'ring'—from now on in Germany I will probably be reckoned among the crazy."[122] For Nietzsche, *Zarathustra* is the "fulfillment" of the free spirit,[123] and what immediately follows it, *Beyond Good and Evil* and *On the Genealogy of Morals*, signifies "a kind of preliminary *glossary* in which the most important innovations of concepts and values of that book occur . . . at some time and are provided with names." But the first Part of the *Revaluation of All Values*, namely *The Antichrist*, is likewise still characterized in the foreword as a book that belongs to those who understand *Zarathustra*; and *Zarathustra* itself is characterized as a work that is "difficult to understand,"[124] a work for the understanding of which it is necessary to stand "with one foot *beyond* life."[125] "There is nothing by me more serious and also nothing more cheerful; I wish from my heart that *this* color—which does not at all need to be a mixed color—might become more and more my 'natural' color."[126] The significance of *Zarathustra* is repeatedly indicated, finally, with exuberant words in *Ecce Homo*,[127] and it is said there that *Ecce Homo*, too, contains no word "that I had not already said five years earlier through Zarathustra's mouth." Corresponding to the evaluation of *Zarathustra* in the retrospective view of *Ecce Homo* are numerous remarks in letters from the time when *Zarathustra* was written: *Zarathustra* is a "fifth

Gospel"; it deals with a "tremendous synthesis," and never before has
he traveled with such sails over such a sea. With *Zarathustra*, Nietzsche writes, he has for the first time given shape to his "main idea," and
perhaps also to himself.[128] It would, on the other hand, be a futile effort to try to bring the notes that stem from quite different times and
have been published under the title *The Will to Power*, into one mold
that could make this mass of fragments into a work.

The correlate to the special position of *Zarathustra*—a position distinguished by the notion of the eternal recurrence—in the whole of
Nietzsche's philosophy, is the special form of philosophic speech in the
parable.[129] In order not to be merely a metaphorical phrasing in an
elaborate parable (and thus to be, as it were, merely words), the *speech*
of the parable must be the same as what it expresses, that is, as *Being*.

> The involuntariness of image, of parable, is strangest of all; one no longer has
> any concept of what is an image or a parable: everything offers itself as the
> nearest, the most correct, the simplest expression. It actually seems, to recall
> something Zarathustra says, as if the things themselves approached and of-
> fered themselves for the parable (—"Here all things come caressingly to your
> discourse and flatter you; for they want to ride on your back. Here you ride on
> every parable to every truth. Here the words and word-shrines of all Being
> open up before you; here all Being wishes to become word, all becoming wishes
> to learn from you how to speak—"). This is *my* experience of inspiration.[130]

If, however, Being itself wants to become word in everything that
is, then even the "most ordinary" speaks of "things unheard-of," and
the allegorical character of speech would be justified by the fact that
Nietzsche, as the initiate of the "highest kind of Being," has become
the same as the latter. The inspired trueness of speech in the necessary
accident of the parable indicates the questionable truth of Nietzsche's
relationship to a divine Being. Only if the highest kind of Being, the
god Dionysus, speaks through Nietzsche (who acts the role of Dionysus) does the truth of Being also speak through Nietzsche's parable.
But how can we decide whether Nietzsche was the persona of a god—
or the "actor of his own ideal"?[131] Zarathustra's speeches contain, right
next to parables of poetic immediacy and simplicity, the most contrived
transcriptions, allegories, and mannerisms.[132] And as soon as the poetically unifying power to allegorize abandons him and he wants to justify his teaching, what previously appeared to be a highest necessity
becomes "fragment" and "accident" again. The unity in the metaphysical parable of the eternal recurrence splits into a double equation, one
on the side of man, the other on the side of the world. The *problem* of

the teaching of the return is, however, the *unity* of this *schism* between the human will to a goal and the goalless revolving of the world.

What at first must strike our attention in the fundamental conception of *Zarathustra*, that is, in the idea of the eternal recurrence, is the anxiously shaken and secretively cautious way in which Nietzsche's letters and notes report on the emergence of "his" idea.[133] This idea is at first not *conceived,* but rather is an ecstatic "experience in thought," the weight, meaning, and importance of which will then be weighed, developed, and justified in multiple experiments. Nietzsche dates his "great health"[134] from the time of this idea. The "great health" plays with everything out of the fullness of Being, so that with this playing the "real seriousness" begins, the "real question-mark" is set down, and the "destiny of the soul turns around." When Möbius in his pathography dates the first signs of insanity at the origin of *Zarathustra,* this determination only seemingly contradicts Nietzsche's self-interpretation; for with the idea of the eternal recurrence, Nietzsche is in fact "beyond man and time," ecstatically removed from himself.

The idea of the eternal recurrence is the "crisis" of nihilism. In this crisis it is decided whether man still wants to be-there at all. It is repeatedly said, as a characterization of the age in which the idea of the eternal recurrence brings everything to the point of "breaking open": "It is time," that is, "*highest time.*" This highest time is as ambiguous as the idea of the recurrence insofar as the latter is the self-overcoming of nihilism. Both the cry of distress of the shepherd (and of all higher men who have despaired of existence) and the "stroke of the clock at the great noon" and at midnight[135] resound at the highest time; the clock's stroke, as the declaration of the time at the point of a highest perfection,[136] is already heard in *The Wanderer,* and then brings redemption from perfected nihilism. In the same double meaning, the hour of the highest time is also a "most silent hour," namely of silent desperation[137] or of silent bliss.[138] In the decisive, critical moment of the great noon—after the temporary noon of the philosophy of the morning—a cessation of time occurs. As the time of a unique decision, once and forever, the *moment* has—*eternity.*[139] To this extent "noon and eternity" is the characteristic time and the ever recurring title for the idea of the eternal recurrence. The proclamation of noon and eternity through the expression "it is time" occurs for the first time in the chapter "Of Great Events." This narrative of Zarathustra's superhuman journey to hell is a continuation of an aphorism from *Human, All-Too-Human* entitled "The Journey to Hades." At first, however, it is only Zarathustra's shadow that travels through the "gate to the under-world" to the heart of the earth. In the dark heart of the earth, where the nothing appears to one as a volcanically erupting depth, Zarathustra has a discussion with the fire hound[140] and says: The earth has a skin, this skin has diseases, and one of these diseases is called "man"—and another, "fire hound." The meaning of this "secret" is as follows: the sickness "man," which is a sickness unto death, is not yet on the path to convalescence in a great health as long as its origin and center (where the dog of the depth howls) themselves still get their nutrition too much from the "surface of the earth." Not only is pessimism that no longer wills, one such superficial depth, but so (and just as much) is revolutionary, political optimism; both are untrue to the earth. The dog of the underworld is at most a "ventriloquist" of the earth, like the advocates of the "backworld."[141, T47]

Another fire hound really speaks from the heart of the earth, namely the one that knows that the unlighted heart of the earth, like the night-eye of life,[142] in truth consists of bright, laughing gold; because the depth of the abyss and the height of the light in the whole of Being are—like shadow and light, too, on the surface of the earth—one and the same "abyss of light."[143] But why did the ghost who is the "shadow" of Zarathustra cry, "at about the hour of noon," "it is time" and in fact "highest" time? *For what* is it the highest time, if not for the com-pletion[T48] and therewith the overcoming of nihilism in a "most silent hour," which is the time of the truly great events and not only of noisy ones? At this time the sickness "man" truly "erupts," but at the same time heals, too, in a great health.

In the next chapter a "prophet" explains the sickness over being human as nihilism. His belief in disbelief teaches: everything is empty, everything is equal, for the man of the present there is no longer a future.

> Indeed we have harvested: but why did all our fruit turn rotten and brown? What fell down from the evil moon last night? In vain was all our work; our wine has turned to poison; an evil eye has seared yellow our fields and hearts.
>
> We have all become dry, and if fire descends on us, we are scattered like dusty ashes;—indeed, we have made the fire itself weary.
>
> All our wells have dried up; even the sea has withdrawn. All the ground would crack, but the depth refuses to devour!
>
> "Alas, where is there still a sea in which one might drown?": thus are we wailing—across shallow swamps.[144]

The sea in which nihilism can drown is the sea of "powers that rage and surge within themselves," the Dionysian double-world of the eternal recurrence of the same, to which the soul of Zarathustra—who likewise is called a "sea," in which the self-contempt of man should drown—corresponds. Zarathustra takes to heart the prophecy of him who says "everything is the same, nothing pays off, the world has no meaning, knowledge strangles," "no searching helps, there are also no blessed isles anymore." He takes this prophecy so much to heart that out of sadness he does not eat or drink and loses his speech for three days—until the abyss speaks to him again, at one with the opposite message of the eternal recurrence. He falls into a deep sleep and then relates a dream, which is a puzzling premonition of his redemption from the sickness unto death.

> I had turned my back on all life, thus I dreamed. I had become a night watchman and a guardian of tombs over there upon the lonely mountain-castle of death.
> Up there I guarded death's coffins; the musty vaults were full of such spoils of victory. Life that had been overcome looked at me out of glass coffins.
> I breathed the odor of dusty eternities: sweltering and dusty lay my soul. And who could have aired his soul there, anyway!
> The brightness of midnight was always about me; loneliness crouched next to it; and as a third, death-rattle silence, the worst of my friends.
> I had keys, the rustiest of all keys; and I knew how to use them to open the most creaking of all gates.
> Like a wickedly angry croaking, the sound ran through the long corridors when the gate's wings moved: fiendishly cried this bird, angry at being awakened.
> Yet still more terrible and heart-constricting was the moment when silence returned and it grew silent about me, and I sat alone in this treacherous muteness.
> Thus time passed and crawled, if time still existed—how should I know! But eventually that happened which awakened me.[145]

A roaring wind ripped the gate open and cast in a black coffin, which burst and, amidst terrible laughter, spewed out a thousand grimaces. Who carried his ashes to the mountain here? A disciple unriddles the dream for Zarathustra. Zarathustra himself is the one who, as the advocate of revolving life, also rips open the gate of the castles of death.

> "Henceforth children's laughter will always well forth from coffins; henceforth a strong wind will always come triumphantly unto all weariness of death: of this you yourself are our surety and prophet!
> "Verily, *it was them that you dreamed of*: your enemies themselves; that was your most difficult dream! But as you woke from them and came to your senses, thus they are to awaken from themselves—and come to you."[146]

Zarathustra looks at the interpreter of the dream and shakes his head. Does that mean that the disciple has interpreted it incorrectly?[147] Or is

Zarathustra only surprised at his precocious wisdom? The answer to this question follows from Zarathustra's own question, "Who carries his ashes to the mountain?" As a wanderer Zarathustra carried to the mountain his own ashes, as the scorched remnants of his first liberation; only to carry his "fire into the valleys," just the opposite now, after the last metamorphosis into the child.[148] And only then did the ghost of the backworldly[T49] sermon of death retreat.[149, T50] *Before* this redemption through the self-overcoming of nihilism, Zarathustra finds himself, still unchanged, between the nihilistic and the Dionysian truth, and what gushes forth from the coffins of death is therefore not yet the liberated laughter of one who has awakened into childhood again, but only the laughter of children's ugly grimaces. The interpretation of the disciple is thus in itself not false but not yet timely, because the riddle of the dream about the castle of death does not yet contain the "vision" of the eternal recurrence. The sea in which he can drown is yet to be shown to the prophet of nihilism.

The following chapter, "Of Redemption," treats the redemption into the childish innocence of human being-there in the whole of what is, which is the world. Zarathustra wants "to unify poetically" and "collect" what was previously a fragment and a dreadful accident about being human. He wants to redeem man from the accident and from the "punishment" of existence, to redeem him by means of the knowledge that in the accident itself, necessity rules, and that existence as such is just as purposeless as, in itself, it is innocent.[150] But this redemption does not become intelligible until after the unriddling of Zarathustra's "vision," which is the prophecy of the eternal recurrence and of nihilism. This prophecy is prepared for in the "Most Silent Hour," with which the second Part of *Zarathustra* closes. In this most silent hour, a sacrifice is demanded of Zarathustra that he is unwilling to make; this sacrifice is Nietzsche's unachieved Gethsemane.

Zarathustra is finally "unwillingly obedient, ready to go" into his last loneliness, through which (in the sequel) the meaning of Being discloses itself to him. It was already a kind of most silent hour, when Zarathustra sat dreaming in the castle of death, so that time—"if time still existed"—passed by him like nothing. This cessation of time now returns, altered.

Yesterday, toward evening, *my most silent hour* spoke to me: that is the name of my terrible mistress.

And thus it happened; for I must tell you everything lest your hearts harden against me for departing suddenly!

Do you know the fright of him who falls asleep?—

He is frightened down to his very toes, because the ground gives under him and the dream begins.

This I say to you as a parable. Yesterday, in the most silent hour, the ground gave under me: the dream began.

The hand of the clock moved, the clock of my life drew a breath—; never had I heard such quiet around me: so that my heart took fright.

Then it spoke to me without voice: "*You know it, Zarathustra!*"—

And I cried with fright at this whispering, and the blood left my face: but I remained mute.

Then it spoke to me again with voice: "You know it, Zarathustra, but you do not speak it!"—

And at last I answered defiantly: "Yes, I know it, but I do not want to speak it!"

Then it spoke to me again without voice: "You do not *want* to, Zarathustra? Is this really true? Do not hide in your defiance!"—

And I cried and trembled like a child and spoke: "Alas, I would like to, but how can I? Let me off from this! It is beyond my strength!"

Then it spoke to me again without voice: "What do you matter, Zarathustra? Speak your word and break to pieces!"—

And I answered, "Alas, is it *my* word? Who am *I*? I await the worthier one; I am not worthy even of being broken to pieces by it."[151]

What Zarathustra "knows" but cannot will is that one can voluntarily destroy one's existence; whereas later, in the sight of life, he knows that life recurs precisely in sacrifice.[152] Zarathustra's real word is the freedom toward death,[153] which freedom is *at one* with the will to the eternal recurrence. But the recurrence is not proclaimable until after the temptation to destroy oneself has already been overcome. In the most silent hour, which is his temptation, Zarathustra is encouraged to walk as a shadow of what must come and in this way to walk ahead. He reflects for a long time and finally answers: "I do not want to." A cruel laughter then occurs, and for the last time the voice cries, "Your fruits are ripe, Zarathustra, but you are not ripe for your fruits."[154] That is: he is in danger of becoming too old for his truths and victories, and then of not being free any longer to die at the right time out of a free decision.[155] After Zarathustra has resisted the temptation, he lies on the ground as though dead, and once again he must go back into his last loneliness. For he still has "something to say" and "something to give," thanks to the "double silence" of the most extreme abandonment and of the coming bliss. With that the second Part of *Zarathustra* logically ends; and after a pause in which the decision ripens, the third Part begins with Zarathustra's most silent and steepest wandering to a final peak. This peak is as much at one with his deepest abyss as the prophecy of the eternal recurrence is at one with nihilism.

Before the "wanderer" himself becomes a "shadow" by the free

spirit's liberation of himself from the first liberation to the childish innocence of reborn existence, Zarathustra sets off on his last wandering.
This last wandering leads him, at midnight, away from the blessed isles[156]
to the peak of the highest mountain, and is a reversal of the journey
that previously led Zarathustra's shadow, at noon, away from the same
isles to the heart of the earth. But this wandering—as much as it belongs to Zarathustra as a liberated spirit—has had its time. For in the
end the wandering is but an "emergency makeshift" to overcome the
heaviness that is the burden of existence. The climber does carry this
burden high, but he never throws it off.[157] On this last path to greatness and loneliness, which is something different from the abandonment[158] of the most silent hour,[159] peak and abyss become one for him.
This path is passable only so to speak, because behind it the foot of the
wanderer himself erases the path, and above it is written "impossibility." Zarathustra must *climb over himself* in order to be able to climb
up further and thus to overcome humanity as such—to overcome the
sickness "man" and the punishment "existence." The danger to which
he thus subjects himself is not the usual dizziness on a precipitous
path, where the climber's glance falls downward and his hand grasps
upward; rather, his danger is that his glance hurls into the height and
his hand would like to hold on to the depth.[160] The super-human wanderer Zarathustra becomes giddy before this "double will" to Being as
well as to the nothing; from a great distance he finally sees under himself, "beyond man and time," the whole fact "man." But to this end
Zarathustra must once again go down into the darkest tides of suffering[161] over the gravity of existence and learn to look away from himself
in order to behold the whole of Being.

On the ship on which Zarathustra leaves the blessed isles on the
morning after that midnight, he relates to the bold attempters of the
open sea the riddle he *saw*, his loneliest "vision," which concludes his
attempt with the truth.

Not long ago I walked gloomily through the deadly pallor of dusk—gloomy
and hard, with lips pressed together. Not only *one* sun had set for me. A path
that ascended defiantly through scree, malicious, lonely, not cheered by herb
or shrub . . . this path crunched under the defiance of my foot.

Striding silently over the mocking clatter of pebbles, crushing the rock that
made it slip, my foot forced its way upward.

Upward—defying the spirit that drew it . . . toward the abyss, the spirit of
gravity, my devil and archenemy.

Upward—although he sat on me, half dwarf, half mole, lame, making lame,
dripping lead . . . through my ear, into my brain.

"O Zarathustra," he whispered mockingly, syllable by syllable, "you philosopher's stone! You threw yourself up high; but every stone that is thrown must—fall!

"O Zarathustra, you philosopher's stone, you slingstone. . . . It was you yourself whom you threw so high,—but every stone that is thrown—must fall!

"Sentenced to yourself and to your own stoning—O Zarathustra, far indeed have you thrown the stone, but it will fall back onto *you*!"[162]

But how can man plan himself, in a superhuman way, out of his thrownness?[T51] Does the courage that says, "Dwarf! It is *you* or *I*!" suffice for this purpose? Courage, it is said, strikes dead even the dizziness at abysses, as well as suffering and pity, even death—by saying, "Was that life? Well then! Once more!"[163]

At this critical turning point of thought, from denial of death to unconditional affirmation of one's own existence in the whole of Being, the previous Either-Or is reversed, and Zarathustra now says to the dwarf, "It is *I* or *you*!" For the dwarf cannot bear Zarathustra's most abysmal idea of the eternal recurrence; but Zarathustra—who, in carrying up the dwarf, carried up the burden of his existence—can indeed bear the most abysmal idea. The dwarf jumps off Zarathustra's shoulders and sits on a stone. "But there was a gateway just where we had stopped." In the symbol of the gateway, the idea of the eternal recurrence is first demonstrated. Over it is inscribed what it is temporarily, namely a "moment," at which it is noon and eternity, because in that moment time comes to completion. Two temporal paths meet at the gateway "moment." One runs back interminably, infinitely, and to that extent "eternally" in a straight line back in time; the other, likewise interminably and infinitely forward in time. At the gateway the two paths collide with each other head-on.

"But whoever would follow one of them, on and on, farther and farther: do you believe, dwarf, that these paths contradict each other eternally?"—

"All that is straight lies," murmured the dwarf contemptuously. "All truth is crooked; time itself is a circle."

"You spirit of gravity," I said angrily, "do not make things too easy for yourself!"[164]

The dwarf makes it too easy for himself with truth because he himself is only the burden of existence, the burden that has jumped down but not been overcome, and because the real difficulty consists in bringing the vision of the eternally revolving world into harmony with the purposeful willing of the man of the future.

"Must not whatever *can* walk, have walked on this lane before? Must not whatever *can* happen, have happened; have been done; have passed by before?

"And if everything has been there before—what do you think, dwarf, of this moment? Must not this gateway, too—have been there before? And are not all things knotted together so firmly that this moment draws after it *all* that is to come? *Therefore*—even itself?

"For whatever of all things *can* walk—in this long lane *out there*, too—it *must* walk once more!—

"And this slow spider that crawls in the moonlight, and this moonlight itself, and I and you in the gateway, whispering together, whispering of eternal things—must not all of us have been there before?

"—and return and walk in that other lane, out there before us, in this long, dreadful lane—must we not eternally return?"

Thus I spoke, more and more softly; for I was afraid of my own ideas and ulterior motives. Then, suddenly, I heard a dog howl nearby.[165]

The dog, in whose pitiful howling an experience from Nietzsche's youth recurs, is an intimation of the cry of distress of the higher men that is to come. They call after Zarathustra as the overcomer of man. For a while the answer is thereby delayed to the question, already developed previously and to be developed later,[166] whether the freedom of "willing" and "ability" does not, in the end, encounter the necessity of "compulsion" in "*amor fati*."

At first dwarf and gateway, spider and whisper have disappeared in a most desolate moonshine. "But there lay a man" with the figure of a shepherd. A heavy, black snake hung out of his mouth. Zarathustra's hand tore at the snake in vain. Then Zarathustra's nausea and pity cried out of him, "Bite! Bite its head off!" The shepherd did it, no longer a shepherd, no longer a man, but one who has changed. He laughed as no man had ever laughed before, and the recuperated Zarathustra also laughed as one who has changed. The interpretation of this twofold vision of the gateway and the shepherd emerges from Zarathustra's own convalescence from his sickness unto death.[167] Zarathustra's temptation to self-destruction presents itself to the world around him as the mortal danger of a shepherd who cannot heal himself from the sickness unto death because he is a "man," as distinguished from him who will climb over himself and overcome "himself," that is, the sickness "man," by means of a realization. The symbol of this realization is the snake of eternity, the snake that has wound around itself in rings. The vision of the shepherd is thus a "foreseeing" of that redemption which Zarathustra himself, as one who has recuperated, experiences. He experiences redemption by calling up his most abysmal idea—and thereby becoming the advocate of the circle. (Previously he had already encountered the circle for a moment in the image of the gateway as the point of intersection of the dimensions of time.) Where modern man "does not know which way to turn," Zarathustra finds the "exit from two thousand years of mendacity." As the overcomer of man and time, he finds this exit by joining the two endlessly straight paths, which end in the nothing, into the eternal circle of Being. Thinking this *"circulus vitiosus deus"*[T52] is, "for human bones," a "spinning illness"[168] to be sure. But it is an illness only because the man of the Christian age thinks of an imperishability, a timeless "eternal life," when he thinks of eternity; whereas the "eternal vitality"[169] is an eternal recurrence of the same that justifies precisely what comes into being and passes away as such.[170]

When Zarathustra hears the laughter of the transformed shepherd, he says, "How could I bear to keep living! And how could I bear to die now!"—that is, before a last such metamorphosis of the most extreme mortal danger into the highest will to life. He then leaves the isle, in order to be solitary again with the pure sky and the open sea, which in changing from day into night and from low tide into high tide are an image of the eternal recurrence.[171]

The wanderer's shadow, the longest repose,[T53] and the most silent hour all say to Zarathustra that it is the highest time, namely for the completion of nihilism. The wind, which previously tore open the gate to the castle of death, in order to throw Zarathustra a coffin, now blows through the keyhole and says, " 'Come!' Cunningly, the door flew open and said to me, 'Go!' " namely out into life.[172] And this time the past burst its tombs in order to be reborn from death into life.[173] It is now time for this last metamorphosis. "But I—did not hear, until at last my abyss stirred and my idea bit me." Previously Zarathustra had been bitten in the neck by his idea in the form of an adder, and the humane shepherd had bitten off the head of the same idea in order not to be strangled by it. Up to now Zarathustra has only *carried* his idea, as the burden of existence, upward; now he wants *to summon it up* for the first time. That is, he wants to call up precisely that idea of the meaningless boredom of existence, that idea which pulls downward, the obverse of which is the long repose[T54] of the eternal recurrence. For this purpose he still must overcome himself, to this final "excess courage."[174, T55] The decisive hour of his great noon has not yet come.[175] A preliminary peace in uncertainty, and "involuntary bliss," still delays the freely willed decision[176] by means of which the illness "man" convalesces.

The unity of abyss and peak presents itself "before sunrise" in the *abyss of light* of the heavens. The abyss of light is the "light" to Zarathustra's "fire" (out of the ashes that were carried to the mountain) and the "sister soul" to Zarathustra's double insight into the "in vain" and the "well, then"[T56] of nihilism and recurrence. "To throw myself into your height—that is *my* depth! To hide in your purity—that is *my* innocence."[T57] But to this end his own will would have to be able to fly into the innocence, high-spiritedness,[T58] and chance[T59] of the heavens; in order, like the heavens, to stand over every single thing as its own heaven, as its "round roof," "azure bell," and "eternal security." *For that purpose* Zarathustra, who too often had mastered himself,[177] struggled to get his hands free to give his "Yes and Amen" blessing to everything that is, already was, and will be again, too. It is *this* freedom that Zarathustra's final, superhuman "sun's will" wants. But not everything may be put into words "before the day,"[T60] and it is not yet day in the sense of the great noon, *after* sunrise.—On the open sea and in sight of the heavens, Zarathustra has forgotten man, and wants to learn what has happened to him in the meantime. Man has more and more approached the last man who has declined but thereby announces at the same time the closeness of the great noon[178] of the man who has climbed over himself. Zarathustra, sitting before "half-written" tablets of the new law, still waits for his redemption through a will for which necessity is freedom itself, and all time a blissful mockery of eternal moments.[179] A skiff of death stands there. With it one can ferry over into the great nothing—"perhaps," however, also into the great Being at the great noon.[180] At last Zarathustra's "final will"[181] is ready to recover from the nothing and toward Being. He calls his most abysmal idea up into the light of day and thus becomes the advocate of revolving life, in which joy[T61] and suffering are one and the same, although only joy wants itself again and again in all eternity.

In coming into contact with his idea, Zarathustra wavers even now between approaching and retreating. After Zarathustra has given his hand to his most abysmal idea, he falls down, just as after the most silent hour, like a dead man, sick from his own convalescence. Afterward Zarathustra stands there as Zarathustra-Dionysus, or in another plan as "Caesar." The decisive moment is eternalized. The knowledge that dawns on him in this moment is that of *the eternal recurrence as the truth of nihilism.* Both mean: everything is without purpose, everything is without meaning. His animals proclaim to him the truth of the recurrence:

"Everything goes, everything comes back; eternally rolls the wheel of Being. Everything dies, everything blossoms again; eternally runs the year of Being.

"Everything breaks, everything is joined anew; eternally the same house of Being is built. Everything parts, everything greets every other thing again; eternally the ring of Being remains faithful to itself.

"In every Now, Being begins; round every Here rolls the sphere There. The center is everywhere. Bent is the path of eternity."[182]

Zarathustra's animals know before he himself does, who he is and consequently must become, namely the teacher of the eternal recurrence of eternally self-renewing life; because they themselves are natural and periodic living things. They "bear" this idea, which corresponds to their nature. In contrast, for man this idea is at first unbearable.[183] What an animal is by birth, man can become only through a rebirth, through an overcoming of himself, by means of which the "wise man" and the "animal" draw near to each other and produce a new type, who knows himself to be responsible for everything that lives. But because man is neither perfect like a wise man nor whole like an animal, the necessity of teaching the eternal recurrence signifies for Zarathustra his "greatest danger and illness," from which he must convalesce. Therefore the first proclamation of the eternal recurrence is given by Zarathustra's animals, and in a speech that talks of the "convalescent."

Zarathustra is reborn thereby, however, not to a new life in the Christian sense of another and better life, but to the equal and selfsame life "in the greatest and also in the smallest"—for the "small" man, too, returns eternally; likewise, the hour of the great noon and the proclamation that occurs in that hour:

"to teach again the eternal recurrence of all things—

"to speak again the word of the great noon of earth and man, to proclaim the superman again to men.

"I spoke my word, I break into pieces on my word: thus my eternal lot wants it—as a proclaimer I perish!

"The hour has now come when he who goes under should bless himself. Thus—*ends* Zarathustra's going under."[184]

Zarathustra's downgoing began when he climbed down to men from his mountain in order to teach them the superman, who by overcoming himself is able to will the eternal recurrence.

Now Zarathustra can say *Today* like *Someday* and *Formerly,* and he can dance his dance beyond all Here and There and Over There. His transformed spirit now says No as the storm says No, and Yes as the open heaven says Yes. Silent like a light, he goes through storms of negation; and what the sunrise promised and the prologue already proclaims, is fulfilled and completed at noon and eternity. His melancholy reposes in the bliss of future Dionysian songs. And with a final philosophic cheerfulness, the skiff of death of the past now glides onto silent seas, and is willingly moved by the sea of Being. The skiff belongs to the divine winegrower Dionysus, who cuts the ripened fruits with a diamond winegrower's-knife.[185] Only now the truth of the *one* life is viewed, by looking at the eternal recurrence of the same. The Yes and Amen song[186] and the twice recurring song of eternity[187] consequently close the third and fourth Parts of *Zarathustra.* The further contents thereof present the redemption of the *other* men, who are "higher men" inasmuch as they despair and despise themselves. They all are transformed at the ass festival, where the always same Yea-Yuh of the ass makes a travesty of the Dionysian Yes to the whole of Being. But these are not yet Zarathustra's disciples but only preliminary men of the great nausea and therefore of the great longing—"remnants of God," as they are called in an allusion to the notion in the Old Testament of the Chosen People. They all still suffer over themselves, but not basically over humanity as such. The three metamorphoses of the same spirit, with which Zarathustra's speech begins, are completed in an anti-Christian way with the teaching of the eternal recurrence of the same in the fullness of time. Zarathustra's teaching gives the weak a "Thou shalt," the strong an "I will"; and to those liberated even from willing, it gives back the "Yes and Amen" to the simple necessity of being-thus-and-not-different, the necessity of the highest star of Being.[188] Under the "shield of necessity," the accident of one's own existence is again at home in the whole of Being. Therewith Nietzsche has—seemingly—discovered the "new possibilities of life" for the sake of which he had, initially, repeated pre-Socratic philosophy; in order to renew, in the end, the ancient view of the world on the peak of anti-Christian modernity.

But how, with the freedom of the will that has sprung from the Christian understanding of existence, can one will again the necessity of simple being-thus-and-not-different, except through a *willing of what must be*—which as a double will denies both? The whole *problem* of a *creative willing* of the eternal *recurrence of the same*[189] is contained in this double will that wills against itself. In *Zarathustra,* the chapter "On Redemption" deals with the solution to this problem.

What Nietzsche's "last will" wills is not only a destiny of its own but *destiny* itself *as fate*—"a destiny standing on a destiny."[190] If the human will—and man *is* "will" since no God commands him any more to do what he "ought"—would limit itself, as a "creative" will to power, to do its own work, the true teaching of willing and of freedom would be the same: "Willing liberates, for willing is creating."[191] But is not every human willing attached to a for-the-sake-of[T62] that the new teaching precisely denies?[192] Or is the human *will to create* something like a natural *power of creation,* a power that, because it is as it is and cannot be different, creates naturally, playfully, *without* any for-the-sake-of? Or can the human will that creates the future creatively "re-create itself"? To be sure, creation is "the great redemption from suffering and the lightening of the burden of life." But "that the creator may be, suffering is needed and much metamorphosis,"[193] namely the most difficult and final metamorphosis into the child who creates at play, to whom everything becomes light and easy that to the manly will was still heavy and difficult. That is, were the will *only* a liberator that creates the future in the realm of the possible and re-creates what is his lot into what is his need, then the "necessity" of the will would consist only in the "turn of necessity"[194, T63] but not also in the blessing Yes to the highest star of Being, which is an eternal, *inescapable* fate that comes on its own to the will.[195] This "own Yes" to the "Yes of Being"—"As such, everything that is says the Yes"—does not have the meaning of an affirmative willing toward something for the sake of which the will wills. Rather, it has the sense of a "Yes and Amen" that "wills" nothing more and nothing less than a simple final *sealing* (no longer conditioned by something else) of the necessity of its own existence in the whole of what is by nature. This "Yes and Amen" is unattainable for every "Yes" that is reciprocally conditioned by a "No," every "well, Yes, but No." The simple necessity of being-thus-and-not-different surpasses every being-necessary-for-something.

But how does Zarathustra's relentless "sun's will" toward fate[196] fly into the high-spiritedness, innocence, and chance of the heavens in order to return to all things the "oldest nobility of the world"?[197]—unless by means of a freedom of willing that is more than merely courageous, a freedom that transforms (again) the first liberation from "Thou shalt" to "I will" and re-creates it into the creative play of a child of the world, who now "wills" only so to speak.

For the creator to be the child that is to be newly born, he must also want to be the mother who gives birth and the pangs of the birth-giver.[198]

But how can the adult will of the liberated spirit give itself rebirth to a childlike existence in the midst of the things that are, if that will does not also will *back* to what already was and cannot be different any more? The temporal problem in the willing of the eternal recurrence (as the self-redemption from the craving for the "Different," for the "No," and for the "Nothing") is therefore the *redemption from what is past,* from all "*it was.*"

Zarathustra sees everything that has passed away to be abandoned, and this is a twofold way. Some force the past down to the status of a portent paving the way for their decayed "today."[199] For others, the past ends with the grandfather. Neither redeems from what is past.

> This is my pity that I see for all that is past: it is abandoned
> —to the pleasure, the spirit, the madness of every generation . . . that comes along and reinterprets all that has been as a bridge to itself!
> A great power-lord might come along, a shrewd monster who, according to his favor and disfavor, might constrain and strain all that is past: until it became a bridge to him, a harbinger and herald and cockcrow.
> This, however, is the other danger and what prompts my other pity:— whoever is of the rabble thinks back as far as the grandfather;—with the grandfather, however, time ends.
> Thus all that has passed away is abandoned: for one day the rabble might become master and drown all time in shallow waters.[200]

But what is past would also be abandoned and unredeemed if it were only what had already happened, once and forever, which no longer allows of being willed. The fact of human existence would remain a "fragment" and a "riddle" if man had to accept his own always-having-been-there-already as a meaningless accident in the whole of Being. "And how could I bear to be a man if man were not also poet and guesser of riddles and the redeemer of the accident!" The accident that man redeems is the accident that being-there itself is, *because being-there always has already fallen into the world and been there before it willed itself.*[T64]

> "To redeem those who lived in the past and to recreate all 'it was' into a 'thus I willed it!'—that alone I would call redemption!
> "Will—that is the name of the liberator and joy-bringer; thus I taught you, my friends! But now learn this, too: the will itself is still a prisoner.
> "Willing liberates; but what is it that puts even the liberator himself in fetters?

"'It was'—that is the name of the will's gnashing of teeth and loneliest melancholy.

"Powerless against what has been done,—it is an angry spectator of all that is past.

"The will cannot will backward; and that it cannot break time and time's covetousness,—that is the will's loneliest melancholy.

"Willing liberates; what means does the will devise for itself to get rid of its melancholy and to mock its dungeon?

"Alas, every prisoner becomes a fool! And the imprisoned will redeems itself foolishly.

"That time does not run backward, that is the will's wrath; 'what was'— that is the name of the stone that the will cannot move.

"And so it moves stones out of wrath and displeasure, and wreaks revenge on whatever does not feel wrath and displeasure as it does.

"Thus the will, a liberator, took to hurting; and on everything that can suffer, it wreaks revenge for its inability to go backward.

"This, indeed this alone, is *revenge* itself: the will's ill will against time and its 'it was.'"[201]

What Nietzsche has, with regard to morality, illuminated psychologically as "*ressentiment*" and "a slave rebellion in morals" is made evident here with regard to being-there as such in its significance in principle for all willing. The impotent revenge on the inability to will backward to the "it was" of the deed that has already happened makes guilt and punishment out of existence, the "punishment 'existence.'" The vengeful will seeks after guilt, that is, after what is to blame for the fact that there is anything at all that is already there and thus and not different. The vengeful will punishes existence, seemingly rightly, by a punitive revenge on the fact that all human willing—and man *is* essentially will—has an uncrossable border and an irremovable stumbling block in what is not willed, not owing to, and not caused by the will. The revenge calls itself "punishment" with regard to its own desire to find guilt. But if it were recognized once and for all that no one—also no willing God as *causa prima*[T65] of the world—is to blame for being there at all and being as he is, then existence would regain its natural innocence again in the whole of living Being. Existence has forfeited this innocence through the spirit of revenge. The opposition of revenge and "blessing" or of ill will and "*amor fati*" corresponds to the opposition of guilt and innocence. The vengeful ill will transforms itself into the "good will" of that ring (in the last aphorism of *The Will to Power*) which is a cycle that runs forward as well as backward, a cycle of the world that wills itself. The "wrestling" of the human will, which wrestling is a self-conquering, transforms itself into the unconstrained blessing of that entirely different "ring"[T66] which is the eternal recurrence of all that is. But as long as the wrestling and conquering will only wills the future and therefore has an ill will toward everything that already exists without this wrestling-conquering will, the willing existence will again and again become guilt and punishment for itself. Existence becomes "eternally crime and guilt again" for itself precisely because it is *not* itself guilty of bringing about the fact of its own being-there; but as a will that is, it *wants* to be guilty thereof and nevertheless *cannot* be.[202] Therefore the will, as ill will toward the burden of existence that has always already fallen to the will, rolls "stone upon stone." And "cloud upon cloud rolls over the spirit, until eventually madness preaches: 'Everything passes away; therefore, everything deserves to pass away.'"[T67] That is, indignation[T68] over the already past time of the already done deed devaluates the latter[T69] into transience; unless, that is, "the will finally redeems itself" as in Schopenhauer's metaphysics, and "willing becomes not willing." In opposition to the latter, Zarathustra's creative will says to the stone, which is the burden of existence that plans itself in vain, "*But thus I willed it*" and will it again into all eternity! But when did he speak thus? And when will it happen that the creative will to the future also exerts itself for what already exists without that will? And who taught the will to will backward in place of not willing and the bringing of joy instead of hurting? Zarathustra answers this question as the teacher of the eternal recurrence. For in willing the eternally recurring cycle of time and of Being, the will that wills thus also develops from a straight movement into a circle that wills forward as well as backward. The movement of this circle is not open to the future, as is the movement of willing that sets goals and purposes. Rather, this circular movement is closed within itself, and the will in all that is willed accordingly wills exclusively itself and constantly the same and always the whole. The riddle "man" finds its solution in this temporal whole of the ring, which does not conquer by struggling[T70] but instead freely and easily wills itself again and again. Zarathustra does not teach just this and that but the one thing needful. But what could be more necessary for the "fragment" and "accident" man than his completion and insertion into the necessary whole of Being? Zarathustra seeks and walks on a path on which man is to insert himself, through a turn of necessity,[T71] into the highest necessity of all that is. But this reversal and return of the human will and its willfulness into the necessary whole of natural Being is difficult for the modern European. It is difficult for him to the same extent that he has separated and liberated himself from the "ways of heaven" and of earth, so that the unquestioning foundation of Eastern wisdom[202a] becomes a problem for him, the solution to which requires a turning of the will. The future-willing will of the superhuman Zarathustra must turn itself against itself in order to be able to will the eternal recurrence. Nietzsche calls this inverted will, which continues to will what it always has to will, "*amor fati.*" In "*amor fati*" the whole of time and of Being unites into the future—which has already been once—of a Being that is still evolving.[203]

Only in the love of fate does the creative will, too, com-plete[T72] itself. (The creative will creates its own destiny out of everything that falls to it as something different.) For if the will "cooks" every accident "in its own pot" in order to call it welcome as *its own* nourishment[204]—that cooking does make the strange accident into the will's own destiny, to be sure, but it does not make the latter into fate.[205] The will that wills precisely the fate of the eternal recurrence "in order to gain the highest strength"[206] welcomes eternal fate in its own temporal destiny; and what falls to the will is no arbitrary individual case,[T73] but instead affiliation with the whole of the world. The accidental destiny of one's own existence is necessary in the highest sense of fatality only when that destiny willingly inserts itself into the fatality of all that is. Zarathustra's "soul" is the "highest type" of *all* that is because it only reflects the highest law and essence of the world. It is

the soul that has the longest ladder and can reach down deepest;
the most comprehensive soul, which can run and stray and roam farthest within itself;
the most necessary soul, which joyfully plunges itself into chance;
the soul that, while being, wills into becoming; the soul that has, yet wants to will and desire—
the soul that flees itself and catches up with itself in the widest circles;
the wisest soul, which folly talks to most sweetly;
the soul that loves itself most, in which all things have their stream and counterstream and low and high tides—.[207]

Zarathustra's soul is the eternal Yes to the Yes of Being.[208] But "that is the concept of the Dionysian itself," and its formula is not will *to destiny* and still less will *to power,* but "*amor fati.*"[209] "Loving" the absolute or fatal necessity is no longer a willing but—judged by willing—a willingness that no longer wills anything, in which willing as such is abolished. In this reflection, Nietzsche coincides with Schelling's insight that in the greatest unrest and energy of life, the real goal is nevertheless always a condition in which the will no longer wills anything. For, as long as the will still wills something, it involuntarily drives what is willed before itself as if in a constant flight, so that man destroys what is willed precisely by means of his willing and cannot achieve the freedom that he is.[210] "Pure integrity," for which the "child" is the symbol in Schelling, too, can no longer be the goal of a willing but can only be an event and a metamorphosis that happens of itself.

The accident of Being-there—the accident that is deprived of its innocence by the belief in willed, purposeful creation of Being out of the nothing—is "redeemed" in *amor fati*, because Zarathustra-Dionysus grasps precisely in accident what in the whole is as it must be. And when in *Ecce Homo*[211] Nietzsche presents as the highest necessity what coincided, seemingly through mere accident, in his life—his birth date with that of Frederick William IV, his first seeking with the finding of Schopenhauer, the completion of the first Part of *Zarathustra* with Wagner's hour of death, the decisive flashes of inspiration for his works with particular places of residence, and more such "sublime accidents"— even here he does nothing else but "poetically unify" what is fragment and riddle and horrid accident—as long, that is, as the riddle of the accident "being-there" does not yet have the "appearance" of the highest necessity. Yet this necessity does not exclude, but rather includes, the "chance"[T74] character of the whole of what is or of the "world," and the fact that the whole and the world have their "oldest nobility" in that accidental character.

But why does Zarathustra's speech on the redemption of willing suddenly break off in alarm at the decisive question about the possibility of willing backward? And why does he speak to his disciples differently than to himself?[T75] Perhaps because it remains undecided, before his most silent hour, whether he will redeem himself in this way or the other way, *into* the "privilege of existence"[212] or *from* the punishment of existence? The revaluation of "punishment" into a "privilege" and of "revenge" into a "blessing" presupposes that fundamental and comprehensive revaluation which consists in the reversal of the innate nihilism of mere willing into the love of fate of the eternal recurrence. If all things have originally been baptized in the "fountain of eternity"[213] and under the highest star of Being, then good and evil, too, are only "interim shadows" by the light abyss of heaven. The abyss of heaven stands over each thing as its own; while under it "purpose" and "guilt," the whither and whence of existence, evaporate in the innocence of the purpose-free whole.[214] Whether good and evil are at all true, whether they belong to the unshrouded character of existence—those questions are at first and at last decided by the total character of Being.

> There is an old illusion that is called good and evil. So far the wheel of this illusion has revolved around prophets and stargazers. Once one believed in prophets and stargazers. And *therefore* one believed: "Everything is destiny: Thou shalt, because Thou must!"
>
> Then one again mistrusted all prophets and stargazers, and *therefore* one believed: "Everything is freedom: you can, because you will."
>
> O my brothers, so far there have been only illusions about stars and the future, not knowledge; and *therefore* there have been only illusions so far, not knowledge, about good and evil![215]

Nietzsche's own teaching, which likewise is a "prophecy" with regard to the whole of what is, reflects mistrust of the old prophecy according to which everything is destiny, but not less the new prophecy according to which everything is freedom. The reason for this mistrust is that the true knowledge of what is, is the insight into the original unity of this willing and that compulsion, as well as into the original unity of accident and necessity. In his school essay of 1862, Nietzsche had already reflected that freedom could perhaps be only the "highest potentiality of fate." But how is it possible, with the modern freedom to be able to will, to will again that old intimacy with what must be and cannot be different, so that the compulsion of fate (which was once written in the stars) transforms itself, by means of a *willing* of *compulsion*,[216] into one's own destiny, so as finally to be able to say: "Ego-fate"; "I myself am fate and have been conditioning existence for eternities";[217] "I myself belong to the causes of the eternal recurrence"? For that purpose, would not the new prophecy itself have to be the unity of the prophecies from the stars[218] of the heavens, and of the truth of the nothing that is the last result of the freedom of one's own capabilities? Is, then, the whole that the new prophecy expresses, a "heavenly nothing"?[219] And is not the correlate to this interlacing also the double path on which the double will comes to its double truth, namely through a *decision* and an *inspiration*? A decision of the will (which at the most extreme end of freedom still prefers to will the nothing rather than not to will) and an inspiration (in which the highest star of Being gives itself to the thus decided will)—these two together form the problematical access to Nietzsche's double truth. This truth, as a teaching of the self-overcoming of nihilism, is Nietzsche's "*credo quia absurdum*."[T76]

Nothing, that is, has ever made a deeper impression on the German soul, nothing has "tempted" it more, than this most dangerous of all conclusions, which to every proper speaker of Romance languages is a sin against the spirit: *credo quia absurdum est*—with this, German logic makes its first appearance in the history of Christian dogma; but even today, a millennium later, we contemporary Germans sense . . . something of truth, of the *possibility* of truth, behind the famous real-dialectical basic tenet with which Hegel in his time helped the German spirit to victory over Europe: "contradiction moves the world, all things are self-contradictory"—we are plainly pessimists, even right down into logic. . . . Perhaps German pessimism has yet to take its last step? Perhaps it must once again set its *credo* and its *absurdum* next to each other in a terrible way?[220]

Even if these sentences immediately refer only to the self-overcoming of morality, they nevertheless already characterize the self-overcoming of nihilism, which is the real problem of the above passage. This passage at the same time indicates what Nietzsche knew about the present, namely that at bottom nothing at all other than the self-overcoming of nihilism is thought today—where thinking still occurs at all.[221]

The belief in the productive power of contradiction characterizes not only Hegel's formal dialectic and Schelling's construction of the universe but also Nietzsche's reversal of nihilism into the willing of the eternal recurrence. The same faith in the absurd lies at the bottom of Kierkegaard's paradoxical leap from the sickness unto death into Christian faith as well as at the bottom of Marx's theory of crisis, according to which only at the critical climax of the most extreme self-alienation can the change into complete self-reacquisition succeed. They all draw nourishment from Saint Paul's dialectic in the relationship of sin and grace, even if they pretend to be anti-Christian.

### The Double Equation for the Allegory of the Eternal Recurrence

The superhuman identity[T77] of the philosopher Nietzsche with *Dionysus philosophus* lies at the bottom of the metaphysical claim of the parables of *Zarathustra*. But if it is incredible that a radical "at-tempter" of the nineteenth century is the playacted *persona* of a Greek god, then Nietzsche's divine mask, too, is a human "mask" that falls away; and "ahead of the round dance" strides the "horrid necessity" and not an eternal fate. The parable, then, is so little the involuntary revelation of the naked truth that it rather cloaks the truth in its bareness.

As the self-overcoming of nihilism, the teaching of the ring of rings has the twofold aspect of an existence that has decided for the nothing and of a self-willing world of destruction and creation. By ceaselessly re-willing this world that in itself has been doubled, the existence of man frees itself from its own nihilism and regains its lost world:[222] the most authentic *need* of human existence turns into "*necessity.*" The problematical character of "the overcomer and the overcome" that is embraced in the foregoing becomes quite *obvious* when Nietzsche attempts to explain his parable that has been poetically unified. As soon as the poetic power of allegorizing leaves him, the whole decomposes into two contradictory parts, which only conflict holds together. For the tendency to eternalize existence that has become ephemeral does not enter into the circuit of the eternal cycle of the natural world—unless the temporal will of human existence that has become eccentric were to fly in superhuman fashion into the heaven of the pre-Copernican world, in order to circle along in the middle of Being.

The metaphor of the eternal recurrence is therefore equatable with something twofold: on the one hand, with an "ethical gravity" by means of which human existence that has become goalless obtains a goal again, beyond itself; and on the other hand, with a natural-scientific "fact" in the goalless self-contained existence[T78] of the world of forces. Consequently, the teaching of the recurrence presents itself first as the fixing of an ideal goal for the willing man—and then it replaces the Christian belief in immortality with the will to self-eternalization—and second as the ascertainment of a physical fact in the unwilled being-thus-and-not-different of the physical world. With the latter, the teaching replaces ancient cosmology with modern physics. This double explicability as an *atheistic religion* and as a *physical metaphysics* shows that in its totality the teaching is the *unity of a conflict* between the *nihilistic* existence of the man who has rid himself of God and the *positivistic* presence of physical energy. Qua natural scientist, however, Nietzsche is a philosophizing dilettante, and as the founder of a religion, he is a "hermaphrodite of sickness and will to power."[223]

In accordance with the twofold equation into which the parable divides, the Dionysian equality of the "equally powerful" and "equally blissful"[224] in all change breaks up into the *nihilistic* "Everything is the same or equal" of an existence alienated from the world and into the *positivistic* indifference of a world alienated from man. That existence which has become instable and goalless and this world that has become inapprehensible and unsensory combine in the willing of the eternal recurrence. The cosmic cycle of the recurrence is indifferent to all human willing.

*The anthropological equation.* Modern man is generally characterized by Nietzsche as something that "does not know which way to turn" because modern man no longer has a goal in terms of which he can plan his life. Nietzsche therefore wants the teaching of the return to be a "plan of a new way to live." We are the "heirs and masters of millennia," but we lack any particular will to the *future,* we lack a new purpose and direction. All previous determinations of value have been destroyed, because our values, purposes, and goals stem from the most varied tablets of goods of human history; our values, purposes, and goals mutually weaken and destroy themselves. Modernity is sick from having no Yes and no No anymore, from not knowing in what direction to engage its bravery. "In our atmosphere was a thunderstorm; the nature we are became dark—*for we had no path.* Formula for our happiness: a Yes, a No, a straight line, a goal"[225]—thus not at all a periodic, goalless revolving that runs back into itself. Such a "new purpose" is not given by itself, it is always there only if man gives it to himself. "All goals have been destroyed. Men must *give* themselves a goal. It was an error to suppose that men *have* a goal: they have given themselves all goals. But the *preconditions* for all earlier goals have been destroyed."[226] Nietzsche confronts this view of modernity with the "idea" of the eternal recurrence.

*My innovations.*—Further development of pessimism: . . .

1. My *endeavor* to oppose decay and increasing weakness of personality. I sought a new *center.*

2. Impossibility of this endeavor *recognized.*

3. *Thereupon I advanced further down the road of disintegration—where I found new sources of strength for individuals. We have to be destroyers!*—I perceived that the state of *disintegration,* in which *individual* natures[T79] *can* perfect themselves *as never before*—is an image and *isolated example of existence in general.* In opposition to the paralyzing sense of general disintegration and incompleteness, I set forth the *eternal return.*[227]

The eternal return is to give humanity a goal that goes beyond the present state of man, yet not into an otherworldly "backworld," but instead into humanity's own continuation. Man *as such* must be raised above himself. That is the human meaning both of the "superman"[228] out of whom Nietzsche teaches the recurrence, and of the "new determinations of value" of the will to power. Then man becomes the "lord of the earth" and the legislator of the future in a new human world ordered according to rank and power. "Who should be the lord of the earth? That is the *refrain* of my practical philosophy."[229] Nietzsche sees the "deep unfruitfulness of the nineteenth century" in the fact that he still has met no man who has actually brought a new "ideal." He compares our epoch to the Alexandrian culture, which in his opinion perished because "with all its useful discoveries . . . ," it "was nevertheless not capable of giving *this* world and *this* life the final *importance*." According to Nietzsche, this decay in humanity should be guided so "that something will come of it." From all the foregoing arises the historical, *anthropological* meaning of the teaching of the eternal recurrence as a highest "ethical gravity" on the willing (that has become goalless) of an existence that has become "ephemeral." The teaching of the recurrence should strike modernity with the "heaviest stress," namely that of *responsibility* for the future. But it should precisely not unburden existence by means of a "positively turned irresponsibility" toward the innocence of existence. Ever since religious faith has decreased, it must be asked, "How do we give gravity to the inner life?" And the teaching of the return should burden human existence anew, as a "heavy" and "disciplining" idea. The new burden arises through the categorical imperative: live in every moment so that you *could* will that moment back again over and over. The teaching of the return is supposed to remodel our image of man through a new stipulation of man in his passions; and the model for this teaching is Zarathustra, because he is the highest type of man, who commands himself and has been well disciplined and bred. The already mapped-out image of an "exaltation of man" presents itself in him. For there have already been men who have been raised above themselves, in antiquity[230] and in antiquity's Renaissance. In the modern world, Napoleon and Goethe[231] are such more-than-human human beings.[232]

As a counterweight to the "*modernity*" of decayed Christianity, the idea of the return is thus a *historically* conceived idea, and in accordance with its purpose it is directed to the *future* of European man. The idea of the return occurs when it is necessary for all Europe and every individual to decide whether they want to descend to the last man or to ascend to the overcoming of man. The teaching of the return sets free the hidden nihilism that results from the death of God. It puts "all and no one," that is, every individual, before the logically consequent question "whether his will 'wills' toward decline,"[233] whether European man still wants to exist at all. As such an Either-Or, the teaching of the return resolves the undecided ambiguity in modern existence.

The teaching of the eternal return is, consequently, not at all a teaching of something that with simple necessity is thus and not different. Rather, it is supposed to teach something with the "tendency"[234] to create new horizons by means of a new purpose,[235] in agreement with the basically experimental character of Nietzsche's philosophy. The teaching is a sculpting "hammer" in the hand of the mightiest man, who is the mightiest because he has overcome in himself the will to the nothing. And as a "philosophy of the hammer," the teaching aims at the eternalization of *this* existence as opposed to its vaporization in the technical bustle of existence. The teaching reflects Nietzsche's desire to raise this finite existence to an eternal "significance." "That emperor constantly kept himself aware of the transitoriness of all things in order not to take them too seriously and in order to stay peaceful among them. To me, on the contrary, everything seems much too valuable to be allowed to be so ephemeral: I seek an eternity for each and every thing."[236] The teaching *is* what it can "*signify*" to man, because what it teaches is no theoretical truth at all but a practical postulate. "The task is to live in such a way that you must *wish* to live again." The recurrence is consequently no event that is impending in the future, but it is also no recurring of the same again and again. Rather, it is a *will to rebirth,* to a "*vita nuova,*"[T80] for "our task confronts us in every moment," and one should "seek" after the eternalization of this existence. This life "shall be" your eternal life.[237] "*That we could bear our immortality—that would be the highest thing.*" The immediate "result" of the teaching should accordingly be "*a replacement for the belief in immortality.*"[238]

If it is borne, the idea of the eternal recurrence increases the good will to life. It bars the previous evasions, both into the beyond of the backworld and into the nothing, as well as into the blind secularization of man who becomes unquestionable unto himself.[239] With the help of the recurrence, "absolute skepticism" is to be overcome—that skepticism which has discovered, "nothing is true; everything is permitted," that skepticism for which the normal practice is letting oneself go. In opposition to that letting oneself go, one should take on the burden of wishing and willing that everything recur in always the same way.

The whole teaching thus seems to be above all an experiment of the human will and, as an attempt at the eternalization of our deeds and nondeeds, to be an atheistic gospel. "Let us imprint the likeness of eternity upon *our* life! This idea contains more than all religions that despise this life as ephemeral and have taught the faithful to focus their gaze on an indeterminate *other* life."[240] In transforming the alienated "Thou shalt" of the Christian faith into one's *own "Thou shalt" of an "I will,"* the teaching of the recurrence is a self-made legislation and religion.

The *time* of the eternal recurrence is, then, not the "eternal present" of a goalless revolving in which past still becomes and future already was; it is rather the future time of a goal that liberates from the burden of the past and arises from the will to the future.[241] "Eternity," then, does not have the meaning of an eternal *recurrence* of the *same,* but it is the willed goal of a will to eternal-ization.[T81]

On the basis of the educational character of Nietzsche's teaching, one could understand it subjectively as a "fiction" in the sense of: "*as if*" there were an—objective—return.[242] But this character of the teaching manifests only *one* side of the recurrence, the anthropological side, without the affiliated other side, which pertains to the world—the side that has already made itself conspicuous within the compass of the aphorisms quoted hitherto. Where Nietzsche writes, "My teaching says: the task is to live in such a way that you must *wish* to live again," there follows a dash—which, however, announces a break in Nietzsche's thought[T82]—and then: "you will do so [live again] *in any case!*" With a different emphasis but the same meaning, Nietzsche writes Overbeck on 10 March 1884 regarding the idea of the return: "*If it is true,* or rather: if it is believed to be true—then *everything* changes and spins around, and *all* previous values are devalued." But how can one believe, wish, and will something that excludes and renders superfluous, through the irrevocability of its fatality, every willing, wishing, and believing?

"But if everything is necessary, what can I control about my actions?" That idea and belief is a gravity that, next to all other weights, presses on you, and does so more than the others do. You say that nutrition, place, atmosphere, society change you and determine you. Well, your opinions do so still more, for these destine you for this nutrition, place, atmosphere, society.—If you incorporate into yourself the idea of ideas, it will transform you. The question with everything that you want to do: "is it such that I want to do it innumerable times?"—that is the *greatest* gravity.

In the same sense Nietzsche says:

Let us examine how the *idea* that *something repeats* itself has functioned up to now (the year, for example, or periodic illnesses, awakening, sleeping, etc.). If the repetition of the circle is even just a probability or possibility, the *idea of a possibility*, too, can shake us and modify us; not only perceptions or particular expectation can do this! What an influence the *possibility* of eternal damnation has had![243]

But the fact that the mere idea of a possibility can "have an influence" does not abolish the distinction between an actual recurrence (say, of day and night or of wakefulness and sleep) and a recurrence that is only thought as a possibility. And if, on the other hand, it were certain that at all events everything recurs, then the demand "to live as if" would lose all reasonable meaning. Also, the expectation of an event that will occur once in the future (as of the Last Judgment) would neither shake nor modify man if the believer were not certain, regarding the event, that some such thing will actually occur. But Nietzsche's teaching contains exactly this irreconcilable double-meaning of a practical-moral postulate and of a theoretical statement, even in regard to itself; his teaching teaches in the sense of a demand and simultaneously in the sense of a teachable knowledge that everything recurs precisely so—"Sirius[T83] and the spider and your ideas in this hour and this idea of yours that everything returns."[244] Through this second, cosmological meaning there arises a fundamental absurdity in the whole of the super-human teaching. For if human life is turned upside down again and again like an hourglass, and if human existence including human ideas is only *one* ring in the great ring of the eternal recurrence of all that is—what sense would it then still make to want to get above oneself, to will a European future, to "will" anything at all? This contradiction emerges all the more strikingly inasmuch as Nietzsche develops the one meaning as an *ethical imperative* and the other as a *scientific theory*.

*The cosmological equation.*    The scientific principle of the conservation of energy requires the eternal recurrence.[245] The victory of the scientific spirit over the religious, God-inventing spirit should find expression in the recurrence.[246] It is the "most scientific of all possible hypotheses," a "new conception of the world," which says:

The world exists; it is not something that becomes, not something that passes away. Or rather: it becomes, it passes away, but it has never begun to become and never ceased to pass away—it *preserves* itself in both. . . . The world lives on itself: its excrements are its nourishment.[247]

The teaching of the recurrence affirms, instead of a *progressus* or *regressus ex infinito* or *in infinitum* conceived as *final,* the goalless cycle—goalless because it has no beginning and no end—of a specific quantity of self-maintaining force. The world has neither origin nor goal, for it is not the creation of an arbitrary God who once created Being out of the nothing; instead, in every moment the world is beginning and end at the same time, a constant alteration of the same.[248]

Consequently the number of states, alterations, combinations, and developments of this force is, to be sure, tremendously large and practically "immeasurable," but in any case also determinate and not infinite. But the time in which the universe exercises its force is infinite, that is, the power is eternally the same and eternally active;—up to this moment an eternity has already elapsed, that is, all possible developments must *have* already *been there. Consequently,* the development of this very moment must be a repetition, and likewise the one that gave birth to it and the one that arises out of it and thus forward and backward further! Everything has been there countless times inasmuch as the total state of all forces always recurs.[249]

This goalless recurrence should not be understood merely as a lack of meaning and of any goal; it should rather be understood in a positive way.

The old habit, however, of associating a goal with every event and a guiding, creating God with the world, is so powerful that it requires effort for a thinker not to fall into thinking of the very aimlessness of the world as intended. This notion—that the world thus intentionally *avoids* a goal and even knows artifices for keeping itself from entering into a cycle—must occur to all those who would like to decree onto the world the ability to introduce *eternal novelty;* i.e., to decree onto a finite, definite, unchangeable force of constant size, such as "the world" is, the miraculous capacity to introduce *infinite* novelty in its forms and states. The world, even if it is no longer a god, is still supposed to be capable of the divine power of creation, the power of infinite transformations; it is supposed willfully to *prevent* itself from returning to any of its old forms; it is supposed to possess not only the intention but the *means* of *guarding* against any repetition; to that end it is supposed to *control* every one of its movements at every moment so as to avoid goals, final states, repetitions—and whatever else may follow from such an unforgivably crazy way of thinking and wishing. It is still the old religious way of thinking and wishing, a kind of longing to believe that *in some way* the world is after all like the old . . .[T84] infinite, boundless-creative God—that in some way "the old God still lives"—that longing of Spinoza which was expressed in the words *"deus sive natura."*[T85] . . . What, then, is the principle and belief with which the decisive change, the now attained *preponderance* of the scientific spirit over the religious . . . spirit, is most definitely formulated? Is it not: the world, as force, may not be thought of as unlimited, for it *cannot* be so thought of;—we forbid ourselves the concept of an *infinite* force as *incompatible with the concept "force."* Thus—the world also lacks the capacity to introduce eternal novelty.[250]

On the other hand, this conception of the world is not automatically a mechanistic view;

for if it were that, it would not condition an infinite recurrence of identical cases, but a final state. *Because* the world has not reached a final state, we must consider mechanistic explanation to be an imperfect and merely provisional hypothesis.[251]

The world, understood as a certain definite quantity of force and as a certain definite number of centers of force, has to pass through a calculable number of combinations "in the great dice game of its existence."

In infinite time, every possible combination would at some time or another be realized; more: it would be realized an infinite number of times. And since between every combination and its next recurrence all other possible combinations would have to take place, and each of these combinations conditions the entire sequence of combinations in the same series, a circular movement of absolutely identical series would thus be demonstrated: the world as a cycle that has already repeated itself infinitely often and plays its game *in infinitum*.[252]

Man necessarily plays along in the world's game, but not because he has completed in himself the third metamorphosis from "I will" to the "I am" of the child who begins anew; but rather because human existence, too, is only *one* ring *in* the great ring of the eternal recurrence of all that is.

Man! Your whole life will be turned over again and again like an hourglass and will run out again and again,—there is a big minute of time, meanwhile, until all conditions out of which you have developed in the world's cycle, combine again. And then you will find every pain and pleasure and every friend and enemy and every hope and every error and every blade of grass and every ray of the sun again, the whole nexus of all things. This ring in which you are a bead, shines again and again. And in every ring of human existence altogether there is always an hour when the mightiest idea appears to first one, then many, then all, the idea, namely, of the eternal return of all things:—for humanity, every such time is the hour of the *noon*.[253]

This eternal recurrence of the same, which also comprehends the emergence of the idea of it, is neither meaningful and valuable nor meaningless and valueless, for its value is "equal in value" in every moment. Or to express it in a different way: this becoming *has no value whatever,* because it lacks everything by which it might be measured and in relation to which the word "value" would have meaning. *The total value of the world is not assessable;* consequently, philosophic pessimism belongs among the comic things.[254]

The eternal recurrence is a "primordial law" that is not subject to becoming, that is, it is already primevally posited with the specific amount of force of Being in the universe. Even the natural phenomena of periodic cycles and repetitions—for example, of the stars and seasons, the always identically recurring alternation of day and night or of the tides—already conceal the original essence of the law of the eternal recurrence, which is mathematically ascertainable.[255]

In the elated closing aphorism of *The Will to Power,* however, the physical formulations are outstripped by the vividness of the Dionysian view of the world. The characterization of Zarathustra's soul corresponds to this Dionysian view.

And do you know what the "world" is to me? Shall I show it to you in my mirror? This world: a monster of energy, without beginning, without end; a firm, iron magnitude of force that does not grow bigger or smaller, that does not expand itself but only transforms itself; as a whole, of unalterable size, a household without expenses or losses, but likewise without increase, without income; enclosed by the "nothing" as by its boundary; not something blurry or wasted, not something endlessly extended, but set in a definite space as a definite force, and not in a space that might be "empty" somewhere, but rather as force everywhere, as a play of forces and of waves of forces, at the same time one and many, increasing here and at the same time decreasing there, a sea of forces tossing and flowing together, eternally changing, eternally flooding back, with an ebb and flow of its forms; drifting out of the simplest forms toward the most complex, out of what is most silent, most rigid, coldest, toward the hottest, most turbulent, most self-contradictory, and then again returning home to the simple out of this abundance, out of the play of contradictions back to the joy of concord, still affirming itself in this sameness of its courses and its years, blessing itself as what must return eternally, as a becoming that knows no satiety, no disgust, no weariness—: this, my *Dionysian* world of the eternally self-creating, the eternally self-destroying, this mystery world of the twofold voluptuous delight, my "beyond good and evil" without goal, unless a goal lies in the happiness of the circle; without will, unless a ring has a good will toward itself—do you want a *name* for this world? A *solution* for all its riddles? A light[T86] for you, too, you best-concealed, strongest, most intrepid, most midnightly men?—*This world is the will to power—and nothing besides!* And you yourselves, too, are this will to power—and nothing besides![256]

But why is the physical world, and not only the man of a particular epoch, a will to self-overcoming and to climbing over oneself, in view of the fact that the basic character of the physical world consists in necessarily being as it is, *without* will and goal—"unless" a ring has a good will to itself and "unless" a goal lies in the happiness of the re-volving? How does man's will to power and possession, to control and self-control, to overcoming and self-overcoming, harmonize with this world of cosmic rhythms, which only *so to speak* "wills" itself—unless man and world be *one* unseparated "life," the secret of which is that it must always overcome itself anew? Nietzsche declares it so in *Zara-thustra,* and he understands the will to power—which on its part is a will to command and a will to obey in *everything* living—as a way of self-overcoming of the life that *all* living things have in common.[257] But the question is: Is this "*life*" (so understood) one with "*wisdom*" and the same as the life that Zarathustra as knower intends to aban-don,[258] but no longer wants to abandon after he is familiar with the "vi-sion" of his "riddle"? Does not the *one* talk of *the life* conceal the com-pletely different meanings of the "again and again" of self-overcoming and the "again and again" of selfless recurrence? For how could it be one and the same life that [on the one hand] must overcome "itself" in man as a willing being and that [on the other hand] always of its own accord returns, with the simple necessity of nature, in the natural world? Or is the *repeated self-overcoming* originally a self-overcoming in the existence of *man,* and the *naturally necessary recurrence* a recur-rence in the Being of the *world*?[259] For it is understandable that life "must always overcome itself" only insofar as life—as human life—has in itself the will to the nothing; and the superhuman solution that Nietzsche has found in *Zarathustra* for the overcoming of the will to the nothing is the *will* to the eternal recurrence, but not the eternal recurrence itself. Only on the basis of this problematic connection of nihilism and recurrence are the different meanings of temporal "again and again" and eternal "again and again," in the life of man and in the life of the world, also understandable. It is not life but rather Nietz-sche's ownmost existence that always had to overcome itself anew and that interpreted life as a whole from that experience. "My writings speak *only* of my overcomings."[260] "My strongest quality is self-overcoming. But I also am most in need of it—I was always at the abyss."[261]

The *problem* in the teaching of the eternal recurrence, which is the peak of this abyss, is, however, the unity of this discord. This discord finds expression just as much in the anthropological mode of present-ing the eternal recurrence as in the cosmological mode. In the anthro-pological mode it is expressed in the contradiction between the "Thou shalt" and one's *own will* and the remark, "You will do so in any case." And in the cosmological mode it comes to light in the supposition that the Dionysian *world* of the eternal recurrence is supposed to be a "will to power" and nothing besides.

Klages[262]—who adopts Nietzsche's rhythmically moved world of cosmic life and, in opposition to the "world of images," wants to show precisely in the case of Nietzsche the impotence of the spiritual will to power—has indicated that the last aphorism of *The Will to Power* breaks, through its final clause, into two parts. Klages can see in this break only a "dreadful derailment," because he himself wants to recognize only the truth of the one, cosmic side of existence. But in fact there is a problem at hand here that can be solved neither by a division of Nietzsche's double will into a spiritual will to power and a "pathetic necessity" nor by reducing Nietzsche's entire philosophy to the mere "will *as* power" (Baeumler). The existence of this problem and the inadequacy of such solutions are proved by the fact that Nietzsche himself composed the conclusion of the aphorism in question in two different ways.

### Second Draft (published in *The Will to Power*)

. . . unless a ring has a good will toward itself—do you want a *name* for this world? A *solution* for all its riddles? A light[T87] for you, too, you best-concealed, strongest, most intrepid, most midnightly men?—*This world is the will to power—and nothing besides!* And you yourselves, too, are this will to power—and nothing besides![263]

### First Draft (communicated in an appendix)

. . . unless a ring has a good will always to turn around itself on its own, old course, and to turn only around itself; this, *my* world,—who is bright enough to look at it without wanting to be blind? Strong enough to hold his soul against this mirror? His own mirror against the Dionysus mirror? His own solution against the Dionysus riddle? And must not the man who would be capable of that then have to do still more? Would he not *himself* have to become betrothed to the "ring of rings"? With a solemn vow to his own *return*? With the ring of eternal self-blessing, self-affirmation? With the will to willing-again-and-once-more? To the willing-back of all things that have ever been? To the willing forth toward everything that must ever be? Do you know now what *the world* is to me? And what *I* will, when I—"will" *this* world?[264]

In the first draft the *problem* of a willing of the eternal recurrence (in the image of the reciprocal mirroring of world-constitution and self-conduct) is seemingly resolved in that the self-willing of the world is conceived from the standpoint of the eternal recurrence as a willing-of-itself-again-and-again, and the human will, as a will that wills backward as well as forward, likewise moves in a circle. But in the second draft, the dubiousness of a willing fatality is concealed rather than brought up with the abrupt formula of the "will to power," which is supposed to be simply the same in man and in the world. In the end the sloganized formulation of life as a "will to power" does not at all reveal the always recurring cycle as the total character of life, but instead reveals the unique historical situation within which Nietzsche has considered the *one nature* of all things in the nineteenth century. The dubiousness of a willing of the eternal recurrence in the sense of the will to power becomes completely clear where Nietzsche wants to give—in order to justify his teaching—*natural-scientific* proof for the world as viewed from the Dionysian perspective[265] and conceives the willing of the eternal recurrence as *ethically* required.

In order to justify his teaching scientifically, Nietzsche dealt with Dühring, Julius Robert Mayer, Boscovich, and probably also Helmholtz,[266] and weighed a plan to study physics and mathematics at the University of Vienna or the University of Paris. This effort at a scientific justification is no strange eccentricity but the necessary consequence of Nietzsche's desire to teach something. Whoever wishes to generate a communicable philosophic teaching cannot satisfy himself with a mere reference to an ecstatic vision or a plan; he must attempt to clarify and solve in his teaching the riddle of his vision and to justify his vision in a carefully reasoned way. The attempt at a natural-scientific justification of the eternal recurrence as the temporal structure of the physical world should not be taken any less seriously than the other attempt, that is, to develop the eternal recurrence as an ethical postulate. Both attempts show that in the seeming unity of world-constitution and self-conduct, the two sides that that unity is supposed to unify are poles apart. The teaching of the eternal recurrence is equally essentially an *atheistic substitute for religion* and a *"physical metaphysics."*[267] As the unity of both, it is the attempt to tie the existence of modern man, which has become eccentric, back into the natural whole of the world.[268]

### The Problematic Unity in the Discord of the Double Equation

The contradiction in the presentation of the teaching of the return can be epitomized, for the sake of clarifying it methodically, as a fundamental discord in the relationship to the world that the man has who is liberated to the "I will" and therewith to the nothing. It is indirect evidence of the decay of modern man in his relations with God and the world that Nietzsche wants to restore a lost unity and order in the whole of Being through a *cosmic* interpretation of the will to power. The essential impulse of the philosophical efforts of the last three centuries has arisen from the separation of what is in the whole into an outer world, an inner world, and a backworld. Since Descartes's doubt of God and his differentiation between man ( *res cogitans*[T88] ) and world ( *res extensa*[T89] ) according to being oneself and being other; up to the mediation of man and world, self and other through Hegel; and from there up to Nietzsche's attempt at a "*re-betrothal*" of the world, philosophy has been one single attempt to regain a lost world. What Nietzsche with his teaching of the eternal recurrence of the same wants to restore on the peak of modernity—after the disintegration (which began with Descartes) of the Christian interpretation of existence—is the pre-Socratic view of the world. In this attempt to philosophize over a distance of two millennia, he remains tied both to the positivism and to the nihilism of his century, in the vain effort to unite at a new depth two separated yet corresponding spheres, namely the sphere of an unchanging quantum of forces and the sphere of the nihilistic energy of modern existence. The purpose of this effort to unite the two spheres is to tie the untied freedom, at its outermost edge, back into the always same law of the revolving world. In the condensed parable this experiment seems to succeed, whereas in the reflective analysis, the poetically unified whole falls apart again into its two parts. But because both are nevertheless parts of a willed whole, in each of the two lines of interpretation—with regard to man and with regard to the world—the respective other line comes to view: the not at all "divine" circle of Nietzsche's own *existence* shines into the mechanistic recurrence of the same, and Nietzsche's hopeless existence tentatively plans itself into fate, as if his solitary ego belonged to the necessary conditions of the always same structure of the physical world.

Nietzsche last discusses the questionable position of man toward the world, with regard to the true apprehension of the apparent world, in *The Will to Power* under the title "Truth and Appearance." But in this discussion he does not, in the principal attempt to formulate the question, get beyond his very first plan on "Truth and Lie in the Extramoral Sense."

In some remote corner of the universe ( poured out, glittering, in innumerable solar systems), there once was a star on which sagacious animals invented knowledge. That was the haughtiest and most mendacious minute of "world history": yet only a minute. After nature had drawn a few breaths, the star grew cold, and the sagacious animals had to die.—Someone might invent such a fable and still not have illustrated sufficiently how wretched, how shadowy and fleeting, how aimless and arbitrary the human intellect appears within nature. There have been eternities when it did not exist; when it is gone, nothing will have happened. For this intellect has no further mission that would lead beyond human life.[269]

The natural world is "in itself," man in the natural world is only "for himself," and thus truth on the whole seems to be thoroughly blocked from the view of man, who is thrown into the world. One does not understand "where, in all the world, at this constellation, the drive to truth comes from!" Man lives confined within his own "room of consciousness" and at the same time thrown into the natural world. But "nature threw away the key" with which the entrance to nature could become accessible, and "woe to the calamitous inquisitiveness that once manages to see through a crack out of and down from the room of consciousness," and then divines that man hangs, as though on the "back of a tiger," in "dreams." As a substitute for this truth that is blocked from him, man dresses up the world, lays down generally valid, conventional, and life-preserving truths. In truth these "truths" are illusions that are not known as such—they are thus the most extreme opposite to a true expression of Being in the allegorical emergence of the world in speech.

Nietzsche characterizes as follows the *aporia*[T90] that results for the problem of truth from this schism: the forbidden truth is veiled by means of a permitted lie, and the forbidden lie occurs where the permitted truth has its domain. Either the individual who wants to recognize the forbidden truth must sacrifice *himself*—or he must sacrifice *the world*. In a plan from the time of *Zarathustra*, it is said less pointedly:

Blindness is temporarily necessary for us, and we must leave certain articles of faith and errors untouched—as long as they *preserve* us in life. We must be *without conscience* with regard to truth and error as long as *life* is at stake— *with the very purpose* of then . . . spending life again in the service of truth. This is our ebb and flow, the energy of our contraction and expansion.[270]

Error—that is, the drive to veil the truth, which is inherent in the human will to truth—can actually be eliminated only together with the life of the one who apprehends, because the "final" unveiling of Being will not bear "incorporation." Thus it is said already in the Empedocles fragment of 1870–71[271] that Empedocles, having advanced through all the stages of knowledge, finally directs the last stage against himself; becomes insane; and, before disappearing in the crater, proclaims the truth of rebirth. Nietzsche, too, was unable to bear the incorporation of his doubt about truth, and he searched for a way out of epistemological nihilism that would eliminate the disproportion between the will to truth and the unavoidable lie. In the end he thought he had found the key that unlocks the nature of all things. What Zarathustra prophesies is the unanimous agreement of everything that is in *one* highest type of Being,[272] which determines the soul of Zarathustra just as much as it determines the Dionysian world of his soul. But why should man not be able to bear his consent to the "Yes of Being" if he really were embedded into the whole of the world and if he were of the same type as all naturally necessary Being? That Nietzsche did not bear up under his own "wisdom" in his "life";[273] and that at midnight, between the first and twelfth "strokes of the clock of Being," when life was dearer to him than all his wisdom, he considered abandoning life just for that reason—this speaks in favor of his first plan, according to which man is in contradiction to the universe because in the existence of the man who knows, natural life is split. Nietzsche's last plan, too, is likewise split. Merely qua "plan," Nietzsche's world is already abysmally distant from the ancient cosmos, which did not partake of that "monstrous dumbness" which teaches man "to *cease* to be man."[274]

A later plan for *The Will to Power* agrees with the *aporia* of truth and lie in the "extramoral," that is, cosmic sense. This plan characterizes nihilism (the self-overcoming of which is the eternal recurrence) by means of the following alternative:

The opposition of the world that we revere and the world that we live, that we are, is now dawning. What remains is to do away either with our revering or with ourselves. The latter is nihilism.[275]

In *Twilight of the Idols,* Nietzsche used the formula "End of the Longest Error" for the end of this dawning opposition between the world that we are and the world that we esteem. He coined this formula in the belief that the opposition between that "true" world and this "apparent" world[276] is, with Zarathustra's teaching, at an end.

*How the "True World" Finally Became a Fable*
The History of an Error

1. The true world: attainable for the wise man, the pious man, the virtuous man—he lives in it, *he is it.* (Oldest form of the idea . . . A circumlocution for the sentence, "I, Plato, *am* the truth.")[T91]

2. The true world: unattainable for now, but promised for the wise man, the pious man, the virtuous man ("for the sinner who repents"). (Progress of the idea: it becomes more subtle, insidious, incomprehensible . . . it becomes Christian . . . )

3. The true world: unattainable, indemonstrable, unpromisable; but the very idea of it a consolation, an obligation, an imperative. (At bottom, the old sun, but seen through mist and skepticism. The idea has become elusive, pale, Nordic, Königsbergian.)

4. The true world—unattainable? At any rate unattained. And qua unattained, also *unknown*. Consequently, not consoling, redeeming, or obligating: to what could something unknown obligate us? . . . (Gray morning. The first yawn of reason. The cockcrow of positivism.)

5. The "true" world—an idea that is no longer useful for anything, not even obligating—an idea that has become . . . superfluous—*consequently,* a refuted idea: let us abolish it! (Bright day; . . . return of *bon sens*[T92] and of cheerfulness; Plato's embarrassed blush; pandemonium of all free spirits.)

6. The true world we have abolished: what world has remained? the apparent one perhaps? . . . But no! *With the true world we have also abolished the apparent one!* (Noon; moment of the briefest shadow; end of the longest error; high point of humanity; INCIPIT ZARATHUSTRA.)

On the basis of this abolition of the true world *and* of the apparent world, it is now no longer necessary to abolish ourselves! But what follows from that for Nietzsche's own philosophic position in the history of the decay of the metaphysical backworld? Apparently this: Zarathustra's last wisdom stands (at the end of the world that has become a fable to that wisdom) *before the beginning of the world*, because he himself *is* world again if his parables are true, and the "noon for man" is at the same time a "noon for the earth."[277] The continuation that is only hinted at in the final section above would, if elaborated, have to read as follows: *I,* Nietzsche-Zarathustra, *am* the truth of the *world,* for I am the first over the whole history of the longest error to have rediscovered the world before Plato. I will nothing at all but this eternally recurring world, which is no longer alienated from me and is at the same time my ego and my fate. For I will even myself again eternally, as one ring within the great ring of the self-willing world.[278]

To speak of man as *one* "ring" within the great ring of the world, however, poetically unifies what already falls apart in Nietzsche's own attempt at speculative explication. In several sketches that lie far apart from one another, the unsolved problems in the relationship between man and world appear quite clearly. The "subjectivity" of the world, it is once said in Nietzsche's writings,[279] is not an anthropomorphic subjectivity but rather a "mundane" one. Man belongs to the essence of the physical world in his highest and lowest elements, but we have access to the physical world only through ourselves. This human access, however, does not humanize the world, but brings to light that our own comportment toward the world is always world-forming and creative because "*creation* belongs to the inalienable and constant characteristics of the world itself."[280] Put differently, "We are the figures in God's dream who guess how he dreams"—an image that means the same as the passage, "It is not *our* perspectives in which we see things; but we see things in the perspectives of a being of like sort but *greater* than ourselves: *we peer into his images.*"[281] Contradicting this mundane understanding of man (out of the essence of the world that needs no God because it is already creative itself ), Nietzsche at another time says the opposite: the philosopher does not seek the truth of the world but its "metamorphosis into man," the "world as man."[282] This reversal of the line of vision makes a humanized world out of the cosmic ego. The correlate to this humanized world is Zarathustra's stress on heaven, earth, and world as "*his*" heaven, "*his*" earth, and "*his*" world—as if the world belonged to the creative will of man and not man, including his capacity to will, to the world. The idea of the world "as man," thought out to its most extreme end, runs as follows in a note from the time of *Zarathustra*: "We want to penetrate nature with what is human and to redeem nature from the divine masquerade. We want to take what we need from nature in order to dream *beyond* man. Something that is *more magnificent* than storm and mountains and sea should now arise—but as the son of man!"[283] What could be more alienated from an original and natural relationship to the world of nature than this willing to outstrip the physical powers of the cosmos by means of an anti-Christian "son of man" who transfers his will to power and self-overcoming into the whole of the world in order to be able to stand firm against the world? Out of this alienation arises Zarathustra's longing "to say No like the storm and to say Yes as the open heaven says Yes"—a longing and evasion toward nature, as a letter of the twenty-two-year-old Nietzsche to Carl von Gersdorff (7 April 1866) already reveals. But the world of heaven says neither Yes nor No. It speaks to man only in the language of silence.

   Nietzsche's extreme attempt at a re-betrothal of the old, natural world was condemned to failure, because in the nineteenth century that attempt could not be undertaken in any other way than with the

means of the post-Copernican world and on the peak of modernity.
As the earth becomes eccentric in the whole of the world, there arises
a boundless tension in the human will to dominate the world and to
bring it home, for the world reacts by constantly expanding and growing more distant. And how should man still be able to remain "close,
true, and trusting" to the earth[284] and know himself in "eternal security" under the "azure cover" of the world of heaven, if every day brings
new discoveries that are no longer compatible with the *old* world that
was naturally ordered and only "surrounded" by the "nothing"? Since
man in fact became the "aerial navigator of the spirit"[285] and the "lord
of the earth," a dehumanization of man has occurred and a boundless
overstepping of the visible world toward a physical construction of the
world. This construction can be conceived mathematically, to be sure,
but it cannot be lived in. Nietzsche, too, asked himself, in his journey
of discovery into the untested, the anxious question, "Where is this
powerful appetite dragging us?" And he closed *The Dawn* with the
question whether it should not perhaps also be his lot "to be wrecked
on infinity," only to discover a "blessed isle," finally, in the province of
*Zarathustra*.[286] Only this *island* still represents that old, Mediterranean world for which the new Columbus was "not simple and silent
enough."[287]

The discord in the double presentation of the parable of the eternal
recurrence is crystallized in the symbol of the "*noon*." "Noon and eternity" signifies not only the cessation of time in which the world shows
itself as perfect, but also and above all the critical "center" in which
the man of a particular epoch should decide whether he will still will
himself in the future. Noon is the time in which the sun—also the
sun of knowledge—stands highest, and at the same time it is a "highest time" in the sense of a most extreme distress and danger. No dialectic of "correspondence," however flexible, can offset this contradiction
into which the parable of the noon decomposes as soon as one takes it
literally and thinks it through.

*Zarathustra*'s Prologue already presupposes the last "metamorphosis," which the first speech calls a "new beginning" and at the same time
a "self-propelled wheel." But how is a new beginning supposed to be
able to begin if the "first movement" stems from no decision, but instead is a circle without beginning and end in which everything has already been decided forever? The bearer of these conflicting modes of
motion is the "child," whose productive "creation" is a "game." After
Zarathustra's heart has at last changed, he is an "awakened man" be-

cause he has become a child. As a transformed, awakened man, he steps
before the sun at dawn and says, "You great star! What would your
happiness be if you did not have those for whom you shine!" This un-
childlike form of address to the sun is repeated at the beginning of the
last speech of the whole *Zarathustra,* where Zarathustra himself now
comes out of his cave "glowing and strong like a morning sun." His
will, too, is called an "inexorable sun's will," because the will (which is
turned by necessity[T93]) of the man who overcomes and climbs over
himself, wills its own setting for a new beginning in the morning, just
like the sun in the evening. Noon—which comes again and again, when
the sun stands highest, and which is the time of a highest omnipresence—is evoked in Zarathustra's last words as a "sign" of what is coming, as "*his* morning." Zarathustra, this childlike superman, takes the
superfluity from the great star and blesses the star for it. A few lines
later, however, he speaks from the reverse perspective to the sun regarding his own superfluity, which he wants to give away to men:[288]
"So bless me then!" Who blesses whom, here? And to whom does the
superfluity originally belong? Apparently to both: to the sun, the eternal prototype of the world of heaven; and to Zarathustra, who *as* the
teacher of the superman and of the "great" noon at noon, wills the eternal recurrence. To be sure, Zarathustra needs the blessing of the sun,
which is "the highest star of Being," in order to be able, himself, to
bless it. But this reciprocal relationship originates, nevertheless, in the
Zarathustra who grants blessings, who fancies himself to be like a sun.

Or is Zarathustra's desire to bestow, his will and abundance, only
the reflection of that so-called self-willing and self-giving-away of natural life, which appears at noon in the god of nature Pan? Or is the literal
correspondence of "noon of earth" to "noon of man,"[289] of the world
of heaven to the superman, of the noon sun to the sun's will, of the
light of heaven to Zarathustra's fire, only a fictitious parable and thus a
"poet's trick"? He who reads Zarathustra's parables attentively will not
be able to close his eyes to the impression that the claim of one's own
willing that, as a human willing, thinks about the future, consistently
takes precedence over the casual perception of the world. Nietzsche-
Zarathustra knows, to be sure, that he has lost the world, but he can
gain it back only by creating it as "his" world and re-creating all that is
in itself and for itself into an "in and for me."[290] Nietzsche-Zarathustra
only temporarily gets out of this circle of his own will in rare moments.
Instead of thinking with Goethe that no human eye could behold the
sun unless that eye itself be sunlike, for Zarathustra the sun is an eye

whose "happiness" would be null if it did not have Them for whom it shines.

The noon, where it first comes up for discussion, is only reminiscently the hour of the great Pan, and in its foremost meaning is the critical "*center*" of a life surrounded "by death."[291] The wanderer does see the great Pan sleeping in a hidden glade and does see all the things of nature with an expression of eternity on their faces, but—it only "seems" so to him. He does want nothing in this eternal moment, and his demanding, repose-craving heart does stand still, but not because he perceives the physical breath of a perfect world but because "death" touches him "with wakeful eyes." He feels happy, but it is a "heavy, difficult" happiness. His happiness is not the natural fruit of repose and of immersion into the totality of life, but the delusive result of the "craving for rest" by an existence that is never entirely capable of forgetting itself. Even at the hour of Pan's noon, the eye of this existence is still not closed as in sleep, but awake and open. The shadowy wanderer who is en route to a goal is not capable of actually abandoning himself unconditionally to the total life of nature—not even for a moment. The mood that originally characterizes the hour of Pan[292] and is determined by motionless silence, a scorching noon blaze, a deathlike sleep, and envelopment by divine and demonic powers, changes into a mood in which death with wakeful eyes and a webbed envelopment in a "net of light" are predominant. Nietzsche's characterization of the noon is therefore always ambiguous: the mood of Pan is constantly thwarted and set out of tune by the completely unheathen and unnatural idea that the hour of noon is a time of "decision." "As if by magic, something wholly new, wholly different has developed out of age-old words and images—as if someone had ignited a Bengalese fire on a bright day: Everything becomes pallid, everything appears as though on the brink of decline and death. Warmth and color disappear, the shadows of the end crawl over the earth, anxiety creeps into our heart[s]."[293]

The set of problems that were indicated in *The Wanderer and His Shadow* becomes quite clear in *Zarathustra*. The eschatological pathos of the language of the New Testament reverses[T94] the ancient reminiscences. The last section of the last speech of the first Part of *Zarathustra* gives the first detailed reference to the noon. The message of the New Testament is present in the form of a parody in Nietzsche's "fifth gospel," even in its details.[294] It is about the master's parting from his disciples. The promise of the return belongs to the departure. When

Zarathustra will be with his disciples for the third time, that will be the time to celebrate the "great" noon, an eschatological event. Whereas what happens again and again by nature becomes manifest in the hour of Pan, with the great noon of the Antichrist Zarathustra, something completely new and final commences. Noon is not the time in which gods and demons reveal themselves in the plant and animal life of the world, but instead the center of a path to be hiked through. Noon is the "center of a road" between beast and superman; the superman, in turn, first appears when all gods are already dead. What reveals itself at noon is not the world of Pan, the god of nature, but a "last will" and a "highest hope" for the self-redemption of man. Zarathustra must go down and bless himself in order to become a man who crosses over in transit to a last goal. This going down and crossing over, which is often referred to, clashes deeply with the experience of *the* noon, when the world is complete and time stands still. The proclamation of the noon (which, as high point of a crisis, is a critical center) takes place in the expectation of what is coming, which in turn is determined by the future of a task. At the coming, great noon it is to be decided whether man wants to descend to the last man or to ascend to the superman. A metamorphosis occurs unexpectedly in Nietzsche's presentation of the noon and of the eternal recurrence: out of what by nature comes *again and again,* develops something that is supposed to be decisive *once and forever.* Likewise, the "moment," too, is not eternal because what is forever shows itself in the moment, but because the moment (as a decisive moment) determines in advance what will be in the future.

The language of biblical eschatology also determines the end of the speeches "On Virtue That Makes Small" and "On Passing By." Zarathustra's noon resembles more the doomsday of the prophets and apostles than the noon at which isolated existence sinks back into the total life of nature. "Seen through the eyes of the ancients," remarks Karl Schlechta quite correctly, "the 'great noon' is a blasphemy beyond all bounds." The great noon of *Thus Spoke Zarathustra* is the hour of the superman, just as the eternal recurrence is his teaching. As a result of this linking of the experience of noon to the teaching of the superman and to his willing of the eternal recurrence, the elemental meaning of the noon disintegrates into a transition to a "new morning." And what was originally characterized by heathen piety receives an anti-Christian meaning that, absurdly, now also determines the old idea of the return as such. Zarathustra returns, with this sun and with this earth—"not" to a new or better life but to the selfsame life.[295] The critical center does not always repeat itself but only "every time" that the "will to the future" arises, says Nietzsche in a note on *Zarathustra* from the literary remains. What recurs is thus a decision that must always be willed anew and that concerns the future nature[T95] of man. Zarathustra is "wholly will to the noon," and his talk of the world of heaven, earth, and noon of earth cannot gloss over the fact that what is immediately at issue for him is not the natural world but the overcoming of contemporary humanity. Even as a gay messenger, he remains a critic who thinks first and finally of a crisis. The "world" of *Thus Spoke Zarathustra* is the shadow world of a redeemer figure whose "dancing" and "laughter" lack all power of persuasion. Only Zarathustra's "wandering" corresponds to Nietzsche's human reality.

In the penultimate aphorism of the second essay of *On the Genealogy of Morals,* the problematical meaning of the noon is expressed even more acutely. Here the "great noon" is simply one and the same with the "great decision" by the "man of the future," who is supposed to redeem us from the Christian ideal and its nihilistic results.[296] The redeeming man of the future, as Antichrist and antinihilist, is supposed to give back to the earth (as man's home) its "goal" and to man his "highest hope." The title "Noon and Eternity," originally meant for *Zarathustra,* is defined in the subtitle, "Plan of a New Way to Live." That is: nothing everlasting or eternal reveals itself at noon; rather, at noon a new way to live is resolved upon, a type of life that is strong enough to be able to will the eternal recurrence. Zarathustra thus teaches two things: as the redeeming man of the future, he proclaims a new way of existence; and as the teacher of the eternal recurrence of the same, he teaches ("beyond man and time") the highest law of the whole life of the world. But as a critical center, the noon is not the always recurring time of something everlasting, but rather the moment of decision at which previous history parts from the history of the future. The teaching of the eternal recurrence is supposed to be an interpretation of the physical world and at the same time the "turning point of history."

In the later self-interpretation of his *Untimely Meditation* on Richard Wagner, Nietzsche in *Ecce Homo* expressly interprets the idea of the noon world-*historically* and projects it into the future. As the rival and heir of Wagner, Nietzsche wants to have transformed the "idea of Bayreuth" into that of the "great noon," at which his disciples will someday gather for a feast. Likewise, looking back on *The Dawn,* he characterizes as his task: "to prepare a moment of the highest self-examination of humanity, a *great noon* when humanity looks back and looks out [to the future]." A noon that has to be prepared for as a world-historical task cannot, however, be the same as *the* noon at which the natural world presents itself in its always same perfection to him who precisely does not look back and out to the future but contemplates or looks upon the world. The "seer" and the "man who wills" are only seemingly one and the same in Zarathustra. The "world" that the author of *Ecce Homo* wants to break into two pieces—into a pre-Nietzschean and post-Nietzschean world[297]—is not the omnipresent physical world, within which world history is something infinitesimal, but the contemporary world of human history. The time of this latter world is measured not by the recurrence of the sun but by the single, nonrecurring event of God's revelation in Christ, whose place is now taken by *Ecce Homo,* with which Nietzsche's anti-Christian chronology begins.

Only once,[298] in the speech of Zarathustra expressly entitled "At Noon," in the center of the final Part of the book, does the convincing tone of a "strange drunkenness" stream into the equally pallid and over-lit landscape of *Zarathustra*; and the world becomes perceptible again, as from time immemorial: when man wills nothing any more, "his soul stretches out" and becomes silent, so that it hears the voice of muteness, in a "time without goal." Here the noon of Pan is not the critical center of a demanding decision by means of which the man of the future divorces himself in anti-Christian fashion from man so far, but rather a veritable noon event in which human existence engages.

But why does Zarathustra's "soul" speak even here against Zarathustra himself, that is, against his "ego," which still wills and interrupts the noon nap, only to "wake its fill"[T96] and go farther instead of standing still? And why is the noon also the *abyss* of noon and midnight?[299] Does this double characterization of the highest center suggest the co-presence of the critical time—in which the abyss of the nihilism of an existence that has become goalless wants to overcome itself—also at the hour of the perfect noon? To be sure, the worldly hour of Pan, too, is abysmal and threatened by uncanny powers. But what is abysmal in the mythical noon is not the bottomlessness which Nietzsche feels at his "noon of life," when it is time, highest time, namely for redemption from the distress and isolation in which he created for himself, as his only partner, the character Zarathustra.[300] The experience of the noon, at which Zarathustra together with the superman teaches the eternal return, does not lead Nietzsche to demand an eternal recurrence of the same, forlorn life; rather, it causes him to yearn for the solution by means of death. The noonday sun stabs Zarathustra in the center of his own life, in his heart, and he wishes that it would break—after such happiness. The poem of the magician betrays how dubious this "happiness" is; the magician's "last" happiness likewise consists in the breaking of his heart when an unknown executioner-god stabs into it. The relaxed cheerfulness at the hour of the noon hence proves itself to be the "most secret anticipatory delight" of death. Just as the rising of the sun indicates a descent with several meanings, so does the seemingly perfect noon (at the time of the highest position of the sun), too, complete itself only when "the sun is sinking." In the poem thus named, the "strange drunkenness" of the speech at noon finds its final explanation.

### 1.

Not for long will you thirst yet,
  Burnt heart!
Promise is in the air,
From unfamiliar mouths it blows on me,
  —The great coolness comes . . .
My sun stood hot over me at noon:
My greetings for coming,
  You sudden winds,
You cool spirits of the afternoon!

The air moves in a strange and pure way.
Does not the night, with a wry
  Seducer's glance,
Watch me from the corner of her eye? . . .
Stay strong, my stout heart!
Ask not: why?—

### 2.

Day of my life!
The sun is sinking.
The smooth flood already
  Is gilded.
Warm breathes the rock:
  Did happiness take its noonday sleep
On it at noon?
  In green lights
The brown abyss's play still evokes happiness.

Day of my life!
The eve is looming!

Your eye already glows
  Half-broken,
The teardrops
  of your dew already surge,
Your love's purple
  already runs quietly over white seas,
Your last lingering bliss . . .

### 3.

Cheerfulness golden, come!
  You, death's
Most secret, sweetest anticipatory delight!
—Did I run down my path too swiftly?
Only now, when my foot has become weary,
  Your glance overtakes me,
  Your happiness overtakes me.

All around are only wave and play.
  Whatever was heavy
Sank into blue oblivion,—
Now my boat lies idle.
Storm and voyage—how it has forgotten that!
  Wish and hope drowned,
  Smooth lie soul and sea.

*Seventh* loneliness!
  Never did I feel
Sweet certainty[T97] nearer to me,
Never warmer the sun's look.
—Does not the ice of my peak still glow?
  A light silver, a fish,
  My skiff now swims out . . . [T98]

Only now, around evening, when the day of his life came to an end, did Nietzsche experience as a "seventh loneliness" what appeared to Zarathustra—in harmony with the biblical creation story—as the "evening" of a seventh day. Inexplicably to Zarathustra himself, this evening came "exactly at noon," because at the time of the greatest brightness, the night, too, already enveloped him. The alarmed, oft-repeated question at noon, "But what is happening to me?" is answered with the sinking sun by the transition into resolving and redeeming insanity. Only insanity—and not a "final will" or "highest self-examination"—liberated Nietzsche from the delusion that he could and must decide the destiny of Europe, or even of "humanity."

# 4

# The Anti-Christian
# Repetition of Antiquity
# on the Peak of Modernity

*He who would be wise about old origins . . . will finally
search for sources of the future and for new origins.*

If Nietzsche's prophecy were a mere "poet's trick" and
its origin nothing but a private experience, it would neither be intrinsi-
cally systematic nor have a historical position in the whole of Western
philosophy. This position is characterized, equally briefly and all too
clearly, by the concluding formulation of *Ecce Homo*: "Have I been
understood? *Dionysus versus the Crucified.*" Nietzsche is not against the
Crucified because he wants to be rid of suffering, however, but because
he wants it in another, Dionysian way.[1] Only as a disciple of Dionysus-
Zagreus is he an opponent of the Crucified, who wants an overcoming
of suffering and of death in an opposite way. The revaluation of all values, too, must be understood in this sense. Zarathustra's teaching of
the eternal recurrence, which also concludes the plans for *The Will to
Power,* already *is* the revaluation of all previous, Christian values, because it draws the most extreme consequences from the death of the
Christian God. In consideration of the foregoing, Nietzsche in *Ecce
Homo* knows himself to be a European destiny.

I know my fate. One day my name will be associated with the memory of . . . a
crisis without equal on earth, the most profound collision of conscience, a decision that was conjured up *against* everything that had been believed, demanded, hallowed so far. I am no man, I am dynamite.—Yet for all that, there

is nothing in me of a founder of a religion. . . . I do not *want* any "believers"; I think I am too malicious to believe in myself, I never speak to masses. . . . I have an alarming fear that one day I will be pronounced *holy*. . . . I do not want to be a holy man, sooner even a buffoon. . . . Yet in spite of that—or rather, *not* in spite of it, because so far nothing has been more mendacious than holy men—the truth speaks out of me.—But my truth is *terrible*; for so far one has called the *lie* the truth. *Revaluation of all values*: that is my formula for an act of supreme self-awareness on the part of humanity, an act that has become flesh and genius in me. It is my fate that I have to be the first *decent* human being, that I know myself [to stand] in opposition to the mendacity of millennia. . . . I was the first to *discover* the truth by being the first to experience the lie as a lie. . . . I contradict as has never been contradicted before and am nevertheless the opposite of a No-saying spirit . . . only beginning with me are there hopes again. In all that, I am necessarily also the man of calamitous fate. For when truth enters into a fight with the lie of millennia, we shall have upheavals, a convulsion of earthquakes . . . the like of which has never been dreamed of. The concept of politics will have merged entirely with a war of spirits; all power structures of the old society will have been exploded—all of them are based on the lie; there will be wars the like of which have never yet been seen on earth. It is only beginning with me that there are *great politics* on earth.[2]

Which truth it is that speaks through Nietzsche is not specified here. The name that comes closest to it is the remaining *nothing,* the nullity of the highest values of our whole morality so far. Without God, the Christian morality no longer has any sanction. At first, however, the "discovery" that Christian morality is "antinature" is no positive discovery of a new land of the soul, but instead "a real catastrophe" in which all previous judgments of value perish.

He who enlightens about it is a *force majeure*,[T99] a destiny—he breaks the history of mankind in two. One lives *before* him, or one lives *after* him. . . . The lightning bolt of truth struck precisely what stood tallest so far: let whoever comprehends *what* has been destroyed here see whether anything at all is left in his hands. Everything that has hitherto been called "truth" has been recognized as the most . . . subterranean form of lie. . . . Whoever uncovers morality also uncovers the unworthiness of all values that are or have been believed; he no longer sees anything venerable in the most venerated types of man, even in those pronounced *holy*; he sees in them the most calamitous type of abortion—calamitous *because they exerted such fascination*. . . . The concept "God" invented as a counterconcept to life,—the whole deadly hostility to life synthesized into a gruesome unity . . . in this concept![3]

But if Nietzsche's decision against everything previously believed in is an explosive that breaks in two the history of European humanity so far, he harks back (in anticipation of the history that comes after him) behind the history that preceded him, "with a voice that bridges millennia."[4] Accordingly, in *Twilight of the Idols* he explicitly attributes his teaching to what he "owes to the ancients." Therewith he repeats the "tragic mentality" of antiquity; the restoration and "transposition" of that mentality into a philosophic pathos[5] was already the theme of *The Birth of Tragedy* and of *Philosophy in the Tragic Age of the Greeks*. By means of this return to the old world, Nietzsche thought that he had found the exit "from whole millennia of labyrinth." He found this exit in contrast with modern man, who "is everything that does not know which way to turn," who knows, that is, neither any way out of Christianity, which has become empty, nor into the new world of a most ancient Being. The "new possibilities of life," which are indicated for the first time in the studies on pre-Socratic philosophy, seem finally to have proved really possible with the teaching of the eternal recurrence as a plan of a new way to live. On that basis Nietzsche, in the aftermath, sees himself as a precursor.

Let us look ahead a century; let us suppose that my attempt to assassinate two millennia of antinature . . . will succeed. That new party of life . . . will again make possible that *excess of life* on earth from which the Dionysian state, too, will have to awaken again. I promise a *tragic* age: the highest art in saying Yes to life, tragedy, will be reborn when humanity has weathered the consciousness of the hardest but most necessary wars *without suffering from it*.[6]

The restoration of antiquity, however, occurs at the peak of modernity. Modernity linked Nietzsche to Wagner and also separated him from Wagner.

And is not this precisely what we are coming back to, we daredevils of the spirit who have climbed the highest and most dangerous peak of present thought and looked around from up there—we who have *looked down* from up there? Are we not, precisely in this respect, Greeks?[7]

In order to render understandable the historical meaning of this movement, which stretches beyond Christianity in going back behind the Christian origins, Nietzsche in *Ecce Homo* referred to a passage of the *Untimely Meditation* on Wagner, which more than all other passages elucidates in advance the world-*historical* meaning of his future teaching.

The history of the development of culture since the Greeks is short enough if one takes into consideration the real path actually covered. . . . The Hellenization of the world and, in order to make that possible, the Orientalization of the Hellenic—the double task of the great Alexander—is still the last great event; the old question of whether a foreign culture can be transferred at all is still the problem with which the more recent cultures struggle. It is the rhythmic play of those two factors against each other that in particular has determined the course of history thus far. Christianity, for example, appears therein as a piece of Oriental antiquity, which was brought to the end by man in thought and deed, with extravagant thoroughness. . . . The earth, which so far has been well enough Orientalized, longs for Hellenization again. . . . Thus a series of *anti-Alexanders* has now become necessary, men who have the mightiest power to pull together and bind, to reach for the most distant threads and to guard the fabric from blowing apart. Not to undo the Gordian knot of Greek culture as Alexander did, so that its ends flew to all parts of the world, but *to tie it after it has been undone*—that is now the task. I recognize in Wagner such an anti-Alexander; he spellbinds and unites what was isolated, weak, and loose; he has, if a medical term is permitted, an *astringent* power; to this extent he belongs to the quite great cultural forces. He rules over the arts, the religions, the various national histories, and is nevertheless the opposite . . . of a spirit that merely compiles and orders; for he molds together and animates what has been assembled, he is a *simplifier of the world*.[8]

Such a simplified world is the ring—not only of the Nibelung, but also of the eternal recurrence.[9] The "fragment" "man" completes himself in the whole of this world-historical ring by means of a will that wills to get out to what else can be by willing back to what already was. In this will Nietzsche found himself to be at one with the basic intention of German philosophy.

German philosophy as a whole . . . is the most fundamental form of *romanticism* and homesickness there has been hitherto: the longing for the best that ever was. One is no longer at home anywhere; at last one longs to return to that place in which one can somehow be at home, because it is the only place in which one would want to be at home: and that is the *Greek* world! But it is in precisely that direction that all bridges are demolished—*except* the rainbow bridges of concepts! And these lead everywhere, into all the homes and "fatherlands" there were for Greek souls! To be sure, one must be very subtle, very light, very thin to step across these bridges! But what happiness lies already in this will to spirituality, to ghostliness almost! How far it takes one from "pressure and stress," from the mechanistic awkwardness of the natural sciences, from the market hubbub of "modern ideas"! One wants to go *back,* through the church fathers to the Greeks, from the north to the south, from the formulas to the Forms; one still relishes the exit from antiquity, Christianity, as an entrance to it, as a goodly piece of the old world itself, as a glittering mosaic of ancient concepts and ancient value judgments. Arabesques, flourishes, rococo of scholastic abstractions—still better, that is to say subtler and thinner, than the peasant and mob reality of the European north, still a protest of higher spirituality against the peasants' war and mob rebellion that has become master of spiritual taste in northern Europe and has found its leader in the great "unspiritual man," Luther: in this respect, German philosophy is a piece of counter-Reformation, even of Renaissance, at least of will to Renaissance, will *to go on* with the discovery of antiquity, in the digging up of ancient philosophy, above all of the pre-Socratics, the most deeply buried of all Greek temples! A few centuries hence, perhaps, one will judge that all German philosophizing derives its real dignity from being a gradual reclamation of the soil of antiquity, and that all claims to "originality" must sound petty and ludicrous in relation to that higher claim of the Germans to have joined anew the bond that seemed to be broken, the bond with the Greeks, the hitherto highest type of man. Today we are getting close again to all those fundamental forms of world interpretation invented by the Greek spirit . . . —we are growing *more Greek* day by day; at first, as is only fair, in concepts and evaluations, as it were as Hellenizing ghosts; but one day, let us hope, also with our *bodies*! Herein lies (and has always lain) my hope for the German character![10]

But Nietzsche's metaphysics, too, is a Hellenizing ghost, because it has no carnal foundation in him. The failure of Nietzsche's attempt to retrieve antiquity, therefore, appears most clearly where he himself points to the backgrounds of the Dionysian mysteries (which were by no means "hypothetical"), that is, to their foundation in the sexual will to procreation, by means of which life recurs incarnate.[T100]

What was it that the Hellene guaranteed himself by means of these mysteries? *Eternal* life, the eternal recurrence of life; the future promised and hallowed in the past; the triumphant Yes to life beyond death and change; *true* life as the overall continuation of life through procreation, through the mysteries of sexuality. For the Greeks the sexual symbol was therefore the venerable symbol par excellence, the real profundity in the whole of ancient piety. Every single element in the act of procreation, of pregnancy, and of birth aroused the highest and most solemn feelings. In the doctrine of the mysteries, *pain* is pronounced holy: the "pangs of the woman giving birth" hallow all pain; all becoming and growing—all that guarantees a future—*implies* pain. . . . In order that there may be the eternal joy of creating, that the will to life may eternally affirm itself, the "agony of the woman giving birth" *must* also be there eternally. . . . All this is meant by the word "Dionysus." I know no higher symbolism than this *Greek* symbolism of the Dionysian festivals. Here the most profound instinct of life, that directed toward the future of life, toward the eternity of life, is experienced religiously—and the path itself to life, procreation, is experienced as the holy path. . . . It was Christianity, with its resentment *against* life at the bottom of its heart, that first made something unclean of sexuality: it threw *filth* on the beginning, on the presupposition of our life.[11]

The physical foundation for an eternal recurrence of "this" life is lacking in Nietzsche's philosophy as in his own, noncarnal existence, which was anything *but* a "deified form and self-justification of nature."[12]

But what can be done to reembody Greek "world-affirmation and transfiguration of existence" if even the relationship of Goethe and Winckelmann to the secret of the Greeks had "something unpermitted, almost immodest" about it? Nietzsche's answer is:

> To wait and to prepare oneself; to await the emergence of new sources; to prepare oneself in solitude for strange faces and voices; to wash one's soul ever cleaner from the marketplace dust and marketplace noise of this age; to *overcome* everything Christian . . . and not merely to put it aside—for the Christian doctrine was the counterdoctrine to the Dionysian—; to rediscover the *South* in oneself and to spread out above oneself a bright, glittering mysterious Southern sky; to reconquer Southern health and hidden powerfulness of soul; step by step to become more comprehensive, more supranational, more European, more super-European, more Oriental, finally more *Greek*—for what is Greek was the first great union and synthesis of everything Oriental and on just that account the *inception* of the European soul, the discovery of *our "new world"*—who knows what the man who lives under such imperatives can encounter one day? Perhaps—a *new day!*[13]

The last aphorism of *The Dawn* already deals in a cryptic way with this "new world," too (the desideratum of Nietzsche's teaching), which, as shown, is no completely *new* world but the restoration of the ancient world. The dawn referred to in the title of the work by that name occurs before the sunrise of *Zarathustra*.

> And where do we want to go? Do we want to go *across* the sea? Where is this powerful craving taking us, this craving that counts more for us than any desire? Why exactly in this direction, toward where so far all suns of humanity have *set*? Will they say of us someday that we, too, *headed west in the hope of reaching an India*—but that it was our fate to founder on infinity? . . . Or?—[14]

But why is it an *India* that Nietzsche tries to reach, uncertain though he may be whether he must not founder on the impossibility of this attempt? Does it not contradict the reference to the land of the "nihilistic religion" of Buddhism that Nietzsche in *Ecce Homo* characterizes *The Dawn* as his first *Yes-saying* book, in which no negative word occurs and which eternalizes divine moments? And why does he refer here, too, to the "Indian" epigraph of the book: "There are so many dawns that have not yet glowed"? And why does he ask once more the question, "Where does its author *seek* that new morning . . . with which a day— . . . a whole world of new days!—begins?"

The answer is established by holding together what lies separated in scattered aphorisms as a long train of thought. Another aphorism of *The Dawn* gives a first clue. It has the heading "*In hoc signo vinces,*"[T101] whereby—in a reversal of the Christian meaning—Nietzsche means to say that those coming will conquer under the sign that the redemptive God is dead. In consideration thereof, Buddha is understood as the teacher of a religion of "*self*-redemption." But

how distant Europe still is from this level of culture! When all customs and conventions on which the power of the gods, priests, and redeemers rests are at last destroyed; when, thus, morality in the old sense will have died, then comes—indeed, what comes then?[15]

What comes then is, first, the pure nothing in the obligation to exist. Buddhism and Christianity belong together as the two great "nihilistic movements" in times of the sickening of the will,[16] but

One cannot condemn Christianity enough for having devaluated the *value* of such a *purifying* great nihilistic movement, which was perhaps already in progress, through the idea of the immortal private person; likewise through the hope of resurrection; in short, through continual deterrence from the *deed of nihilism*, suicide.[17]

It is the intention of Nietzsche's teaching to set free this purifying movement in Europe. The nihilism that emerged out of the decay of Christianity is thought to the end in Nietzsche's teaching in a way comparable to Indian nihilism. For Christianity

has only now attained to approximately the state of culture in which it can fulfill its original vocation—a *level* to which it *belongs*—in which it can show itself *pure*.[18]

European pessimism of the nineteenth century is just the beginning of pessimism:

it still lacks that tremendous, yearning rigidity of expression (once found in India) in which the nothing is reflected; it is still far too "contrived" and too little "developed"—too much a pessimism of scholars and poets.[19]

The teaching of the eternal return, as the *most extreme* form of nihilism, is "*the European form of Buddhism*"[20] because in that teaching the *energy* of knowing and willing denies the "purpose" of existence.

Nihilism as a symptom that the underprivileged have no solace left; that they destroy in order to be destroyed; that with morality removed they no longer have any reason to "resign themselves"—that they put themselves on the plane of the opposite principle and, for their part, too, *want power* by *compelling* the powerful to be their hangman. This is the European form of Buddhism—*doing No* after all existence has lost its "meaning."[21]

This No-doing, however, is also the precondition of a new Yes-saying to the whole of what is, and in order to be able to do that, man must become more "Greek" again, "for what is Greek was the first great union . . . of everything Oriental and on just that account the *inception* of the European soul, the discovery of *our 'new world.'* "[22] Nietzsche can therefore say that previously the continuation of the revived discovery of the *old* world is "the work of the *new* Columbus."[23]

Thus the riddle is solved of why Nietzsche heads "west," where the sun sets, in order (in following that path) to reach an India in the East—an "India" where the sun emerges anew as eternal Being out of the nothing of "European Buddhism."[24]

Nietzsche's hope for this coming day, which is at the same time a beginning that has already existed, shines even into a last letter to Jacob Burckhardt after insanity overtook Nietzsche. In that letter he once again gives thanks "in every moment" for the *ancient* world—for which, however, men have not been "simple and quiet enough": but he knew well that everything had changed thoroughly.

The illumination and the colors of all things have changed! We no longer entirely understand how the ancients experienced what was most familiar and frequent—for example, the day and waking: since the ancients believed in dreams, waking appeared in a different light. The same goes for the whole of life, which was illumined by death and its significance; our "death" is a completely different death. All experiences radiated differently because a god shone through them; all decisions and perspectives on the remote future, too; for they had oracles and secret portents and believed in prophecy. "Truth" was experienced differently, for in former times the insane person could qualify as its mouthpiece—which makes *us* shudder or laugh. . . . We have given things a new color; we go on painting them continually. But what do all our efforts to date avail when we hold them against the *colored splendor* of that old master!— I mean ancient humanity.[25]

Nietzsche both ended and began his intellectual life with the recollection of the ancient world. The philological papers, especially on the philosophy of Heraclitus, as well as the philosophical revision of these for the planned work on pre-Socratic philosophy, already contain all the principal features of his teaching that emerged ten years later.[26] Nietzsche's critique of Socrates, too, must be understood in terms of this recourse to *pre*-Socratic philosophy; for it concerns not only the Socratic knowledge of virtue but moreover the alienation (that has become world-historical in Socrates) of the natural cosmos from human existence, and of physics from metaphysics.

Nietzsche characterizes Heraclitus[27] and his teaching as follows: Every feature of his life shows "the highest form of pride." Nietzsche poses this pride as the companion of sagacity in the symbol of the eagle. In faith in the truth grasped only by himself, Nietzsche-Heraclitus, through "excessive development" and "by means of a non-arbitrary identification of himself and the truth," brings *his* pride to the point of an elevated pathos. This superhuman self-veneration in Heraclitus has, however, "nothing religious" about it—"for all that," says Nietzsche of himself in *Ecce Homo,* "there is nothing in me of a founder of a religion."

Only in the wildest mountain wasteland, however, can one have a numbing presentiment of the feeling of loneliness that penetrated the Ephesian hermit of the temple of Artemis. No overpowering feeling of pitying agitations, no desire to help, heal, and save, streams out of him. He is a star without an atmosphere. His eye, which blazes when directed inward, is benumbed and icy, as though for show, when it looks outward. All around him, directly adjacent to the citadel of his pride, the waves of insanity and folly crash; he turns away from them with nausea. But men, too, . . . shun such a man as a larva poured out of metal; in a remote sanctuary, under images of gods, next to . . . peaceful, lofty architecture, his character may seem more comprehensible. Among men Heraclitus was, as man, unbelievable; and if he was well seen as he paid attention to the play of noisy children, at all events he thereby pondered what no man had ever pondered on such an occasion: the playing of the great child of the world, Zeus. He did not need men, not even for his findings; nothing that one might ask them about, and nothing that the other wise men had taken pains to ask them about, mattered to him. He spoke with little esteem of such questioning, gathering, in brief "historical" men. "I searched myself and researched myself," he said of himself, with a remark that designates the research of an oracle[28]—

just as Nietzsche himself solves his "riddle." Both seek not "fame" but "eternity," in the belief that their wisdom has an unbounded "effect" and *must* reach to the thousand years of the future, because they themselves are a fate and their wisdom is a knowledge about the highest necessity.

What he viewed, *the doctrine of law in becoming and of play in necessity,* must from now on be viewed eternally: he has raised the curtain of this greatest theatrical play.

As a wise man, Heraclitus has the penetrating glimpse of the *one logos* in everything that is, while the poets are not prophets but deceivers. Like Nietzsche, Heraclitus views the Being of all that is not as a "punishment of what has become" but rather as a "justification of be-coming," a justification that comprehends passing away and destruc-tion. In this eternal process of constant making and becoming, $Dike^{T102}$ rules as the law of necessity. Heraclitus's teaching, like that of Nietz-sche, is "terrible" and "elevating" at the same time. But one needs to have a special power to transform the terrifying effect into one that delights.

In order to regain an impression of Heraclitus's teaching, Nietz-sche recalls "*how natural science now considers these problems,*"[29] and in *Ecce Homo* he still says of the deepest insight of *Zarathustra*—which "in the end" Heraclitus could already have taught[30]—that it is also most rigorously confirmed by "science." A natural-scientific explanation should make Heraclitus's intuition probable as a scientific hypothesis by imagining a changed tempo of sensual perception, by means of which the seemingly constant world disintegrates into a visible "storm of be-coming." Heraclitus, too, has thus seen the becoming of the one *logos* (which essentially appears through a multiplicity of appearances) in ev-erything that is. He no longer separated a "physical" and a "metaphysi-cal" world, a "true" and "apparent" world, as Anaximander had done. Like Nietzsche, he knew only this one world, "screened all around by eternal laws"—under the "shield of necessity." The highest justice re-veals itself in the quarrel between the powers of the world that stream upward and those that stream downward, and the eternal ring of Be-ing reveals itself in the grappling contest of the one and the other.[31] The world is a mixing vessel that must constantly be stirred in order not to putrefy. "Good and evil join in the selfsame, like the harmony of the bow and the lyre." The world-forming play of Zeus (or of the fire with itself) is like the play of a child of the world that again and again constructs and destroys; for it occurs "without any moral attri-bution" in eternally same innocence, comparable to the creation of the artist who *must* create and at the same time surveys his work. The highest necessity rules in this play of heavenly accident, but no teleol-ogy of any kind rules, and thus no causality of any kind either. Nietz-sche's critique of every teleological interpretation (it dates back to his years as a university student [1868])—that is, of the seeming compul-sion to consider the movement of the world and of all that is as if that movement had a purpose laid down by an extra-worldly principle or even laid down by that movement itself—comports with his critique of causality as efficient causation. "The belief in *causae* falls with the belief in τέλη,$^{T103}$ because the seeming compulsion to think causally lies in the seeming inconceivability of purposeless happenings." The eternal recurrence in the cycle of the world, however, knows neither a *causa efficiens* nor a *causa finalis*;[T104] it is simply "fatality." A "tendency" of the whole is ruled out, as is done in Nietzsche's teaching. The child of the world does not act in accordance with any purpose; his willing is not willing "in the popular sense," i.e., a willing directed at purposes, but rather a willing according to an inborn *Dike*.

The eon plans this game with itself, and from time to time the game begins anew.

Not wanton daring, but the drive to play, which always is aroused anew, calls other worlds into life. Once the child throws the toy away; but soon it starts to play again, in an innocent mood. But as soon as the child builds, it ties, assembles, and forms regularly and according to internal rules.[32]

Heraclitus's philosophy knows no "ethical imperative," no "Thou shalt," but also no mere "I will"; for the individual man is himself fate down to his last fiber and altogether "unfree" if one measures freedom by outer compulsion. He occupies no privileged, special place in the whole of the natural world. What differentiates between men is only whether they exist knowingly and willingly or ignorantly and unwillingly in accordance with the *logos* of all that is. The wise man, however, is at one with *logos*, as Nietzsche's Dionysian philosophy is at one with *Dionysus philosophus* himself.

An obligation to know the *logos* because he is man, does not exist. But why is there water, why is there earth? This is for Heraclitus a much more serious problem than to ask why men are so stupid and bad. In the highest man and in the most wrongheaded man, the same immanent regularity and justice reveals itself. But if one wanted to advance the question of Heraclitus, "Why is fire not always fire? Why is it now water, now earth?" he would just answer simply, "It is a game; don't take it so seriously, and above all not morally!" Heraclitus describes only the existing world and takes in that world the contemplative pleasure of the artist looking at his developing work. Only those who have cause not to be satisfied with his natural description of man find him somber, melancholy, . . . morose, pessimistic.[33]

At bottom Heraclitus is what Nietzsche himself wanted to be when he attempted to translate man back into the "language of nature," man's "eternal basic text." He is, that is, "the *opposite* of the pessimist."[34] But on the other hand, he is also no optimist, for he does not deny suffering and unreason; he does not believe in the best of all worlds. What he beholds is the whole of Being, beyond good and evil because beyond man and time altogether.

| | |
|---|---|
| World wheel, while rolling on | World game, the ruling force, |
| skims aim after aim: | blends false and true:[T105] |
| Fate says the sullen one | the eternally fooling force |
| The fool calls it a game. | blend *us* in too.[35] |

But whereas for Heraclitus man is blended into the cosmic law of becoming Being, because as a pre-Socratic man Heraclitus still understood his own existence primally from the standpoint of the Being of the world, Nietzsche finds the new access to the Heraclitean world from the standpoint of an existence that has become pathless and goalless. He repeats antiquity on the peak of anti-Christian modernity.

It was Nietzsche's aversion to Christianity that caused him to want a world that was the foundation of heathen thought both in Greece and in the East. At the end of an exhausted Christianity, he sought "new sources of the future," and found them in the recollection of that ancient world as it was before Christianity. The death of the Christian *God* awakened in Nietzsche a new understanding of the *world*. It is of secondary significance that this world was familiar to him through his studies as a classical philologist. Many experts in antiquity, before him and after him, were well acquainted with the teaching of the eternal cycle as it has been handed down in Heraclitus and Empedocles, Plato and Aristotle, Eudemus and the Stoics; but only Nietzsche recognized in this teaching future possibilities for his own thought, whereas all Christian thought seemed to him reduced to morality. By repeating the idea of the eternal recurrence, he confirmed his own insight that the history of thought again and again fills a basic scheme of possible ways of thinking and returns under the sway of necessity into an age-old "total household of the soul."

Nietzsche did not know that his own *contra Christianos* was an exact repetition of the *contra gentiles* of the church fathers, with reversed valences. Not only the teaching of the eternal recurrence that was polemically debated by Justin, Origen, and Augustine turns up again from the opposite standpoint, but also all the main arguments of the Christian apologists against the heathen philosophers. If one compares Nietzsche's arguments with those of Celsus and Porphyry, it is not difficult to notice how little has been added to the ancient arguments against Christianity, with the exception of the Christian pathos that caused Nietzsche to speak as an "Antichrist" and no longer as a philosopher. For Celsus as for Nietzsche, the Christian faith is crude and absurd. It destroys the reasonableness of the cosmos by an arbitrary usurpation. The Christian religion is for both a revolt of the uneducated people, who have no understanding of aristocratic virtues, citizen duties, and ancestral traditions. Their God is shamelessly curious and all too human, "a God of all dark corners" and a staff for the tired. If the only question of actual significance is the welfare of the soul of every individual, Nietzsche, like Celsus, asks, Why then should there be responsibility for public matters and thankfulness for good birth? These "holy anarchists" called Christians deemed it piety to weaken the *imperium romanum* for so long that the Germans and other barbarians were in a position to subdue it. Nietzsche's *Antichrist* is a repetition of the old charge that the Christians are *hostes humani generis,* a vulgar people of bad upbringing and bad taste. This historical agreement between the ancient and the modern attacks on Christianity demonstrates the lasting significance of the former and the historical significance of the latter, although the ancient attacks had long been forgotten before Nietzsche revived them again.

Because of the changed historical situation, however, the age-old idea of the eternal recurrence does not arise again unchanged, but instead is calamitously modernized. Nietzsche sang his new hymn to the "innocence" of existence with a broken voice—on the basis of a Christian "experience." *Thus Spoke Zarathustra* is a reverse Sermon on the Mount, and less Greek and heathen than the humanism of Goethe and Winckelmann. Nietzsche, too deeply branded by a Christian conscience, was not capable of canceling the "revaluation of all values" that Christianity had brought about against heathendom, and of regaining the lost world in his own existence on the peak of modernity. "As a plant" he was near to the "churchyard," and "as a man" he was born in a Protestant pastorage; and his last self-depiction is still a Christian/anti-Christian *Ecce Homo.*[T106] He was through and through so Christian and anti-Christian, so Protestant and protesting, so demanding and hoping, that only *one* question drove him on: his yearning for the *future* and his *will* to create it, in order to undo the alienation of the world. Zarathustra is the "redeeming man of the future," and Nietzsche's whole philosophy is a "prelude" to the future. No Greek philosopher thought so exclusively in the horizon of the future, and none took himself to be a historical destiny. All Greek myths, genealogies, and histories represent the past as an everlasting foundation. The will to power is equally *un*-Greek: the will to power (as a will to something) wills the future, and is opposed to the eternal cycle of coming into being and passing away apart from will and purpose. For the Greeks the visible circular motion of the heavenly spheres revealed a cosmic logos and a divine perfection. For Nietzsche the eternal recurrence is the "most terrible" idea and the "greatest gravity," because it contradicts his will to a future redemption. Nietzsche wanted to "overcome" the temporality of time in favor of the eternity of the eternal recurrence; the Greeks started with the things that always are and conceived of transitory time as an inferior copy of eternity. For the Greek understanding of man, being a man means in effect being a "mortal," whereas Nietzsche wanted to "eternalize" the fleeting existence of finite man. For the Greeks the eternal recurrence of emergence and decline explained the constant change in nature and history; for Nietzsche the recognition of an eternal recurrence demands an extreme and ecstatic point of view. The Greeks felt fear and reverence before inexorable fate; Nietzsche made the superhuman effort to will and to love fate, in order to re-create the highest necessity into a "turn of necessity." All these superlatives of "highest" and "last" willing and willing back, creating, and re-creating, are just as antinatural as they are un-Greek. They derive from the Judeo-Christian tradition, from the belief that world and man are created by God's almighty will, that God and his human likeness are essentially will. Nothing else is so striking in Nietzsche's thought as the emphasis on our creative essence, creative through the act of will, as with the God of the Old Testament. For the Greeks, the creative element in man was an "imitation of nature" and its natural productive power. Nietzsche lived and thought to the end the metamorphosis of the biblical "Thou shalt" into the modern "I will," but he did not accomplish the decisive step from the "I will" to the "I am" of the cosmic child of the world, which is innocence and forgetting. As a modern man, he was so hopelessly separated from an original "loyalty to the earth" and from the feeling of an eternal security under the vault of heaven, that his effort to "translate" man "back" into nature was condemned to failure from the outset. His teaching breaks apart into two pieces because the will to eternalize the existence of the modern ego (an existence it is thrown into) does not harmonize with the beholding of an eternal cycle of the natural world. All the more astounding is the internal consistency with which Nietzsche became what he was from the beginning, and developed "his" idea in the course of two decades into its ultimate logical conclusions.

# 5

## "How One Becomes What One Is" in the Idea of the Eternal Recurrence

The subtitle of Nietzsche's last self-portrayal, "How One Becomes What One Is," polemically refers—in harmony with the main title, *Ecce Homo*—to the Christian requirement to become new and different by means of a reversal and rebirth. When Nietzsche-Zarathustra becomes the teacher of the eternal recurrence, he, too, is "reborn" because of a reversal, to be sure. But he is reborn not to a new and different life in Christ, but to the always same life of the world, which as an eternal cycle comes back to itself in its becoming. Nietzsche in *Ecce Homo* wants to show how he, too, in the course of his life, only became what he was from the beginning, and to describe how all seeming accidents of this particular life occurred necessarily or were destiny. But if Nietzsche's philosophic destiny is the teaching of the eternal recurrence, it must prove to be the case in the development of this teaching, too, that the *final* problem of his teaching was present from the *beginning* and belongs to those problems about which a thinker does not change his view but rather only learns all there is to learn. Two school essays by the eighteen-year-old Nietzsche on "Fate and History" and on "Freedom of the Will and Fate,"[1] as well as an autobiographical sketch by Nietzsche at nineteen, furnish the evidence that this final problem was indeed present at the outset. What Nietzsche's teaching already declares by intimation in 1872 in the portrayal of Heraclitus and definitively ten years later in *Zarathustra,* is laid out in a preliminary fashion in these related discourses of 1862.[2]

Both essays contain the word "fate," once referring to history, in the other instance to the freedom of willing, because there is history only where men act and want something. In contrast with the freedom of arbitrariness, fate indicates a naturally necessary being-thus-and-not-different that constrains the will. As a will-constraining necessity, fate refers to the history of human willing, but in and of itself it is out of man's reach. Fate belongs in the realm of nature, which is as it is and cannot be different. The problem contained in the connecting "and" in each of the two titles thus concerns the questionable relationship of the history of human willing to the naturally necessary fatality in the whole of the physical world within which there is man, world, history. What preeminently mattered to Nietzsche (who was born "as a man" in a parsonage) about history, was—from his first self-depiction on up to *The Antichrist* and *Ecce Homo*—the history of Christianity and of the type of willing, and of anti-willing aversion, that underlies Christian morality.

The first of the two discourses begins in cognizance of the risk involved in the attempt to find a "freer standpoint" to judge the Christian interpretation of existence and its moral consequences. "Such an attempt is not the work of several weeks, but of a lifetime. For how could one have the power to annihilate the authority of two millennia, the guarantee of the most intelligent men of all ages, by the results of the ruminations of a youth, how could one override, with fantasies and immature ideas, all those lamentations and blessings of a religious development that have had such far-reaching consequences in world history?"—unless it be with Zarathustra's view across millennia. "To dare to go into the sea of doubt without compass and guide"—as a "wanderer" without a goal—"is folly and ruin for undeveloped intellects; most will be tossed about by storms; only very few will," like Nietzsche-Columbus, "discover new lands." "From the middle of the vast Indian Ocean of ideas, one often longs to return to terra firma: how often during fruitless speculations did the longing for history and natural science overcome me!"[3] The first, decisive step toward the liberation of the spirit, which Nietzsche completed fifteen years later with *Human, All-Too-Human,* and the consequential revaluation of all values, initially still takes the form of irresolute doubt. "I have attempted to deny everything," but even demolition is difficult, and construction is still harder. For "the power of habit, the need for the higher, the break with everything that exists, the dissolution of all forms of society, the uncertainty whether two thousand years have not already led humanity astray by means of a delusion, the feeling of one's own audacity and recklessness: all that fights an undecided battle." The question concerning the morality of the prevailing morals arises. But there also already emerges simultaneously the question that goes further: what does the whole system of human morality and its history mean within the "infinite world" that is not already "our" world? Perhaps not more than the result of *one* turn of mind within our social-historical world. But what meaning does "this eternal becoming" have in the infinite whole of the universe? What are the hidden springs in this clockwork? Are they the same as those in the clock that we call history? And are the events merely the clockface that shows how the hand sweeps on from hour to hour, "only to begin its course anew after twelve: a new period of the world begins"—an inchoate idea, which recurs in its maturity in the stillest hour of the great noon, where the "clock of life" takes a breath, the hand sweeps, and the eternal "hourglass of existence" runs out in the eternal "ring of rings," which conflates the conflict of human history and fate? But then what is man in the whole of the self-repeating periods of the world? Is he a mere means to something, or is he himself an end? *If* the innermost spring in the clock of Being were "immanent humanity," then both aspects would be reconciled, and the conflict between the Being of the natural world and the historical existence of man would be eliminated. For us willing human beings, there are given, to begin with, purposes and goals, and we apparently are completely caught in the compass of our historical humanity, locked into the "moral" world with "conscience and a sense of duty." And yet all human history drifts through "ebb and flow" toward an "eternal ocean," toward—the "innocence of becoming." The history of humanity is perhaps merely the smallest circle, even if for us the most central circle, in the infinitely small and infinitely large revolving of natural events, *one* ring in the big ring of universal passing away and coming into being. But how is the human "individual will" in the "circles of world history" related to the "total will"—in case the latter wills anything at all?

"Here that infinitely important problem is intimated, the question of the justification of the individual to a people, of a people to humanity, of humanity to the world; here, too, the fundamental relationship between *fate* and *history*," between freedom and necessity, between wanting and having to do something. To man as such the "highest conception" of "universal history," i.e., of a history that includes events in the natural universe, seems "not to be possible"—yet from a superhuman viewpoint of the world, universal history would seem possible. To gain this viewpoint, man would—like Zarathustra—have to climb over himself and be more than mere man. The great historian and philosopher would have to become a "prophet," a foreseer and reviewer of the whole of what is. Only then could he recognize the fatality in the history of human willing, too, and be free with the highest necessity. "But the position of fate," that is, in relation to historical humanity, "is not yet certain." Therefore there remains the question: are the "events" nothing, and is our "temperament," the color-tone in which we experience them, everything? Does everything only mirror our type of experiencing—or is the mirroring (of what man wants in what the world is) the other way around, and is our temperament merely the expression of the events of the natural world?—a question that is finally answered in the last aphorism of *The Will to Power* to the effect that man holds out his own mirror against the Dionysian mirror.[4] Does not a "fatalistic structure of the skull and spine," as well as habituation and extraction, already make man "against his will" into this particular man? But do we not want ourselves and know ourselves, nevertheless, as self-sufficient human beings? For man is, after all, "never the same again." "As soon as it were possible, however, to overturn the whole past of the world by means of a strong will," i.e., one such that can also will backward, "we would immediately step into the ranks of independent gods"—then the "I will" would be liberated into the "I am" of the child of the world, "and world history would then mean to us nothing but a visionary state of self-withdrawal." But as long as man's "I will" has not yet been freed into the simple existence of the child of the world in the middle of Being, the free will appears only as the "unfettered" and "arbitrary," as the infinitely free, indefinitely dissolute spirit. In contrast with this will, fate is a blind, compelling necessity, *against* the free will. Two different principles then confront each other: Fate preaches, "It is events that determine events," i.e., there is no freedom whatever. The other principle maintains the opposite: Events are nothing without the free will. If the first principle were the only true principle, man would be a plaything of sinister powers, not responsible for his actions and inactions, a necessary link in the chain of events. And he would have to be happy if he did not find out his situation; for if he did so, he would strive, "with an insane desire, to disarrange the world and its mechanism."

But "perhaps" (here Nietzsche concludes his reflection) *our free will* is *"nothing but the highest potency of fate."* Then—as in the previously considered reverse case, in which immanent humanity should also be the law of the world—our human world-history would be one with the events of "matter," "provided that one construe the meaning of this word infinitely broadly," namely so broadly that "matter" means the whole of what always is by nature. Only then would the history of mankind flow in freedom into that "enormous ocean" "where all evolutionary levers of the world find themselves again, united, fused together, all in one." History and fate would then be one, and as "*amor fati*" the will would correspond to freely willed necessity.

In the discourse on "Freedom of the Will and Fate," which was composed somewhat later, the problem of the contradiction and agreement of man and world is raised anew. The freedom of the will at first is (again in the sense of natural-scientific positivism) opposed to the "structure of the brain," over which the spiritual will is powerless. What the will "is capable of" is "fatalistically apportioned" to the will itself. But in philosophizing, Nietzsche immediately goes beyond this positivistic starting point in framing the question, when he continues, "Inasmuch as fate appears to man in the mirror of his own personality, individual freedom of the will and individual fate are two well-matched opponents. We find that peoples who believe in a fate distinguish themselves by vitality and strength of will," whereas resignation to the will of God is usually only a guise for being too timid to confront one's fate resolutely. That is: when it meets the resolute individual will of man, the impersonal fate individualizes into man's personal "destiny," because the free will apportions fate to itself as destiny.

But if fate as boundary-setter nevertheless appears more powerful than the free will, we must not forget two things: first, that fate is only an abstract concept, a force without substance; that for the individual there is only an individual fate; that fate is nothing but a chain of events; that man, as soon as he acts and therewith creates his own events, determines his own fate; that in general, events, as they reach man, are caused by man himself, consciously or unconsciously, and have to suit him. The activity of man does not begin with his birth, however, but already in the embryo and perhaps—who can decide here?—already in parents and ancestors.[5]

With the distinction between conscious and unconscious activities (which is more and more copiously developed in Nietzsche's later writings and leads to unexpected disclosures), the problem of the conflict between fate and freedom seems to approach a solution. Freedom of the will and fate grow closer to each other; each is of itself only an "abstraction." Thus the "strict distinction," i.e., the abstract opposition, of the two disappears in the conscious and unconscious activity of the individual. The activity of man does not begin only after his birth into self-being but already long before this time, in the generations of remote antiquity. With this view of preconscious and unconscious activities, the possibility arises of tying man back into the nature of all that is. "For the individual, the principle of separation, of detachment from the whole, of absolute unrestrictedness lies in the freedom of the will; fate, however, places man back into organic union with the total development," i.e., it puts him back into the whole of what is and by nature always has been. But at the same time fate first compels him, too, to the "free development of a counteractive force" in willing. "The fateless, absolute freedom of the will would make man into a god; the fatalistic principle, into an automaton."

But man is neither a will-less automaton nor a god who freely creates Being out of nothing. He is a being who can experience and willingly affirm the fatality in the whole of Being, even as his own basic character. Such a man would then be capable of "countenancing every moment of existence altogether" and of fitting himself into the whole of what is.[6] Nietzsche finally answers his initial question concerning the relationship of freedom of the will (of history) and fate with the formula "*amor fati*."

Within the context of the question of history and its position vis-à-vis fate, Christian events were from the very beginning the dubious phenomenon that primarily moved Nietzsche. A series of school essays ("On Christianity," 1862; "On the Life of Jesus," 1865; "Ideas on Christianity," 1865–66) as well as several childhood poems ("You Called—Lord, I Am Coming," 1862; "In Front of the Crucifix," 1863; "Now and in Times Past," 1863; "Gethsemane and Golgotha," 1864; "To the Unknown God," 1863–64) manifest a hesitating doubt about the truth of Christianity, which he had originally encountered not as a world-overcoming faith but as "Naumburg virtue." The difference in the mood of the first and of the last of these poems indicates the critical transition from a sentimental faith in the old, familiar God to the invocation of an unknown god. The title refers to the Apostle Paul, who had interpreted the "unknown god" of a heathen inspiration to the effect that this god had revealed himself and become conspicuous in Christ. Exactly this god who had once revealed himself becomes for Nietzsche the unknown god again, to whom Nietzsche feels schismatically bound, both seeking him in flight and fleeing him. In between these two poems is "In Front of the Crucifix," in which the Crucified is challenged to climb down from the cross and the challenger is destroyed by his blasphemy. "To the Unknown God" is already permeated by the will to devotion to a new, "related" god, who forces the beckoner into his service. The ambivalence of the flight[T107] already characterizes the poem on the familiar, crucified God in the reversing lines: "Christ, come here to me!"—"I am coming to you!" and: "I will pull you down with me"—"Pull me up to you from the grave." Twenty years later Nietzsche once again wrote poetic lines, in the last Part of *Zarathustra* ("The Magician"), on his relation to the unknown god. He is an "executioner god," veiled in lightning, who wants to hunt him [the magician] down,[7] [and is] his cruelest but indispensable enemy, who is supposed to render himself and surrender himself to him [the magician]. In a reinterpretation of the poem from *Zarathustra,* renamed as the "Lament of Ariadne,"[8] it is "Dionysus in emerald beauty" who, unveiled in the lightning, makes his appearance at the end. In *Ecce Homo* Nietzsche finally signs his name as "*Dionysus versus the Crucified.*" Soon afterward, in notes to Strindberg, Brandes, and Gast during the period of his insanity, he signs himself as "The Crucified," which could mean on the one hand that the Greek myth already knows Dionysus-Zagreus as a dismembered being, and on the other hand that to Nietzsche as "Antichrist," Dionysus mingles with Christ.— What can be deduced from these various indications of Nietzsche's religiosity? Profundity, insanity, absurdity? In any event, we can conclude that the final word of Nietzsche's *Ecce Homo* is only half as unequivocal as it seems to be if taken literally. Far removed from the unambiguousness of the Voltairean "*Ecrasez l'infâme,*"[T108] which Nietzsche appropriates in this passage, is *his* "curse on Christianity" and his claim to put an end to the "lie" of the Christian era and to start a new calendar with the date of his own *Ecce Homo,* the last day of Christianity. Nietzsche's curse and claim are as ambiguous as the devoutness of a godless man and the atheism of a man who at the beginning and end of his career invokes an unknown god.

The early doubt about the truth of the Christian faith in a superworldly God is not as a "Yes or No" question in the autobiographical sketch of the nineteen-year-old Nietzsche. This sketch contains, at the beginning, the noteworthy sentence, "As plant, I am close to God's acre; as man, born in a parsonage," only to end with the remark that the time has come now for him to seize the reins of events and to make his entrance into life. "And thus man outgrows everything that once embraced him; he does not need to burst his chains, but they drop off unexpectedly when a god commands it; and where is the ring, which ultimately still encircles him? Is it the world? Is it God?" Twenty years later Nietzsche, as the teacher of the great ring of the eternal return, has decided once and for all in favor of the incarnate, physical *world* and against the Christian *God* who is spirit. And he has chosen as his symbol of what encircled him the snake that winds around itself, the snake whose sagacity has, in the eagle, pride as a companion. This snake of the eternity (without beginning or end) of life that revolves into itself, changes repeatedly in Zarathustra's speeches. As a chthonian[T109] power, the snake is a symbol for the earth, but it also winds around the sun. Thus the snake belongs both to the earthly and to the heavenly world and to their eternal life. In relation to mortal man, the snake of eternity at first makes its appearance as the adder that bites Zarathustra in the neck but drinks its deadly poison back out as it licks his wound. In the speech "Of the Vision and the Riddle," the snake of eternally generative and destructive life changes into the black snake of nausea that almost strangled man, who takes the figure of a shepherd (who later proves to be identical with Zarathustra). The talk of a "black flood" and of a "black sea" also corresponds to the snake's nihilistic color. And just as the black snake of strangling nihilism becomes the snake of the eternal recurrence, so does the black sea of deadly melancholy change into the sea of forces that flow into themselves and of the "twofold voluptuous delights" of the eternal recurrence. The snake is, further—in "The Other Dancing Song"—the temptation and seduction of life to itself, the great "binder" and "rewinder" in the darting hair of the dancing maenad,[T110] who would like to lead Zarathustra along "crooked ways" on the path of love. Finally, it is the green, ugly snake in the valley of death, where Zarathustra meets the ugliest man, the murderer of God. But Zarathustra's wisdom consists of changing these different skins of one and the same snake: to save himself, as the shepherd, from the sickness unto death; to redeem himself, as the murderer of God, from self-hate; and finally to eternalize himself by means of love of the eternal ring of Being, so that the inner connection of nihilism, death of God, and eternal recurrence of life is mirrored in the image of the ugly strangler-snake that winds around itself and the sun.

The motif of eternity, which appears in the image of the ring and of the snake that winds around itself, figures playfully at the beginning and end of the *Second Untimely Meditation* (1873–74), too. In this *Meditation,* the temporality of the historical consciousness and of historical existence is expressly treated as a problem. Several passages in the "Discourses on the Future of Our Educational Institutions" (1871–72) touch on this subject, which *Zarathustra* takes up again in the critique of historical education (in the three speeches "On the Land of Education," "On Immaculate Perception," "On Scholars"). The criticism is directed in each case against the decorative "skin of education" of knowledge that comes from mere historical education, in order to oppose to such knowledge "the eternally same intentions of nature" and an interpretation of the "eternally same problems." For that, however, one needs an insouciance regarding the future and the capacity to stand still for a "moment" on the "threshold of the present."[9] The governing viewpoint of Nietzsche's critique of modern education is, already in the discourses on the "future" of modern education, the simple view of something that is always or eternally, in contrast with the twofold view (forward and backward) of what will be and of what has been. Classical education is superior to modern education not because it is, historically, Greek, and as such is an unsurpassable beginning; but instead, because Greek culture and education—today as then—accords with the true nature of the self-educating man. "Culture," Nietzsche says at the close of the *Second Untimely Meditation,* is itself only a cultivated, "improved *physis.*" Culture is subordinate to an "eternal order," toward which the things strive again and again "with a natural gravity." The recollection of *physis* as the Greeks understood it also determines Nietzsche's equivocal concept of "life."

The *Untimely Meditation* "On the Use and Disadvantage of History for Life" distinguishes, with a critical intention, modern, historical education from the unhistorical education of the Greeks. It begins with a reference to an essentially unhistorical life: animals and children, as distinguished from grown men, live "unhistorically," for they are not subject to future and past, but rather live altogether in their self-contained present. The adult lives "historically," for he constantly recalls what was and awaits what will be. His life stretches and scatters forward and backward, while the present moment is only an impermanent now between a "not yet" and a "no longer." The life of the grown man is thus a never completable "*imperfectum*"—which, however, precisely as such is bent on completion and perfection without being able ever to reach them. Therefore one desires in vain the more felicitous life of the animal and the child; both are by nature wholly what they are capable of being, because they are without interruption absorbed in the present of the respective moment:

Consider the herd that graze as they pass by you: they do not know what is meant by yesterday and today, they jump around, eat, rest, digest, jump again, and so on from morning to night and from day to day, brief in their desires and aversions, fettered, that is, to the peg of the moment, and therefore neither melancholy nor weary. When man sees all that, it hits him hard, because he preens himself, before the beast, over his humanity; and yet he looks upon the beast's happiness with jealousy—for he desires that alone, to live neither weary nor in pain, like the beast; but he wants that in vain, because he does not want it as the beast does. Man may once ask the beast, "Why do you not speak to me of your happiness, and only look at me?" The beast wants to reply, too, and say, "That results from the fact that I always forget right away what I wanted to say"—but it then already forgot this answer, too, and was mute: so that man was amazed at its response.

But he also marvels at himself, at his incapacity to learn to forget and his perpetual attachment to what is past; however far or fast he may run, the chain runs with him. It is a marvel: the moment, in one instant there, in the next instant gone, before a nothing, afterward a nothing, nevertheless returns as a ghost and disturbs the tranquillity of a later moment. Continually, a leaf out of the scroll of time separates, falls out, floats away—and suddenly floats back again, into man's lap. Then man says "I remember" and envies the beast that forgets immediately and sees every moment really die, sees it sink back into fog and night and become extinguished forever. Thus the beast lives *unhistorically*: for it is absorbed in the present, like a number, without there remaining any peculiar fraction; the beast does not know how to dissemble, conceals nothing, and appears in every moment altogether as what it is; it is thus altogether incapable of being anything else than honest. Man, on the other hand, resists the big and ever larger burden of the past: this burden weighs him down or bends him sideways, it drags on his gait as an invisible and dark load, which he can deny for the sake of appearance. . . . Therefore he is moved, as if he recalled a lost paradise, at seeing the grazing herd or, in more intimate proximity, at seeing the child, which does not yet have anything past to deny and plays between the fences of past and future in overjoyed blindness. And yet its play must be disturbed: only too early will it be called up out of forgetfulness. Then it will learn to understand the expression "it was," that trigger word with which struggle, suffering, and weariness approach man, to remind him what his existence basically is—a never completable *imperfectum*.[10]

The man who exists historically is never capable of simply existing, because in every moment he constantly (and yet without duration) anticipates what will be and remembers what was. He is unable to "forget." The full significance of the ability to forget first emerges in the speeches of Zarathustra where the symbolic concepts of the *Untimely Meditation* (child at play, threshold of the moment, chain of the past) recur with heightened significance in Zarathustra after he has awakened as a "child," in the gateway "moment," and in the redemption from the "it was" to characterize the third and most difficult "metamorphosis," by means of which the nihilism of the unconditional "I will" overcomes itself into the recognition of the Being that wills itself eternally. What at first appears to be only a pre-human deficiency, the *un*historical life of the animal and child, proves itself—from the superhuman viewpoint of Zarathustra—to be positive perfection. But how can merely not remembering or forgetting be a way to perfection? Only through the willful man's forgetting himself over and in something else that is more comprehensive, more powerful, and more pristine than he himself is. Such a locus of comprehensive embrace was called the "eternal ocean" in Nietzsche's school essay on fate and history, the ocean toward which all human history drifts, so that the accident of human existence, which had fallen out of bounds, withdraws into the necessary whole of the natural world. In the same sense the prophet of nihilism (who teaches, "Everything is empty, everything is equal, everything was") asks in *Zarathustra* about the "sea" in which one could drown, before his "great sadness" changes (in the "Drunken Song") into a desire that wills everything again and again, and the dried-up spring of nihilism becomes the wellspring of eternity. And it is said again the same sense in a poetic fragment of *Zarathustra*:[11] "throw yourself into the sea," for the art of forgetting is divine. In order to be capable of practicing it, the metamorphosis of the willing ego into a child of the world is needed.

The "child," which is only mentioned at the beginning in the *Untimely Meditation,* becomes in the first speech of Zarathustra the Heraclitean child of the world, which—in the polemical reversal of the Christian rebirth into a child to whom the Kingdom of God belongs—is unsophisticated innocence and a new beginning through forgetting. The "threshold of the moment" becomes the "eternal" moment in which time stands still, and this time is a "noon." The undetachable "chain of the past" becomes the "it was" from which the will that wills forward as well as backward redeems itself in the *amor fati.*

Within the *Untimely Meditation,* however, it is not yet a question of redemption through a divine art of forgetting, but only of liberation from a knowledge that injures life. The purpose of this liberation is to restore a natural equilibrium between historical recollection and unhistorical forgetting. Yet here the capacity to perceive *un*historically to a certain degree is emphasized as the more important and more pristine of the two. For it is possible to live happily almost without any memory, but it is impossible to *live* at all without temporarily forgetting. Just as, prior to its emergence into the light, the germ has (in the dark) a hidden development that belongs to organic life, so also do an unilluminated atmosphere, a closed horizon, and the art of forgetting belong to all historical events and to the actions of man. In this art lies also the possibility of "happiness," which is a state of being whole and of perfection. Also the "well-bred man," as Nietzsche describes him in *Ecce Homo,* is a man who knows how to forget.

> He who cannot settle down on the threshold of the moment, forgetting all the past, he who is unable to stand on one point like a goddess of victory without dizziness and fear—he will never know what happiness is, and still worse: he will never do anything that makes others happy.[12]

In settling down on the threshold of the moment, man is able to forget that he is an *imperfectum* and to nullify for a moment the imperfectibility of his historical existence and of the historical consciousness that belongs thereto.

In the last sections of the first Part of the *Untimely Meditation,* the possibility finally is considered of a disposition toward history that is not only relatively *un*historical but *supra*historical. That is, he who has once recognized that every great event in history arises in an unilluminated atmosphere can "perhaps" also rise—at least in his recognition—to a suprahistorical viewpoint from which it becomes apparent that our estimation of the historian's discipline is an extreme overrating of history and an "Occidental prejudice." The suprahistorical viewpoint shows that the decisive question, "What is the point of living at all?" can be answered just as well—or just as badly—whether we ask a man of the first century or a man of the nineteenth. Several decades or even centuries of further historical development can teach nothing essentially new about the essence of the world and of man. The belief that the process of history as such leads to better insights or even is able to solve the problem of history is a perspectival illusion if the world is "completed in every moment" because it has no beginning or end. This suprahistorical viewpoint anticipates what Nietzsche teaches in *Zarathustra* under the title of the eternal recurrence of the same. As opposed to *all* historiological ways of considering history ("monumental," "antiquarian," and "critical"), the wise men of knowledge of all times agree that—beyond the all-too-human perspectives of our willing and unwilling—the opposition between "formerly" and "someday" is canceled in the "omnipresence" of nontransitory types of "eternally same meaning."

As the hundreds of various languages correspond to the same typically firm needs of men, so that someone who understood these needs would be capable of learning nothing new from any language; likewise does the suprahistorical thinker illuminate all history of peoples and of individuals from the inside, clairvoyantly guessing the original meaning of the various hieroglyphs and gradually even tiredly evading the hieroglyphics that are forever streaming in anew: for how, in the endless superfluity of events, is he supposed to avoid bringing on satiation, oversatiation, even nausea![13]

Nietzsche's reflection breaks off with the remark, "But let the unhistorical men have their nausea and their wisdom," in order to turn again to the "active and progressive men" for whom such transhistorical wisdom is a "nausea" because it does not serve the "future" and "life." Wisdom contradicts life as long as life is still understood in the horizon of the will of the future. In the two "dancing songs" of *Zarathustra,* the relationship of life and wisdom is called into question anew, and it is said that they resemble each other to the point that we could mistake one for the other. But Zarathustra, too, who has seemingly reconciled his differences with his wisdom (who knows that every individual thing, too, is exculpated in the eternally recurring whole of what is), is still an "overcomer of the great nausea" at his own wisdom, who cannot help knowing that the "small" and contemptible man, too, always recurs. Nevertheless, Zarathustra never tires of combating the small man with every resource of his wit: as "mob" and "rabble," as "flies of the marketplace" and "tarantulas"—like vermin to be exterminated. Zarathustra would like to be the "man without nausea," it is true, but he also knows that only nausea over man as he has been so far has disclosed to him the new springs of the future that flow into his teaching of the eternal recurrence.

The main theme of the rest of the essay is the threefold relationship of historical knowledge to life. Each of the three kinds of history, "monumental," "antiquarian," and "critical," serves life in its own way without knowing it. The correlate to the first type is the man who is active in a progressive way in his present age and to that end takes from the past, models for the future. To the second type corresponds the man who piously preserves the traditional and knows himself to be one with his origin; to the third, the man who through is critique of the past frees himself from the historical burden of the present, for the possibilities of the future. Nietzsche himself treated the philosophy of history monumentally when he represented philosophy "in the tragic age of the Greeks" as a paragon, and critically when in *Twilight of the Idols* he related the "history of the longest error."—In the discussion of monumental history, there arises for the first time, with odd abruptness, the idea of the eternal recurrence of the literally "same." The monumental type of history presupposes that the greatness that once was there, surely was once *possible,* and thus could also again be possible. But how is that once possible thing of the past supposed to be able to repeat itself exactly as it was before? Strictly speaking, such a repetition can occur only if

the Pythogoreans were right to believe that in equal constellations of the heavenly bodies, the same must repeat itself on earth, too, down to every smallest detail; so that again and again, if the stars have a certain position in relationship to one another, a Stoic will join with an Epicurean and murder Caesar; and again and again, when there is another configuration, Columbus will discover America.[14]

To think such an identical recurrence of the same would require, however, that the astronomers again become astrologers—so far, however (it is said later in *Zarathustra*), men have had only fancies about "stars and future," not knowledge.

At the end of the essay, Nietzsche returns to its beginning:

With the expression "the unhistorical," I characterize the art and power to *forget* and to hem oneself into a bounded *horizon*; I call "transhistorical" the powers that deflect one's glance from becoming toward what gives existence the character of the eternal and equally significant, toward *art* and *religion*. Science . . . sees in . . . these powers opposing powers and forces: for it holds true and right, and therefore scientific, only that view of things which sees something that has become, something historical everywhere, and nowhere, something that is, something eternal; science lives in an inner contradiction, equally opposing the eternalizing powers of art and religion and hating forgetting, the death of knowledge. . . . [15]

Only starting with *Zarathustra* does Nietzsche lift the confinement to art and religion of the "eternalizing powers"—to make these powers henceforth the center of his philosophic teaching. Only as the teacher of the eternal recurrence does Nietzsche develop from an untimely critic of his age into a philosopher who has overcome his age. In the foreword to Nietzsche's very last untimely meditation of all (*The Case of Wagner,* 1888), the overcoming of the temporality of time is characterized as the real task of the philosopher:

What does a philosopher demand of himself first and last? To overcome his age in himself, to become "timeless." With what must he therefore engage in the hardest combat? With what makes just him the child of his age. All right! I as much as Wagner am the child of this age, that is, a *décadent*; except that I comprehended this, that I resisted it. The philosopher in me resisted it.

By means of this will to the overcoming of time, the circle closes, which reaches from the critique of the historical consciousness to the wisdom of philosophic knowledge. Nietzsche is the last within the ancient tradition, and the first within the modern, historical consciousness, who had in what is forever or the eternal a philosophic yardstick by which to measure the experience of time and of the temporal.

# 6

## The Problematic Connection between the Existence of Man and the Being of the World in the History of Modern Philosophy

In the development of Nietzsche's teaching, the problematic unity in the discord between being *man* and being *world* proves to be the *problem* that endures from beginning to end, under the title "Freedom of the Will and Fate." In order systematically to understand this problem, which is expounded in Nietzsche's teaching as a willing of the cosmic recurrence, a clarification of the *historical* position of the problem in the whole of Western philosophy is required. Previously in this book, we have described the history of this problem one-sidedly as the attempt to recapture antiquity on the peak of anti-Christian modernity. The peak of modernity, however, from which Nietzsche regains "*his* world," is determined by the loss of the world.[1] The world has been lost to man in the "desert of his freedom" toward the nothing, and this freedom toward the nothing has itself emerged from the loss of the "Thou shalt." The loss of the "Thou shalt" has its origin in the "death of God." The death of the Christian God is consequently the cause of the possible regaining of the world, just as, inversely, the incursion into the ancient world by Christianity accounts for the loss of the former.

The Christian-modern man, who through his loss of the world has been thrown back onto his own resources, is only casually in the world, as if he were man's inner spiritualization. This "world" that has become *empty* because it has been understood in a Christian way has, with the beginning of modernity and its rediscovery of the world, been *secularized* into the concept of an autonomous "outer world" as

opposed to a no less autonomous "inner world." These two autonomous worlds are no longer united through the faith in God as the
common Creator of man *and* world. Inner world and outer world are
but loosely connected by means of a no-longer-binding "backworld."
As opposed to the *backworld that has become empty*, Nietzsche "wills"
"*this*" world again: that is, a world as it already was before it became—
through belief in "that" world behind the visible world of the senses—
a merely "earthly" this-world. In the will to his own return in the great
ring of the eternally recurring world, Nietzsche held his own mirror
up to the Dionysus mirror and his "own solution" up to the "Dionysus
riddle" of the world that wills itself.

The falling apart of the poetically unified parable into a double equation indicated that Nietzsche's attempt to regain the ancient world remained attached to his modernity. Modernity has its closest origin in
the genesis of the early modern world,[T111] and that genesis is coeval
with the philosophy of Descartes. With Descartes the world that had
become Christian becomes secular. But the critical turning point in the
modern world, namely the complete loss of the world within the secularized world, presents itself philosophically in the extreme nihilism of
Stirner and in the extreme positivism of Marx.

There occurs in Descartes's philosophy,[2] simultaneously with the
mathematical construction of the world, a liberation of human knowledge and of the man who knows about himself from the authority of
the ecclesiastical bond. Nietzsche was able to see very clearly this double position of Descartes in relation to previous faith and to future
knowledge, because Nietzsche was knowingly godless. He saw in Descartes the first philosophic physicist of the world, who "compared the
discoveries of a man of learning with a succession of battles that man
wages against nature."[3]

Logical definiteness, transparency as criterion of truth ("omne illud verum est,
quod clare et distincte percipitur"[T112]—Descartes): here the mechanistic hypothesis of the world is desired and believable.[4]

Granted that he did so with the caution of a "*larvatus*,"[T113] Descartes
made the freedom of philosophizing depend, for the first time, on the
sovereignty of reasonable willing. Just as characteristic as his independent position toward himself and toward the world, however, is his
doubt of the God of the Christian faith. Apart from this doubt, his
new certainty is unintelligible. "Abelard wanted to bring reason into
the ecclesiastical authority; Descartes finally found that *all* authority is

only in reason," whereas the inner problem of Pascal was the "self-overcoming of reason" for the benefit of the Christian faith.[5] Descartes still owed his audacious doubt of Christian authority itself to the spiritual pressure of the Church.[6] He still had a notion of the fact that

> in a Christian-moral basic mode of thought, which believes in a *good* God as the creator of things, only God's veracity *guarantees* us the judgments of our senses. Apart from a religious sanction and guarantee of our senses and rationality—whence should we derive a right to trust in existence![7]

And because the position of knowledge vis-à-vis Being "is dependent on a previous decision about the moral character of existence," Descartes still justifies the "truth of the perception of Being" itself "on the basis of God's nature."[8]

The peculiar result of Descartes's skeptical meditation[9] is the basic ontological distinction between man and world, according to the respective degree of certainty. Man is certain of himself as *"res cogitans"*;[T114] everything else, the whole world *outside* of man, is in itself as *"res extensa"*[T115] uncertain. From Descartes onward, this division of the whole of what is into two divergent types of Being—in the most varied forms of "idealism" and "realism" up to Nietzsche's abolition of the "true" world *and* the "apparent"—dominated the interpretation of human existence in its relationship to the world that is by nature. Since Descartes, the world is considered to be an *external* world, as distinguished from the inner self-being of the thinking man and from his self-conscious fabrication of the world. The extensiveness in the infinite being of the world corresponds to the modern tension in finite humanity, and "since Descartes, man is building bridges" (Dilthey), from the bridgehead of the "I will" over to the world that has become this-worldly and nevertheless has become further removed. At the end of these efforts at bridging over, stands Nietzsche's lost will to "engage" the divorced world again by willing backward to the naïveté of the ancients' certainty of the world. His doubt of Descartes's methodological doubt manifests itself in a characteristic distinction between the first speech of Zarathustra and the first sentences of Descartes's *Principia*. "Because we came into the world as children and made multifarious judgments about sensory objects before we achieved perfect use of our reason, we are accordingly hindered by many prejudices from recognizing the truth. It seems that we cannot free ourselves from these prejudices in any other way than to resolve once in our lives to doubt everything that arouses in us even the slightest suspicion of

uncertainty." Nietzsche doubts this path to the certainty of knowledge and bases his own, new certainty precisely on Zarathustra's finally
"awakening," while on his path to the truth, *into* the child of the
world.[10] Such an awakening is "forgetting" and a "new beginning,"
but not "once" and for all and by means of doubt, but rather again
and again and by means of the play of creation. Having awakened into
a child, Zarathustra is liberated not only from the authority of "Thou
shalt"—from which Descartes was already freed—but also from the "I
will" doubt everything that has so far bound him.

Nietzsche gains this new certainty in relation to the world, which
permits Zarathustra "to plunge into chance with pleasure," by *fundamentally doubting*—on the peak of modernity, where nothing is true
any more—*Descartes's modern doubt once again*. To be sure, Descartes
doubts whether he truly is, for God *could* be a deceiver, but Descartes
assures himself that deceit is not compatible with God's perfection. In
contrast, Nietzsche's "new Enlightenment," for which God is not only
dubious but dead, takes as its "point of departure" the "irony against
Descartes" and his "carelessness" in doubting.[11] For his "I want not
to be deceived" could still be the means of a deeper and more subtle
will to self-deception. This will to self-deception could consist in the
unwillingness of Descartes's will to truth to recognize the semblance
in which the truth of Being appears. His rational reason constructs a
world behind the world that visibly appears,[12] in order to be sure,
within the world thus concocted, of this very world.

Descartes is not radical enough for me. With his demand to have what is certain, and his "I want not to be deceived," we need to ask "why *not*?" In brief,
moral prejudices . . . in favor of certainty against semblance and uncertainty.[13]

Descartes's faith in immediate certainty is itself still a faith in the
power of reason and no original certainty of the world.

We newer men are all opponents of Descartes and defend ourselves against his
dogmatic carelessness in doubting. "Doubting must be done better than Descartes did it!" We find the opposite, the reverse movement against the absolute authority of the goddess "Reason," wherever there are profound men.
Fanatical logicians brought it about that the world is a deception, and that the
path to "Being," to the "unconditional," exist only in thought.[14]

Is certainty at all possible in *knowledge*, or is it based only in Being?
And what is cognizing knowledge in relation to Being?

To whoever brings along already finished articles of faith in answer to these
questions, the Cartesian caution has no meaning whatever anymore: it comes

much too late. Prior to the question of "Being," the question of the value of logic would have to be decided.[15]

For Descartes, "Being" is defined from the outset as being knowable, for he believes in scientific knowledge; but he does not see the unshrouded, true vision of the highest type of Being that lives.

A further step in the definition of the relationship of man and world, beyond the fundamental distinction of Descartes, is taken by Kant. With a view to Descartes's alleged doubt, Nietzsche interprets Kant's categorical imperative in the remark, "Is God supposed to be a deceiver after all, in spite of Descartes?"[16] That is, Kant relies on nothing but reason, which says to him what he "should" do; thus he also no longer needs the dubious assurance of Descartes that God does not deceive him. Whereas Descartes shook ecclesiastical authority for the first time, yet still assured himself of his new certainty theologically, Kant already interprets the commandments of Christian faith as primally commanded by the practical reason. But how are man and world related to each other, if the "true world" behind the actual world has become "unreachable and unprovable," as an imperative that only "obliges"? Does not the whole of Being necessarily divide into two unconnected parts if there is no God any more to hold them together, as the authoritative Creator?

In a prominent place, namely the "resolution" of the *Critique of Practical Reason*, Kant[17] formulated the twofoldness that has developed between man and world, in the famous thesis that there are two things that fill the heart ever anew with admiration and that I immediately connect with the consciousness of my existence: the *starry sky* above me and the *moral law* within me. The difference, however, is as follows according to Kant:

The former begins with the place I take in the external world of the senses and extends into incalculably large dimensions my linkage with worlds across worlds and systems of systems, moreover into boundless ages of their periodic movement, of their beginning and further duration. The second begins with my invisible self, with my personality, and pictures me in a world that is truly infinite, . . . and with this world (therewith, however, simultaneously with all those visible worlds, too) I know myself linked not, as in the other case, accidentally, but universally and necessarily.[18]

In the whole of the countless myriads of worlds, says Kant, I lose my importance as a human being. I am only one natural organism among others. But as a morally responsible, intelligent being who has insight into the whole of what is, however, I am a "life independent" of the whole natural world of the senses. But it also does not suffice to halt admiringly before the system of the sensual world only to gaze upon the starry heaven, and to marvel over the moral law within me. Rather, in both realms of Being, one must conduct investigations, in order to avoid having the consideration of the cosmic world end in astrology, and of the moral world in "superstition and fanaticism."

Fichte took the next step, beyond Kant, in *The Destiny of Man*.[19] For him, moral existence and the natural world are no longer compatible by virtue of being analogously characterized by laws. Instead, their relationship is that of a dialectical antinomy between the naturalness of man and his moral self-being. This inward contradiction in man can only be resolved in a philosophical "faith." The first meditation presents man as one natural organism among others. He, like all else that also is, is by nature "thoroughly determined," and his entire "definition"[T116] seems to lie in this very fact alone. In the whole of objectively given nature, everything in all of its parts is exactly as it is, and it could not be different. Everything is naturally *necessary*. Nothing has the cause of its existence in itself, but everything is in a great web of reciprocal effects by virtue of a natural force that interweaves through everything as the cause of Being of all things that can possibly exist. Every expression of the one natural force in the universe necessarily turns out as it does, "and it is simply impossible for it to be even slightly different from what it is." Every individual man, too, would not exist and be as he is, if everything else, too, did not already exist and develop as it does. I myself am a link in the chain of the strictest natural necessity.

I did not originate by means of myself. It would be the greatest absurdity to suppose that I preexisted myself, in order to bring myself into existence. I became real through another force outside of me. And through which force might that be, other than the universal natural force? For I am, after all, a part of nature. The time of my coming into being and the attributes with which I came into being were determined by this universal natural force. And all the forms in which my inborn fundamental attributes have expressed themselves since and will express themselves as long as I will be, are determined by the same natural force. It was impossible for another to arise instead of me. It is impossible for this one who has by now arisen, to be anything else, in any moment of its existence, than what it is and will be.[20]

This existence of man, in itself innocent, will straightaway be accompanied by consciousness of itself, it is true; but this consciousness, too, necessarily belongs to humanity, just as self-motion belongs to animals and growth to plants.[21]

Thus man has no special destiny[T117] at all that would provide him a special position in the cosmos. Instead, he is always determined by a natural necessity insofar as he is this particular[T118] man and no other.

I am who I am because in this web of the natural whole, only such a being and altogether none other was possible. And a mind that could gain a perfect overview of the inner core of nature would be able, through knowledge of a single human being, to state specifically[T119] which men have ever been and which men will be at any given time; in *one* person he would recognize *all* actual persons. It is my connection with the natural whole, then, that determines everything that I was, am, and will be; and the same mind would be able to deduce without error, out of each possible moment of my existence, what I have been before this moment and what I will be afterward. Everything that I ever am or will be, I am or will be necessarily, and it is impossible that I be something different.[22]

But already in this initial meditation, there arises a contradiction, through which the meditation is reversed. For I am *at the same time* conscious of myself as an autonomous, self-reliant being who can say " I" to himself. Man can decide with self-confident and self-conscious willfulness to do this or that, he can even terminate his own existence by committing suicide. And *im*mediately, my consciousness does not go beyond me at all, for I am not the man-forming natural force itself, but only one of its expressions, which I am conscious of *as my self*. Thereby I appear free to myself, and I appear limited in my free autonomy if, because of "external circumstances," I cannot do what I want to do. Man thus seems to be two things: in himself a naturally necessary expression of the universal natural force, and for himself a free capacity to be. And "because nothing in nature contradicts itself, is only man a contradictory being?" This contradiction is not resolvable on the basis of the first meditation. The second, which approaches the issue from the other end, follows. I myself want to be something for and through myself. I want to be the cause of my own self-determination and to assume the position of the original natural force. But for that purpose man would have to be free from his having always been eternally determined by nature. The consciousness that belongs to freely willing must not be the mere natural determination of man.[T120] And indeed it emerges that the whole world is always a world *for* the consciousness of man, that the world exists not unmediated but mediated by us, e.g., as the sensory world of our senses. Subjectivity is itself always determinative of the natural external world. Immediately certain is only: *I* am conscious of my seeing and feeling something. Everything that "is" is a possible object of my consciousness, for the object *is* an object only insofar as it faces *me*.

This consciousness of the object is accompanied by self-consciousness. *I* can at any given time return from my seeing *something* to my *seeing as such*. The question first asked is thus no longer: How is man situated within the universe? but the opposite: How do I ever get out of the compass of my self-consciousness and world-consciousness to the real things? What "bond" connects me with them? But in respect to myself this question does not come up; because the ego that knows about itself is already simultaneously subject *and* object for itself, a simple identity of both, and the thing seems to be a mere product of my imaginative consciousness. But does not the ego that has become autonomous dissipate into a phantom, too, as the world that is external to me loses it autonomy?

Is this in its entirety the wisdom you made me hope to achieve, and do you glory over thus liberating me?—You liberate me, it is true: you absolve me from all dependence by changing me myself, and everything around me on which I could depend, into nothing. You abolish necessity by abolishing all Being and simply eradicating it.[23]

Thus begins the third and final meditation, on "Faith," which is supposed to lead out of this "logical denial of the world" (as Nietzsche called the epistemological result of his first liberation). What defines man[T121] is not at all mere knowing but knowing action, *believing* in reality. Practically speaking, this belief takes us beyond the nothing of the second meditation.

When I shall act, I shall doubtless know that I act and how I act; but this knowing will not be the acting itself, but will only observe it.—Thus this voice announces to me exactly what I sought: something that is external to knowledge and completely independent of knowledge in its very Being.[24]

This also seems to be the point of connection for the *consciousness* of all reality: the acting ego's actual interest in reality.[25] This interest, however, is morally commanded by the conscience, which summons us to engage in free and active deeds and therewith makes us certain of the world again.

We do not act because we know; instead, we know because we are destined to act. Practical reason is the root of all reason. The laws of action for rational beings are *immediately* certain; their world is certain only *by virtue of the certainty of the laws of action*. We cannot renounce these laws without having the world, and with it ourselves, sink into the absolute nothing. We lift ourselves out of this nothing and keep ourselves above this nothing solely by means of our morality.[26]

Fichte removes the nihilism of freedom through moral positiveness. A divine will that produces itself is discussed at the end of his meditation. It is finally the divine will that mediates between the ego and the nonego of the natural world external to me; the natural world is a planned world, guided by divine providence, and a "moral testing ground" for man, a "school on eternity." In conclusion, the following image of the universe emerges:

To me the universe is no longer that circle which runs back into itself, that play which is repeated incessantly, that monster which devours itself only to give birth to itself again, just as it was already: it has been spiritualized before my eyes, and bears the authentic stamp of the spirit; it is constant progress toward the more perfect, in a straight line that goes into infinity.[27]

The world I just now admired disappears before my eyes and sinks. In all its richness of life, of order, of blossoming that I behold, the world is nevertheless only the curtain by means of which an infinitely more perfect world is concealed from me, and the germ out of which the latter should develop. My faith stops behind this curtain and warms and enlivens this germ. My faith sees nothing particular, but it expects more than it can grasp here below, or ever will be able to grasp in time,[28]

whereas Nietzsche, on the contrary, pulled away the curtain of this *morality* that had lost all sanction, in order to make visible again the self-repeating play of annihilation and creation in the cycle of the world.

In rejoinder to Fichte's "annihilation" of the natural world, Schelling[29] said of Fichte that he is to be sure a great orator who understands how to discuss things to the point of boredom, but that his pure active ego makes of the world a pure nothing.

Such a complete nothing of reality is thus the *prius*[T122] of Mr. Fichte: for the *purity* of his knowledge, it is already disturbing that anything at all exists, that the eternal is in fact real and is also known only *after* it is real—because this very knowledge itself belongs to the reality of the eternal.

Schelling contends that in Fichte, on the contrary, the whole existence of nature amounts to man's purpose in fashioning and managing nature.

The agreement of nature with thought is, according to Fichte's construction, only possible in such a way that nature conforms to the idea; but not in such a way that the truth itself is Being, that Being or nature itself is the truth. . . . In order to achieve this purpose, knowledge of the laws according to which those forces operate, i.e., physics, is necessary (for Fichte). But nature *should* not be *merely* useful and usable for man, which function was nature's first purpose and the economic view; rather, "it *should* at the same time give man a decent environment," i.e. (how can one otherwise explain it?), it should be remodeled into agreeable gardens and estates, beautiful apartments and suitable chattels, which is the second purpose and aesthetic view of nature.—What else can be compatible with such a state of mind and with the notion of such a nature, which is only worth being remodeled into tools and appliances, than the blindest contempt for all nature, the rash opinion that one cannot revile man more harshly than to say of him: it is a natural force that produces and thinks in him[?] . . . He has elevated himself over all natural force and would have clogged this spring in himself long ago, had it ever flowed in him; everyone will attest that nature does not think in *him*—in his presence, how is nature even supposed to get a word in edgewise? If nature started to show the slightest sign of life, he would immediately shout it down and talk it to death with his wisdom. . . . Long ago he crushed the hand of nature in himself; but it remains uncertain, if one listens to him, which of them has done the other the most harm.[30]

Nietzsche always kept aloof from Schelling, who had influence on Nietzsche only derivatively, through Schopenhauer's metaphysics of the will and Eduard von Hartmann's philosophy of the unconscious. Yet Schelling is the sole thinker of German idealism who—in spite of his theogonic[T123] constructions—has a positive relationship to Nietzsche's teaching of the eternal cycle. "What is alive in the highest science," it is said in the introduction to *The Ages of the World*,[31] can only be the "primeval living thing," the prehistoric being that is preceded by none other, and that has no other being but itself, and that must accordingly develop purely out of itself, out of the impulse and willing most proper to it. This primeval and oldest living thing, this "abyss of the past," which always remains present and outlasts everything that once has become, can be known and be told about like a primeval history, because man derives from the same source and has an original (albeit obscure and forgotten) shared knowledge with the creation. This oldest remaining thing is "nature in the most perfect understanding of the word," just as man, too, is a nature—regardless of his freedom. The secret intercourse between the unconsciously knowing "heart" of man and the mind that wants science (the mind that gets the answer to its questions from that witness of what has existed and what is essential, in "whom" knowledge is originally contained, in a hidden and undeveloped way), this silent dialogue between the mind that wants knowledge and the unconsciously knowing heart, is, according to Schelling, the real secret of the philosopher, who seeks a highest and deepest knowledge about the original nature of all things. In this dialogue—as Nietzsche puts it, between "life" and "wisdom"—man's nature achieves effability, self-differentiation, and intelligibility. And if the questioning and examining research could elevate itself into simple narration of the essence and emergence of things, as in Plato's return from disputatious dialectics to the "simplicity of history" of the philosophic myth, then the philosopher would become a seer who with his gaze would join into one "what was, what is, and what will be." For the nature of all events is always one and the same in all living things; and anyone who could relate the history of his own life thoroughly, would have summarized in one essence the history of the universe, too. But most men turn away from the hidden elements of their own interior just as much as from the abysses of the great life which, like all living things, begins in the dark and in terror before it emerges therefrom, tempered, into the light. A contradiction that belongs to its essence operates in this primeval life (which combines human life with the totality of life in the history of the universe): it is at the same time negative and affirmative, destructive and creative, it simultaneously reveals itself and conceals it-self. This double character of primeval, living Being—in Nietzsche's terms, the Dionysian world—has always already been experienced and named, as light and darkness, as heaven and earth, as male and female. As an original whole it is something that in itself is complete and round, closed and terminated, which contains in itself equally the annihilating and the creative primeval force. The "first nature" is a constant activity, a never-halting, revolving movement without beginning and end. The original being wants nothing apart from itself; it is a willing of itself. This life that eternally revolves into itself is a kind of "circle," a "wheel" or "clockwork" that turns incessantly, a movement that al-ways goes forward and backward, a constant alteration of "ebb" and "flow"—all words that Nietzsche, too, used to characterize the basic character of the totality of life. With a reference to Heraclitus, Schelling describes the complete concept of the first nature (which also compre-hends the nature of God) very much as Nietzsche does in the last aphorism of The Will to Power: as a "life that ceaselessly gives birth to itself and consumes itself again, a life that man must [suspect],[T124] not without fright, as the life that hides in everything; although it is now covered up and has outwardly assumed peaceful attributes." By constantly going back to the beginning and by starting over eternally, the primeval nature makes itself into a substance (*id quod substat*), into something that always remains and is fundamental. It is the constant inner machinery and clockwork, "the eternally beginning, eternally becoming time that always swallows itself and always gives birth to itself again."

What decisively distinguishes this conception from Nietzsche's metaphysics of the life that wills itself again and again from Nietzsche's metaphysics is that Schelling does not equate this constant activity of the first nature with the present "world," and still less with a Divine Being. If nature were to come to a halt at its first stage, there would be nothing more than an eternal exhaling and inhaling, a constant alternation of coming into being and passing away, of spreading itself out and going back into itself, and external drive to be, without real existence—that is, without constancy, stability, and self-consciousness.[32] Accordingly, Schelling constructs a theogonic process that redeems the living activity into freedom in God's being, which neither exists nor does not exist but, like pure freedom, is a nothing: a pure will that wills nothing, a will free of obsession and desire that is a pure, natureless spirit. God is the eternal freedom to be, and nature is only the necessary material or possibility of his realization. Nature itself is not God and also not world; it only belongs to the necessary nature of God and to the precondition of the world. Left to its own devices, primeval nature is something that "does not know where to turn," a life of "anxiety" and "repulsiveness," that longs for a steadfast Being. The same applies to man, whose innermost constituent is likewise that wheel of nature, but from which he wants to be redeemed.[33]

It would therefore be wrong to continue the modern (that is, Cartesian) way of picturing man and the world instead of establishing a connection with the old and most ancient again. It would be equally impermissible, however, to stop there, for the abyss of nature would not justify the free being of God and of man who is made in his image. This abyss turns up in man when he is *no longer* in possession of himself, when he is sick or mentally ill, because the governing power of his mind has left him. Man becomes himself only by separating himself, in a "crisis," from his nature and his nature's past, when he resolves and decides once and for all, like lightning, and thereby posits a true beginning. On the other hand, however, any sensible and conscious willing also presupposes a blind and unconscious force of inspiration and at bottom only unfolds this force. Schelling interprets the holy insanity of Dionysian drunkenness in this sense.[34] The Dionysian insanity that rends itself is now still the innermost element of things and the natural force of all procreations, and is controlled only through the light of a higher understanding. For where should the understanding try itself and prove itself, if not in the mastery of insanity? The complete lack of insanity leads not to reason but to idiocy. The basic material of all life and existence, according to Schelling and Nietzsche alike, is the terrible: a blind power and force, a barbaric principle that can be overcome but can never be eliminated, and that is "the foundation of all greatness and beauty."[35]

Schelling's *Ages of the World* contains in passing a polemic against the "empty rattling" of Hegel's formal dialectic and the opinion that one must oppose to the understanding a higher "reason" in order to be able to grasp the absolute, instead of apprehending that the adversary of the understanding is not reason but insanity. Without the "solicitation" of insanity, there would also be no living understanding.

In Hegel's system nature has no original, fundamental, and autonomous meaning. It is the "otherness of the idea." Hegel, conscious of the modern disintegration of man and world, attempted in his dispute with Kant, Fichte, and Schelling to restore the lost unity of self-sameness and otherness in a mediating philosophy of the absolute spirit, which is itself a "second" nature. The result of this mediation is a "state of evolved selfsameness in otherness." But Hegel completed this movement (expressly conscious of the "reconciliation of a perdition") at the end of the Christian epoch of Western philosophy[36] and with a view to the beginning of the modern separation of man and world in the philosophy of Descartes.

Cartesian philosophy has articulated in philosophic form the generally spreading dualism in the culture of the recent history of our Northwestern world. The quieter transformation of men's public life as well as the noisier political and religious revolutions generally, are only different-colored exteriors of this dualism, which is the downfall of all ancient life. Every facet of living nature, and philosophy likewise, had to seek a remedy against Cartesian philosophy as well as against the general culture that expresses it. What has been done by philosophy in this regard has been treated with rage when it was pure and open. When it was more hidden and more intricate, the understanding took possession of the philosophic activity all the more easily and reworked it into the previously mentioned dualistic mold. All sciences have been based on the death of nondualistic life and thought; and what was still scientific, and thus at least subjectively alive in the sciences, time has completely killed. The sciences are the edifice of an understanding that has been abandoned by reason, an understanding that, worst of all, has finally also ruined theology, with the borrowed name either of an enlightening reason or of moral reason. So that—if it is not immediately the spirit of philosophy itself that, immersed and pressed together in this broad ocean, feels all the more strongly the force of its growing pinions—it also is the boredom of the sciences that makes the whole, flat expansion unbearable. For this boredom should arouse at least a longing of riches for a drop of fire, for a concentration of living contemplation, and (after death has been known long enough) for a knowledge of the living, which is possible only through reason.[37]

Hegel's mental strength was not able to delay the history of this disintegration. Precisely by means of his "reconciliation," he made clear for the future that man is separated from the world now that no God holds it together any more and an absolute "spirit" has taken God's place.

With the "crow of the cock of positivism,"[38] this theological backworld fades from view. From Descartes to Hegel, the theological backworld has still prevented the problems already present in man's relationship to the world as an external world, from coming to a head. This culmination of problems did occur in the extreme radicalism of Stirner and Marx. For both of them, there is no longer a natural world by nature at all. To Stirner's "unique man," the world becomes a usable "property," and to the "generic man" of Marx, it becomes a common "means of production" in a human world that must first be produced.

"I've based my existence on nothing" is the motto of Stirner's smug nihilism.[39] *The Unique Man and His Property* (1844) is divided into two chapters, entitled "The Man" and "I." Stirner's problem is neither *the* human being nor *the* world, but "I" as the unique proprietor of my world, which is always my own. Stirner's unique ego—at the most extreme end of a lost faith in God and in the world—creates its world out of the nothing, as God once did.

The divine is the business of God, the human the business of "the human being." My business is neither the divine nor the human . . . but only *what is mine,* and that is not anything general but is—unique, as I am unique.[40]

And now I take the world as what it is to Me, as Mine, as My property: I refer everything to Myself.[41]

In making this remark, Stirner knows himself to be at the beginning of a new epoch. From the standpoint of this epoch he distinguishes the old world of antiquity and the new world of Christianity. Political, social, and humanistic liberalism he knew to be the final form of Christianity. To the ancients the "world" was a truth, and Christianity discovered its lie. To the moderns the "spirit" became the truth, and

Stirner, drawing the logical conclusion of Feuerback and Bruno Bauer, discovered its lie.

> If the ancients have nothing to show but worldly wisdom, the moderns never brought or bring it further than theological learning. We will . . . see that even the most recent rebellions against God are nothing more than the most extreme exertions of "theologians' learning," i.e., theological insurrections.[42]

Finally the humanitarian man still seemed to be a divine truth, but this "man" on whom post-Hegelian philosophy relies is only a pregnant phrase. Stirner surpasses this slogan with his "absolute phrase" of the "unique man," who is supposed to be the end of all phrases and empty talk. Stirner discovers that not only philosophy from Descartes to Hegel is a hidden theology, but also the "pious atheism" of the unchristian philosophy of Bauer and Feuerbach. He makes this discovery because he sets himself resolutely onto nothing, and for him neither the "spirit," which was originally God, nor the "human being," nor anything else, is the "highest being."

> What is venerated as the highest being—the dispute over that issue can conceivably be meaningful only as long as even the most bitter opponents concede to one another the main proposition that there is a highest being, to whom a cult or service is due. If someone smiles sympathetically over the whole battle about a highest being, like a Christian, say, during the verbal battle of a Shiite with a Sunni . . . , the hypothesis of a highest being would be empty to him, and the dispute on this basis would be a vain game. Whether the one God or the Trinity, whether the Lutheran God of the *être suprême*[T125] or not God at all but "the human being" may represent the highest being, makes no difference whatever to him who denies the highest being itself, for in his eyes those servants of a highest being are all—pious people: the most rabid atheist no less than the most religious Christian.[43]

They all still pray to idols and are possessed by monomanias. The difference between the faith of Luther, the *cogitare* of Descartes, and the self-knowing spirit of Hegel comes to nought, for they all do not yet know the naked and altogether common human being. They all still believe in something divine and eternal in man.

> Hence the Lutheran Hegel succeeded in completely implementing the concept in everything. Reason, i.e., holy spirit, is in everything, or "the real is rational."[44]

For two thousand years men have tried to desecrate the "Holy Spirit," but it is still there as a spirit that has become profane and "more humane," and now appears more attractive as the "spirit of the age" or as the "spirit of humanity"—until it finally goes about dressed only in rags.

> In humane liberalism, shabbiness is perfected. We must first . . . descend to the most shabby if We want to achieve ownness,[T126] for We must take off everything alien. But nothing seems shabbier than the naked—human being.
>     It is more than shabbiness, however, if I throw away man, too, because I feel that even he is alien to Me and that I may Myself not be conceited about that. That is no longer mere shabbiness, because even the last rag has fallen off, and thus the real nakedness, the denuding from everything alien, stands there. The shabby rogue has shaken off shabbiness himself and thus has stopped being what he was.[45]

With that the second Part begins. Here Stirner no longer critically deals with the man of the old and new world, but with the ego as the proprietor of his property. The epigraph to this part reads:

> At the entrance to the new age stands the "God-in-man." At the exit of this age, will only the God in the God-in-man vanish, and can the God-in-man really die, if only God dies in him? One did not think of this question and supposed oneself to be finished upon having brought the work of the Enlightenment, the overcoming of God, to a victorious conclusion in our day. One did not notice that man has killed God only to become now—"the only God on high." The *Beyond outside of Us* has, to be sure, been swept away, and the great endeavor of the Enlighteners has been completed. But the *Beyond within Us* has become a new heaven and summons us to a new storming of heavens; God had to make room, not for Us, however, but for—the human being. How can you believe that the God-in-man has died before, in addition to the God in him, the man in him, too, has died?[46]

But what does the Ego do after man has died, too, together with God, who previously determined humanity? Man's doing is nothing else than a "squandering" in each instance, a consuming and utilizing of himself and of the world as his property. It is necessary to achieve a "restamping" of Christian values and to honor anew everything of Christian values and to honor anew everything that is Own: Self-Interest, Obstinacy, Willfulness, Self-Love, and Property.[T127]

> Ownness includes in itself everything that is one's own[T128] and honors again what Christian language dishonored. But ownness also has no alien yardstick, for it is no *idea* at all (like freedom, morality, humanity, etc.). Ownness is only a description of the —*owner*.[47, T129]

Feuerbach's "human being" is only a conjured-up generic being; the owner, by contrast, is a real individual being. My own task is not to realize the "universally human" but to be self-sufficient.

As Ego, man no longer has a "vocation," a "task," or a "destiny" at all. Instead, he is exclusively the owner of what he can in fact make his own.

One has always supposed it necessary to define Me in terms of something exterior to what is Mine, so that one finally unreasonably demanded of Me that I should be preoccupied with the human because I = Man. This is the Christian magic circle. Fichte's Ego, too, is the same being, external to me; for Ego is Everyone, and if only this Ego has rights, it is "the Ego" and is not I.[T130] But I am not one Ego next to other Egos, I am the sole Ego: I am unique. Accordingly, my needs and my actions, too, in brief everything about me, is unique. And only qua this unique Ego do I take possession of everything, as I only exercise and develop myself as this unique Ego. I do not develop qua man and I do not develop man; rather, qua Ego I develop—Myself.
That is the meaning of the—*unique man*.[48]

Only with that is the "magic circle" of the Christian tension between essence and existence broken. The disenchanted man has value neither as a participator in the Christian Kingdom of God nor as *chargé d'affaires* in Hegel's spiritualized world-empire. Rather, the unique man is for himself already a "world history," one for whom the rest of world history is his property, and "that goes beyond what is Christian." Thus "in the unique man the owner returns into his creative nothing, out of which he is born."

If I rely on Myself, the unique man, then my existence is based on the transitory, mortal creator who consumes himself, and I may say:
"I've based my existence on nothing."[49]

This nihilistic position changed radically into the no less extreme positivism of Marx, who subjected Stirner's work to a fundamental critique in *The German Ideology* (1845–46) under the ironic title "Saint Max." By canonizing him, Marx means to say that Stirner, too, is possessed by the "spirit," because he is the most radical ideologue of the decadent bourgeois society, i.e., a society of "isolated individuals." Stirner's unique man liberates himself not from the real, "material," conditions of existence but merely from imaginary conditions of consciousness that he himself never sees through, because he is trapped in the principle of his bourgeois world, that is, in private egoism. Stirner only absolutizes the contemporary private man and his private property to the absolute "category" of *the* individual and property per se. But it is not consciousness that determines Being, but rather social Being that determines even the theoretical consciousness of the individual. Only a universal emancipation of the self-alienated masses could also liberate Stirner's unique man and really give him the world as his own in a "realm" of freedom; whereas Stirner believes himself able to found, "without large expenses," a world empire that is most properly his own. His very critique of liberalism still moves in the liberal idioms. These idioms, however, are in reality only the idealistic expression of the real interests of the bourgeoisie. He fails to recognize that man will become another being only when his actual living conditions change. For man's power is not measured by particular individuality; instead, the latter is measured by the power of human society. The bourgeois individual, however, is incapable—even just in his imagination—of freeing himself from private property. The actual appropriation of the world of commodities, alienated from man, can only come about through a total upheaval of the relations of production in society. Only through this revolution would it be possible to free the individual man, too, to be himself, whereas Stirner's owner is only the *negation of freedom from all ties*. The communist society then takes the place of Stirner's "association of egoists." Communist society expropriates the owner together with his property, in order really to give man as the "generic being" the world as his own again.—When Marx speaks of the "world," he means exclusively the historical world of man living in society. To "historical" materialism, nature is no original substance but only material and utilizable capital of the relations of production in human history, and thus is no different in principle from Stirner's "property." The difference lies only in the different definition of the proprietor: the "unique man" or "generic man." What interests Marx about an apple is not that nature produces such things in a natural way, but that this natural product was cultivated and imported and merchandised as a commodity for money by men, at a particular time and under particular economic and social relations. To historical thought, which reduces the world to the co-world of men and their environmental world, it is an uninteresting truism that man, the producer of his world and therewith of himself, exists and produces by nature. The exclusive interest in sociohistorical production, however, is as common to the bourgeois-capitalist private individual and to the communist, generic man as the "world" in which they act and think as producers and consumers.

With these two products of extreme disintegration that come from Hegel's absolute philosophy of the subjective *and* objective spirit— both equally far removed from the *natural* world and the *nature* of man—the ancient cosmos and the Christian hierarchy are completely at an end. Stirner and Marx philosophize against each other in the same "desert of freedom." The "man" whom Marx calls alienated from himself must "change" the whole of the existing world through a world revolution in order to be at home again in a human world; the "I" that Stirner calls free and exempt from all ties, conversely, does not know anything else to do but return into his nothing in order to consume the world (just as it is) for his own purposes, insofar as the world is usable for him.

What Nietzsche—in spite of the Reich established in the interim—saw before him thirty years later was the world, which had lost all culture, of an existence that had become goalless, an existence placed without commitment into an extrahuman world of forces. Nietzsche radicalized this "peace of disintegration" (into which entered "all the spiritual powers of the old, bound world") to the point of a resolute nihilism, in order to find his way back, in the reversal of nihilism, to the world that has always existed and is still always becoming. For:

What is the vanity of the most vain man compared with *that* vanity which the most modest man possesses in view of his feeling himself to be "man" in nature and the world![50]

# 7

## The Eternal Recurrence of the Same and the Repetition of the Selfsame

The problematical character of Nietzsche's reversal of the will to the nothing into a willing of the eternal recurrence (p. 56ff.) unfolded in the double interpretation of the parable with regard to the human aspect and to the aspect of the world (p. 82f.). This discord makes the eternal recurrence ambiguous also *as recurrence*: the recurrence means just as much the world's recurrence *of the same* as one's own repetition *of the selfsame*.[T131] The "again and again" of the recurrence has the twofold meaning of a naturally *necessary* "again and again" in the whole of the revolving world, and of a self-overcoming that is again and again *requisite* for man's will to existence (in contrast with the simple necessity that lies in the Being-thus-and-not-different of the physical world) (p. 92f.). The internal connection between the latter "again and again" and the former results from Nietzsche's repetition, on the peak of modernity, of the ancient view of the world; so that for him the teaching of the eternal recurrence of the same signifies no immediate view of the natural world, but the most extreme form of nihilism and its overcoming by means of itself. A self-overcoming that is always repeated anew, changes in a decisive moment (which, as perfect "noon" and as critical "center," is likewise ambiguous, p. 100ff.) by means of a final metamorphosis into a game of the worlds that is always the same. The willing human being is always mixed into the necessity of this game of the worlds. In the anthropological interpretation, the eternally same recurrence appeared as an ethical task, renewing itself in every moment, for the willing man for whom this teaching is to

replace the Christian belief in immortality. In the cosmological interpretation, by contrast, the recurrence appeared not as a "plan for a new
way to live" and a "will to rebirth" but as destruction and rebirth that
happens by nature and that is completely indifferent to all plans made
by man out of his thrownness.[T132] The man who has been freed from
the will to free will and has awakened into the child is not only accidentally thrown into existence once and for all, only to be annihilated,
finally—freely or unfreely—but he has always been there and also will
always recur, in the whole of the revolving time of the world. Consequently, Nietzsche's attempt to overcome nihilism in the existence of
finite man is at the same time an attempt to overcome time, which is
innate to the accident of finite existence, and his philosophic movement on the whole is a movement from the temporally transitory to the
eternally recurring Being. However, Nietzsche wants to "believe" in
the eternal recurrence of the same precisely because it is "absurd" to
make eternal Being emerge out of the temporal nothing and the highest affirmation emerge out of the deepest negation. As the overcomer of
man and of time, which belongs to man, Nietzsche-Zarathustra teaches
the eternal recurrence of the same "beyond man and time."

This doctrine, Nietzsche's *"credo quia absurdum,"* can be made still
clearer if one puts the problematical character of a free will to the eternally necessary recurrence into a pertinent context with the philosophic
willing of two other thinkers of the nineteenth century. Not just arbitrarily do these two men allow of comparison with Nietzsche; rather,
through their common radicalism, they are on a par with him. These
two other "existing" thinkers who likewise went to the extremes are
Søren Kierkegaard and Otto Weininger. They match Nietzsche in the
despairing seriousness with which they thought over (before him and
after him) the question "To be or not to be?" In their way they completed the same movement that he did: from the temporal nothing to
eternal Being. The fundamental meaning that the teaching of the eternal recurrence of the same has for Nietzsche's philosophical experiment corresponds to a religiously oriented experiment of "repetition"
in Kierkegaard and an ethical speculation on the "unidirectionality of
time"[T133] in Weininger.

Weininger[1] saw in Nietzsche a "seeker" who became a priest in *Zarathustra*. "Nietzsche was for a long time a seeker; not until he became
Zarathustra did he put on the priest's robe, and then those speeches
climbed down from the mountain, testifying to how much certainty
he gained through the metamorphosis. The *experiences* of the priest (as

the seer!) are *more intense* than those of the seeker; and therefore he is more sure of himself; he feels himself the chosen apostle of the sun, moon, and stars, and listens only in order to understand their speech as wholly as he feels it his duty to do."[2] However, Nietzsche did not win, in his battle with himself, that "*gaya scienza*" and "*serenità*"[T134] which he "would so much have liked to have achieved after he had come to know the Riviera." That Nietzsche failed in this respect and why he did so are explained by the fact that the will to power denies the "will to value."[3] To be sure, man is for Weininger, too, essentially will and as such a movement between Nonbeing and Being.[4] But in order to be able wholly to will oneself, one must have an *ethical* will to overcome *culpable* existence and thus exactly what Nietzsche's teaching of the innocence of becoming denies. Weininger formulates with a rigorousness reminiscent of Kierkegaard: "Man lives until he enters either the absolute or the nothing. He himself *determines* in *freedom* his future life: he chooses God or the nothing. He destroys himself or creates himself for eternal life. A *double* progress is possible for him: into eternal life . . . and into eternal destruction. He always advances, however, in one of these two directions: there is no third."[5] Here Weininger conceives self-destruction as the slightest of cowardices and as an escape from the destruction of somebody else.[6] "Fear is the obverse of *all* will. Forward, something; backward, nothing. Therefore it is uncanny, in walking along a path, to turn around suddenly and become aware of the stretch that one has covered (the unidirectionality of time). Thus I do believe that fear is kindred to immorality; it is just that the feeling of chaos grows, the more one wants to be cosmos. The nothing is the periphery of the something; and if man becomes everything, if he becomes God, he thus has no more peripheries and no more fear. But shortly before this transition, he probably has to conquer the final, greatest fear."[7] Nietzsche's superhuman will and high-spiritedness[T135] fail to recognize this fear as the obverse of *all* willing. But according to Weininger, even a man's going mad is only possible through his own fault, for "a man *cannot* perish inwardly from anything else but a deficiency of *religion*."[8] And [Nietzsche's] deficiency of religion is also the final reason for Weininger's rejection of Nietzsche's path to the overcoming of nihilism in the existence of modern man. Modern man is "ugly," Weininger once says, because he "hates" himself.

The man who hated himself most, may well have been Nietzsche. His hatred of Wagner and of asceticism, his desire to escape to Bizet and Gottfried Keller, was indeed only a hatred of the Wagnerian and ascetic and the *altogether un-idyllic man* that he himself was. In moral terms, self-hate surely ranks higher than self-love. What was bad was thus Nietzsche's disingenuousness in pre-tending that he had succeeded in that transition (the "convalescence" from Wagner, his "illness")—and this is not the only pose that Nietzsche assumed before all others and before himself. Pascal, who certainly hated himself terri-bly, ranks high above Nietzsche here—he is also, apart from that, never as insipid as Nietzsche can be sometimes. Whereas Pascal was able to express it openly as a principle that *"le moi est haissable,"*[T136] Nietzsche even denied and—he so hated himself—slandered and disparaged his own hatred of him-self—though only as an attribute of Pascal. Only in one passage does Zara-thustra speak candidly about this matter: in the splendid song "Before Sun-rise," which absolutely must be understood as an ethical symbol. . . . It is precisely Nietzsche in whom the hatred of himself originated in the strongest will to affirmation. In him, therefore, this hatred could become both creative and tragic. Creative, for it bid him to seek after what he missed in Schopen-hauer; it forced him to turn away from Schopenhauer, who had not taught him to know Kant. This hatred could also become tragic, for he was not great enough to make his way—independently, on his own power, and in purity—to Kant, whom he had never read. Therefore he never reached *religion*: when he most passionately affirmed life, life disavowed him—that life, that is, which will not let itself be deceived. Nietzsche's ruin is explicable as a result of a defi-ciency of religion. . . . The genius displays this most dreadfully. For the man of genius is the most pious man, and if his *piety* abandons him, then his genius has abandoned him. It was not without a profound reason that for Nietzsche the "unscrupulous man of spirit" became a problem: . . . that is the man "rich in spirit" and he . . . was Nietzsche's danger and abyss, who finally pulled him under. . . . What Nietzsche lacked was *grace*; but without grace the loneliness even of Zarathustra is unbearable. Thus to him logic was no single most pre-cious good but a compulsion from the outside (for he felt himself too weak not to detect danger everywhere); but as for him who denies logic, logic has already abandoned him; he is on the path to lunacy.[9]

That is, Nietzsche's *ethos* lacks the right *logos,* because his philosophy of the eternal recurrence of the same forgets that *man* is not the *world* and is one and the same as *God* only in Jesus Christ.

To Weininger, the true "ethicality" of human life manifests itself pre-eminently in the phenomenon of *recollection,* just as forgetting, con-versely, is an essential precondition of Nietzsche's last metamorphosis.[10] Weininger characterizes as authentic memory—in contrast with mere recollection of what has been learned—the memory of what has been lived through, by virtue of which man can at any time extract "the sum of his life" to the extent that he satisfies his idea. The perfect male char-acter, the universal genius, also has the most perfect memory for him-self and everything else, little or big, that he otherwise has encountered.

Memory, by means of which man can recall his entire existence, gives man the inner continuity that makes responsibility possible and is itself already a moral responsibility. Only because man has a memory can everything he has ever apperceived and experienced become meaningful and remain unforgettable for him; for he thus apperceives it once and for all. The most human man remembers his whole past again in every moment. He does not live transiently and discontinuously like a sexual being that lives merely by nature, without character, from moment to moment.[11]

Thankfulness and piety, too, vis-à-vis one's own past, depend on this reminiscence of one's own life, a life that does not forget what promoted and rescued it. Only through this very continuity of temporal existence, which is a self-remembering existence, does man become truly certain of his existence and understand what it means at all, "that he is there, that he is in the world." And because his previous life is always present to him, everything that is still possible in the future, too, becomes meaningful for him from the outset; and really only he has a destiny in which the meaning of temporal existence on the whole is embraced. "The remanent magnetism that the experiences of a man have in him, is proportional to the significance that they are able to gain for him." One therefore recognizes the character of a man primarily in what he never forgets and what he cannot retain.

This memory that belongs to man's essence makes experiences timeless by preserving them in recollection. In its very conception, memory is an "overcoming of time," although it redeems from what has passed away in an entirely different way than Nietzsche's remorseless "I wanted it thus" liberates from what already has been. Memory is both the condition of and the liberation from the temporality of time. In memory man transcends time although he is in time.[12] For he is not simply "plugged in" to the course of time; instead, by recalling what has happened and making history of himself, he is always withdrawn from the course of events and will be so forever. Memory, as such a detemporalization of always transitory time, is also the precondition for the characteristic human longing for *immortality*, for the overcoming of death as the time that determines existence.

The relationship one has to one's own past, as it is expressed in piety and depends on continuous memory, . . . can be presented in still further contexts, and at the same time be analyzed more deeply. *That is, whether or not a man has a relationship to his past at all is extraordinarily bound up with whether he feels a need for immortality or whether the idea of death would leave him indifferent.*[13]

The complete loss of meaning that the individually fulfilled, fully lived life suffers, if it should come to a complete end forever at death, the *meaninglessness of the whole* in such a case (Goethe, too, expresses this, in other words, to Eckermann [4 February 1829]) leads to the demand for immortality. The genius has the most intense longing for immortality. And this longing, too, converges with all other facts about his nature which were previously disclosed. *Memory is a complete victory over time only if, as in the universal man, it appears in the universal form. The genius is therefore the really timeless man*; at least this and nothing else is his ideal of himself. He is, as just his burning and compelling desire for immortality proves, plainly the man with the strongest longing for timelessness, *with the mightiest will to value.*—One is often astounded at how men of an altogether ordinary, even vulgar nature experience no fear of death. But it thus becomes clear: *it is not the fear of death that produces the need for immortality, but the need for immortality that produces the fear of death.*[14]

But not only the questions of concrete existence that matter to us immediately, but also the problems of formal logic are strongly illuminated by the fundamental significance of memory.

For, the principle of contradiction and the principle of identity are only possible on the basis of a record of the premises to be held identical or not identical. But *he who* records both by comparing them and by separating them is the transcending timeless ego of the autonomous man who is responsible to himself.

Hence *Sex and Character* has its final significance not in a psychology of the sexes but in a psychological penetration of Kant's teaching on the intelligible character. And thus follows, at one with the reference to Kant as the "moral-heroic" philosopher, Weininger's rejection of Nietzsche, too. Nietzsche's Zarathustra sublates the principle "You can, because you want to" into the wholly different principle "I want what I must," so that freedom completes itself only in the love of fate and becomes one with the highest necessity. In opposition to Nietzsche's "how one becomes what one is," Weininger defines the self-becoming of man imperatively as "Be!" But because man in temporal existence never perfectly becomes what he should be according to his own idea, and because he breaks through time only for passing moments, time itself is "immoral."

There is an act, however, that so to speak absorbs the future in itself; that already perceives in advance all *future* relapses into immorality as guilt, no less than every immoral past; and that *thereby grows beyond both*: a timeless positing of the character, the rebirth.[15]

The meaning of this rebirth that first establishes a character[16] does not lie beyond good and evil, but in the necessity for man in temporal existence to take up "again and again" the battle against evil (which is the nothing in existence).

What always will *also* lead to determinism is the fact that the struggle will be forced upon us again and again. In individual cases, the decision may result wholly ethically, man may decide for the good; however, the decision is not lasting, but man must again struggle. Freedom, one could say, exists only for the *moment*. And that belongs to the concept of freedom. For, what kind of freedom would it be that I might have produced and caused for all time by means of one good action in any earlier time[?] . . . It is precisely man's pride that in every moment he can be free anew.[17]

Man could truly overcome time, however, only if (with the "strongest will") he could invest into the moment "all universality of his self" and of the world (which he, as a microcosm, already is). Then the difference between what man *is* and what he *should* be, would be nullified; then man himself would have become divine and not just be alone in proud loneliness on the revolving earth, where he can freely survey the world. Such an autonomy of self-reliance, in Weininger's view, found its classical expression in the "Conclusion" of the *Critique of Practical Reason*. This closeness of man in the whole of the extrahuman world means that man is a one and all.

And therefore he also has a *law* within himself; therefore he is himself all law and no gushing arbitrariness. And he demands of *himself* that he follow this law within himself, this law of his self, that he be *only* law, without looking back behind himself, without looking forward ahead of himself. That is the gruesome greatness: it makes *no further sense* for him to obey the call of duty. Nothing is *super*ordinate to him, the alone, *all-and-one* being.[T137] But he must comply with the relentless, nonnegotiable *categorical* demand *in himself*. "*Redemption!*" he cries, "Peace, just give me peace before the enemy, peace, not this endless wrestling"—and he *frightens*: even in the desire to be redeemed there was cowardice still; in the yearning "*Already!*" there was still desertion, as if he were too small for this battle. "*Why?*" he asks, he screams into the universe—and *blushes*; for he just wanted *happiness* again, the recognition of battle, the other man who would reward him. *Kant's* loneliest man does not laugh and does not dance, he does not howl and does not rejoice; he does not need to make noise because outer space is too profoundly silent. The meaninglessness of a world "of chance" is not duty for him, but *his* duty is for him *the meaning of the universe*. To say yes to *this* loneliness, that is the "Dionysian" element in *Kant*; only that is morality.[18]

The will to the free will pridefully disdains the last metamorphosis of Zarathustra. On the basis of this position that Kant made possible, the cycle of Being and of time—that is, eternal recurrence of the same—

signifies for Weininger the nonmoral and meaningless movement par excellence that denies the true Being of man.

While the earth on which we live, constantly revolves and revolves, man remains untouched by the cosmic dance. His spirit is not bound up mechanically with the whole system; he gazes out freely and gives to the spectacle, or takes from it, its value.[19]

With these remarks, corresponding to the conclusion of the seventh chapter of *Sex and Character*, Weininger concludes his later essay on the "Unidirectionality of Time."

Weininger challenges the perfection of the circle because it is incapable of and does not need any further perfecting. He consequently begins his discussion in the essay by doubting the classical exemplariness of the circular movement, closed in itself.

One has generally accorded an especially high dignity to the *circle* as the most perfect, symmetrical, even form. For millennia the view persisted that the only form of movement worthy of elevated things is the circle, and it is well known that this view still hindered Copernicus from considering the movement of the planets around the sun as anything else but circular. That the planets must move in a circular motion was, to him just as to all his predecessors, an axiom about which no doubt even arose in him. The elevation of the most perfect, imperturbable homogeneity . . . obviously lies at the bottom of this demand. When Kepler's laws gained recognition, one tried to refute the earlier, childish view by smiling at it. Elliptical movement does not, it is true, entirely share the solemnity of law with circular movement; but the dignity of calculability is inherent in the ellipse in the same way that "perfection," the attribute to be made the object of criticism in the present discussion, is inherent in the circle.[20]

There follows a critique of the retrogradeness of circular movement. This critique implicitly presupposes the Christian break with the ancient world, a break that for Weininger is expressed in the moral distinction between *man*, who exists morally, and the *world*, which is there by nature and only symbolically significant. His critique of circular motion takes for granted that the meaning of human existence does not at all emerge in view of the visible world; rather, the "intelligible" meaning of the world emerges, inversely, from the "ethicality" of human life, which is not temporally reversible, but moves unambiguously and unidirectionally, from birth onward, toward death.

The unidirectionality of time is identical with the fact of nonreversibility of *life*, and the riddle of time is identical with the riddle of *life* (although not with the riddle of the world). *Life is not reversible*; there is no way back from death to birth. *The problem of the unidirectionality of time is the question of the meaning of life.*—In the unidirectionality of time lies the reason for the fact that our need for immortality embraces only the future (not backward, the life before our birth). Thus we take little interest in our condition before birth, but very much indeed in our condition after death.[21]

"The ego as will is time," and time is aimed unidirectionally, because the will cannot will backward, so that for the will the past never recurs. Only in wanting to rise to something that has never yet existed and does not yet exist, does the time that for any given moment is still future, bring itself about.

If unidirectional time were not the same as the will, the will could indeed will backward and change the past. (According to Nietzsche's remark, "But what is the will's greatest pain? That it cannot command over the past.") The will would have to be nonwill and the principle of identity would be negated if the will *willed* to change the past or *could* do so;[22] for it is precisely in the will's being will that the gap between past and future (and their eternal differences) is expressed. The will is something aimed, and its direction is the meaning of time. The ego realizes itself as will, i.e., it experiences and unfolds itself in the form of time: time is the form of inner intuition, as Kant taught.—Every will wants the past as *past*; and only the criminal (who no longer wants to look for God, but sinks down) lies, i.e., *murders* the past; *the reversal of time is the radical evil, and fear of this reversal is fear of evil.*[23]

Time—in which above all we live as beings that will—is time aimed at the future, is time of fear and hope. Both types of comportment are related to the irreversibility of unidirectional time, which is established in willing. Thus the final cause of time is man, to the extent that he exists morally as a being who wills the future and longs for immortality. Time is an expression of the ethicality of human life, which wants to overcome time in view of death. By contrast it is unethical not to want to acknowledge the past (in which, after all, all "reasons" and "obligations" are situated) as what it was, i.e., settled, and to want to change and re-create the historical deed that has already happened.

Every *lie* is a *falsification of history*. At first one falsifies one's own history, then that of others. "It is unethical *not* to want to change the *future*, not to want it different, better than the present, i.e., *not* to want *to create*; Will!" Thus the categorical imperative could be formulated. The phenomenon of *repentance* combines both (it is the real expression of the unidirectionality of time): it *affirms* the past guilt, but as *past,* and *denies* it as *future,* i.e., it opposes to guilt the will to improvement in the future.—The future is not yet true, the past is true. The lie is *power-will* over the *past.* The lie can bestow no freedom or existence upon the past, because the present is equally unfree and equally dead. In the present, past and future touch; the present is what man *can* do; he has no *more* power over the past, and he does not *yet* have any over the future. When eternity and present have become one, man has become God, and God is *almighty.*—Thus the lie is unethical, is the *reversal* of time: since the will to alter, here, concerns the past instead of the future. All evil is the abolition of the meaning of time: it forgoes giving life a meaning and despairs about the need to do so.—The will of man creates the future: in making decisions man *anticipates* time, and he takes time *back* in repenting. In man's *will*, which is always a will to eternity, *time is simultaneously posited* and *denied.*[24]

Boredom, by contrast, is an extremely immoral phenomenon, because in boredom the unidirectionality of time appears to have been canceled, and time itself appears to exist outside of ourselves.[25] "Boredom and impatience are the most immoral sentiments there can be. For in them man posits time as *real*; he wants time to elapse without *his* filling it up, without its being a mere phenomenal *form* of his inner liberation and broadening."

If man were nonethical, like revolving motion, he would not be able to see something different in tomorrow than in today, to distinguish the new year from the old, to feel himself depreciated and to feel fear when he finds himself at an earlier point again, like Robinson or like a figure of Tolstoy (in . . . *Master and Servant*). As much as it may provoke smiles when on New Year's Eve the philistine turns from his newspaper and begins to reflect on time,[T138] there is in his reflections nevertheless a certain cosmic feeling . . . for past and transitoriness, to which a promising future is opposed.[26]

But even an eternal recurrence of the same can be recognized and evaluated only on the presupposition of an ego that remembers and evaluates it, and thus of the view of the unidirectionality of time that is the condition of all unambiguousness and truth. If man were conceivable as a periodically recurring existence of the same, he would, like Nietzsche's superman, be beyond man and time, and his will would be a superhuman sun's will that would have flown into the heaven of eternity that always remains the selfsame. But as long as man still wills at all—and that means, wills the future—he cannot will himself to become a periodic being. But time, which is posited by the will, is also not conceivable as a straight line. For on a straight line one can go to and fro, forward and backward at will, whereas the unidirectionality of time consists precisely in the fact that its direction is determined *unambiguously.* Therefore there exists, in the morally assiduous man, a natural resistance to all forms of motion that lead back to the point of departure, to all retrograde and revolving forms of motion. The riddle of the unidirectionality of time, which "is the most profound problem in the universe," can only be solved strictly dualistically and thus not universally. And he who, with Kant, recognizes the meaning and task of human existence in moral progress (which is accomplished in the struggle against merely natural impulses)—he no longer can find, even in admiration of the planetary orbits, any support for the moral existence of man, but sees therein only something completely *foreign* to morality.

In the planets, too, we do not find . . . the dignified support of our existence as moral beings. Yet our moral existence still gains in elevation if it is separated from all individual things of visible nature. If the solar system were conceived particularly in ethical terms, the course of a planet would never be permitted to run back into itself. The moon, too, revolves around the earth in the same movement as that by which the earth revolves around the sun. And in the moon there is surely nothing that is in any way ethical. And Saturn, to which, of all the planets, man surely has the closest relationship, appears (with its rings and moons) as almost the summation of evil.—Perhaps there are heavenly bodies that execute no retrograde movements, on which *astronomy* will founder. But on no account (even in case of the full justification of the types of orbit that run back into themselves) will the starry heaven that Kant put next to the moral law, now have to lose all its majesty in favor of the moral law. One should simply seek no more in the starry heaven than it actually represents to us psychologically: it is the symbol of the *infinity* of the universe—to which we feel ourselves worthy only in the moral law and which alone is worthy of the moral law—and of its painless bliss of light.[27]

Nietzsche, by contrast, considered this bliss not to be guaranteed by the world's being "infinite" (like a moral task) but by the fact that the world is determined like a circle, without beginning or end, that remains the same to itself. This self-sufficient form of circular movement appeared to Weininger's ethical will "laughable or eerie." Considered in moral terms, the circular movement is still worse than the retrograde steps of a crab, the gait of which is, after all, at least not estranged of meaning, but only not positively meaningful and purposeful. Weininger gives the following examples for his thesis:

To go around in circles against one's will, like Robinson, is senseless. To have already experienced a new situation in exactly the same way is eerie. To turn around in circles while dancing the Viennese waltz is an expression of fatalistic indifference. A merry-go-round is oppressive for the adult. It is indecent to say the same thing twice in a row, to repeat oneself. The intention to say this or that in a future moment already prevents the freedom—which should be generated *anew* in every moment—of willing with presence of mind. The magic circle enchains man and robs him of his power to decide. The marriage ring binds and takes from a couple their metaphysical freedom and loneliness. The ring of the Nibelung is the mark of radical evil, of the will to power. And the ring of the magician, turned once around his finger, conveys this power to evil. No *ens metaphysicum*[T139] *wants* revolving motion. What man as such wants is an immortality in freedom, but not an eternal vitality that is a process of the world. In contrast, a genuine metaphysical motif underlies the idea of the "wanderer" (and already the ordinary desire to travel), a motif that does honor to the unidirectionality of time of the willful man.

The supposition of the eternal recurrence of the same, as Oriental and Greek teachings knew it and as Nietzsche again proclaimed it, is thus "everything but a satisfaction of the need for immortality"; it is *only* terrible, but not *also* elevating. What can actually recur in the existence of the man who wills himself is nothing that remains the same by nature but rather the double of his self. The eeriness of this double shows that man is originally at home in the uniqueness of his moral existence and that man wants to rise above himself. The double is eerie because he denies the Once and Never Again of the temporal existence of the individual.[28] The true recurrence is accordingly neither a natural nor a ghostly recurrence of the same, but the again and again self-renewing will to one's own rebirth. Without this rebirth man would age prematurely inwardly, whereas he remains eternally young by means of it—like nature, which however is eternally young because it remains eternally the same, and cannot at all be different from what is always and necessarily is by nature.[29]

In contrast with Weininger's ethical speculation on the unidirectionality of time, Kierkegaard did not simply rule out the possibility of a kind of recurrence as unethical. Rather, he discovered by psychological experiment the possibility of one's own, authentic repetition of the *selfsame* on the very basis of the impossibility of a recurrence of the *same*. It was on this category of "repetition," peculiar to him, that Kierkegaard based his attempt, struggling against official Christendom, to retrieve original Christianity into existence after a history of two thousand years of decay. He attempted to repeat Christianity—which had become alienated from modern, advanced man—by means of recollective practice and appropriation.

Kierkegaard[30] develops his category in his depiction of the love of a young man (whose "secret confidant" Kierkegaard is) by making this love pass through the three stages of aesthetic immediacy, ethical reflection, and religious paradox. Only at the end of the treatise does it become clear what Kierkegaard ultimately intended with the repetition right from the beginning, namely a rebirth—meant in the Christian sense—by means of which man (who has been lost to the world, like Job before God) regains himself.

I am myself again, I again possess this "self," which another man would not wish to pick up from the highway. The fissure that was in my being has been pulled tight; I close myself together again. The anxieties of sympathy that were supported and nourished by my pride no longer crowd in, only to cleave and separate.

Is there not, then, repetition here? Did I not receive everything in duplicate? Did I not receive myself again in exactly such a way that I had to feel the meaning thereof doubled? And what is a recovery of an earthly good that is irrelevant for the destiny of the spirit, in comparison with such a repetition? Only the children did Job not get in duplicate, because a man cannot be doubled in such a way. Here only a repetition of the spirit is possible, even if this will never be as perfect in temporal existence as in eternity, which is the true repetition.[31]

To receive oneself again in order to be able wholly to will oneself, however, is also the tendency of Weininger's ethical will that says: "If man had not lost himself at birth, he would not have to seek himself and find himself again." But in temporal existence man is again and again compelled to complete, in fear and hope, the movement from temporal Nonbeing to eternal Being. For both, this proposition holds: man chooses either God or the nothing if original sin is the decisive fact in man's existence.

Kierkegaard's repetition is a retrieval of oneself out of the world's spell. It essentially completes itself in recollection, which is at the same time an inward growth. In Kierkegaard this recollection serves a function analogous to that of memory in Weininger. Repetition, as the recalling of oneself again,[T140] is the opposite of the self-forgetting of the man who rises unbroken in the natural world; as if he himself, being in the world, were also *of* the world. Kierkegaard not only understands himself as a "microcosm" in relation to the great world, but he especially satisfies his fancy by "behaving as macrocosmically as possible" in his "so microcosmic existence" and by "thus having the whole world in a nutshell that is greater than the whole world, and yet no greater than the individual can fill up."[32] In truth, however, his confidant exists neither microcosmically nor macrocosmically, but in an "unspeakable fear of the world," because his dull, meaningless existence nauseates him.

One sticks one's finger into the earth in order to smell what kind of country one is in. I stick my finger into existence—it smells like nothing whatever.

Where am I? What is that supposed to mean: world? What does this word sig-nify? Who has allured me into the whole and abandons me there now? Who am I? How did I come into the world? Why was I not asked, why was I not made familiar with mores and customs, but set in a row as if I had been pur-chased by a salesman of souls? How did I become an interested party in the big enterprise that they call reality? Why should I be an interested party? Is that not a matter of free choice? And if I am compelled to be that, where is the conductor to whom I could make a comment? Is there no conductor?[33]

This conductor, who finally reconciles him again with being-there[T141] as such, is God. In view of God, the religious movement of repetition, too, takes a unidirectional orientation in the form of a return to the original ground of Being of creaturely existence. What is peculiar to this retrograde repetition is neither a *revolving* that runs back into it-self nor a *mere recollection,* but the fact that it is the true *movement for-ward.* The paradox of the religious repetition, in express contrast with the ancient recollection, is that it does not *re*call something that has al-ready existed; instead, in genuine repetition one "recollects forward." Therefore, Kierkegaard introduces his category by opposing it to the Greek *anamnēsis*[T142] on the one hand and to Hegel's mediation on the other. Hegel's dialectical ontology has the Christian existential move-ment from Nonbeing to Being happen only as a mental "transition" in Greek concepts, but does not consummate it existentially in the leap from desperation into faith.

Kierkegaard's discussion takes its point of departure in nothing less than a brief presentation of the beginning and end of Western philos-ophy as a whole, in order to determine the historical locus of the repe-tition. This fact shows what significance repetition has as a matter of principle within Kierkegaard's own task.

When the Eleatics denied movement, Diogenes appeared, as everyone knows, as their opponent. He really [just] made his appearance,[T143] for he said not a word, but only walked back and forth several times, whereby he believed he had refuted them. When I had devoted myself for a long time (at least occa-sionally) to the problem of whether a repetition is possible and what meaning it might have, whether something gains or loses thereby, it suddenly occurred to me: you can travel to Berlin, where you have been once before, and convince yourself whether a repetition is possible and what it means. At home in my apartment, I would almost have come to a halt over this problem. One may say what one will about this matter; it will surely get a very important role in more modern philosophy, for *repetition* is a decisive expression for what "recol-lection" was among the Greeks. As they taught that all knowing is a remem-bering, modern philosophy will teach that all of life is a repetition. The only modern philosopher who has had an inkling of this is Leibniz. Repetition and recollection is the same movement, but in opposite directions, for what one remembers, has been and is backwardly repeated; in contrast, in the case of genuine repetition, one remembers forward. Accordingly, if it is possible, repetition makes a man happy, whereas recollection makes him unhappy, assuming, that is, that he allows himself time for life and does not immediately seek, in the hour of his birth, an excuse to steal out of life again, for example because he has forgotten something.[34]

As opposed to forgetting, repetition serves recollection of the meaning of existence, in order to opt into existence. Repetition is clothing that cannot be worn out, clothing that fits the body firmly and softly. Courage is required to choose and to desire this movement that is adjusted to inner existence; and when one has circumnavigated existence, it will become evident whether one has enough courage to grasp that the whole of life is basically a repetition, a retrieval and fetching back of the lost self. Repetition is the ethical reality and the seriousness of existence. According to Nietzsche's teaching, the seriousness of existence conversely begins with the innocent game of "eternal self-creation, of eternal self-destruction."[35] Nietzsche's doctrine expresses the most extreme convergence of the world of becoming and the world of Being, because by means of the eternal recurrence of the same, Eleatic Being is transferred into Heraclitean becoming. And unlike Nietzsche's doctrine, in Kierkegaard's writings it is said:

If one is somewhat familiar with modern philosophy and not entirely ignorant of Greek thought, one will easily see that precisely this category makes clear the relationship of the Eleatics to Heraclitus, and that repetition is really what one erroneously called "mediation." . . . The Greek development of the doctrine of Being and of nothing, the development of the "moment," of "what is not," and so forth, says to Hegel: "Save your breath!" "Mediation" is a foreign word; "*Gjentagelse*" (repetition) is a good Danish word, and I congratulate the Danish language for a philosophic term. In our time it is not explained how mediation comes about, whether it results from the movement of the two moments and in what sense it is already contained in these in advance, or whether it is something new that supervenes and then—what? In this regard the Greek reflection on the concept of *kinesis*, which corresponds to the modern category "transition,"[T144] is eminently noteworthy. The dialectic or repetition is easy. For what is[T145] repeated, has been; otherwise, it could not be repeated; but precisely the fact that it has been, makes the repetition into something new. When the Greeks said every recognition is a recollection, they said: the whole existence that is there, has been there. When one says that life is a repetition, one says: the existence that has been there, comes into being now. If one does not have the category of recollection or repetition, life altogether disintegrates into an empty, contentless noise. Recollection is the ethnic view of life; repetition, the modern view. Repetition is the *interest* of metaphysics and at the same time the interest on which metaphysics founders. Repetition is the motto in every ethical view. Repetition is the *condicio sine qua non* for every dogmatical problem.[36]

Hegel's philosophy only appears to join this movement that is required for the seriousness of existence. In reality his philosophy only makes a lot of "fuss"[T146] over movement, and insofar as it realizes a movement, this occurs in immanence. But repetition is and remains aimed at transcendence, by means of which man not only circumnavigates his existence but also rises above himself.[37]

Repetition is therefore neither a naturally necessary recurrence nor a merely moral rebirth, but a movement to be chosen religiously, a movement that man cannot accomplish out of his own moral strength. For man does not have in himself the "Archimedean point" from which the world can be overcome. Likewise, repetition[T147] differs from every objective as well as every subjective replication,[T148] from every recurrence or even repetition of the *same* whereby nothing new emerges, because a replication *only* repeats[T149] what has already existed but does not renew it in repeating it.[T150] Existential repetition is, in contrast with the ancient category of *anamnesis,* a "new" category that becomes necessary after the completion of classical philosophy in Hegel's system of mediation. Existential repetition leaves behind both the ethnic view of life of antiquity that Nietzsche repeats and the ethical-idealistic view of life of Christian modernity that Weininger repeats; and because existential repetition is generally concerned with the ownmost Being and Nonbeing, it leaves speculative ontology stranded on the "interest" of metaphysics. The model for existential repetition is neither Heraclitus nor Kant, but Job, from whom everything was taken to which man can usually cling, and who precisely thereby got everything back from God in double measure.

Kierkegaard attains this possibility of a repetition in which precisely nothing recurs, by testing whether anything so allows of repetition that a "same" recurs therewith. He had already been in Berlin once and now repeats this journey in order to put to the test what meaning repetition can have. In the course of this repetition he recalls how this and that was and looked the first time; but precisely as a *result* of his recollection, he must discover that nothing repeats itself, but everything has become different from what it was. The landlord and the apartment, the theater and the whole mood in which he entered the city the first time, everything has become different with time; so that even what little has remained the same as far as objects are concerned, also no longer fits in, in the new situation, with the retuned environment, and thereby is likewise different than it was before. Insofar as there is a repetition in detail, it is a "topsy-turvy"[T151] repetition, because the whole that sets the direction for all particulars has not remained the same. It is precisely recollection back on what has been, that teaches Kierkegaard the impossibility of a recurrence of the same. But it not only makes a recurrence of the same impossible, it also prevents the possibility of a genuine repetition of the selfsame, the possibility of a recollection forward by means of which what has already been could become new.

When this had repeated itself for several days, I became so embittered, so weary of the repetition, that I resolved to travel home again. My discovery was not significant, and yet it was peculiar, for I had discovered that there is not repetition at all, and I had convinced myself of this by repeating this in all possible ways.[38]

At home, too, he again finds everything different from what he had expected and counted on. Life seems to recapture for itself, in the irresistible progress of time, everything that it has once given us—without ever making a repetition. Happy is the small child that has not yet chosen itself and therefore has also not yet lost itself, the child that in its naive self-concern lets the adults see to it that nothing shall happen to it, the child that stays the same even in the greatest mortal danger and continues unchanged to play with itself.[39] But Kierkegaard does not draw from this observation Nietzsche's conclusion of a willed return to a new beginning with the innocence of childhood existence. Rather, for Kierkegaard this childhood existence is only a premature image of the true, Christian concern in which man knows himself to be in the hand of God and leaves the whole of world history to Providence.

And yet Kierkegaard, too, has experienced these short moments of the best happiness in which Nietzsche's teaching of "noon and eternity" culminates. For what is it other than a Dionysian "noon," when Kierkegaard portrays the "dizzying maximum" of transient well-being?

I was once on the verge of it [the maximum]. I got up one morning and felt unusually good. In the course of the morning, this well-being increased, contrary to every analogous instance. At one o'clock on the dot, I was on the peak and had a presentiment of the dizzying maximum, which one finds recorded on no measure of well-being, not even on a poetic thermometer. My body had lost its earthly weight; I felt as though I had no body, precisely because every function enjoyed its full satisfaction, every nerve rejoiced on account of itself and the whole; while every pulsebeat recalled, like the restlessness of the organism, the voluptuousness of the moment and announced it. My gait glided lightly, not like the flight of a bird that cuts through the air and abandons the earth, but like the surging of the wind over the crops, like the blessedly yearning cradle of the sea, like the dreamy gliding of the cloud. My essence was transparency like the deep brooding of the sea, like the self-satisfied muteness of the night, like the soliloquizing silence of the noon. Every mood rested in my soul with a melodic resonance. Every idea came to mind, and did so with the ceremoniousness of bliss, the most foolish fancy no less than the richest idea. Every impression was anticipated before it came, and therefore awakened in myself. It was as though the whole of existence was in love with me and everything trembled in destiny-laden relation to my Being. Everything was ominous in me and everything was puzzlingly radiant in my microscopic bliss, which transfigured everything in itself, even what is disagreeable, the most boring remark, the moment of the loathsome, the most fatal collision.—As I said, at one o'clock on the dot I was on the peak, where I had a presentiment of the very highest peaks.[40]

But man cannot maintain himself on this peak of existence permanently; such a "nothing" as a particle of dust in his eye hurls him just as quickly from the peak of bliss down into the abyss of desperation again. An absolute satisfaction seems to be altogether unattainable. And therefore Kierkegaard—as "Constantius," who wants to sustain the eternally constant in "God's unchangeability"—abandons once and for all the hope of being absolutely satisfied with himself and the world even for just a passing moment. Disappointed by the untenability of such a "bliss against one's will," he performs a resolute renunciation, and he becomes enthusiastic about the idea of repetition, the daily bread of human existence. The "true humanity" of human existence for Kierkegaard is Christian humanity, and the measure of human existence is the eternity of God.

# 8

## The Critical Yardstick for Nietzsche's Experiment

Nietzsche fancied himself to have affirmed the accident of his own existence through his teaching of "*this*" world (the highest star of which is necessity) and to have found the answer to his question, "Do you now know what *the world* is to me? And what *I* will, when I will *this* world?" Nietzsche's will to *this* world is negatively conditioned by his critical aversion to the meta-physical "backworld" of Christian Platonism; and positively, by the longing for that "ancient" world as it was before the incursion of Christianity, that "greatest misfortune" of the world.[1] But did Nietzsche really succeed in making himself at home in this world, short of that "backworld," in the innocence of the new beginning of a Greek child of the world? "Or" did the "new Columbus" deceive himself, in his circumnavigation of the spiritual world, regarding his direction? and did he finally get back—only from the other side—to the place from which his will was supposed to lead him away? Is his world thus once again that "backworld" on which he has turned his back, that "backworld" which is a "heavenly nothing" and "colorful smoke before the eyes of a divine unsatisfied man"? Did not Zarathustra, too, with his "plan for a new way to live," cast his delusion "beyond man, like all the backworldly,"[T152] his "vision" coming to him, just like that "ghost," not from The Beyond but out of "his own ashes and fire"?

In the chapter "On the Backworldly," Zarathustra himself explains what happened when his nausea gave him wings and powers to divine the sources of things. For the way in which Nietzsche redeems himself from the will to nothing is just as absurd as the reverse self-redemption from the will to life in Schopenhauer's metaphysics, to which the talk of the "backworldly" alludes. What corresponds to man's redemption from the *cosmic necessity* to will in a blissful nothing is, in Nietzsche's case, redemption from the human *capacity* to will, in a "bliss against one's will"; and the superman, out of whom Nietzsche teaches the doctrine of the recurrence, is an "ecstatic nihilist."[2] What is said of the "backworldly" as an explanation of "what happened" applies to Zarathustra himself.

I overcame myself, the sufferer; I carried my own ashes to the mountain, I invented a brighter flame for myself. . . .

It was suffering and incapacity that created all backworlds—this and that brief madness of bliss which only the sufferer experiences.

Weariness that wants to reach the ultimate with one leap, with one fatal leap, a poor, ignorant weariness that does not even want to will anymore: this created all gods and "backworlds."

. . . It was the body that despaired of the body—it touched the ultimate walls with the fingers of a deluded spirit. . . . It was the body that despaired of the earth—it heard the belly of Being speak to it.

It wanted to crash through these ultimate walls with its head . . . —over there to "that world."

But "that world" is well concealed from man—that . . . inhuman world which is a heavenly nothing; and the belly of Being does not speak to man at all, except as man.

Verily, all Being is hard to prove and hard to induce to speak. Tell me, my brothers, is not the strangest of all things still what is best proved?

Indeed, this ego and the ego's contradiction and confusion still speak most honestly of its Being—this creating, willing, valuing ego, which is the measure and value of things,

if, that is, "*middle and measure*" are lost in man's relationship to the world and man is as if thrown into a world that no longer befriends him. At the gateway of a decisive moment, Nietzsche's will decided for the self-willing of the world and against indignation at accidental existence. In superhuman fashion, Nietzsche's will sets itself into harmony with the world. But because Nietzsche was no superman, the redemption occurred just as he himself said: "In man everything superhuman makes its appearance as illness and insanity."[3] Therefore he can rightly say of himself that it was "his destiny" to teach the eternal recurrence, this "superhuman view of the world."

Nietzsche, who himself wore the prosaic garb of a middle-class man of the nineteenth century, reports to us that Empedocles went about in a purple robe with a golden belt, in shoes of ore, and with a Delphic

crown on his head. Surrounded by his people, he went mad and announced, before disappearing into a crater, the truth of the rebirth; a
friend died with him.[4] The difference between this mythical death of a
philosopher and Nietzsche's own end in insanity (out of which a man
by the name of Langbehn attempted, as a "friend," to revive him into
mental life[5]) is as great as that between Aeschylus and Wagner. Instead
of disappearing into the center of Aetna, Nietzsche was enclosed by the
protective walls of a sickroom. For ten years he lived on naturally, "like
a black, half-destroyed fortress sitting alone on its mountain, reflective
and silent enough—so that even the birds are afraid of this silence,"[6]
as a painting by Stoeving shows Nietzsche. "On Fort Gonzaga outside
of Messina. Condition of the deepest reflection. Everything done in order to set myself far away; no longer bound by either love or hate. As
on an old fortress. Signs of wars; also of earthquakes. Forgetting."[7]

Nietzsche had gone to this extreme, and the proposition applies
to him that "the spell that fights on our behalf is *the magic of the extreme,* the seduction that everything extreme exercises."[8] A boundless
accumulation of superlatives and "*über-*" ("over-," "super-") words in
the speeches of *Zarathustra* accords with this observation about extremes—*Übermensch, Überart, Überheld, Übermut, Über-Drache, Über-
Selige, Über-Mitleidige, Über-Güte, Über-Reichtum, Über-Zeit*[T153]—which
all together point to the primary term "*Überwindung*" (overcoming),
and characterize Nietzsche's radicalism as extremism. But extreme positions are not "radical" in the literal sense, but rather rootless. Only
complete rootlessness could make Nietzsche believe that extreme positions are in turn "superseded" only by extreme, but contrary, positions. Between the extreme of nihilism and the opposite extreme of the
eternal recurrence, as well as between the superman and the last man,
all medium concepts (which according to Schelling's understanding are
the only ones that really clarify and explain[9]) are lacking in Nietzsche's
teaching. Nietzsche's will to affirm *unconditionally* his own existence
in the whole of what is and even to become a periodically recurring
being himself, also belongs to the extreme positions. This demand for
eternalization, however, mismeasures the dimensions of mortal man.

But as a friend of the Greeks, Nietzsche also knew that in the long
run it is not those who overdo to the extreme who prove themselves
the strongest, but "the most moderate" who, because they are sure of
their power, have no "*need*" for extreme tenets of faith[10]—and so it is,
too, with regard to the possible overcoming of man.

*To find measure and center in the stiving beyond humanity:* the *highest and most vigorous type of man* must *be found! Depict* the highest tendency constantly in the *small:* perfection, maturity, . . . health, a mild radiation of power. Work like an artist on the daily work, in every work bring us to perfection.[11]

Measure and center, however, are exactly what Nietzsche's attempt to overcome man thoroughly lacks. Strindberg sent him the Horatian warning too late:

> Rectius vives, Licini, neque altum
> Semper urgendo, neque dum procellos
> Cantus horrescis, nimium premendo
> Litus iniquum.[T154]

> Interdum iuvat insanire! Vale et Fave![T155]

Only as an empty chasm between man's existence, which has become goalless, and a world that has become natureless, is there a center; and only the will has, by sheer force, spanned this chasm and therefore always named the world "its own." "There are many paths and ways of self-overcoming: see to that yourself! But only a jester thinks, 'Man can also be *jumped over'* "[12] instead of being overcome step by step "without haste." In this latter the Greeks are admirable.[13] According to Nietzsche's understanding, they alone were real, well-bred men of manly moderation, such as Zarathustra's superman wants to be.[14] Whereas the ancient man held to center and measure[15] because he was violent by nature, modern man is overstrained to the extreme—in order not to be mediocre.

Nietzsche foresaw as the danger of the age that "world government" could fall into the hands of the mediocre, because in a *"mesquin"*[T156] age the mediocre are the surviving men of the future.

In such an extreme movement regarding tempo and means as our civilization represents, men's gravity shifts: the gravity of *those* men who matter most, who have, as it were, the task of compensating for the whole vast danger of such a morbid movement;—they will become procrastinators par excellence, slow to adapt, reluctant to let go, and relatively enduring in the midst of this tremendous change and mixture of elements. In such circumstances, gravity necessarily shifts to the *mediocre:* against the dominion of the mob and of the eccentric (both usually allied), *mediocrity* consolidates itself as the guarantee and bearer of the future. Thus emerges a new opponent for *exceptional men*—or alternatively a new seduction. Provided they do not accommodate themselves to the mob and sing songs to please the instincts of the "disinherited," they will need to be "mediocre" and "solid." They know: *mediocritas* is also *aurea.*[T157] . . .

And once more . . . the entire *worn-out* world of the ideal gains a body of gifted advocates. . . . Result: mediocrity acquires spirit, wit, genius—it becomes entertaining, it seduces.[16]

But there is an opposite seduction, and Nietzsche did not, in his detachment, escape it; although he himself jotted down that "hatred of mediocrity" is unworthy of a philosopher and is "almost a question mark on his right to philosophy."[17] It belongs to philosophy to recognize the justification of mediocrity as the "*first* necessity in order that there may be exceptions."

Mediocrity itself is legitimate not only in its relationship to him who is exceptional but also independently thereof, that is, in itself. It indicates, albeit in a mediocre fashion, by its own gravity that center and measure are the highest form of—exception that reposes in itself. Nothing is as rare as a real normality that has its center in itself because amidst the world it is in harmony with itself. But only a few know the inner strength and signs of measure and center, and these few shun public talk of it.

All others hardly listen when this is spoken of, and believe that the discussion concerns boredom and mediocrity: still excluding those, perhaps, who once perceived a prompting reminder-sound from that realm, but stopped up their ears against it. The recollection thereof now makes them angry and exasperated.[18]

Only in the image of the well-bred man did Nietzsche temporarily possess the human due proportion that is equally distant from the extreme idea of the last man and from the opposite idea of the superman through whom Nietzsche teaches the recurrence.

What is it, fundamentally, that allows us to recognize *good breeding*? That a well-bred human being pleases our senses, that he is carved from wood that is hard, delicate, and fragrant at the same time. He has a taste only for what is good for him; his pleasure, his delight ceases where the measure of what is good for him is transgressed. He guesses what remedies avail against harm; he exploits bad accidents to his advantage; what does not kill him makes him stronger. Instinctively, he collects from everything he sees, hears, lives through, *his* sum: he is a principle of selection, he discards much. He is always in *his own* company, whether he associates with books, human beings, or landscapes: he honors by *choosing*, by *admitting*, by *trusting*. He reacts slowly to all kinds of stimuli, with that slowness which long caution and deliberate pride have bred in him: he examines the stimulus that approaches him, he is far from meeting it halfway. He believes neither in "misfortune" nor in "guilt": he comes to terms with himself, with others; he knows how to *forget*—he is strong enough; hence everything must turn out for the best for him.[19]

The instinct of the well-bred man says, "*The world is perfect*," and even "the imperfection, the *beneath*-us of every kind" still belongs to the whole of Being, which always already was what it will always still be. To gain the distance that is necessary in order to keep a proper remove from the beneath-us of every kind without "indignation over the total aspect of things," Nietzsche recalls how much already has turned out well and how rich this earth is in "little, good, perfect things," in what has turned out well. "Place little, good, perfect things around you, O higher men! Their golden ripeness heals the heart. What is perfect teaches hope."[20]

But the time of perfect Being is a "time without goal,"[21] the hour of "noon" that is the divine moment in which Nietzsche-Zarathustra beheld the eternal recurrence.

But at the noon hour, when the sun stood straight over Zarathustra's head, he came to an old crooked and knotty tree that was embraced, and hidden from itself, by the rich love of a grapevine; and yellow grapes hung from it in abundance, inviting the wanderer. Then he felt the desire to quench a slight thirst and to break off a grape; but even as he was stretching out his arm to do so, he felt a still greater desire for something else: namely, to lie down beside the tree at the perfect noon hour, and to sleep. . . .

Falling asleep, however, Zarathustra spoke thus to his heart:

Silence! Silence! Did not the world become perfect just now? But what is happening to me?

As a delicate wind dances unseen on an inlaid sea, light, feather-light, thus—sleep dances on me.

My eyes he does not close, my soul he leaves awake. Light he is, verily, feather-light.

He persuades me, I know not how. He teaches me inwardly with flattering hands, he compels me. Yes, he compels me and makes my soul stretch out:

—how she is becoming long and tired, my strange soul. Did the eve of a seventh day come to her at noon? Has she already roamed blissfully among good and ripe things too long?

She stretches out long, long—longer! She lies still, my strange soul. Too much that is good has she tasted; this golden sadness oppresses her, she makes a little face.

—Like a ship that has sailed into its quietest cove—now it leans against the earth, tired of the long voyages and the uncertain seas. Is not the earth more faithful?

The way such a ship moors on, and nestles against the land—it suffices that a spider spins its thread to it from the land: no stronger ropes are needed here.

Like such a tired ship in the quietest cove, I, too, now rest close to the earth, faithful, trusting, waiting, tied to it with the softest threads.

O happiness! O happiness! Would you care to sing, O my soul? You are lying in the grass. But this is the secret solemn hour when no shepherd plays his pipe.

Refrain! Hot noon sleeps on the meadows. Do not sing! Silence! The world is perfect.

Do not sing, you winged one in the grass, O my soul! Do not even whisper! Behold—silence!—the old noon sleeps, he moves his mouth: is he not just now drinking a drop of happiness—

—an old brown drop of golden happiness, golden wine? It flits over him, his happiness laughs. Thus—laughs a god. Silence!

—"O happiness, how little is sufficient for happiness!" Thus I spoke once and thought myself sagacious. But it was a blasphemy: *that* I have learned now. Sagacious fools speak better.

Precisely the least, the softest, lightest, a lizard's rustling, a breath, a flash, a moment's glance—it is *little* that makes the *best* kind of happiness. Silence!

What happened to me? Listen! Did time perhaps fly away? Do I not fall? Did I not fall—listen!—into the well of eternity?

What is happening to me? Silence! I am stung, alas—in the heart? In the heart? Oh break, break, heart, after such happiness, after such a sting. . . .

"When will you drink this drop of dew that has fallen upon all earthly things?—When will you drink this strange soul?—

—When, well of eternity? You cheerful, dreadful abyss of noon! When will you drink my soul back into yourself?"

Thus spoke Zarathustra, and he got up from his resting place at the tree as from a strange drunkenness.[22]

This well of eternity has the same double meaning as Nietzsche's whole philosophy: it is an "abyss of noon," cheerful and at the same time hideous. The highest Being, like the deepest nothing, appears in this well of eternity once again. In Nietzsche's experiment this duality finds its philosophic expression in Zarathustra's teaching of the eternal recurrence of the same as the self-overcoming of nihilism.

But Nietzsche is not Zarathustra, and even Zarathustra is not yet a superman, but only teaches the superman, on the way to him; Zarathustra is only a "prelude" and "example." Nietzsche speaks in the *role* of Zarathustra, just as the speech of the ancient actor resounds through the mask of a *persona*. This mask itself has, in turn, various faces, depending on how it is worn by the actor. Zarathustra's entrance and appearance recall Nietzsche's characterization of *Heraclitus* and *Emped-ocles*. But Zarathustra—whose teaching takes for granted that God is dead, and who is himself, therefore, "the godless man"—also already speaks as the *Antichrist*; and as the history of his self-redemption develops further, his name is the first name of the god *Dionysus*. On the other hand the "Dionysus Dithyrambs" are the "songs of Zarathustra" "that he sang to himself so that he might bear his last loneliness." Last but not least, Zarathustra speaks of Friedrich Nietzsche himself. Zarathustra is Nietzsche as he wanted to see himself, a Savior-and-Redeemer figure for which Nietzsche was, as a human being, no match. Zarathustra's superiority to the "spirit of gravity" expresses itself in dancing and laughter; in a letter to Overbeck, Nietzsche writes that he would like to "laugh himself to death!!!" Zarathustra plumes himself on frivolity and abundance; Nietzsche confesses that his *Zarathustra* is wrested from the greatest privation and the most severe suffering. Zarathustra speaks as the advocate of life, which Nietzsche felt as a burden that he desperately wanted to cast off.—Zarathustra is Nietzsche's consciously desired reproach and at the same time a projection out of the depth of the unconscious. The ever recurring question, "But what happened to me?" demonstrates that in all conscious willing on the part of Nietzsche-Zarathustra, something occurs of itself, something that cannot be willed.

One can therefore read the parables of *Thus Spoke Zarathustra* in manifold ways: as a succession of demanding speeches in which Nietzsche draws up in thought a decisive experience and molds it into a philosophic teaching, or alternatively as a set of dreamlike, ascending images that—psychologically analyzed—yield the hidden history of suffering of a man who imagines the problem of his existence in shadowy and halcyon landscapes and enigmatic figures, in whom he just as much reveals and exposes himself as he conceals and masks himself. The ropedancer and the buffoon of the Prologue, the pale criminal and the shadow, the dwarf and the shepherd, the magician and the daughters of the wilderness, volcanic underworld and azure world of heaven, coffin and skiff, snake and eagle are the sorts of figures and configurations that allow of both philosophical and psychological interpretation. In both cases choice and discrimination are required to be able to distinguish empty pathos from the passionate stream that holds together the all-too-many speeches. The philosophic interpretation, like every proper interpretation, takes its bearings by what Nietzsche himself consciously wanted to say and teach in the figure of Zarathustra. The psychological explanation for the most part adheres to what remains unsaid in all that is said and what is involuntarily expressed, against the conscious intention of the author. Without depreciating the possible fertility of a psychological interpretation—to which Nietzsche himself opened the way as did no one before him—we have limited ourselves to the possibilities of a conceptual analysis of the parables in view of the basic philosophic framework of Nietzsche's teaching. We thus have circumscribed the boundless possibilities of the interpretative art according to Nietzsche's philosophic self-consciousness and self-understanding.

In the first Part of *Zarathustra,* Zarathustra only teaches the *"super-man"* as the self-overcoming of the ordinary man hitherto. The superman is his "highest idea" and his "last will," and remains so even after the proclamation of the eternal recurrence, because only the superman can call up and endure this idea. The teaching of the superman and of the eternal recurrence presupposes that one already knows that *God* is *dead,* namely the God who up to now has excessively elevated and ordained humanity. The relationship of man to superman is not that of a gradual development from the one to the other and only experimentally the goal of a methodical breeding of the "type" superman; it is a lightning-swift "metamorphosis" of the self-satisfied man, whose humanity is stamped by the traditional marks of humanity (longing for happiness, reasonableness, virtue, justice, pity). The humanitarian man is a dull "cloud," out of which, in the moment of metamorphosis, the superman strikes like an illuminating, cleansing, and searing "thunderbolt." The superman *is* nothing short of this thunderbolt of illumination and purification, and at the same time he is called an "insanity," because everything superhuman about man appears as illness and insanity.[23] Finally, however, the meaning of humanity reveals itself not already in the super*man,* but in what is really *supra*human,[T158] in a new god, Dionysus, who discloses himself in the lightning.[24]

At first the meaning of humanity does not yet refer to a new God but to this earth of ours. The superman is the "meaning of the earth"; the "body," too, speaks of the meaning of the earth. The figure of Zarathustra is conceived as a real, well-bred, handsome human being who towers above the ill-bred and ugly sufferers, who suffer over themselves and with others. In order to be able to teach the meaning of the earth, a critique is needed of all metaphysical "backworlds" of Christian Platonism and of the traditional notion of God, according to which God is a supraterrestrial and supernatural, incorporeal "spirit." "Loyalty to the earth" can be taught within the compass of the Judeo-Christian tradition and its shadowy aftereffects only if man has gotten rid of this God. Granted, many new gods are still possible, and only the "moral" God is actually dead, but Zarathustra believes neither in old gods nor in new gods: "Zarathustra says, he *would*—; but Zarathustra *will* not. . . . One should understand him correctly."

Only as the godless one can and must Zarathustra teach the self-overcoming of man toward the superman, because man without his orientation by the Christian God and God-in-man is no longer man in the previous sense, and not yet man in a new and future sense. Man no longer stands firm and must therefore be firmly determined anew. He has become the "undetermined animal."[25] In the transition to the superman, Zarathustra wants, in place of the heavenly realm that has become unbelievable, an "earthly realm" and the eternal recurrence of this earthly life. What Zarathustra pedagogically and truly prophesies[T159] is, however, at first not yet the abysmal thought of the eternal recurrence but the *nihilism* that has emerged out of the death of God. Only as the "conqueror of God and of the nothing" is he able to prophesy truly the reverse teaching, by means of which the lost loyalty to the earth is to be restored. However, how little the earth itself, in its own nature, gets a chance to speak in this loyalty to the earth is shown by the fact that Nietzsche, thinking of the future lords of the earth, speaks of the *realm* of the earth and of the "goal" of the earth. Thus the idea of the superman gets the significance in world politics, "that the earth will someday be the earth of the superman." The superman stands above the caste of men called to dominion and administers with them the "government of the earth."

Nietzsche teaches by talking and talks by writing a book: "a book for all and none." At first he talks in the marketplace to everyone, and just thereby to no one.[26] In this marketplace of the rabble that wants the "last man," he get no audience; and so he later turns to the "higher" men, whose cry of distress summoned him, and who can hear him because they share with him a similar (although not the same) distress. He still waits for his children and those like him. To the higher men belongs also the ugliest, self-hating man, who killed God and who thus colludes with Zarathustra. In all these and other figures, Nietzsche talks not only to others but also with and of himself, in a dialogue between his "soul" and his "will," or between his "self" and his "ego." He himself is the ropedancer who has made danger his profession, as opposed to the ropemaker (in the speech "On Free Death") who in going backward drags out the threads of life. He himself is also the jester who jumps over the ropedancer, so that the latter loses his head and falls to his death. Nietzsche himself is the wanderer and the shadow that likewise wanders and seeks its home, the shadow that is sick over the futility of its search. Nietzsche himself is also the shepherd whom nausea at humanity strangled, and the magician who knows that he is pursued by an unknown god—because as Nietzsche-Zarathustra altogether, he

is divided into multiple roles and split to his innermost core, to the border of schizophrenia.

Of what and how does Nietzsche speak through Zarathustra? He
speaks like a Christian preacher of "redemption," which is the main
theme in the work not only of Wagner[27] but also of Nietzsche. As a
preacher against Christianity and its redeemer, Zarathustra is not only
the godless one but also "the long-promised Antichrist."[28] In literary
form and in content, *Thus Spoke Zarathustra* is an anti-Christian gospel and an inverted Sermon on the Mount. The profusion of reminiscences of well-known biblical passages needs no elucidation. One must
distinguish (a) the imitation of biblical style and the parallel use of biblical parables from (b) the simple negation of, and (c) the parodic reversal of, the scriptural meaning of these parables.[29] Several typical examples can serve to represent the three Nietzschean uses of the language
of the New Testament.

a) "And only where graves are, are there resurrections."—John 12:24.
   "And I love those who do not want to preserve themselves."—Matt.
16:25.
   "I would have something else to say to you."—John 16:12.

b) "That happened when the most godless word emanated from a god himself—the word: 'There is One God! Thou shalt have no other god beside
me!'"—Exodus 20:3.
   "When you have an enemy, do not requite him evil with good: for that
would shame him."—Matt. 5:44.
   "Not a few who want to cast out their devil leap thereby, themselves, into
the herd of swine."—Matt. 8:31.

c) "What is most difficult . . . ? To climb high mountains, in order to tempt
the Tempter?"—Matt. 4:1, 8.
   "And all those are like me who give themselves their will and get rid of all
humility."—Matt. 12:50.
   "This crown of the laughter, this garland of roses: I myself set this crown
upon myself, I myself canonized my laughter."—Matt. 29:29.

The whole *Zarathustra* is, from Zarathustra's first appearance to the
commemoration at the ass festival, the tedious story of an ever-delayed
redemption that is supposed to redeem man from his previous Redeemer. The question asked by Nietzsche, "Who is Zarathustra?" can
therefore not be answered by reverting to the beginnings of Greek
metaphysics. Rather, one also must constantly have in view that with
Christianity a *new* beginning occurred. This new beginning so much
dominated Nietzsche's thought that his first and last principle is the

opposition of "world" and "God," or of "Dionysus" and the "Crucified." Almost every line of Zarathustra's Prologue essentially refers to
Christianity, albeit not always with the excessive clarity of the last sentence of *Ecce Homo*. Zarathustra wants to empty the cup of the golden
excess, whereas Christ, who also left the lake of his homeland when he
was thirty years old, empties the goblet of bitter suffering. Zarathustra,
the teacher of the eternal recurrence of the same, is accompanied by a
proud eagle—the symbol of John the Evangelist—and around its neck
is wound the snake of eternity. This image stands in contrast with that
other superman who teaches the unique, nonrecurring rebirth out of
a change of one's ways[T160] and whose symbol is the humble sacrificial
lamb. The correlates to the pride and sagacity of the eagle and the snake
are the humility and sagacity of the dove and the snake in the New Testament. The eagle of Zarathustra is the animal that swoops down upon
lambs from its heights and bears a grudge against all "lamb souls," and
the eagle is overjoyed to tear apart the God in man who is a "*God
as sheep*" (*agnus Dei*[T161]).[30] In the curious configuration of the snake
wound around the neck of the eagle, there already comes to light the
forced contrivance of Nietzsche's whole teaching of a willing of the cosmic revolving. For how is that "friendship" between the proudest animal of the heights and the most sagacious animal of the earth (the
friendship simulated by the double image of the animals) supposed to
last if the eagle embodies the proud will to soar up into the heights,
and the earthbound snake (which, however, is also wound around the
sun) embodies the eternal recurrence of the same?—unless the eternal
recurrence of the same could be willed with the wings of pride because
this individual willing complies with the cosmic will. The "self-willing"
of the ring of the eternal recurrence, however, is as little a proud willing as the circling of the eagle makes it into a being wound around
itself. The *one* word "will" obscures the distinction between the two
wills just as the play on words regarding the "flexibility vis-à-vis need
that is at the same time necessity"[T162] obscures the irreconcilability of
"being thus and not different" with a willed "turn of necessity."[T163]
And did not Zarathustra himself have a sound presentiment, expressed
in the last sentence of the Prologue, that one day the sagacity of the
snake could abandon him, and then his pride will fly with folly? In
Zarathustra's very last speech, the talk is no longer of a snake but only
of Zarathustra's eagle and of a laughing lion. The lion, as a predator,
symbolizes the metamorphosis from "Thou shalt" to "I will" in the
first speech, and thus precisely does not bring the redemptive solution,

the proclamation of which is the often-interrupted but lasting theme of *Zarathustra*.

Zarathustra, the godless teacher of the superman and of the eternal recurrence, wants to bring the gospel to proclaim a "gay science" that emerges out of the death of God. This proclamation is preached, in accordance with Nietzsche's insight that in Germany there is only "*one* type of public and *roughly* skillful speech," namely that delivered from the pulpit:

In Germany the preacher alone knew what a syllable or word weighs and how a sentence strikes, leaps, plunges, runs, runs out; he alone had a conscience in his ears. . . . The masterpiece of Germany's greatest preacher, the *Bible,* has so far been the best German book. Compared with Luther's Bible, almost anything else is mere "literature": something that did not grow in Germany and therefore also did not and does not grow into German hearts—as the Bible did.[31]

But why can Zarathustra's speeches neither persuade the heart nor convince the understanding? Because they are the fabrication of a writer whose strong point is the critical fine-honing of the aphorism. By contrast, his proclamation is an embarrassing mixture of the language of the New Testament and the musical dramas of Wagner with Nietzsche's own, great linguistic art. Nietzsche speaks in an immediately persuasive way not as the proclaimer of a fifth Gospel, but where he talks the "language of the thawing wind." To be able to learn something from Nietzsche's teaching, it is necessary to disregard the way in which it is delivered and to condense it to its principal and productive motive: the motif of "overcoming," not only of one's own time and of oneself, but of the temporality of time altogether, toward the eternity of the eternal recurrence of the same. "The true eternity is not the one that excludes all time, but the one that itself holds time (eternal time) in submission. True eternity is the overcoming of time."[32] What Schelling conceives, with a speculative-theogonic intention, in these propositions is conceived anew by Nietzsche after the "cockcrow of positivism" and applied to his own relationship to time. For the first thing that a philosopher must demand of himself, according to Nietzsche, is that he overcome his time in himself, in order to behold his time's highest measures of value. The test of whether one has overcome one's time is whether one has gotten over even one's aversion for one's time.[33] Nietzsche passed this test exactly to the extent that he succeeded in making his teaching of eternity believable. But how can the truth of his teaching be confirmed and demonstrated, if not in comparison with the "primal text" of nature, wherein the recurrence of the same comes to light again and again in the natural phenomena? "We all do not know how deep and high *physis*[T164] reaches" and how much man is "wholly nature" in his highest as well as lowest urges and powers. Even his knowledge displays a "perfect analogy" to the organic process of selecting and estimating, of acquiring, transforming, and excreting. Nietzsche's writings are a "Prelude to a Philosophy of the Future" not because Nietzsche thought of a future change in the essence of man that one could prepare for or even will, and which he tried to bring about by thinking up the superman. Rather, his writings constitute such a prelude because Nietzsche, in recalling the pre-Socratic *physikoi*,[T165] engages in the great attempt to "translate" man "back" into the *nature* of all things; and because in metaphysics, which had become supraworldly and backworldly, he tries to gain acknowledgment again of the everlasting *physis* of the world and the "great reason of the body" as what is fundamental and exists always, remains the same and recurs.[34] In this tendency to "return to nature," Nietzsche is, in spite of his opposition to a sentimental concept of nature, the Rousseau of the nineteenth century.

Our thesis is that the teaching—absurd to all modern (natural-scientific, historical, and existential) thought—of the eternal recurrence is the core of Nietzsche's whole philosophy. This thesis must, it is true, at first seem as strange as Schelling's contention[35] that the proof of God's existence is the "remnant of genuine philosophy" in Descartes's doubting meditation. But the paradox of both contentions loses its offensiveness as soon as one understands that a teaching about man is groundless if it does not have as a supporting basis either a metaphysical *God* or the *physis* of the world; for man does not exist through his own powers.[T166] And because for Nietzsche the transworldly God was dead, he had to ask anew the old cosmological question about the eternity of the world,[36] as opposed to its single creation. What can be learned from his teaching is not ready-made results but rather the indispensability of certain issues of the philosophy of nature that result, historically, from the fact that the old, biblical God is dead for modern man's consciousness. Each of these philosophic issues refers, within the historical conditionality of Nietzsche's anti-Christian thought,[36a] to the loss of a theological answer. These issues accordingly lend themselves to summary in the following alternatives:

1. that everything depends exclusively on the Being of the *world*—if the belief in *God* as the Creator of the world is no longer alive;

2. that the *Being* of this world that has always existed already is a self-moved, original *physis*—if Being does not arise, in a miraculous way, out of *nothing*;

3. that the physical world is *eternal*—if it has no original *beginning* and no purposeful *end*;

4. that the eternity of an *always* existing physical world is an eternal *time*—if it is not the *timeless eternity* of a transworldly and supernatural God;

5. that *man* is of *nature* and of the *world*—if he is not *created in the image* of a supernatural and transworldly God;

6. that the question of the relationship of the *everlasting* Being of the physical world to the *finite* existence of *man* cannot be avoided—if the answer on the relationship of man and world is not already given by faith in the *common* creation and coordination of world and man by God;

7. that the *accident* of all de facto being-there necessarily becomes a problem if the faith in *Providence* and its secularized forms is no longer believable;

8. that what is enigmatic about the accident "man" cannot be solved if man is not integrated into the eternal whole of what is by nature.

Nietzsche had to ask the questions laid down in these theses because he decided against God and for the world, and within this world experienced with the most extreme radicalness what it means that since Copernicus, man falls out of a center into an x, that is: the absolute contingency of modern existence in the world.[37] "We still struggle step by step with the giant Accident," by virtue of whose dominion over the whole of mankind, the lack of meaning prevails.[38] "And how could I bear to be man, if man were not also . . . the redeemer of the accident?" In order to redeem from the detached, ab-solute accident "man" who appears like a "sickness of the earth," Zarathustra's teaching teaches that this lost fragment "man" should be taken back into the "chance" of the whole of the world that has always been and is still becoming, with a necessary revolving that is equally distant from caprice and compulsion. Thus man cannot be compelled by anything else because he is himself already the whole, and stems from no caprice because he is a self-willing fatality. The highest, unconditional "*fatalism*" is identical with "*accident*" and the "*creative*."[39] The teaching of the eternal recurrence completes this fatalism so understood by putting the isolated human being back into the whole, just as accidental as it is necessary, of the creative life of the world. Nietzsche therefore doubts not only the opposition to the world by man who disparages the world ("man *against* the world") but also the juxtaposition of the two ("man *and* world").[40] We ourselves *are* already world—but not because we exist as part of the world around us and because the world is only a determinant of human existence, but because all incorporation, opposition, and juxtaposition is always outstripped by the all-encompassing Being of the living, physical world, which is a constant cycle of coming into being and passing away, of creation and destruction. What is distinctive about humanity does not lie in a special meta-physical quality, but only in the fact that man has a special *consciousness* of himself and the world. But this consciousness is no Being of its own, but belongs to what it becomes conscious of. Almost everything is and happens in man as in the world, apart from it.[41] The unmistakable intention of Nietzsche's notes for his planned main work—in which the revaluation has a foundation in the philosophy of nature and essentially in biology—is to show "the absolute homogeneity in all that happens." The question of how to overcome the accident "man" gets its answer (if at all) only out of the whole of what is, which Nietzsche calls the "total character of life." The eternal recurrence is a recurrence of what is always the same, that is: of life that is uniform and of equal power in everything living. The structure and problematical character of the teaching of the eternal recurrence and the relationship of that teaching to the will to power do not lend themselves to useful discussion if—in presupposing an abstract concept of Being—one disregards the fact that the decisive point of all Nietzsche's teachings is designated by the word "life," which for its part aims at a *physis* that carries and dominates everything, generates and destroys.

Within the "primal law" of the eternal recurrence of life that is uniform and of equal power in everything living, the total character of life differentiates itself according to fullness or poverty of life, strength or weakness, ascent or decline. As little as Nietzsche ever pondered ontologically the difference between Being and what is,[42] just as much did he make thematic the difference within all living Being (without the liveliness of which there would be no Being at all)[43]—from *Of the Use and Disadvantage of History "for Life"*[T167] up to the notes for *The Will to Power*. Nietzsche labels the distinction of life (which is one and of equal power in everything) according to ascent and decline, as his "main differentiation." It is out of this distinction that the apparently more comprehensive distinction between "Being" and "becoming" must, in Nietzsche's view, be interpreted.[44] In a prominent passage, in the first chapter of *Ecce Homo* ("Why I Am So Wise"), he calls himself the "teacher par excellence" regarding this distinction. And one cannot deny to him that he has his ownmost mastery in exegesis that differentiates the signs of ascent and decline—be it in philosophy and religion, morals and politics, science and art, literature and music. The formation and transposition of perspectives for ascent and decline—to look "toward *healthier* concepts and values from the optics of the sick, and on the other hand to look down, on the contrary, out of the fullness and self-certainty of *rich* life into the secret work of the instinct of *décadence*"—was his "longest exercise," his "authentic experience," and also the "first reason" why a revaluation of values became at all possible for him. For revaluation presupposes in every case that within the total character of life one is capable of distinguishing what is full of life from what is poor in life, the well-bred from the ill-bred, and the good from the bad. The reversal of the will to the nothing into the willing of the eternal recurrence, however, is also—and this above all—a revaluation according to this main distinction.

But if the main distinction is a distinction within life that preserves itself and grows, increases and subsides again, then nihilism, too, cannot *originally* arise only from the "death of God," that is, out of the fact that faith in God is no longer credible. Faith and disbelief, seen from Nietzsche's point of view, are not types of behavior, with their formulation within themselves, of the man who is willing or unwilling to have faith; rather, they must be interpreted—like every conscious behavior and also every interpretation of the world—as a sign or symptom for something more original and hidden: for growth or decay of the life force. It belongs to Nietzsche's "total insight"[45] that even nihilism is no unique historical event but an ever-recurring appearance of life that is homogeneous and of equal power and inexhaustible in nature and history, life that rebuilds itself as it destroys itself. There have always been nihilistic movements, too, and the indications of dissolution and decline belong in the periods of transition to new conditions of existence.

Zarathustra's crossing, too, from previous man to the superman and from nihilism to the willing of the eternal recurrence should be understood in the sense of such a transition. This transition is not yet set in motion by Zarathustra's decision one morning to go down for the sake of a new ascent, but his *decision* is at the same time an "inspiration" or impulse, and it comes to pass as an *event*. Man is on the way to the superman not because Zarathustra undertakes, out of his own will, to create the future and to go over to something else, but because he is being "changed"—through the creative power of life that ascends and declines. Yet on the other hand he is only being changed if he wants to change himself. Zarathustra's will is—in case Zarathustra-Dionysus is the highest type of *all* that is—a creative accident and a necessary willing. And what overcomes itself to affirm the eternal recurrence is—in case *all* life is self-overcoming—also not man (who no longer believes in God and therefore would rather will the nothing than not will) but life, which is homogeneous and of equal power and significance in all that is. But if nihilism is at first and at last not at all the "consequence" of the fact that God is no longer believed in but a "symptom" and "logic" of a "physiological" *décadence*,[46] then also the self-overcoming of nihilism toward the willing of the eternal recurrence can result only from life's self-regeneration in man and the removal of the nihilistic condition by virtue of life's creative, transforming force. Just as the nonarbitrary event of change corresponds to one's own willing of self-change, so does regeneration on the part of cosmic life correspond to one's will to rebirth. Both the devaluation and the revaluation of all previous values occur in human willing and evaluation; but this willing and evaluation is accomplished in advance by the essence of life, which is itself already a self-willing and evaluation. "Life itself forces us to fix values; life itself evaluates through us *when* we fix values."[47]

The tension and the contradiction within this postulated correspondence between the finite existence of the willing man and the eternal Being of the world that wills itself produce the problematic conflict in the willing of the eternal recurrence. Only within this *conflicting* correspondence can Nietzsche on the one hand think that man moves the whole of nature if he is completely mankind,[48] and on the other hand adhere to the view that in the whole of what is, man is a mere "incident" and altogether a natural fatality. Or, summarized in a single sentence of two words, "*ego-fate*,"[49] namely the fate of the eternal recurrence. This sentence, too, on being unfolded, signifies something twofold, conflicting, and self-contradictory: I myself have for eternities conditioned the fatality of *all* existence and its eternal recurrence, and I myself am only *one* conditioned fatality in the whole of the cycle of the natural world. Put in moral terms: I am responsible for everything's being there and being as it is, and there is no being there that would be responsible for its being as it is and its being there. The contradiction between both sets of assertions could only be nullified and brought to a noncontradictory correspondence if Nietzsche succeeded in flying beyond all going, going over, and going under, into the innocence of heaven.

Nietzsche wanted to have no mere disciples for his questionable teaching of the eternal recurrence, which aimed at a *"kosmos anthropos."*[50, T168] He knew he was only a "railing by the stream," but no "crutch" on which one could support oneself. At the end of the Foreword to *Ecce Homo* he repeated—in reminiscence of the Christian expectation of the return of the Lord—what Zarathustra says at the end of the first Part of *Zarathustra* and also uses as the motto of the second Part:

> One repays a teacher badly if one always remains nothing but a pupil. And why do you not want to pluck at my wreath?
>
> You revere me. But what if your reverence tumbles one day? Beware lest a statue slay you.
>
> You say you believe in Zarathustra? But what matters Zarathustra? You are my believers—but what matter all believers? You had not sought yourselves: and you found me. Thus do all believers; therefore all faith amounts to so little.
>
> Now I bid you lose me and find yourselves; and only when you have all denied me will I return to you.[51]

In the same sense Nietzsche wrote Georg Brandes after the commencement of his insanity: "After you discovered me, it was not difficult to find me; the problem now is to lose me. . . . The Crucified One."

On the same day Nietzsche confessed in a note to Jacob Burckhardt, "Now you are—thou art—[T169] our great greatest teacher. . . . " Nothing is more human in Nietzsche's superhuman claim than this willing abdication for the benefit of a wiser and older man. To be sure, Burckhardt took notice of and respected the younger and more passionate man with an ironic resistance,[T170] but he was never, as Nietzsche fancied, his friend. Burckhardt, who for a half-century was really a teacher in a high sense, did not make it difficult for his pupils not to remain tied to him. His skepticism, caution, and reserve demanded neither believers nor venerators, not even discipleship and allegiance. What attracted Nietzsche to Burckhardt was his human maturity, the *"attained* freedom of the spirit." What separated Nietzsche from Burckhardt as well as from Overbeck was that Nietzsche could not grasp why they did not share his distress, although they were not at all untouched by the distress of the age. He wrote Overbeck on 2 July 1885, that is, after finishing the last Part of *Zarathustra,* from Sils Maria: "My 'philosophy,' if I have the right so to call what mistreats me into the roots of my being, is *no longer* communicable, at least not by means of print. Occasionally I long to have a secret conference with you and Jacob Burckhardt, more to ask how you avoid this distress than to relate news. . . . For me my life now consists in the *wish* that all things may be *different* from how I grasp them; and that someone would make *my* 'truths' unbelievable to me."[52]

# Appendix

## On the History of the Interpretation
## of Nietzsche (1894–1954)

The very titles of most interpretations of Nietzsche demonstrate, through their juxtapositions of terms, what perplexity has resulted from the effort to understand Nietzsche's work in his *own* terms. Riehl deals with Nietzsche as "artist" and "thinker"; Joel with Nietzsche "and romanticism"; Simmel with Nietzsche "and Schopenhauer"; Hildebrandt with Wagner's and Nietzsche's mutual "struggle against the nineteenth century"; Bertram with the "legend" Nietzsche; Klages with Nietzsche's "psychological accomplishments"; Baeumler with Nietzsche as philosopher "and politician." For them all, the concern is either not at all, or only within narrow limits, Nietzsche's *philosophic teaching*.

At first the powerful influence of Nietzsche's stirring writings overshadowed by far the intellectual confrontation with them. The impact of his literary production extended less to philosophy than to the totality of European literature and the European way of thinking. A Danish literary historian, Georg Brandes, was the first to hold public lectures on Nietzsche in 1888, and an Italian, Gabriele D'Annunzio, proclaimed Nietzsche's glory in the year of his death in a poem, "*Per la morte di un distruttore.*"[T171] We are indebted to the French literary historian Charles Andler for the most comprehensive presentation of Nietzsche's life and writings. André Gide and Antoine de Saint-Exupéry, D. H. Lawrence and T. E. Lawrence, Stefan George and Rilke, Rudolf Pannwitz and Oswald

Spengler, Robert Musil and Thomas Mann, Gottfried Benn and Ernst Jünger—they are all unthinkable without Nietzsche. For half a century Nietzsche has been a slogan that one therefore did not take literally.

A first attempt to grasp the change in the image of Nietzsche insofar as he concerns Germany occurs in a work by Gisela Deesz.[1] The author comes to the conclusion that at first it occurred to no one to consider Nietzsche with a view to his philosophic position. In the first decade of his influence, Nietzsche was regarded preeminently as a moralist; thereafter, under the imprint of Stefan George, as a prophet of the coming century and as a critic of the century past; and only after World War I did he emerge clearly as a thinker.

The question whether this or that Nietzsche—Simmel's or Baeumler's, Jaspers's or Heidegger's—is the "authentic" one allows of an answer only if one has previously asked what Nietzsche is for himself. In the present exegesis the test of Nietzsche's contention was made by taking bearings from Nietzsche himself, who tells us that he is the teacher of the eternal recurrence. Accordingly, the following critique of the previous presentations of Nietzsche can be limited to pointing out in each case the problematic point at which the interpretation of his teaching fails to convince. Thus only those authors will be considered who have expressly dealt with the problems of the eternal recurrence. They are, in the main: Lou Andreas-Salomé, Oskar Ewald, Georg Simmel, Ernst Bertram, Charles Andler, Ludwig Klages, Alfred Baeumler, Erika Emmerich, Thierry Maulnier, Karl Jaspers, Ludwig Giesz, Martin Heidegger.

# 1.

Lou Andreas-Salomé[2] in her book depicts above all Nietzsche himself, albeit "in his works." She thereby limits her interpretation of the problem of his philosophy to the set of problems that concern the philosopher personally. Her presentation appeared in 1894, that is, still before the publication of Nietzsche's self-presentation in *Ecce Homo*. All the more astounding is the circumspection and maturity of her characterization. In the following fifty years there has appeared no depiction of Nietzsche that joins the central issue more directly, but also none that is now paid so little attention.[T172] What is presented by Baeumler as a new discovery, namely the "system" of Nietzsche, is already clearly elaborated here; and it is elaborated without giving up the teaching of the return, by means of which alone Nietzsche's philosophy has a central focus.

Andreas-Salomé characterizes first Nietzsche's "nature," then his "changes," and finally the "system." "If one considers his ideas in their flux and diversity, then they appear almost immeasurable and much too complicated; if on the contrary one tries to pare out of them what always remains the same in the flux, one then is astounded at the simplicity and constancy of his problems" (pp. 74f.; cf. pp. 10 and 237). At the end Nietzsche returns to his point of departure, so that the circle of his intellectual existence closes (pp. 49, 137ff., 153f.). The repetitious basic character of his nature is seen in a discord that reverts into itself without ever reaching beyond itself.

Thus he achieved the exact opposite of what he strove for, not a higher unity of his being, but the innermost bifurcation thereof, not the integration of all impulses . . . into a unified individual, but their dissociation into the "*dividual.*" A health was nevertheless reached, but with the means of sickness; a real adoration, but with the means of deception; a real self-assertion and self-elevation, but with the means of self-laceration. (P. 35; cf. pp. 117, 147f., 248)

The drive toward self-destruction generates out of itself the opposite drive, toward self-apotheosis, just as the latter reverts back into the former. Andreas-Salomé thinks she discerns a "rupture of faith" as the final motive for this discord.

His entire development emanated as it were from his loss of faith, that is, from "emotion over the death of God," that enormous emotion which resounds right into the last work (which Nietzsche composed while already on the threshold of insanity), the fourth Part of his *Thus Spoke Zarathustra. The possibility of finding a replacement for the lost God in the most varied forms of self-divinization,* that is the history of his mind, of his works, of his illness. (Pp. 38f. and 213)

His work becomes the more universal in its claim, the more it becomes identical with Nietzsche's ownmost destiny (pp. 143f.). Accordingly, the presentation of the teaching of the return (pp. 220ff.) mainly serves the explanation of Nietzsche's intellectual destiny and not the clarification of the actual problems of that teaching, which locate the return in the context of European philosophy. The teaching of the eternal return is recognized as the foundation and conclusion of Nietzsche's whole experiment, and the core of the idea of the return is the reversal of suffering into the most extreme transfiguration of existence.

To me the hours are unforgettable in which he first confided it to me, as a secret, as something he unspeakably dreaded to see verified . . . : only with a soft voice and with all signs of the deepest horror did he speak of it. And in fact he suffered so deeply from life that the certainty of the eternal recurrence of life had to entail something ghastly for him. The quintessence of the teaching of the return, the radiating apotheosis of life that Nietzsche afterward set forth, forms such a profound contrast with his own tortured perception of life that it charms us like an eerie mask. . . . Everything that Nietzsche thought, felt, lived after the genesis of his idea of the return, arises from this discord within himself, and moves between "cursing with gnashed teeth the demon of the eternity of life" and the expectation of that "tremendous moment" which gives one the strength to pronounce the words, "You are a god and never did I hear anything more divine!" (Pp. 222f.)

The idea of the return was therefore at first no theoretical conviction but rather a personal fear that then turned into its opposite. In Andreas-Salomé's view it was what Nietzsche knew as "metaphysician" in the first period of his creativity and what he missed and himself destroyed as "empiricist" in the second, that drove him into the "mysticism" of his teaching (p. 225), into a mystical "philosophy of will" (p. 131). Nietzsche intensifies pessimism into a resolute nihilism in order "to use the most extreme weariness and pain from living as a *springboard* from which he wants to plunge into the depths of his mysticism." This leap occurs in fact in the onset of insanity as the meaningful end of Nietzsche's constant self-exaltation.[T173] What previously was called his final danger becomes his final refuge; his foot obliterates the path behind him and above him stands written, "Impossibility."

Only through this result does the irreconcilable contradiction become clear to us in its entire magnificence. The contradiction lay in Nietzsche's introducing his philosophy of the future with a "gay science," in his calling it a good news destined to justify life forever in its whole strength, abundance, and eternity—and in his setting forth the *eternal return* of life as the highest idea of that philosophy. Only now do we recognize fully the victorious optimism that reposes over his last works like the touching smile of a child—an optimism that displays as its obverse, however, the face of a hero who conceals his features, disfigured by horror. . . . The great thing is: he knew that he was perishing, and yet he took his leave with a laughing mouth, "garlanded with roses," excusing life, vindicating it, transfiguring it. His spiritual life died out in Dionysian dithyrambs, and what they were supposed to drown out in their jubilation was a cry of pain. They are the last rape of Nietzsche by Zarathustra. (Pp. 261f.)

"There is also *revenge* therein, revenge on life itself, if a grave sufferer *takes life under his protection*" (XIV, 105). Andreas-Salomé believes herself able to dispense with the "theoretical contours" of the idea of the return in favor of the elaboration of the "ethical and religious conclusions that Nietzsche ostensibly draws from that idea; whereas in reality the ethical and religious constitute the inner presupposition of the eternal return" (p. 226). Because she simplifies the problem of the teaching of the return, a bias results for Andreas-Salomé, as if the authentic and sole meaning of the teaching were the superhuman *creation* of the world (pp. 231ff.); whereas in reality the will to the fate of the self-willing and eternally recurring world presupposes a "re-creation" of the will. Only thereby can the superhuman will will the Dionysian world of the recurrence, the Dionysian world that itself lacks will and goal. Consequently, Nietzsche's final will is not only a will to self-eternalization but just as much a will to the radical breaking asunder of individuation, which is already the problem of *The Birth of Tragedy* (*The Birth of Tragedy*, 10 and 16); and his teaching is on the whole the attempt to tie man's existence, which has become free unto itself, back from the outermost edge of freedom unto the nothing—into the Being of the naturally necessary world. But that attempt is, to say it with Nietzsche, "the most tragic of all histories with a heavenly solution" (XIV, 302).

## 2.

In contrast with that first presentation of Nietzsche's intellectual personality, Oskar Ewald[3] consciously interposed himself "between Nietzsche and his ideas" in order to discuss impartially the basic ideas of his philosophy and only then to "test" Nietzsche (cf. especially pp. 67ff., the interpretation of the "Drunken Song"). He does not want to "cite" Nietzsche, but to "think" his ideas "out to the end" in their "logical and ethical content" (pp. 6 and 83). In this way Ewald supposes he will grasp the *principle* on which rests the contradiction between the idea of the superman and the idea of the eternal recurrence. The goal is to erect the "*system* of contradictions" that supports Nietzsche's philosophy but also causes it to fail.

The fundamental ideas that are decisive for Ewald's analysis, superman and eternal return, are first shown to be contradictory with regard to their opposite temporal forms: radical "evolution" (p. 47) and eternal recurrence of the same. The so-called superman does not have any fixed social, political, or biological content or goal. Rather, the superman is an unswerving will *to* the superman, an ethical "appeal," a "psychological function" (p. 18), a "postulate to permanence" (p. 17), yet not an object. In contrast with the always already completed infinity of the ring of the eternal recurrence, the superman presupposes an unconcluded, infinite span of time. With the superman Nietzsche wants to cancel the past and create the *future*; with the eternal recurrence he wants, on the contrary, to vindicate the *past* in the future. This contradiction remains, however, only while one deals with both ideas "dogmatically" and "realistically" instead of "critically" and "idealistically" (p. 29). What matters is to "*fathom*" the contradiction and "to deepen it to the point of *unity*" (p. 34). Ewald contends that the *ethical ideality* of both ideas is the common source of the apparent contradictories. As an idea the superman is not something apart from and above us, but an "*immanent* ideal" (pp. 48ff.), an always present "possibility" a "living potentiality" in man that expresses a moral ideal, in opposition to the possibility of the last man. But the idea of the eternal return, too, is not to be taken realistically, its "value" is likewise that of a "symbol" (pp. 55ff.), and as the superman is the symbol of the "infinity of desire," so is the eternal recurrence only the concrete condensation and sensual embodiment of this subjective infinity and the necessary complement thereto. As a cosmological theory understood objectively and metaphysically, however, the recurrence is a "wild assertion" (p. 60), "unfounded" and "meaningless" (p. 87). Aphorism 341 of *The Gay Science* contains the key to understanding the recurrence; i.e., as the "greatest gravity" it is a binding imperative, but not the true *logos* of the Being of all that is. "Thus the eternal recurrence, too, like the superman, becomes an *ideality* and a *symbol*" (p. 62); both ideas have a fundamentally ethical meaning. Translated into an imperative the superman means, "Act as if you wanted to generate the superman out of yourself by actualizing him in yourself"; and the eternal recurrence means, "Act as if every moment possessed the value of eternity and you embraced all the future in this one, indivisible present" (pp. 71f.). The endless heightening of the consciousness of *responsibility*—also for what already was—is the psychological function of both teachings. "The eternal return is the *symbol of the superman,* and on the other hand the superman becomes an *organ of the idea of an eternal return*" (p. 77). But whereas both ideas are only "illustrative devices" for the sake of "giving a concrete form to moral truths," there is still a difference between them: the superman is a postulate that is *also* supposed to actualize itself, albeit as idea, whereas the eternal return remains meaningful *only* as long as it is meant strictly symbolically and one refrains from giving it any meaning of its own or making it real (p. 87).

Nietzsche's teaching becomes untenable only where the presentation of that teaching extends beyond its symbolic ideality to reality (pp.

74ff.). After *Zarathustra,* which is essentially symbolic, Nietzsche wanted to make "more" out of his teaching and thus lessened its weight. He "coarsened" the "idea" of his teaching into a "Being" (p. 79). But because the teaching is only tenable as an ethical concept of value, one must interpose oneself between Nietzsche and his teaching and, for the sake of saving him philosophically, "declare him incompetent." The superman, too, in Nietzsche is often more than an idea to be actualized, inasmuch as it acquires a particular historical content; but precisely when one supplies such a content to the idea, one hollows out its "ethical core." The core of his teaching is *the problem of immortality* (pp. 81ff.), which is a "value problem" because immortality consists in the "untransitory intrinsic value of the moral personality." Immortality is an expression of the imperative that man is to eternalize his existence ethically. Ewald calls this man who actualizes the idea of immortality as a value idea, the "historical" man as distinguished from the "elementary" man (pp. 100ff.). Only the historical man can be a superman and affirm the eternal recurrence of the same as an idea of value. In Nietzsche and his philosophy, however, elementary man is in a fundamental conflict with historical man, and the truth of Nietzsche's teaching becomes a lie when he attributes meaning and reality to the eternal return in itself. That is the absurdity of Nietzsche's teaching, which in and of itself makes sense. This contradiction is mirrored in the central contrast between *accident* and (ethical) *law* (p. 73 note and p. 136). When Nietzsche elevates what is "by accident" to the oldest nobility of the world and affirms the innocence of the accident, his teaching begins to "alternate" between the poles of accident and moral law, between irresponsibility and responsibility of and for oneself. Nothing remains, finally, of the "great symbol" of the eternal recurrence other than "the crudely realistic conceptual shell," because the immortality of man is to become immanent in what happens in the world (p. 139).

Thus Nietzsche removes the nerve of the fundamental idea of his teaching. . . . Precisely what is supposed to make possible the independence of man from the compulsion of objective Being is given up. This abandonment occurs in order to force man to submit to the yoke of a geometrical axiom to which he must subordinate his intellectual point of view and the motives of his will. Nietzsche displaces into the world of objects what is supposed to belong to the subject as inalienable property. . . . Man was not himself to lay the sublime yardstick of the eternal recurrence alongside his experiences, but instead the eternal recurrence applied the yardstick to man himself, from the outside, as a reality that does not need man at all. In the recurrence it is no longer man who affirms his life, but the recurrence that affirms man's life. With the symbol the activity of moral valuation is abandoned to accident and catastrophe. (Pp. 140ff.)

Ewald's critique proceeds from the presupposition that the "vital nerve of all metaphysics" is the "problem of value" (p. 96). Therefore he takes the yardstick of his critique not from Nietzsche but from Kant's *Critique of Practical Reason* (pp. 7 and 71), which under Weininger's influence he then modifies in the vein of philosophy of value. The "misunderstanding" of Nietzsche's teaching, however, is not Nietzsche's fault but Ewald's, whose fundamental distinctions (reality and ideality, Being and ought, natural accident and ethical law) are still *short* of Nietzsche's "Prelude to a Philosophy of the Future."[T174] The historical meaning of Nietzsche's "Yes" to the "Yes of Being"—which "Yes" is exactly not a "hopeful longing" (p. 141)—is, however, nothing other than the abolition of the duality, handed down since Descartes, of man and world, of inner and outer world, of "true" and "apparent" world in such a way that precisely the accident of one's own existence becomes one with the highest necessity in the whole of Being. Only when one understands Nietzsche's philosophy as an idealistic ethics does that philosophy alternate within the contradiction between accident and law; whereas according to its philosophic intention, Nietzsche's thought is a most extreme attempt to regain a lost *world* (p. 66). Only by emphasizing *the* contradiction—which consists in Nietzsche's repetition of the *ancient* view of the Being of the world on the peak of *modernity* and thus a Greek cosmology on the ground of a post-Christian anthropology of willing—is it possible to reconstruct also that "system of contradictions" which is the goal of Ewald's analysis.

Ewald's rigorously reasoned interpretation of Nietzsche's teaching according to its ethical function was first proposed in an inadequate way by Ernst Horneffer,[4] and then, in a more or less diluted fashion, it entered into the subsequent presentations by Aloise Riehl,[5] Arthur Drews,[6] Richard Moritz Meyer,[7] Raoul Richter,[8] Karl Heckel,[9] and above all Simmel.

## 3.

Simmel,[10] arguing logically, reduces the meaning of Nietzsche's teaching to its *ethical tendency*; he interprets that doctrine, like Ewald, according to the side that Nietzsche calls the "ethical gravity" of his teaching. But in Simmel's view this moral idea has no "real" meaning, but stands rather in insoluble contradiction to his cosmological claim. This other side is only a "magnifying glass" for emphasizing the moral importance of every action and omission in every moment. The magnifier is comparable to the maxim of Fichte, "The empirical ego ought to be disposed in such a way as it could be disposed eternally." As a "touchstone" of human action, Nietzsche's idea reduces to a conceptual "function," while the teaching of recurrence itself and the agitation with which Nietzsche speaks of that teaching is for Simmel explicable only in terms of a "certain imprecision in its logical conception."

If one thinks it out to the end with complete rigor, the inner meaning of the teaching of eternal recurrence disappears completely, because the . . . repetitions of the exactly same do not at all allow of any *synthesis* of these repetitions. If an experience in my existence repeats itself, this repetition as such can acquire the most enormous significance for me. But that significance obtains only because I therewith remember the first experience, only if the second experience happens to a state of my Being or consciousness after that state has been modified by the first. But if one were to invent a fictitious case—empirically impossible—in which the second experience happened to me in the absolutely same state as did the first, my reaction to the second experience would be the absolutely same one as my reaction to the first, and it could not have the slightest significance for me that the second is a repetition. . . . But matters are no different in the case of the recurrence of total existence generally.—Only for an onlooker . . . who embraces in his consciousness the multiplicity of the repetitions does the recurrence mean something; in its reality in and for itself, for the one who lives through those experiences, the recurrence is nothing. Only the *idea* of the eternal recurrence has an ethical-psychological meaning. . . . (Pp. 251ff.)

The contradiction between the idea of the eternal recurrence of the same and that of the superman is abolished by the fact that the latter as well as the former "in its real meaning is only a regulator and touchstone for our behavior." For Simmel the superman is not the name for a last metamorphosis, by means of which Zarathustra awakens into childhood, but rather an endless-infinite "task" in the Kantian sense. The teaching of the superman has the meaning of the imperative: in every moment to live "as if we would live thus eternally, i.e., as if there were an eternal return" (p. 254). The will to a most extreme moral "responsibility" thus seems to be the "final motif of the most astonishing teaching of Nietzsche." But in reality the whole problem of that teaching consists in regaining, by means of a most extreme justification of existence before the bar of one's own self, a most extreme *ir*responsibility, in order to exist, that is, to-be-there,[T175] amidst the innocence of the revolving world. Simmel recognizes that "of all doctrines of Nietzsche" the teaching of the eternal recurrence "is the one that still has the most metaphysical significance," but that knowledge does not prevent him from interpreting the meaning of the recurrence in terms of its "fundamental moral intention."

This interpretation of the eternal return as an ethical regulator is supplemented by means of a metaphysical speculation. For the teaching of the return is further said to be the attempt to grasp *Being* in the form of *becoming* and indeterminate infinity in the form of determinate finitude. The symbol for this attempt is the ring, for a circle, exactly because of its finite circumference, in itself permits of an infinitely repeatable motion. To Simmel, though, the attempt to comprehend Being and infinity is a speculation that subsists on the vagueness of such abstract concepts as finite and infinite, Being and becoming. Simmel does not attempt to find any *connection* between the teaching of the recurrence as subjective-ethical gravity and as objective-metaphysical speculation, even though the interpretation in the sense of a *fiction* rests upon the *objective* claim of the idea of the recurrence. For only under the presupposition of a recurrence thought to occur in fact can the idea of recurrence become a fiction in the sense of the imperative to live as if there were—in fact—an eternal recurrence.

## 4.

Bertram[11] begins with the assertion: everything that has been is only an allegory. Accordingly he wants to understand Nietzsche, too, not in terms of the historical problems of his philosophic existence but as a kind of legend, as a "symbol," an "emblem," a "figure." The ancient heroic myths and the medieval legends of the saints serve Bertram as models for this transfiguration. Bertram accomplishes the transition from the historical to the mythical by means of a loose discourse in the "just like" of the allegory transmitted by literature. The historical insight of Hegel and Burckhardt that nothing distinguishes us so much from antiquity as precisely the lack of a truly mythical way of thinking, is ignored in Bertram's presentation. There he would like to give the impression that the mythical viewpoint is possible at any time, whereas for him it is an alexandrine metaphor. Bertram forces Nietzsche's philosophical problems together into an emblem that, by conjoining words, obscures the obvious break in Nietzsche's philosophy and existence. To him Nietzsche is a "believing doubter," a "god-seeking blasphemer" with the will to a "godless divine" man, and Nietzsche's whole figure is a prophetic "beginning of the end"—formulas that are just as correct as they are empty. Bertram's essential intention is to present this "double-souledness" in order to make clear thereby the "undecidable, swaying balance-scales of his being and of his values" (p. 10). In accordance with this synopsis of Nietzsche's frequently broken existence, Bertram never attacks Nietzsche's work at any point in a material way. He only paraphrases Nietzsche through vague similes with emblematic headings: Arion, Judas, Weimar, Napoleon, mask, anecdote, Indian summer, Claude Lorrain, Venice, Portofino, etc. The question never arises whether an existence as problematic as Nietzsche's can at all be depicted "by means of a figure." Instead, everything remains in an undecided state of suspense, even though precisely Nietzsche, like no one else, and up to the point of insanity, wanted to bring about spiritual "decisions." It is true that Bertram intends by means of his translation of the historical into the legendary to serve the historical efficacy of Nietzsche. In reality, however, Bertram weakens that efficacy to the point of complete inefficacy by using numerous emblems to intercept Nietzsche's unique spiritual impact.

The inappropriateness in principle of this sort of presentation for the type of subject being presented feeds on George's[12] poetical image of Nietzsche and becomes especially evident in the closing chapter "Eleusis," which deals with Nietzsche's end in insanity as if madness had, as it were, carried him off to the gods.[13] The cynicism with which the last Nietzsche speaks of himself and of all great things is, however, still truer than the poetic veil that Bertram spreads over that cynicism. The correlate to the total character of this presentation is the irresolute way in which Bertram speaks in passing of Nietzsche's teaching. He calls it a "pseudo-revelation" and a "deluded mystery" and sees in it a "symbolization of the feeling of dizziness" at the sight of the "return to harbor," to oneself. The problem of Nietzsche's teaching is not clarified thereby, but artfully concealed.[14]

## 5.

Charles Andler[15] limited the purpose of his comprehensive presentation to a historical understanding of Nietzsche. Within the context of his intention as a literary historian, Andler was the first to examine Nietzsche's teaching from every angle for its sources and for parallels. That teaching is a *"vision cosmologique"*[T176] that is to lift man above himself.

> On n'avait pas compris jusqu'ici qu'on pût admettre à la fois le Retour éternel et la Surhumain. Il semblait que la grand vision de l'Homme régénéré n'apparût qu'au bout d'une route droite et ascendante. Comment pouvait-il y avoir cette ascension droite dans l'éternel retour? C'est que le temps a un rayon de cour- bure. Dans l'infini toutes les lignes droites reviennent sur elles-mêmes. La fa- talité du retour éternel rend possible la contingence pure, puisqu'en visant le futur, tous nos actes modifient leur passé. La décision par laquelle nous ac- ceptons de revivre notre présent est l'acte immensément libre qui justifie les mondes, non par son contenu, mais par sa liberté.
>
> . . . Le Retour éternel est la gage de notre Surhumanité. La Surhumanité nous permet d'accepter le Retour éternel. On ne séparera plus ces deux idées. (IV, pp. 316f.)[T177]

These two *"mystères"*[T178] complement each other. But *how* they unite into a whole does not become clear in Andler's analysis, because he overlooks the rupture between the "I will" and the self-willing world that Nietzsche wants to affirm in a super-human way. For Andler the whole of the teaching remains "une grande intuition mystique, dont la valeur ne dépend pas de son contenu."[T179] But what value can a teach- ing have if one disregards what it as such contains?

The real problem of the recurrence is seen by Andler in Nietzsche's desire that the teaching liberate from a twofold gravity in existence: from the *"pesanteur physique"* and from the *"pesanteur du passé"* (VI, p. 67),[T180] and in particular to liberate by means of two simultaneous resurrections.

> Il y a donc deux aspects du retour éternel, et aucun commentateur ne le a vus. La physique suffit a démontrer le retour éternel de monde matériel, Nietzsche à la suite de la sagesse orientale essaiera une descente dans l'Hadès pour abolir le passé, où dorment les morts oubliés. Il ne faut pas confondre les deux résurrec- tions, mais elles sont simultanées; et cette simultanéité nous délivre du fardeau le plus lourd à porter après la Pesanteur: le fardeau du Passé. (VI, p. 62)[T181]

But how can the two lines of interpretation, one taking its bearings from the universe and the other from man, be reconciled?

> De cette deuxième théorie emboîtée dans l'autre, comment discuter? Elle tra- duit le sentiment profond de Nietzsche devant l'univers. (P. 74)[T182]

For Andler this riddle is solved by the insight that one must already have become superhuman in order to be able to see as one Nietzsche's twofold teaching of the eternal cycle of the world and of the will to self-eternalization. "Que ferons-nous de cette libre éternité? Mais que pouvons-nous en faire, si ce n'est devenir surhumains?" ( p. 76).[T183] The whole teaching thus remains a "last secret" that does not permit of *rational* articulation.

> C'est un beau poème incommunicable. Par lui, Nietzsche sort de son refuge solitaire et sombre, et se montre à nous dans une clarté qui n'appartient qu'à lui. Nous n'en retiendrons que la fascinante émotion qui lui fait sentir son union avec la nature et avec l'humanité. ( VI, p. 386)[T184]

Just here, however, where Andler's presentation stops, the philosophic problem (which cannot be grasped by literary history) begins. For with what does Nietzsche's very first version—in the two essays about "History and Fate" and "Freedom of the Will and Fate" of 1862—of his final idea deal if not precisely the questionable *discrepancy* between "*nature*" and "*humanité*,"[T185] so that the motif for Nietzsche's tendency to *unify* the divided spheres is the *discord* between "*nature*" and "*humanité*." Only once is Nietzsche's attempt to overcome this modern discord fairly accurately characterized:

> Il prétend plonger du fond de l'abîme irrationnel et gravir la cime de l'affranchissement rationnel. Inépuisable effort, et sans doute contradictoire, mais qui traduit un puissant besoin moderne. Nietzsche n'est pas la seule victime de cette intime désunion qui aspire à retrouver l'intégrité intérieure. Peut-être seulement en a-t-il souffert plus que personne. Les temps actuels n'ont pas de tragédie, parce que leur mysticisme résorbe constamment l'affirmation héroïque. Les tragédies contemporaines sont donc, au fond, des poèmes lyriques; et c'est pourquoi, dans le Zarathoustra, la tragédie qu'il contenait n'a pu se dégager de la musique verbale, où elle flotte comme son reflet. ( VI, p. 58)[16, T186]

## 6.

Klages's[17] book stands out because of the methodical rigor of his prosecution of *one* basic idea. This idea extends back to the time of Klages's membership in the "Cosmic Circle" and was first expressed in a text on George (1902), where it is said, "It is not in the brain, the seat of *consciousness*, but in the *blood* that the wave of frenzy swells." The same discord underlies his theoretical foundation of graphology, where he analyzes handwriting in search of a twofold source. As movements of expression that have concrete shape, they point on the one

hand to an original agitation of body and soul and on the other hand to
a supervening shaping-force that arbitrarily regulates those nonarbitrary
impulses. In conformity with this double source, out of a vitality that is
by nature cosmic and a headstrong spirit, out of original abundance of
life (or perhaps poverty of life) and derivative regulation of life or sub-
limation, the explication of a script has in general a double meaning.
According to Klages, Nietzsche's handwriting is to the greatest extent
vital or besouled and at the same time intentionally sublimated; in the
most beautiful way it unifies shaping-force and movement of expression: life *and* spirit.[18]

Klages applies this basic distinction to Nietzsche's philosophy, so
as—in odd contradiction to his analysis of Nietzsche's handwriting—to
show throughout that in his existence and philosophy two *ir*reconcil-
able powers are coupled: a spiritual will to power and a "pathic" necessity to experience the rhythmically moved, cosmic life. The philosophy
of Klages solves this basic conflict by means of the negation of the power
of the "spirit." For him, Nietzsche's work accordingly divides into two
halves: he sees its "achievement" in the fact that that work is a philosophy of the "orgiastic"; the great error consists in Nietzsche's desire that
his work should be simultaneously a philosophy of the will to power.
That Nietzsche himself unites both in "*amor fati*" as his own Yes to
the "Yes of Being," and *how* he joins both into one, as well as the inner
connection of the will to power with the teaching of the eternal recurrence—all these fall outside Klages's strictly limited scope. His revealing
and ever repetitive artifice of interpretation consists in the stubbornly
maintained distinction of what in Nietzsche's work is "undistorted" expression of original life from what in that work is consciously willed,
what is true insight from what is falsifying humbug. And it is not Nietzsche's philosophical works that Klages ultimately regards as a true expression of originally experienced "reality," but some "ecstatic" poems
(n. 46). The Nietzsche positively evaluated by Klages is therefore not at
all Nietzsche as a philosophic personality (= soul bound up with spirit)
but Nietzsche insofar as he is an expression of cosmic life that is "alien
to spirit or (!) original." Taking cosmic life as the starting point, the individual existence receives the privative characterization of an "ephemeral bearer" of universal life. Spirit, according to Klages, has come to
ascendancy with the historical man of the Christian interpretation of existence, whereas the dominance of the "body" or of the "soul" was the
foundation for the heathen view of life. Nietzsche is said to owe his

positive discoveries without exception to his heathen side, and all his errors to the Christian side.

This conflict reaches its peak, by this account, in Nietzsche's teaching of the eternal recurrence of the same. What is in truth expressed in that teaching is the opposite of what it is intended to be; it is not an affirmation of Heraclitean-Dionysian Being, but a negation of suicide.

If one puts oneself into the mood of a thinker who seizes upon ever more imploring formulas in order to prove to himself his *affirmation* of life against the desperation that threatens him—out of the unhappy certitude that in him, too, the *one* [will] belongs to the *haters* of life—with suicide, one knows why he had to end with the teaching of the return, although that teaching is nothing but desperation once more. With the declaration, "I want to live this selfsame life, a thousand times wrested from the will to self-destruction, thousands and thousands of times *again*," he has accomplished the most extreme thing that can be contrived—not, to be sure, in the affirmation of life, but in the *negation of its negation*. It is the formula for defense of the most inflexible self-affirmation against the tendency toward self-*destruction*. (P. 216)[19]

Klages is completely right when he says, "Whoever traverses Nietzsche's work with *this* knowledge in hand will make astonishing discoveries," because the lights of Nietzsche's Dionysian exuberance shine before the fathomless darkness of despair. And thus Klages explains Nietzsche's end in insanity, too, in terms of his "adhering to two points of view that are mortal enemies of each other, that of the unconditional affirmation of life and that of the unconditional affirmation of the will," which is the enemy of all life. For what is more absurd and more impossible, asks Klages, than "to say Yes and No in one breath"?

And yet just this *unity* of "abyss and peak" and the "marriage of light and darkness" is the peculiar fundamental character of Nietzsche's whole philosophy, which comes to a peak in the double prophecy of nihilism and the eternal recurrence. The critical question that therefore should be put to Klages and his interpretation of Nietzsche would be the question of the *originality of the thought of suicide*. Klages is blind to the *essential* "negativity of the spirit," which according to Hegel's insight consists above all in "the ability to abstract" from everything that is. Klages sees in the negativity of the spirit a mere un-nature and not also the strange "prerogative" of man whose nature surmounts itself.[20] Only because man, as a being that "wills," has the freedom unto nothing does he also have the freedom unto Being and can he himself also still affirm what always already is, and thereby exist positively. If for man the thought of suicide were really against his nature, he would as a natural living being be incapable of either negating or affirming life on the whole, and thus there would be neither an affirmative nor a negative "philosophy"—of life. The meaning of Nietzsche's philosophy depends exactly on the fact that he was *not* free, "as the people are," to separate "soul and body" and still less "soul and spirit" (foreword to *The Gay Science*, par. 3). Therefore he had to search for a "self-overcoming of nihilism." Such an attempt is as "natural" for man as it is natural for a plant simply to grow by nature and for an animal to move itself. When Overbeck fetched Nietzsche in Turin, the latter was in an orgiastic condition. But his handwriting at that time had become not—as Klages's theory would lead one to expect—an expression of a pure rhythm of life but rather the script of a "spiritually" disturbed man whose *human* life was thereby at an end, whereas the decline of his vitality did not begin until several years later. During the period of mental illness, Nietzsche was certainly not "translated back into the language of nature," "*homo natura*"; for it belongs to the nature of *man* that he can be a No-sayer *and* advocate. And when Klages's spirit listens to the "flute calls of the primordial world" in order to free himself from the negativity that lives within *him*, he, too, is an ambiguous advocate of life[T187] and not merely a mouthpiece of the cosmically moved world.

## 7.

Baeumler,[21] in contrast with Bertram, wants to say something "nonlegendary" and unified about Nietzsche as philosopher. For this purpose he combines Nietzsche's aphorisms onto a "single plane of interpretation." But this plane is laid out so that, for the sake of producing the unified "system," it makes Nietzsche into someone "nonunified." Baeumler, in differentiating Nietzsche's whole philosophy in terms of what in it is experienced "musically" and what is conceived "philosophically," claims to expose the outline of a buried temple and "to roll back onto one another" again some of its "column segments." This athletic attempt to restore the "true" Nietzsche is to be taken seriously not only because Baeumler at the time of the Third Reich was the official advocate and editor of Nietzsche's works, but also because in earlier times he proved his own ability in a piece he wrote on Kant's *Critique of Judgment* and in an introduction to Bachofen. All the more compellingly does the question suggest itself to the contemporary: how is it possible that Baeumler contrives an interpretation that eliminates Nietzsche's real "teaching" from the whole of his philosophy as if it were a stumbling block and makes a "system" out of what remains? Baeumler's interpretation of Nietzsche's path to wisdom as a "path of will" provides the answer to that question. "Force against force" is seen as the fundamental character of Nietzsche's life, and the "world as a struggle" is portrayed as his view of the world. His philosophy is nothing but deed that ends with his collapse, "while swinging the sword," in his "Siegfried attack on the urbanity of the West"! Apparently Baeumler, too, wanted to swing the sword with fresh and gay science, and because Nietzsche's teaching of the eternal recurrence of the same and the conclusion of *Zarathustra* II and III did not suit that purpose, Baeumler had to devise a fitting interpretation of Nietzsche.

The formula that Baeumler coins for Nietzsche's worldview and that came into use in many variations is that of "*heroic realism.*" He is infinitely remote from all "blessed isles," on which Nietzsche-Zarathustra achieved an "act of highest self-reflection." Baeumler completely misunderstands the type of Nietzsche's heroism because he does not see it together with its seeming opposite, Nietzsche's penchant for sorrow and for peaceful seclusion. Sils Maria and the southern countryside, where *Zarathustra* and *The Will to Power* were written, are for Nietzsche an "eternally heroic idyll," and he uses the compound "heroic-idyllic" (e.g., in *Briefe* IV, p. 114, and *The Wanderer and His Shadow,* aph. 295) in the same sense as Hölderlin does. The heroic man, however, is for Nietzsche the one who "is accustomed to sorrow and seeks sorrow." In Baeumler's depiction of Nietzsche's "landscape of ideas," one notices nothing of a heroic idyll and a heroic sorrow taken upon oneself; both drown in Baeumler's aimless "struggle." His will to struggle is blind to the perfect hour of "noon and eternity." What Baeumler wants to acknowledge is only the philosophy of the "forenoon." Granted, he relies principally on Nietzsche's incomplete final work, *The Will to Power,* but in such a way that he separates it from *Zarathustra,* even though he himself reproduces in his edition of the literary remains the plans for *The Will to Power,* which contain the teaching of *Zarathustra* as the conclusion that is fundamental to the whole project. As a consequence of this arbitrary expurgation of the teaching of the return from the context of *the will to power,*[22] Baeumler is forced to assimilate the "innocence of becoming," which originally results from the eternal recurrence, into a will to power *without* an eternal recurrence and to see in the will to power only the "will *as* power." The will as power takes over the function of the eternal recurrence, and in place of the self-willing Dionysian world, without a will to any thing and without a goal, Baeumler now says (pp. 47ff.) of the will as such that it wills nothing at all, not even "power," but only itself; it is already the innocence of eternal becoming that, as a cycle, lacks beginning and goal. This will made innocent is the dubious foundation of Baeumler's entire interpretation of Nietzsche's beheaded philosophy. In truth, however, the problem of the will does not first arise in *The Will to Power*, but already in the chapter in *Zarathustra* entitled "On Redemption," that is, redemption from willing straight ahead. The will is redeemed from its own re-willing not by the mere lack of purpose and goal but by willing backward to the circle of the circular motion that wills ahead as well as backward. Only in the ring of this eternal recurrence of the same can the existence of the agonal, "wrestling" man, too, "will itself" beyond the first liberation from the "Thou shalt." Nietzsche's formula for this willing of the eternal recurrence is no mere will to "destiny" but *"amor fati,"* whereas Baeumler can picture under the term "love" not love of eternity but only a bourgeois sentimentality (p. 66).[23] Consequently the chapter in *Zarathustra* on the "Seven Seals," like the "Drunken Song" in which the other dancing song recurs, itself remains a book with seven seals for him. The Yes-and-Amen song seems to him to stand in opposition "to all philosophical positions of Nietzsche" (p. 82), whereas in reality the song justifies all "wandering and mountain-climbing" in the morning as a "makeshift" and positively underpins the critique of the will to power. As a result of this resolute misunderstanding of Nietzsche's "system," Baeumler's concept of the "innocence of becoming" is merely another word for a will that goes "into the dark," a will that does not—as in the case of Nietzsche—attempt "to turn" irresponsibility into something "positive," but only wants *not* to "accept responsibility" any longer and is self-confident because it does not know what and why it wills at all (p. 48).[24] This will is at bottom nothing other than an "explosion of force." And despite Baeumler's great effort to equate his heroic will with the innocence of becoming, it comes to light again and again that his will "as power" wills powerfully, to be sure, but has not thought much about the connection of Nietzsche's will with the eternal return; Baeumler himself calls this willing "action," "struggle," and "passion."

*The Will to Power.* A book for *thinking,* nothing more: it belongs to those to whom thinking gives *pleasure,* nothing more. . . . That the book is written in

German is at least untimely: I should have liked to have written it in French so that it might not appear to reinforce any aspirations to German empire. The Germans of today are no longer thinkers: something else gives them pleasure and impresses them. To them the will to power as a principle would indeed be comprehensible. (XIV, 420; cf. *Briefe* I, p. 534)

Baeumler on the contrary sees in Nietzsche's supposed teaching of the will "the most perfect expression of his Germanism" (p. 49). Nietzsche's Heraclitean—but not Dionysian—world, too, in which struggle and victory is everything, is called "primally German." Although Baeumler thinks it important that in this continuing struggle a "highest justice" and an "eternal order" of the world is produced, this reflection applies only to Nietzsche's presentation of the world of Heraclitus and not to Baeumler's world, which lacks the law of the eternal recurrence. It is impossible to see how a highest justice should be produced through mere explosions of force. What Nietzsche as a classical philologist first points out with Heraclitus is exactly the same as what he later teaches under the name Dionysus. And again one must ask: How does an expert on Nietzsche like Baeumler arrive at the *opposition* of the Heraclitean to the Dionysian world and at the assertion, "When the concept of the eternal return appears, the Heraclitean character of the world disappears"? And further:

In truth this idea [of the eternal recurrence], seen from the standpoint of Nietzsche's *system,* is without importance. We have to regard the idea as the expression of a most personal experience. The idea [of recurrence] stands unconnected with the fundamental idea of the "will to power"; indeed, the former would, taken seriously, dissolve the cohesion of the philosophy of the will to power. (P. 80)

A substantial integration of the idea of the return into the system seems to him impossible. The eternal return is an erratic boulder, for the return is a "religious conception," whereas the system is a strictly philosophical, coherent web of thought, and it is impossible to recognize the "world as struggle" in Nietzsche's Dionysian double world. But that this recognition is impossible does not necessarily speak for Baeumler's interpretation. "Dynamic quanta, in a relation of tension to all other dynamic quanta"—*that,* according to Baeumler, is Nietzsche's really authoritative formula for his world (p. 84). But *why* is Baeumler blind to the philosophic content of *Zarathustra* and to Nietzsche's Dionysian world? To this question the final sentence of the note to the section on the eternal recurrence gives the answer: because on the path via the Dionysian teaching of the eternal recurrence, one "only" lands in the "confusing problems" of Nietzsche's existence! These problems, however, are problems not only of Nietzsche's existence but just as much of Nietzsche's philosophy, and they also are confusing only for one who wants arbitrarily to simplify them by means of the division of Nietzsche's "system" into "music" and "philosophy." With that division Baeumler himself lapses into the view, which he opposed, of Nietzsche as a "poet-philosopher," although on the other hand Baeumler ascertains that precisely from *Zarathustra* on, Nietzsche's work becomes a system. But his fighting spirit has allegedly left him no time tranquilly to develop the existing train of thought. Correctly formulated, the question would not be, as Baeumler puts it, "What will come of the production of a creative thinker if he simultaneously has the drive to act?" but rather, What will come of an *interpretation* of Nietzsche if the interpreter is willing to toe the line as a philosopher? Answer: an interpretation that reduces Nietzsche's philosophy to the will to power and makes his philosophic ideas on European politics serviceable for the tendencies of present-day Germany. The knowledge of truth, Baeumler says, depends on the "pathos" and on the "*force* of the thinker" (p. 77)—but what good does all "force" do a philosopher if that force is not one of *thought,* and be it only in the capacity to follow the thought of Nietzsche's philosophy! Baeumler believes himself with his force to be very superior to Bertram's "legend" Nietzsche. But it does not make any principal difference whether one glorifies Nietzsche's philosophic experiment into a legend; or, like Klages, explains it (at the cost of the will to power) as an "orgiastic" philosophy of body and soul; or, like Baeumler, explains away the teaching of the eternal recurrence in favor of a "heroic realism."

# 8.

Erika Emmerich,[25] who is of the opinion that Baeumler's twisted interpretation of Nietzsche the *politician* "proved" for the first time that Nietzsche's Heraclitean philosophy is the intellectual "foundation" of the National Socialist movement (p. 71),[26] simplifies the problem in Nietzsche's *philosophy* in the opposite way from Baeumler's: she integrates Nietzsche's whole philosophy into the teaching of the eternal recurrence and neatly interprets the will to power, too, in terms of that teaching. For the purpose of this simplification she distinguishes between what in Nietzsche's philosophy is "originally experienced" as "Being" and what is only concocted later on the plane of the things that are. In the original experience (pp. 44, 46) of the truth of Being, Nietzsche becomes one with the Dionysian world (pp. 80f. and 84). "The truth that the world is" is the same as the truth that man is, and accordingly the will to truthfulness accords "originally" with the truth of the Being of all the things that are. That is, the whole *problem* of one's own willing of the eternal recurrence is eliminated by Emmerich. "If man is thus 'in the whole,' then the 'essence' of the world is also his essence: will to power *and* eternal return" (p. 81). But precisely this "if" is as *questionable* as the willing backward in willing forward, by means of which the will redeems itself from itself. Emmerich fails to appreciate the magnitude of the nihilistic motif (p. 28) in the tendency to self-eternalization because she is of the erroneous opinion that Nietzsche from a certain moment on had "wrested himself free from" nihilism once and for all (p. 37), namely after the discovery that nothing is true any longer and therefore everything is allowed. In truth, however, Nietzsche so little freed himself from nihilism at any time that even his teaching of the eternal recurrence is the "self-overcoming" of nihilism. Only on the ground and soil of nihilism, i.e., of groundlessness, do the will to power—as the revaluation of all former and now devalued values—and the eternal recurrence belong together systematically, because that teaching itself already is based upon the principle of a revaluation that reverses nihilism.

In Emmerich's interpretation, will to power and eternal recurrence belong together not through the self-overcoming of nihilism but in the "superman." In her view the superman is nothing other than "life in man" (p. 100), without any regard to the problem of an "overcoming of man," in the context of which alone the "superman" makes sense. "In original experience the truthful = superman" (p. 103). In Emmerich's interpretation this constantly repeated appeal to "original experience" solves in one stroke the whole, protracted riddle that Nietzsche attempted to solve up to the brink of insanity, only to find himself crushed, finally, "between two nothings." The whole set of problems in Nietzsche's attempt to "rebetroth the world" by means of a "self-overcoming of man" disappears in Emmerich's presentation through the equation of man and cosmic fatality.

## 9.

Thierry Maulnier[27] regards the attempt to identify man and world as specifically "German," because he himself as a Frenchman follows the tradition of Descartes, as his introduction immediately shows (p. 17). In the light of this classical construction of the world, Nietzsche's Dionysian philosophy has to appear to be a new "mysticism," which subjects to blind fatality the freedom of human willing and capability.

En effet, la théorie moniste du monde dont Nietzsche fait sa philosophie dernière,—il est curieux que l'esprit allemand, moniste par essence, ne puisse parvenir à la définition d'une dualité irréductible sans chercher à la résoudre par la synthèse—, cette théorie l'amène à étendre et à enrichir son humanisme jusqu'à rendre compte de l'univers; il n'est satisfait de sa définition du héros que si elle lui explique aussi les infusoires et les planètes, la morale tragique n'acquiert toute sa valeur que rattachée et soumise à un enchaînement cosmique. Dès lors, la pureté tragique cesse d'être un moyen d'opposer l'homme ou de l'exposer à la fatalité, elle doit découvrir en lui cette fatalité, et le dernier mot de l'idéal humain ne saurait être que de prendre conscience de l'univers en soi-même. Le point extrême de la purification intérieure, l'expérience totale de l'héroïsme ne consistent donc pas à l'éloigner le plus possible de la nature, mais à égaler la nature, à se fondre en elle, à la sentir vivre en soi. . . . Le dualité fondamentale, principe du combat chrétien et du combat tragique, de l'homme et du destin, de la liberté et de la nature, est en fin de compte résolue, l'homme n'a été affranchi que pour l'orgie dionysienne. (Pp. 254ff.)[T188]

The Dionysian excess signifies an incomprehensible renunciation of what makes man into man, namely, *esprit, conscience, jugement, raisonnement, volonté* (p. 286), in contradistinction to the "*instinct élémentaire.*"[T189]

En réalité, cette conscience que l'effort de Nietzsche a tendu, dès les origines, à restaurer dans sa richesse, sa lucidité, son autonomie suprêmes, n'a plus désormais sa place dans l'univers dionysien. Le contact est désormais trop étroit, et l'enchaînement trop nécessaire, entre les fatalités cosmiques et les gestes de l'homme, il n'y a plus, dans la substance du monde, de fissure où la liberté humaine puisse insérer le jeu de ses délibérations ou de ses négations. (P. 258)[T190]

In Maulnier man's "*conscience*" opposes the world's "*mécanisme*"; "*dignité humaine*" opposes "*vie élémentaire*"; "*volonté,*" "*instinct*"; "*valeurs humaines,*" "*phénomènes naturels*"; and "*déterminisme,*" which results from "*fatalité,*" the "*liberté*"[T191] of the self-aware man—in contrast with which Zarathustra's soul is the most necessary soul, which throws itself with pleasure into accident and knows itself to be "free" precisely in *amor fati*. But if this is an "*absurdité logique*"[T192] the question rightly arises:

. . . si, en anéantissant dans cette force profonde de l'univers l'autonomie de la volonté humaine, Nietzsche n'a pas rendu la tragédie impossible en voulant la rendre plus pure. Car la tragédie suppose précisément une fatalité étrangère à l'homme, une volonté irréductible au destin, puisqu'elle suppose conflit de l'un et de l'autre. . . . Or, dans le mysticisme nietzschéen, la Moira surhumaine et les actes du héros suivent les mêmes voies inflexibles. La fatalité n'est tragique qu'autant que l'homme n'y consent point; la fatalité des cristaux et des plantes n'est point tragique, les planètes ne sont point en conflit avec leurs el- lipses. Un des plus grands efforts pour exalter et former l'héroïsme aboutit à placer l'homme au rang des phénomènes. Dès lors, tout ce qui était acquis n'est pas loin d'être perdu. (Pp. 266f.)[T193]

In affirming the cosmic recurrence, Nietzsche sacrifices to "*commu- nion*"[T194] with the world that is by nature, the greatness—hard-won by himself—of the heroically struggling man.

On a déjà remarqué combien tout ceci est allemand, comme est allemand tout ce qui déséquilibre vers la synthèse deux expériences inconciliables. Comme Gœthe, comme Hölderlin, comme Novalis, Nietzsche sombre dans la tentation panthéiste. . . . Dès lors, l'homme dont la dignité est sans doute le refus de l'in- nocence universelle, est devenu un moment de l'innocence universelle. . . . On ne nie pas la grandeur de cet homme nouveau, enthousiaste de l'univers, en- chaîné à un passé et à un futur illimités, nécessaire en chaque instant au monde qui finit, et au monde qui va naître, également lourd d'un héritage et d'une postérité de cosmogonies. Mais cette grandeur, faite de la nécessité de l'homme dans l'univers, et de la gratitude qui la reconnaît, cette grandeur n'est rien que la grandeur même du monde, reflétée en nous. Cette grandeur est certaine; mais Pascal en avait défini une autre, que toute celle-là liguée écraserait en vain. (Pp. 267ff.; cf. p. 281)[T195]

Nietzsche's passion is

presque scandaleux en celui qui avait porté si haut les exigences proprement humaines. On déplore que l'effort le plus douloureux pour l'affranchissement de l'homme, pour la violence de l'âme et la pureté des désirs, que les réflexions les plus subtiles, les plus longues disciplines, les plus dures chastetés n'aient con- duit Nietzsche qu'à une ferveur magnifique mais facile, à peine différente de cette extase de vivre qu'un enfant atteint avec sa seule spontanéité. (P. 268)[T196]

With this third metamorphosis into the child that makes a new beginning, Nietzsche denies himself, as "*le prince des libérations*," by

means of a "*renaissance des idoles*,"[T197] as the two main titles of Maulnier's book suggest. Only after Nietzsche has been forsaken by his mind
and will does he correspond in fact to his last "*mystique pour une om-
bre*" (pp. 271ff.).[T198]

Un homme, qui n'était plus Nietzsche, allait vivre sans heurt d'une vie enfin accordée au rythme du monde. La maladie avait eu raison de l'esprit sans s'atta-
quer aux mécanismes organiques fondamentaux. La supposition de Nietzsche,
que la conscience n'est pas nécessaire à l'accomplissement des actions néces-
saires à la vie, était vérifiée sur lui-même. La conscience, "petite lumière à la surface de la vie," s'était éteinte; la vie continuait, ordonnée toujours, consentante,
épousant pleinement l'évolution du monde: le corps qu'elle animait n'était plus
qu'un fragment du mécanisme universel. Mais la fragile lueur qui en lui s'était
éteinte était l'élément souverain dans lequel Nietzsche avait méconnu le seul ad-
versaire supérieur en dignité et parfois en puissance à la fatalité. Le monde avait
reconquis une parcelle de la liberté humaine. (P. 298)[T199]

The reason for Nietzsche's deserting himself lies in his finally suc-
cumbing after all, on the tragic path via the "*concupiscence de la dou-
leur*" (pp. 223ff.),[T200] to the romantic temptation: the wish to find a
bliss. He reunites what he previously separated, "*la création de la joie*"
(pp. 193ff.) with the "*création du bonheur*" (pp. 42, 57, 204ff.).[T201]

Nietzsche pourra crier son mépris à *Rousseau*, et . . . parler de "cet avorton" qui
"voulait lui aussi le retour à la nature." Ce n'est pas d'avoir voulu le retour à la
nature en effet qu'il lui fera reproche. C'est d'avoir cru que la nature est égalité,
alors que la nature est inégalité et guerre, c'est d'avoir voulu, dans la nature,
retrouver la morale, alors qu'il faut en elle échapper à la morale. Ainsi, pour
juger la civilisation, Nietzsche reprend les principes de Rousseau et les renverse.
Comme Rousseau, . . . il cherche le salut dans un retour aux vertus de l'homme
naturel. (P. 250)[T202]

Nietzsche's cosmic ecstasy seems to have been his last refuge in the
face of the complete loss of the world.

Il n'y a pas d'univers autour de Nietzsche; dans les villes où il erre, il ne cherche
qu'un climat plus propice à ses nerfs, des refuges plus favorables à son travail;
s'il demande une jeune fille en mariage, c'est après avoir reconnu en elle une
disciple; s'il tombe malade, c'est de trop penser; s'il trouve ou perd un ami,
c'est dans des discussions philosophiques; la campagne, pour lui, n'est que solitude; son ciel . . . est sans nuages ni rêves . . . il est seulement la carrière pure et
vide où son vol intellectuel sera le plus direct et le moins retardé. . . . La plus
physique des innocences, le sommeil, ne lui est pas, elle-même, accordée sans
réserve; il doit l'acheter avec du chloral. . . . Il n'y a rien dans ce corps, dans ce
regard, dans ces lèvres, qui soit fait pour les ordinaires relations humaines,
geste, étreinte ou discours: "Celui qui a perdu le monde doit gagner son propre

monde." Il n'y a rien autour de Nietzsche: jamais un penseur n'est resté ainsi implacablement enfermé en lui-même.

. . . ce philosophe de la vie n'avait négligé que de vivre.

. . . N'étant pas capable de sauver sa solitude à travers les occupations, les amours, les relations mondaines, il doit se séparer du monde. (Pp. 33 and 290)[T203]

Precisely in this strict isolation and "magnificent fear of the world" (pp. 8 and 189) and in bearing up against a dreary universe, the *liberating* Nietzsche reached his utmost philosophic heroism, which drove him "à imaginer un monde plus douloureux, plus écrasant, plus étouffant que le monde ressenti. . . . Il importe, pour la création de la joie, que le monde abandonne l'homme, . . . qu'il n'ait pas de fin ni de sens, qu'il ne nous emmène nulle part" (p. 212).[T204] Such a world is that of the eternal recurrence, in the cycle of which nothing is mirrored but the *circulus vitiosus* of Nietzsche's own, hopeless existence.

Il est vain, parce qu'il est facile, de chercher ce qu'a d'arbitraire et de puéril la doctrine du Retour Éternel; il suffit de constater qu'elle était le terme normal de la philosophie de la solitude et sa fatalité métaphysique: non l'explication la plus ingénieuse, ou la plus vraisemblable, ou la plus consolante du monde, mais l'explication la plus terrible. Or, le plus terrible seul était cherché. (P. 213)[T205]

In overstepping the tragic ideal, Nietzsche also abandoned his method of destruction (pp. 62ff., 77, 86ff., 92), which stood in the service of the most extreme liberation and was supposed to give back to man "*sa tragédie perdue*," in radical renunciation of "*salut*" and "*bonheur*."[T206] For the tragic man is always "*à la recherche de la mort*" (p. 164); he is free "*pour vivre et mourir intégralment*" (p. 61)[T207] and "le créateur de la tragédie nouvelle n'a rien voulu définir à l'homme qu'un digne chemin vers la mort" (p. 137),[T208] whereas Nietzsche finally willed the eternal recurrence and no longer "*une provocation inlassable à la fatalité*" (p. 165).[T209]

But perhaps Maulnier does not perceive the inner necessity of Nietzsche's third metamorphosis only because the *héroïsme* "rationaliste" (p. 271)[T210] has not yet been in that "desert" of freedom where what matters is to find a new bond. Not Descartes already, but rather Nietzsche found it necessary, at the most extreme edge of freedom unto the nothing, to turn the need of the will[T211] toward the affirmation of a highest necessity.

Maulnier's counterpart to Bertram's dialectical synthesis of Nietzsche's contradiction shows, as no other presentation does, how much

Nietzsche is a *German* event; for here a Frenchman speaks to us who rejects all essential elements of the real philosophy of Nietzsche:

les cultes informes du surhumain, de l'innocence, de l'Éternel Retour, qui ne peuvent que le déformer et l'appauvrir. Bien plus: trompé par le mysticisme germanique dont il se croit à tort affranchi, victime de l'héritage romantique qu'il a renié en vain, il ne va pas tarder à altérer l'essence tragique elle-même de son héros, qu'il veut définir et purifier. (P. 224)[T212]

Maulnier finds not only Nietzsche's critique of Germanism to be extremely German—"c'est une Allemagne qu'il oppose à l'Allemagne, ce sont des cultes à ses cultes, des ivresses à ses ivresses, c'est l'Éternel Retour au Devenir, et le Walhalla de Dionysos au Walhalla de Wotan"[T213]— but also his renewal of antiquity:

Dans la Grèce à laquelle il recourt, c'est le germanisme grec qu'il découvre: non la Grèce, mais cette colonie allemande que les peintres, les philosophes, les poètes de son pays ont établie en Grèce, et dont le territoire, laissant Athènes et Platon, va de Delphes à Eleusis, et d'Orphée à Empédocle: Grèce de mythes, d'orgies, de mystères, de philosophies hasardeuses, de formules et d'initiations, Grèce réelle, sans doute, mais non la Grèce. (Pp. 277f.)[T214]

What the German lacks, according to Maulnier, is exactly the sense of the "moment" that is noon and eternity.

Le sens de l'instant est proprement méditerranéen, le pouvoir de saisir dans le temps une présence immédiate, une amitié. . . . Pour une philosophie des métamorphoses, le présent n'est qu'une abstraction, un point du temps, "un pont et un passage" du passé à l'avenir: pour nous, le présent est la réalité la plus réelle. Un monde inlassablement tendu vers le dépassement de lui-même n'accorde à aucune existence de valeur pure et incomparable. La sagesse méditerranéenne fait au contraire de chaque minute, non un passage, mais un aboutissement, lui attache un prix absolu et irréductible, y enferme une volupté atteinte et epuisée de façon irréparable: chaque instant reçoit ainsi . . . une valeur en soi, une magnifique inutilité. Signe remarquable: M. André Gide, prenant à Nietzsche les grandes lignes de son attitude de vie, complète en un point cette attitude, et c'est en créant une philosophie de l'instant. Tout l'esthétisme latin de la perfection dérive, en somme, d'une appréhension du présent particulièrement vive et violente: toute perfection est l'instant éternisé. Il manque à Nietzsche cette divination. . . . Le héros nietzschéen connaît la volonté de puissance, non pas l'action. Au delà du sens de l'être, c'est chez Nietzsche le sens de l'instant qui fait défaut; au delà du sens l'instant, le sens de l'acte. Toute philosophie du devenir ignore l'acte. (Pp. 283ff.)[T215]

Nietzsche's attempt at a solution is "monistic" because, as an *"esprit allemand, déséquilibré par essence,"*[T216] he was unable to resist the temptation de réunir en faisceau les forces ennemies du destin et de l'homme, pour le combat tragique magistralement opposées. Il faut que l'homme s'intègre à une théorie moniste du monde, cesse d'avoir une autre réalité que celle d'un moment du mouvement universel. Il est accordé au monde, lors même qu'il le juge, ou qu'il en est écrasé. Ainsi la philosophie de la puissance se trouve conduite à la négation d'un pouvoir humain propre et différént des forces naturelles, d'une liberté de choisir, de peser et de refuser. Elle ne pourra triompher qu'en réalisant l'accord le plus intime et le plus spontané des décisions de l'âme aux mouvements du monde: l'innocence est maintenant son but. Ainsi, l'image du grand civilisé de type césarien tend, dans les derniers ouvrages de Nietzsche, à s'effacer devant celle de l'instictif barbare. (P. 249)[T217]

# 10.

Karl Jaspers's[28] thought carried the imprint of Nietzsche and Kirkegaard from the *Psychologie der Weltanschauungen* ("Psychology of Worldviews") on up to the development of his *Philosophy* (1932). The viewpoint for the interpretation of Nietzsche's doctrine as the teaching of "philosophizing," however, is not taken from Nietzsche's own attempt to establish a new position toward the whole of Being, but out of the existential philosophy of Jaspers. The tripartition that he makes, into world orientation, elucidation of existence, and metaphysics ("ciphers" of transcendence), derives in turn from the traditional distinction of "world" (nature), "man" (soul), and "God," and found its last philosophic expression in Kant. Under the title "The World as Pure Immanence," Jaspers does take note of Nietzsche's observation that the "true world" of Christian-Platonic transcendence was a "history of the longest error," but rather than take this understanding as the positive guide of the interpretation, Jaspers rejects this view as a philosophic deficiency. In the closing division he distinguishes, it is true, between "How Nietzsche Understands His Thought and Himself," and "How Nietzsche Is Understood by Us." But when presenting Nietzsche's self-understanding, Jaspers already presupposes the basic concepts of his own philosophizing, so that the essential distinction of the one body of thought from the other vanishes. Nietzsche, it is said, has dared to take the most varied positions, but only to relativize them again by means of a dialectical negation. What remains of Nietzsche's teaching is therefore only the path as such, his constant being-on-the-way, and what does not allow of being reduced to this movement are unphilosophic absolutizations of empirical matters and superficial rigidifications. Nietzsche's truth is in Jaspers's view not to be found in any stage of this path, such as at the end or on the height of *Zarathustra,* but exclusively in the total movement of his transcending thought. Even in the "increasingly rigidifying teachings" of the superman, of the eternal recurrence, and of the will to power, one may not overlook the questioning, however infrequent. "Nietzsche's real philosophizing prevails only where every teaching can become relative at once" ( p. 281). Lacking this aspect of manifold ambiguity that cannot be eliminated, Nietzsche would not remain himself. For on his path from the nothing to Being, he would press on, beyond all particular things, toward indeterminate "origins and limits."

But if anything is clear about Nietzsche's going and going across, going down and going beyond himself, it is his original and final will to the "ring of the world"—in opposition to a Christian transcendence, however evanescent. This decisive alternative between "God" and "world" is dialectically neutralized by Jaspers by means of a system of contradictions that he points out and relativizes, and the two are dissolved as alternatives by means of the only seemingly undogmatic method of fundamentally and totally relativizing them. In the light of this method, all positions and negations of Nietzsche's thought likewise appear as forms of "transcending." Seen from this standpoint, which is actually no standpoint but a "suspension," Nietzsche's "hierarchies of life" change into "possibilities of existence." The meaning of Nietzsche's overcomings is supposedly that he never devoted himself to anything once and for all. But where Nietzsche nevertheless firmly sets an unambiguous Yes and No, Jaspers can recognize only dogmatic rigidifications of a transcending movement, in relation to which everything positively stipulated is banal. For Jaspers the sought "whole" of Nietzsche's philosophy is an "indeterminate, boundless thing" that remains if one leaves all determinate positions and negations out of consideration. The trouble that Jaspers goes to in order to demonstrate this thesis cannot gloss over the central importance for Nietzsche of a radical decision, or the fact that his work is more than a "dizzying movement" and an "evocation of infinity."

Judged by Jaspers's existentialist thought, the idea of the eternal recurrence of the same becomes a mere "cipher" of transcendence, and qua thought becomes a transcending the origin and goal of which is neither God nor the world. True, his discussion of the teaching of the return begins with the statement that this idea was more decisive for Nietzsche than any other; but Jaspers's interpretation of the eternal return does not show why this idea and no other could become so important for Nietzsche. In Jaspers's presentation the problems of the teaching of the return reduce to its being on the one hand the existential expression of godlessness and on the other hand its aiming at a pre-Kantian metaphysics. That such an attempt necessarily must fail, however, would only be proved if the transcendental, critical idealism that Jaspers adopts in his philosophy in an existentially altered form were the final and definitive word on the truth of the world. As a result of Jaspers's presupposition of the Kantian scheme of God, man, and world—kept together only by [man's] consciousness—the possible truth of the idea of the eternal recurrence reduces to the formal transcending into an indeterminate transcendence, which in Nietzsche is hidden behind the Being of the visible world of the senses. By wanting to grasp with his will what can only be conceived as a symbol, Nietzsche himself brings it about, in Jaspers's view, that the symbol becomes a mere mask. But as much as Nietzsche's paths lead into an "airless space," just as little are they empty, in Jaspers's opinion, for the impetus and goal of Nietzsche's intellectual movement is said to be the "historicity of existence"—and not the attempt to regain a lost world. What Nietzsche is and does, according to Jaspers, remains "open," that is, as open as is genuine consciousness of Being, and as Being itself. What is explosive in Nietzsche's philosophy is as it were macerated in Jaspers and, in an elaborate net of colorless concepts, is robbed of its historical efficacy. Jaspers's helplessness vis-à-vis the assault that Nietzsche is, takes the pose of a "comprehensive" tour through a conceptual world of forms. The will to a decision in Nietzsche and Kierkegaard, whose opposition and relatedness Jaspers has displayed so clearly, is dissolved by Jaspers himself into a "philosophic faith" that sways without concrete content between godlessness and faith in Christian revelation (*Vernunft und Existenz*, pp. 101ff.; *Nietzsche*, pp. 388ff.).

## 11.

Following the precedent of Jaspers, Ludwig Giesz[29] interprets Nietzsche's teachings of the superman, of the eternal recurrence, and of the will to power out of the "existential dialectic" of being oneself (pp. 160ff.). He applies this method so exclusively that he sacrifices the character of these teachings as signs of possible transcendence. All three teachings are traced back to the single formula of "self-overcoming," because in Giesz's opinion this formula defines not only the idea of the superman but also the will to power conceived as universal and the eternal recurrence of the same in the whole of the living world. Eternal recurrence and will to power are merely regarded as the "functional expression" of a constitution of the self, of its self-referential creativity. The eternal recurrence is an interpretation in which nothing but the world image of a particular humanity (pp. 61, 66, 162f.) and a "dialectic of inwardness" interpret and hypostasize themselves. The circular temporality of the eternal recurrence is based in the "reflexivity" of self-overcoming, which is at once the basic character of the will to power (pp. 23, 159). Appealing to Zarathustra's speech "On the Backworldly," Giesz binds his interpretation of Nietzsche to the assertion that the "belly of Being" does not speak to man at all, unless it be as man (pp. 37, 62). He overlooks the fact that this speech polemicizes against the backworldly and that the continuation of *Zarathustra* in the image of the eternal recurrence wants to articulate Being itself, and not only man and his reflexiveness. Moreover, Zarathustra's speech to his animals, who first proclaim his teaching to him, is by no means meant only scoldingly (pp. 130, 140). Certainly Zarathustra's world is "his" world and accords with his soul (pp. 49, 161), but that does not mean that the cosmological problem of the eternal recurrence can be reduced to the subject that teaches and bears the recurrence. The "mirroring" of world and man is in principle reciprocal and ambiguous. That mirroring cannot be fixed at *one* end, in the subjectivity of self-overcoming, because the goal of self-overcoming is just this: to free oneself from the will to the nothing, in favor of willing the fatality of all Being, and from a self-conscious and lost-to-the-world "I will" to become a self-forgetting child of the world. In the presentation of Giesz, on the contrary, the world as will to power and its temporal mode of being is only an "illustrative allegory" of the creative man who as creator makes the world into his own world. The eternal recurrence just articulates in terms of the world at large the same turning backward that also lies in the willing backward of the creative will, so that the "wheel that rolls out of itself" of the child and the eternal wheel of Being exactly correspond to each other—as if it were not precisely this *having* and *wanting* to correspond that presents the whole problem of overcoming a contradiction based not only in man himself but also in his relationship to the world.

By reducing the problem of the questionable unity of world and man (who is a fragment, accident, and riddle in the whole of Being) to *one* side of the will to power as subjective self-overcoming, Giesz can declare that the relationship between superman, will to power, and eternal recurrence is "no problem at all," that they optimally harmonize with one another and complete one another (pp. 126, 131). But if the teaching of the eternal recurrence really only expressed the dialectic of self-overcoming (= will to power) in world time, and if the circular world time of the eternal recurrence were really based in the subjective reflexiveness of self-overcoming (p. 159), it would be incomprehensible that five hundred pages of *Zarathustra* were needed to complete the last of the three metamorphoses and, after all going and going across fails, finally "to fly into" the eternal heaven. (Walter Kaufmann's *Nietzsche: Philosopher, Psychologist, Antichrist* [1950]—much less forcefully, but with the same tendency—also develops Nietzsche's philosophy out of self-overcoming, understood anthropologically.)

## 12.

Martin Heidegger's[30] thought, like that of Jaspers, moves on paths that transcend all the things that are and that express nothing ascertainable of Being itself. He, too, reads his own thought into that of Nietzsche in order to interpret himself in Nietzsche. But the kinship of the two Nietzsche interpretations is already exhausted in this formal similarity. More essential and striking is their opposite posture and intention. While Jaspers has Nietzsche's teaching sway, as a cipher of transcendence, in the movement of a transcending that relativizes everything, and while he embraces Nietzsche's entire work from all sides, Heidegger bores himself into Nietzsche's work from a particular point by selecting isolated propositions and seminal terms or sayings, the meaning of which is dogmatically delimited without regard for possible contrary propositions and terms or sayings. The intention of this delimiting interpretation is to emphasize the question of Being.

Nietzsche is for Heidegger the most exciting figure of that "previous" thought which still immediately concerns us, and *Zarathustra* is that work in which Nietzsche's "only" idea, the eternal recurrence of the same, is thought. This single thing that Nietzsche has to say, according to Heidegger, allows neither of proof nor of contradiction, but it also is not an object of faith. It can be brought to view only through questioning and thinking, and at bottom this observation holds true of every essential idea within any essential body of thought: "something sighted, but a riddle—question-worthy" (*Vorträge und Aufsätze*, p. 119). The question is all the more decisive whether Nietzsche's teaching comes to view for Heidegger as Nietzsche himself saw it, namely as the primordial law of all *living* Being. Considering the closing observation in the lecture "Who Is Nietzsche's Zarathustra?" we may presume from the outset that this [faithfulness to the author's intention] does not obtain here. For, when might Nietzsche ever have thought that the essence of modern technology, of the revolving engine, could be an "embodiment of the eternal recurrence of the same"?[T218] And how does Heidegger understand the reversal of the will to the nothing into the willing of the eternal recurrence and the resulting revaluation of all values, if he asserts the unity of the teaching of the superman, of the eternal recurrence, and of the will to power without considering even by way of allusion the contradiction that lies at the bottom of the correspondence desired by Nietzsche between the Being of the world and the existence of man? For Heidegger, Nietzsche's reversal and revaluation mean something merely negative, because every overturning moves within the domain of its opposite, that which has been overturned (*Holzwege*, pp. 200, 214, 242). Because of the overturning accomplished by Nietzsche, there is nothing left to metaphysics except to turn[T219] into essential insubstantiality;[T220] for the removal of the suprasensual also eliminates the merely sensual and therewith the distinction between the two. In [the writings of] Nietzsche himself, however, the abolition of the "true" world ends not at all in the insubstantial[T221] but rather in a new beginning, at "noon," which—as the moment of the perfection of the world and time—is an eternity. This self-interpretation of Nietzsche does not prevent Heidegger from contending that Nietzsche has so little overcome metaphysics (i.e., Christian Platonism) that, on account of his mere countermovement against nihilism, he has remained hopelessly entangled in metaphysics and in the nihilistic consequences of metaphysics. To be sure, Heidegger's Nietzsche has experienced "some features" of nihilism on the path of the overturning, but he has still interpreted nihilism nihilistically; and he has as little recognized the "essence" of nihilism, the hiddenness of the truth of Being, as has any metaphysics before him (*Holzwege*, p. 244). His revaluation of previous values only consummates, once and for all, the preceding devaluation of the highest values so far. Trapped in the horizon of the will to power that wills itself, that is, in the perspective of value and of setting of value, Heidegger's Nietzsche no longer recognized his own new setting of values as nihilism.—One wonders how a thinker who himself accomplished a "turning" and who insists on the circular structure of all disclosure can fail to acknowledge that an attempt at the "overcoming" of nihilism cannot begin without presuppositions, short of nihilism. Rather, as Nietzsche knew and said, an attempt at the overcoming of nihilism sublates in itself what is to be overcome. If any philosopher of modernity went so far as to think—beyond all historical thought in terms of epochs, ages, and plights of the world—of an eternal same, the necessity of which arises from no "future need" but from the eternal law of all becoming Being, that philosopher was Nietzsche, when he attempted to "translate" man (who had become eccentric) "back" into the "basic text" of nature.

Despite Nietzsche's express statement that the total character of life and of the living world can*not* be assessed and evaluated, Heidegger interprets Nietzsche's philosophy as a "metaphysics of values" and interprets value as a "point of view," the simple meaning of which he artfully misinterprets. But the conception of the world that Nietzsche envisions, and which he attempts to develop on the foundation of *Zarathustra* in *The Will to Power,* is characterized by the idea that life as will to power cannot be devalued, because "in every moment" life is wholly what it is, and remains equally powerful and signifies the same through all alteration. Heidegger's interpretative approach in terms of the concept of value is a prejudgment decisive for everything further. He interprets the noon, which is eternity, not as Nietzsche experienced and understood it but instead purely negatively, as a "transitoriness brought to a halt." Anyone who reads what Nietzsche says about the noon, however, can only be astonished at what Heidegger reads into it that was neither said nor intended. He leaves out of consideration, in his interpretation of what is "essential" in Nietzsche's teaching, the fact that Nietzsche closes the third and fourth Parts of *Zarathustra* with a commemoration of eternity. This eternity is no "securing of continuance" but an eternal recurrence of the same coming into being and passing away. As an eternal recurrence of the same, Nietzsche's eternity appears in Heidegger's interpretation only in that the will to power—the vantage point from which he one-sidedly interprets the teaching of the return—secures the lasting continuance of itself for a willing that is "as homogeneous and regular as possible."[T222] The will, as the same, thus comes back constantly onto itself as the same; and the way in which the things that are exist in the whole (the *essentia* of which is the will to power), that is, their *existentia*, is the eternal recurrence of the same. But because Heidegger has left behind him the traditional distinction between *essentia* and *existentia,* his interpretation of the two key terms of Nietzsche's metaphysics, "will to power" and "eternal recurrence," comes to the conclusion that Nietzsche conceived nothing at all that was essentially new, but instead completed what has been a leading theme for metaphysics since olden times: the definition of the things that are in their Being through an "essence" and an "existence" both of which have still not been contemplated. The relationship between will to power and eternal recurrence thus conceived is not discussed further by Heidegger.

It cannot be disputed that Nietzsche conceived of eternity as a being-always, and thus not as timelessness but rather as the lasting present or "presence" of a becoming that always is of the same type, power, and meaning ( *Was heißt Denken?* pp. 40ff.; *Vorträge und Aufsätze,* p. 109). But the question is whether this Nietzschean view is a deficiency and a failure to reach Being, or rather the eternal-temporal or everlasting truth of Being. In the end it is a deficiency in *wisdom* in whoever does not want to admit that knowledge only brings itself to wholeness and fullness when it knows the world as "perfect," i.e., when it comprehends that in every moment of a "today," the "former time" and the "someday hence" are as joined together as are all the things that are in the wheel of Being. "Everything goes, everything comes back; the wheel of Being rolls eternally. Everything dies, everything blossoms again; the year of Being runs on eternally. Everything breaks, everything is put together anew; the same house of Being builds itself eternally. Everything separates, everything greets itself again; the ring of Being remains true to itself eternally. In every split second, Being begins; the ball There rolls itself around every Here. The center is everywhere. Crooked is the pathway of eternity."[T223] This first proclamation of Zarathustra's teaching, uttered by his animals, is certainly nothing absolutely new, but rather repeats from the modern viewpoint on volition what metaphysics has thought since olden days.[T224] But then who tells us that truth changes from time to time through some "other fate of Being" and does not—like the Being of all the things that are—always remain the same and therefore also return in time in the consciousness of those who know? Had Nietzsche only reflected on what is evidently the concern of the time "now," in the age of the will to power and of the coming reign over the earth, he would have remained an untimely critic of his time. Only by freeing himself from the sickness of his age[T225] did he become "a convalescent," who as a last lover of wisdom knew about what is always, which always recurs because it remains the same in all alteration and change of the things that are.

# References

*Nietzsche's Werke* (Divisions I and II) in sixteen volumes of the Großoktav and Kleinoktav edition.

*Nietzsche's Werke,* Division III (Philologica), Vol. 3 = Vol. XIX of the Großoktav edition.

Nietzsche, *Jugendschriften,* Musarion edition (1923), and *Werke und Briefe: Historisch-Kritische Gesamtausgabe* (1933ff.).

*Friedrich Nietzsches Gesammelte Briefe,* 5 vols. [cited as *Br.*], and *Die Briefe Peter Gasts an Friedrich Nietzsche,* 2 vols. (1923–1924).

*Friedrich Nietzsches Briefwechsel mit Franz Overbeck* (1916).

## Sources on Nietzsche

C. A. Bernoulli, *Franz Overbeck und Friedrich Nietzsche,* 2 vols. (1908).

E. Förster-Nietzsche, *Das Leben Friedrich Nietzsches,* Kleine Ausgabe, 2 vols. (1925). [Cited as "Biogr." in Author's Notes below.]

E. F. Podach, *Nietzsches Zusammenbruch* (1930).

## Writings on Nietzsche's Attack on Christianity

W. Solovjeff, "Dichtung oder Wahrheit," in *Ausgewählte Werke,* Vol. I (1914).

J. N. Figgis, *The Will to Freedom; or, The Gospel of Nietzsche and the Gospel of Christ* (New York, 1917).

L. Schestow, *Dostojewski und Nietzsche* (1924).

K. Jaspers, *Nietzsche und das Christentum* (1938).

H. de Lubac, *Le drame de l'humanisme athée* (Paris, 1945).

M. Carrouges, *La mystique du Surhomme* (Paris, 1948).

W. Nigg, *Religiöse Denker* (1952), pp. 219ff.

G.-G. Grau, *Christicher Glaube und intellektuelle Redlichkeit: Eine religions-philosophische Studie über Nietzsche* (Frankfurt a.M., 1958).

M. Heidegger, *Nietzsche*, 2 vols. (Pfullingen, 1961).

Except as otherwise noted, citations from the works published by Nietzsche himself (Vols. I–VIII) provide title and aphorism number; from the *Nachlaß* (Vols. IX–XVI), except as otherwise noted, volume and page number; from *Zarathustra* (Vol. VI), volume and page number.

Vol. XX, the Index of the Großoktavausgabe, contains a cross-listing of pages to the edition published by Kröner Verlag. F. Würzbach provides a bibliography in *Literarische Berichte aus dem Gebiete der Philosophie*, Heft 26 (Erfurt, 1932).

# Abbreviations

| | |
|---|---|
| *The Birth of Tragedy (Die Geburt der Tragödie)* | = *G.d.T.* |
| *Human, All-Too-Human (Menschliches, Allzumenschliches)* | = *M.A.M.* |
| *The Wanderer and His Shadow (Der Wanderer und Sein Schatten)* | = *W.u.Sch.* |
| *The Dawn of Day (Morgenröte)* | = *M.* |
| *The Gay Science (Die fröhliche Wissenschaft)* | = *F.W.* |
| *Beyond Good and Evil ( Jenseits von Gut und Böse)* | = *J.* |
| *On the Genealogy of Morals (Zur Genealogie der Moral)* | = *G.d.M.* |
| *Twilight of the Idols (Götzendämmerung)* | = *G.D.* |
| *The Antichrist (Der Antichrist)* | = *A.* |
| *Ecce Homo* | = *E.H.* |

The Author's Notes (pp. 233–258 below) contain, besides simple citations and notes, references to the most important parallel passages for the respective basic concepts treated.

# Author's Notes

The vignette under the title of the book depicts "Dionysus in the Ship" after a Greek vase of Exekias. Cf. the conclusion of the poem "The Sun Sets," pp. 106–107.

## Foreword to the First Edition

1. *E.H.,* "Why I Am So Wise" (XV, 9).
2. *Br.* I, p. 515.

## Foreword to the Second Edition

1. Almost exactly half a century later the following attempts to reach a new understanding of Nietzsche appeared: C. G. Jung, "Eine psychologische Analyse von Nietzsches Zarathustra" (1935–1939; [then] unpublished transcripts of seminars); K. Löwith, *Nietzsches Philosophie der ewigen Wiederkunft des Gleichen* (1935); K. Jaspers, *Nietzsche* (1936); M. Heidegger's "Vorlesungen über Nietzsche" (1936ff.), out of which essential parts were published in *Holzwege*, *Was heißt Denken,* and *Vorträge und Aufsätze.*
2. Letter to Overbeck, 28 December 1888.
3. Stefan George, *Siebenter Ring*; R. Oehler, *Die Zukunft der Nietzsche-Bewegung* (1938); Heidegger, *Holzwege,* pp. 230, 233.
4. The author's thanks for the first edition of a book that could not be publicly distributed under the political circumstances of that time are due the owner of the press "Die Runde," Mr. Gerhard Bahlsen.

5. Last letter to J. Burckhardt, dated 6 January 1889. Facsimile reproduced in E. Podach, *Nietzsches Zusammenbruch* (1930).
6. See C. A. Bernoulli, *Overbeck und Nietzsche* (1908), II, 251, cf. *M.* §14.
7. XIV, 359.

# 1. Nietzsche's Philosophy: A System in Aphorisms

1. IX, 340ff.; XVI, 245.
2. XII, 191.
3. XIV, 319; cf. *F.W.* 347 and XVI, 84.
4. *J.* 42.
5. VI, 286.
6. XVI, 383.
7. *J.* 209 and 210.
8. XI, 159.
9. *W.u.Sch.* 213; cf. XIV, 352f.
10. XV, 91.
11. XIV, 354.
12. XIII, 72f. and *M.* 453.
13. XIV, 353f.
14. *M.* 318.
15. XIII, 55.
16. XIII, 57, and VI, 439.
17. XIII, 54ff.
18. XIII, 34f.
19. *J.* 20.
20. XIII, 58.
21. *J.* 231.
22. XIII, 154.
23. XIII, 73.
24. *G.D.,* "Skirmishes of an Untimely Man," 51.
25. X, 216ff.; 290ff.
26. Cf. XV, 95, and Rohde's letter of 24 March 1874.
27. VI, 183ff. and 186ff.; cf. 288f.
28. X, 216ff.
29. *Br.* III, p. 281; cf. p. 306.
30. *Br.* IV, p. 170.
31. *Br.* I, p. 487.
32. *Br.* IV, p. 347.
33. *Br.* IV, p. 434.
34. Prologue to *G.d.M.*
35. Prologue to *M.*
36. See XIV, 362.
37. Regarding the problem of *J.* see above all VI, 131ff.; 274ff. On the

problem of *G.d.M.* see above all VI, 41ff., 88ff., 127ff. Concerning the problem of the *W.z.M.* see VI, 63ff., 84, 105ff., 147, 165ff., 197ff.

38. Preface to *G.d.M.*

39. F. Overbeck, *Christentum und Kultur* (Basel, 1919), pp. 282f. and Bernoulli I, pp. 227f.

## 2. The Division of Nietzsche's Writings into Periods

1. Prologue to *M.A.M.* II, 2.
2. Cf. among other passages *Br.* IV, pp. 17, 114, and 293.
3. Cf. XV, 82.
4. See, e.g., XIV, 308f.
5. *Br.* II, p. 568f.; *Br.* III, p. 365.
6. Prologue to *M.A.M.* II.
7. See further: Prologue to *M.A.M.* II, 1 and 7; XIV, 371ff.; XV, 61.
8. X, 241ff.
9. X, 233ff.
10. XV, 102f.
11. See Baeumler's edition of the posthumously published "Die Unschuld des Werdens" I, pp. xiiiff.
12. XIII, 39f.
13. Cf. VI, 27ff. and 142: "Gone is the hesitant gloom of my spring! Gone the malice of my snowflakes in June! Summer I became entirely, and summer noon."
14. VI, 397; *G.d.M.* III, 24; XII, 406 and 410; XIII, 361; XVI, 413f.
15. VI, 34 and 150.
16. VI, 11, 35, 108, 218; cf. XII, 391; *G.d.M.* II, 16.
17. Cf. VI, 125; XII, 412, and XVI, 328, where the third level is characterized as the "*I am*" of the Greek gods, whereas in *Zarathustra* a characterization corresponding to the "Thou shalt" and "I will" is lacking. With the creative-destructive play of the child of the world compare XII, 409, where Zarathustra in a "cosmic speech" breaks his completed work asunder, only to put it together again anew, again and again.
18. *W.z.M.,* aph. 1041.
19. Cf. Rohde's letter of 16 June 1878, in which he predicts for Nietzsche, for the purpose of reaching his goal, the retrograde path (*Br.* II, p. 546).

## 3. The Unifying Fundamental Idea in Nietzsche's Philosophy

1. On the connection between romanticism, postivism, and nihilism, cf. XVI, 448: "Between 1830 and 1850 the romantic faith in love and the future

changed into the desire for the nothing." Cf. also the political criticism of romanticism by A. Ruge, "Der Protestantismus und die Romantik," *Hallische Jahrbücher für deutsche Wissenschaft und Kunst*, Vol. 2 (1839), and Carl Schmitt, *Politische Romantik* (1925).

2. Concerning contemporary judgment of *M.A.M.* see above all the letters of J. Burckhardt (*Br.* III, pp. 174ff.) and E. Rohde (*Br.* II, pp. 543ff.). On the distinction between free spirit [*Freigeist*] and agnosticism [*Freidenkertum*]: *J.* 44; XIV, 396ff.; XV, 489.

3. See XV, 73ff.

4. XI, 8f.

5. *M.A.M.* I, 225.

6. *M.A.M.* II, 113.

7. XI, 19.

8. *W.u.Sch.* 5, 16, 350; cf. L. Klages, *Die psychologischen Errungenschaften Nietzsches* (1926), Chapter V.

9. On Nietzsche's concept of freedom as "will to assume responsibility for oneself" see above all *G.D.*, "Skirmishes," 38; *J.* 19; XVI, 204, in opposition to which his *authentic* concept of freedom from *Zarathustra* onward is developed out of the relationship between *accident* and *necessity*.

10. VI, 92; X, 147; XIV, 394; XV, 23.

11. Prologue to *M.A.M.* I, 3.

12. Prologue to *M.A.M.* II, 5.

13. Typical representatives of this activated, "heroic" nihilism after World War I were above all E. Jünger and O. Spengler; see E. Jünger, *Das abenteurliche Herz* (1929), pp. 23f., 180f., 186ff., 236ff.

14. Prologue to *M.A.M.* I, 2.

15. *M.A.M.* I, 638.

16. XIV, 393.

17. See below, p. 56ff.

18. *W.u.Sch.* 308; cf. VI, 400ff.

19. Cf. *M.A.M.* II, 408 ("Journey to Hell").

20. Cf. the poem of the same title. The dialogue between the Wanderer and his Shadow that expresses the idea ("albeit in a shadowy fashion") that the Shadow is as much as the light is, continues in the dialogue between Zarathustra and the Wanderer-Shadow and ends in that between Nietzsche and Dionysus (*J.* 295).

21. XV, 9f.

22. *W.u.Sch.* 213; see above, pp. 13–14.

23. XV, 467.

24. XIV, 388f.

25. XI, 9.

26. Cf. the poem "The Wanderer" and *W.u.Sch.* as well as XIV, 306.

27. XII, 223; cf. VI, 229.

28. See *Br.* II, p. 582.

29. VI, 191 and 196.

30. VI, 223, 395ff.

31. VI, 396ff. and 223. Cf., on the other hand, p. 317, where the nihilistic

meaning of the eternal "everywhere" and "nowhere" changes into the eternally same; see below, pp. 72–73.

32. *M.* 56.

33. *F.W.* 377.

34. XV, 74.

35. The closing statement of *E.H.* also refers to Voltaire: "Ecrasez l'infâme" ["Crush the infamy"].

36. *M.* 477.

37. *J.* 41.

38. Poem "Between Birds of Prey."

39. A letter of 1866 already contains a first indication of this tendency: "Yesterday an imposing thunderstorm filled the sky; I hurried to a nearby mountain . . . , [and] high up I found a cottage, a man who slaughtered two kids, and his boys. The storm discharged most violently with gales and hail; I felt an incomparable upward surge, and I correctly perceived that we understand nature rightly only when we must flee to her from our troubles and afflictions. What was man and his restless willing to me! What was the eternal 'Thou shalt,' 'Thou shalt not' to me! How different were the lightning, the gale, the hail: free powers, without ethics! How happy, how mighty they are, pure will, undarkened by the intellect!" (*Br.* I, pp. 25f.; cf.—twenty years later—in *W.z.M.*, aph. 332ff.).

40. See further the author's *Von Hegel zu Nietzsche*, 3d ed. (1954).

41. *Principles of the Philosophy of the Future*, Principle 21; *Briefw. und Nachlaß*, ed. K. Grün, I, pp. 407f.

42. *F.W.* 357.

43. XV, 70.

44. Cf. on the decline of antiquity *M.A.M.* I, 141; *M.* 71; *A.* 58ff.; and further Bruno Bauer, *Christus und die Caesaren* (Berlin, 1877).

45. X, 343ff.

46. Cf. K. Hecker, *Mensch und Masse* (1933), where the tendency toward "change" is pointed out, with particular reference to K. Immermann, as a general tendency of the times in the entire post-Hegelian literature of the Young Germans.

47. VI, 63ff. and 105ff.; cf. IX, 73; XII, 230 and 351.

48. XV, 112 and *A.* 10.

49. Cf. *Phänomenologie*, ed. Lasson (1907), p. 483; *Religionsphilosophie, Werke*, XII, 228ff.

50. *Werke* I, p. 153.

51. XV, 34, 323 and 328ff.

52. Cf. also the author's *Heidegger: Denker in dürftiger Zeit* (1953), pp. 92ff.

53. VI, 456.

54. *M.* 92.

55. X, 289f.; cf. IX, 112, 211; X, 408.

56. Cf. also the final aphorism of the first book of *M.*: "*In hoc signo vinces*" [Latin for "By this sign [the Cross] you will conquer"].

57. *F.W.* 125.

58. XIII, 316f.

59. On the history of the concepts "superman" and "God-in-man," see *Zeitschrift für deutsche Wortforschung* I, 1 (1900), pp. 3ff., and the references by D. Tschizewskij in "Hegel und Nietzsche," *Revue d'histoire de la philosophie*, Vol. 3, no. 3 (1929) and *Dostojevskij-Studien* (Reichenberg, 1931).

60. VI, 115 and 418.

61. Cf. Burckhardt's characterization of Nietzsche, *Br.* III, pp. 174, 180, and 186.

62. XIV, 262; cf. XII, 417f.

63. VI, 388, 406, 418.

64. VI, 43 and 315.

65. See with regard thereto A. Gide, "Ariadne," *Jahrbuch der Nietzsche-Gesellschaft*, 1925, and R. Guardini's Dostoyevsky book, *Der Mensch und der Glaube* (Leipzig, 1933).

66. VI, 387.

67. Cf. VI, 127 and *F.W.* 274.

68. *G.d.M.* III, 28.

69. Cf. Nietzsche's remarks on Dühring's book *Der Wert des Lebens*: X, 492ff.

70. XV, 61; cf. also in J. Burckhardt's *Griechische Kulturgeschichte*, ed. Oeri, 4th ed., Vol. II, pp. 349ff.: "Zur Gesamtbilanz des griechischen Lebens."

71. *F.W.* 357.

72. XIII, 363.

73. Cf. regarding this matter frag. 50 of the Dionysus Dithyrambs and *G.d.M.* III, 27 and *J.* 227 with reference to the remaining "*will to truth*," which forbids itself the "lie in the faith in God."

74. *F.W.* 347.

75. See XV, 325.

76. XIV, 319; XVI, 84.

77. XIV, 202ff. and XV, 156.

78. Regarding the inner connection between pessimism, positivism, and nihilism see especially XIV, 341; XV, 147ff., 162, 167, and 194f.; XVI, 448; cf. *F.W.* 347; *M.* 477; VI, 361ff. and frag. 48 of the Dionysus Dithyrambs.

79. VI, 251; on the symbol of the thawing wind, see VI, 55 and 294; cf. *F.W.*, foreword and 377; XIII, 34; XV, 60 and 188.

80. XV, 141ff., 155, and *G.d.M.* III, 27.

81. Prologue to *W.z.M.*

82. XV, 160f.

83. *G.d.M.* III, 1 and 28.

84. *J.* 55; *A.* 7 and 18; cf. XV, 323.

85. XV, 142, and *F.W.* 125.

86. XIV, 208f.

87. Cf. VI, 65; *F.W.* 347.

88. XV, 153.

89. *J.* 56.

90. XVI, 381.

91. XVI, 380f.

92. See further G. Naumann, *Zarathustra-Kommentar* (1899–1901), Part

4, pp. 179ff. The worship of an ass was a favorite charge of late heathendom against Christian congregations. Cf. also P. Labriolle, *La réaction païenne* (Paris, 1934), pp. 193ff.; W. Otto, *Dionysos* (1933), p. 158. Possibly the reference to the ass festival in Lichtenberg (*Gesammelte Werke,* 1802, Vol. IV, p. 537; 1844 ed., Vol. V, p. 326) was known to Nietzsche when he wrote his parody.

93. X, 396; cf. *Br.* IV, pp. 247 and 348.

94. See the Appendix.

95. XVI, 421–436. On the integration of the *W.z.M.* as a "revaluation of all values" into the authoritative philosophy of the eternal recurrence, see XV, 102; XVI, 414f., 435f., and 474.

96. XVI, 422.

97. VI, 203ff. and 210; XV, 80; XVI, 515 and 401f.

98. XV, 182.

99. XVI, 422; XII, 406.

100. XVI, 425.

101. *G.d.M.* II, 24.

102. Cf. *Br.* IV, pp. 178f.

103. XII, 419.

104. Cf. *W.z.M.,* aph. 25.

105. VI, 226.

106. VI, 315.

107. Cf. on the other hand "the evasions hitherto" of the thought of the recurrence: XII, 398f.

108. *F.W.* 370.

109. "The psychological feat of those years was going over a terrible abyss and not looking *down,* thus going and not seeing—in brief, bravely to pass over a danger while believing oneself to be heading for a danger." XIV, 306; cf. VI, 210 and XII, 223, as well as *F.W.* 287 and the poem "The Wanderer."

110. VI, 230 and 462.

111. VI, 315.

112. VI, 10.

113. XIV, 302; XII, 66.

114. XII, 409.

115. XII, 397 and 401.

116. *W.z.M.,* aph. 1041.

117. Nietzsche declares in a letter that far from being a collection of isolated speeches, *Zarathustra* rather consists of hidden, lengthy chains of thought and the depiction of a philosophic problem; in this letter he characterizes his work as "well made" "to speak as a master joiner" (*Br.* IV, pp. 175ff.).

118. *Briefwechsel mit Overbeck,* pp. 199, 216, 240.

119. XV, 85.

120. Plan of 26 August 1881; *Br.* IV, pp. 164 and 210.

121. XII, 413; cf. 409, 412, 418; VI, 105ff.

122. *Br.* IV, pp. 133 and 153.

123. *Br.* IV, p. 149.

124. XIV, 409.

125. XV, 15.

126. *Br.* IV, pp. 132 and 199.

127. XV, 3 and 49.

128. *Briefwechsel mit Overbeck,* pp. 196, 216, 227f., 231, 243.

129. VI, 121.

130. XV, 91; cf. VI, 270f.

131. Cf. on the "problem of the actor" *F.W.* 361 and XV, 356. [See also *J.,* aph. 97.]

132. See further Klages, note 46.

133. See *Br.* IV, p. 70. One could refer to analogous decisive "moments" in the lives of others: Descartes's enigmatic enlightenment on 10 November 1619, Pascal's note of 23 November 1654, Rousseau's portrayal of his enlightenment on the road to Vincennes (letter to Malesherbes of 12 January 1762), Kierkegaard's diary entries of May 1838. But the intellectual experience that "flung" Nietzsche "around" does not become clearer by means of such comparisons. The experience must be explained, if at all, in the context of the thought of *Zarathustra.*

134. *F.W.* 382 and *G.d.M.* II, 24.

135. VI, 469.

136. VI, 400, 402, 469.

137. VI, 215ff., 218.

138. VI, 142, 271.

139. Cf. *W.z.M.,* aph. 1032.

140. The literary connection of the narrative with a passage from the *Blättern von Prevorst* by J. Kerner was first discovered by K. Jung (*Zukunft* of 25 February 1905) and then incorporated by Möbius, Seillière, and Andler into their presentations.

141. When no work is specified, citations of pages in this chapter refer to *Zarathustra.*

142. Cf. the beginning of the "Other Dancing Song."

143. 240; in the poem "Das Feuerzeichen," i.e., *after* Zarathustra's convalescence from the illness "man," the volcanic fire of the depths of the earth changes into a "fire of the heights" under a dark sky, blazing upward with a quiet glow, as a question mark for such men as have answers. Cf. moreover the poem "Ecce Homo" and XII, 352.

144. 197.

145. 199 and 474, where there is likewise, but for the opposite reason, "no time" anymore.

146. 201.

147. Cf. Andler's interpretation in his *Nietzsche: Sa vie et sa pensée* VI (1931), pp. 26ff., which in my opinion, however, does not hold water.

148. 10 and 42.

149. 45 and 63ff.

150. Cf. on the contrary *A.* 25.

151. 215f.

152. 331f.

153. XII, 295: "Heroism is the *good will* to self-decline."

154. 218 and XII, 402f.

155. 105ff.; cf. the plans XIV, 277ff.

156. Cf. further *Br.* IV, p. 169.

157. 229ff.; 241; cf. 281ff.
158. 269f.
159. 269f.
160. 210; cf. *Br.* IV, p. 300.
161. "Without a goal that I regard as unspeakably important I would not have held myself high up in the light and *above* the dark floods! This is actually my only excuse for this type of literature, such as I have been producing since 1876: it is my prescription and my self-brewed medication against weariness with life. What years! What protracted pains! What internal disturbances, cataclysms, loneliness!" *Br.* II, p. 566; cf. *Br.* IV, p. 348 and *Br.* I, p. 445: "My existence is a *horrible burden*; I would have thrown it off myself long ago if I did not conduct the most instructive tests and experiments in the spiritual-moral domain just in this condition of suffering and of almost absolute privation. . . ."
162. 229 and also frag. 71 of the Dionysus Dithyrambs; cf. XII, 399.
163. 230, 420.
164. 231.
165. 232; cf. 465.
166. 206ff., 240ff., 290ff.; further, 17, 125, 210, 312, 364.
167. 314 and 318f. "The great weariness over man—*that* was what strangled me and crawled into my throat; and that was what the prophet prophesied: 'All is equal, nothing is worthwhile, knowledge strangles.'" Cf. *Br.* IV, p. 329.
168. 124.
169. *M.A.M.* II, 408.
170. 125.
171. From here on, the development of the idea proper is disrupted by multiple delays and interruptions, and is first taken up again in the chapter on the convalescent. Cf. XIV, 291, according to which a plan once existed to have the chapter "On Involuntary Bliss" follow immediately the chapter "On Convalescence."
172. 237.
173. 200 and 238.
174. 238 and 242f.
175. 280, 287.
176. 239.
177. Cf. the "Aftersong" to *J.*
178. 252, 280, 314.
179. 289.
180. 301.
181. Cf. the poem by the same title.
182. 317.
183. XII, 408.
184. 322.
185. 327 and the third part of the poem "Die Sonne Sinkt." Cf. the poem "Der geheimnisvolle Nachen," where the same skiff of eternity, still unredeemed and enigmatic, rests upon "black depths," while as a swingboat in "The Other Dancing Song" it gleams at nightly waters; and as a simile for the eternal recurrence, just as it "sinks," it "drinks" from the holy waters of life

and "twinkles again." On the vine as a holy plant of Dionysus, cf. W. Otto, *Dionysos,* pp. 133ff.

186. 334ff.

187. 332f. and 461ff.

188. See the poem "Ruhm und Ewigkeit," which was planned for the close of *E.H.*; cf. the earliest version of the idea in the fragments on Heraclitus: X, 46.

189. Cf. XIV, 267: "We . . . have to *want to become periodic beings*—like existence," i.e., the existence of the natural living beings of the world.

190. See the poem "Letzter Wille."

191. 125, 301.

192. 423.

193. 125.

194. 112 and 312f.

195. See the final part of "Ruhm und Ewigkeit"; cf. *E.H.* XV, 45.

196. 313.

197. 243.

198. 125; cf. 35.

199. 305.

200. 295f.

201. 206f; this passage is repeated in *E.H.* Cf. 113, 144f., 290, and XVI, 201. Unlike the exegesis that here follows, Heidegger (*Was heißt Denken,* pp. 33ff.; *Vorträge und Aufsätze,* pp. 110ff.) interprets "revenge" by going above and beyond what is said.

202. "What a nonsensical notion—to think of oneself as freely choosing one's existence, also even one's being just how one is, thus and so. Background: the demand that there *must* be a being that would have *prevented* a self-despising creature such as I am from coming into being. To feel oneself as a counterargument against God." XVI, 409 and XIV, 219; cf. above all XVI, 201ff.; *G.d.M.* II, 20 and *G.D.,* "The Four Great Errors," 7 and 8.

202a. An Oriental, the Japanese writer S. Natsume, remarks in his marginal comments on Zarathustra's "redemption" by means of a willing backward: "The greatest nonsense that was ever uttered by a human being"; and on the sentence (289) on the necessity that freedom itself is: "This is the practical, ultimate purpose for which so many Zen-Buddhist priests and pupils of Confucius have striven. But they reached a much higher degree of perfection (i.e., of perfect freedom) than any European ever did. Christians have never dreamed that there is such a freedom. Their conceited self-confidence seems to recognize no bounds."

203. "That Everything recurs is the most extreme approximation of a world of becoming to the world of being:—peak of meditation" (*W.z.M.,* aph. 617). And: "Becoming must appear justified at every moment . . . ; what is in the present may absolutely not be justified for the sake of some future thing, nor what is past for the sake of what is in the present" (*W.z.M.,* aph. 708).

204. 250 and 223; cf. XIV, 269.

205. On the distinction between ancient fate and modern destiny cf. Th. Haecker, *Vergil* (1931), pp. 104ff.

206. XIV, 331.

207. XV, 96; VI, 304.

208. "Ruhm und Ewigkeit," 4.

209. XV, 48; on the concept of the Dionysian see above all: the Prologue to *G.d.T.* 4; IX, 85ff.; XV, 61ff.; *F.W.* 370.

210. Schelling, *Die Weltalter,* Reclam ed., p. 68; cf. *Nachlaß* edition of M. Schröter (1946), pp. 217, 227 and *Werke* I/IX, 235.

211. Cf. *Briefwechsel mit Overbeck,* pp. 448, 451.

212. XV, 82.

213. 243.

214. 241.

215. 294f.

216. See frags. 20 and 58 of the Dionysus Dithyrambs.

217. XIV, 331; XII, 408 and, with reference to the recurrence and to the teaching thereof: VI, 322.

218. Cf. *Br.* IV, p. 199.

219. 43.

220. Prologue to *M.,* pars. 3 and 4.

221. XIV, 403.

222. 35.

223. Foreword to *E.H.*

224. XVI, 387.

225. *A.* I.

226. XII, 357ff.; XVI, 287.

227. XV, 443. Cf. XV, 184f.

228. VI, 87, 288, 311.

229. XII, 406ff.

230. X, 367f.; *A.* 3.

231. *G.D.,* "Skirmishes," 48 and 49.

232. X, 366ff.

233. XVI, 393.

234. XII, 426.

235. XVI, 100.

236. XVI, 398.

237. XII, 66ff.

238. XII, 398.

239. XII, 64; cf. X, 188.

240. XII, 66ff.

241. Precisely this will to the future is eliminated, however, by means of the teaching of the eternal recurrence of the same. Nietzsche writes Brandes in 1888: "That is, I am wont to forget now and then that I live. An accident, a question, reminded me in recent days that in me a main concept of life is downright obliterated, the concept 'future.' No desire, no little cloud of desire ahead of me! A smooth surface! Why should a day from my seventieth year of life not be exactly the same as my days of today?—Is it that I have lived too long close to death, so that I no longer open my eyes to the beautiful possibilities?—But it is certain that I now limit myself to thinking from today until tomorrow . . . and no day further! That [approach] may be inefficient, impractical, perhaps also unchristian—that preacher of the Sermon on the Mount

forbade just this concern 'for the morrow'—but it seems to me to be philosophic to the highest degree" (*Br.* III, pp. 307f.).

242. See G. Simmel, *Schopenhauer und Nietzsche* (Leipzig, 1907), pp. 251ff.

243. XII, 64f.

244. XII, 62.

245. XVI, 398.

246. XII, 53 and 57; XV, 63 and 182; XVI, 397; *F.W.* 335.

247. XVI, 399.

248. Cf. VI, 274.

249. XII, 51.

250. XVI, 396f.; cf. XII, 57 and 60; XVI, 130ff., 167ff.

251. XVI, 401.

252. XVI, 400f.; cf. XII, 62ff.

253. XII, 63.

254. XVI, 168.

255. XII, 61; with Nietzsche's attempt at a mathematical justification compare Kant's arguments in the first thesis of the antinomy of *The Critique of Pure Reason* as well as Schopenhauer's critique thereof, *Welt als Wille und Vorstellung* I, pp. 586f.; and O. Becker, "Nietzsche's Beweise für seine Lehre von der ewigen Wiederkunft," in *Blätter für deutsche Philosophie,* Vol. 9, no. 4 (1936).

256. XVI, 401f.; cf. the very first formulation of the Dionysian view of the world, under the name of a Heraclitean view: X, 30ff. and XIX, 167ff.

257. VI, 165ff., 84ff.

258. VI, 331; cf. XII, 392.

259. Cf. O. Becker, *Mathematische Existenz* (Halle, 1927), pp. 664ff. and 757ff.

260. Prologue to *M.A.M.* II.

261. XII, 221; cf. *Br.* IV, p. 176: "An image that occurs in almost all my writings, 'elevated above oneself,'—has become reality—and oh if you knew what '*oneself*' means here!" Cf. moreover Klages, Chapters IX and XIV, particularly p. 204: "All in all, *Zarathustra* is a visionary, eerie exegesis of the relative word 'super/over' {*über*]. Superabundance, supergoodness, supertime, supertype, superriches, superhero, overdrinking, those are several of the large number of 'super/over words,' some newly coined, some used again and again; and there are just as many readings of the one thing exclusively meant: the *overcoming.*"

262. Pp. 175ff.

263. XVI, 402.

264. XVI, 515. In another aphorism, the connection of this will to willing-again-and-yet-again with the will to the nothing becomes visible through the following: in that aphorism the image of the reflection of the world in an eye that is bright enough to behold the world is applied to the *nothing* instead of to the *world* (XV, 162).

265. Cf. XIV, 282: "Zarathustra says: 'I am the desire of the mistral wind, of electricity, of the height, of the change of the seasons' . . ."

266. See *Jugendschriften,* Musarion ed., I, p. 427 and XIX, p. 176. Whether

Nietzsche was familiar with the essay by Helmholtz about the preservation of energy is, according to information provided by the Nietzsche Archive, no longer ascertainable with certainty; cf. Biogr. II, p. 136; Nietzsche's comments on J. R. Mayer vary from the greatest expectation to the greatest disappointment; *Br.* IV, pp. 60A, 63, 102f.; cf. P. Gast's *Briefe an Nietzsche,* Vol. I, pp. 122, 163, 172, 174, 179, 202, 243, 245. See also XII, 432 (note to no. 105) and further: Andler, Vol. IV, pp. 254ff. The piece written by Abel Rey, *Le retour éternel et la philosophie de la physique* (1927), to which Andler refers, has not been accessible to me. A. Mittasch provides the most extensive presentation of Nietzsche's philosophy of nature: *Nietzsche als Naturphilosoph* (1952).

267. The expression was coined by P. J. Möbius, who is also the only man who as a natural scientist saw in a rough but clear outline what it means that Nietzsche believed in natural science: "Without the woe of absolute physics one does not understand Nietzsche's destiny. It seems that Nietzsche was like those who understand nothing at all about the natural sciences, but for just that reason have a powerful respect for the assertions of 'renowned natural-scientific researchers.' Whereas they otherwise believe nothing at all, they believe every word of the representatives of modern science. Nietzsche, too, bowed to natural science and then screamed, 'There is no metaphysics!' . . ." "At the beginning the freshness of youth, the enthusiasm for Wagner and Schopenhauer and for a new cultural movement, carried Nietzsche across this wasteland. But when he strayed from these ideals, he found himself in a meaningless world, hardened, and cried out, 'God is dead, everything is nonsense!' And then he wanted to become the revaluer of all values. In truth, however, desperation speaks out of him. It drove him around until he devised a wretched surrogate for metaphysics—the superman and the eternal recurrence . . . "

268. With the intention of accomplishing such a translation back, Nietzsche speaks of the necessity of a "naturalizing of man" (XV, 228) and of a "naturalizing of morals."

269. X, 189. Cf. XVI, 3ff.

270. XII, 48.

271. IX, 130ff.; XIX, 189ff.; *Jugendschr.,* p. 34; cf. XII, 391ff.

272. See XVI, 386f.: "The word 'Dionysian' expresses: an impulse toward unity, a grasping beyond person, beyond the everyday, beyond society, beyond reality, beyond the abyss of passing away: the passionate-painful swelling over into darker, fuller, more hovering conditions; an ecstatic affirmation of the total character of life, as of what is the same, equally powerful, equally blessed, in all change; the great, pantheistic sharing of joy and of suffering, which also approves and sanctifies the most terrible and questionable qualities of life; the eternal will to procreation, to fertility, to recurrence; the feeling of unity that comes from the necessity of creation and destruction." On the distinction between Dionysian pantheism and traditional pantheism see XV, 182f. and 442.

273. Cf. VI, 156ff. and 331, as well as 151 and 364; *M.A.M.* I, 109 and *Br.* I, p. 360: "In my opinion the *will to knowledge* is left over as the last region of the will to life, as an intermediate domain between willing and no longer willing. . . ."

274. *M.* 423 and 426.

275. XVI, 417. Cf. XV, 146f.

276. Cf. thereon G. Teichmüller, *Die wirkliche und die scheinbare Welt* (Breslau, 1882) and also Andler, Vol. II, pp. 118ff.

277. Cf. XV, 122.

278. Cf. L. Andreas-Salomé, *Nietzsche in seinem Werken* (Vienna, 1894; new printing, 1911; 3d ed., Dresden, 1924), pp. 165ff.

279. IX, 191.

280. XIII, 77 and 228.

281. XII, 361.

282. X, 172f.; XIII, 76; XVI, 100.

283. XII, 361.

284. VI, 402.

285. *M.* 575.

286. VI, 123, 352.

287. See Nietzsche's final letter to J. Burckhardt in Podach, *Nietzsches Zusammenbruch.*

288. Cf. the poem "Von der Armut des Reichsten."

289. 322.

290. 35 and 347.

291. *W.u.Sch.* 308; cf. letter of 11 September 1879 to Gast.

292. See on the following F. Bollnow, *Das Wesen der Stimmungen* (1943), pp. 195ff.; K. Schlechta, *Nietzsches großer Mittag* (1954), pp. 66f.

293. Schlechta, p. 32.

294. Schlechta, pp. 47ff., 54.

295. 322.

296. See above, p. 56.

297. Letters to Strindberg of 7 December 1888 and to Gast of 9 December 1888.

298. See below, p. 180f.

299. See above, p. 63f.; Schlechta, pp. 16ff.

300. *J.,* "Aftersong."

# 4. The Anti-Christian Repetition of Antiquity on the Peak of Modernity

1. "It is *not* a difference regarding martyrdom—it is only that martyrdom has a different meaning. Life itself, its eternal fertility and recurrence, determines the torment, the destruction, the will to annihilation. In the other case [i.e., Christianity], suffering, the 'Crucified as the innocent,' is considered an objection against this life, as a formula for condemning it. One guesses: the problem is that of the meaning of suffering, whether it has a Christian or a tragic meaning. In the first case, suffering is to be the path to a holy Being; in the latter case, *Being is regarded as holy enough* even to justify an enormity of suffering. The tragic man still affirms the harshest suffering: he is strong, full,

deifying enough to do so; the Christian negates even the happiest lot on the earth: he is weak, poor, disinherited enough to suffer over life in any form. God on the Cross is a curse upon life, a cue to redeem oneself from life;— Dionysus cut to pieces is a *promise* of life: he will be eternally reborn and will come home from the destruction" (XVI, 391f.).

2. XV, 116f.; *A*. 1.

3. XV, 125f.

4. XV, 3.

5. XV, 65.

6. XV, 65f.

7. Prologue to *F.W.*; *Br*. IV, p. 270.

8. *Richard Wagner in Bayreuth*, sec. 4. The particular figure in which Nietzsche saw a reborn piece of antiquity is Napoleon, whose historical task he viewed as the simplification of the world by binding the European peoples. Cf. on this matter XV, 111 and the chapter on Napoleon in E. Bertram, *Nietzsche: Versuch einer Mythologie* (1918), pp. 201ff.

9. "*The Ring of the Nibelung* is an enormous system of thought without the conceptual form of thought. Perhaps a philosopher could juxtapose it with something corresponding to it completely, a work that would lack image and action and would speak to us merely in concepts; then one would have the same thing presented in two disparate spheres . . ." (*Richard Wagner in Bayreuth*, sec. 9).

10. XV, pp. 444f.; cf. Hegel, *Werke* XIII, pp. 172ff.; cf. X, 96.

11. *G.D.*, "What I Owe to the Ancients," 4 and "Morality as Antinature."

12. XVI, 388f.: "The mind is then likewise quite at home in the senses, as the senses are quite at home in the mind; and everything that happens only in the one has to elicit a fine, extraordinary happiness and play in the other as well. And likewise, vice versa! . . . It is likely that among such perfect and well-turned-out men finally the most sensual functions of all are transfigured by an allegorizing ecstasy of the highest spirituality; they sense in themselves a kind of *deification of the body* and are most remote from the ascetics' philosophy of the maxim 'God is a spirit.' . . . From that height of joy, where man [is] himself and feels himself altogether as a deified form and self-justification of nature, down to the joy of healthy farmers and of healthy, half-human beasts: the Greek named this whole, long, enormous, light-and-color ladder of *happiness*— not without the thankful shiver of one who is initiated into a secret, not without much caution and pious silence—with the divine name *Dionysus*."—Cf. IX, 131ff., the following pieces from the fragment on Empedocles: "Das Weib als die Natur" ("Woman as nature")—"Empedokles schaudert vor der Natur" ("Empedocles shudders before nature")—"Er wird als Gott Dionysos verehrt" ("He is revered as the god Dionysus")—"Flieht Dionysos vor Ariadne?" ("Does Dionysus flee Ariadne?").

13. XVI, 390.

14. On the historical-philological question of the origin of the cult of Dionysus in the Orient, cf. Schelling, *Sämtliche Werke* I, 9, pp. 328ff. and recently W. Otto, *Dionysos,* pp. 51ff.

15. *M*. 96.

16. *F.W.* 347; *A*. 22, 23, 42, 51.

17. XV, 325 and 186; cf. *F.W.* 131.

18. XV, 304; cf. 318.

19. XV, 162.

20. XV, 182.

21. XV, 185.

22. XVI, 390.

23. XVI, 339; cf. also the last verse of "Das Feuerzeichen" and also frag. 12 of the Dionysus Dithyrambs.

24. Cf. further L. Andreas-Salomé, pp. 137 and 228; Andler, IV, pp. 244ff.

25. *F.W.* 152; cf. VI, 44 and also J. Burckhardt, *Griechische Kulturgeschichte,* ed. J. Oeri, 4th ed., II, pp. 279ff.

26. XIX, 167ff.; X, 30ff. Cf. also J. J. Ruedorffer, "Nietzsche und die Philosophie im tragischen Zeitalter der Griechen," in *Vom Schicksal des deutschen Geistes* (Berlin: Die Runde, 1934).

27. On Nietzsche's interpretation of Heraclitus see Karl Reinhardt, *Parmenides und die Geschichte der griechischen Philosophie* (Bonn, 1916), and L. Binswanger, "Heraklits Auffassung des Menschen," *Die Antike* XI, pp. 1ff. Excellent sources of the ancient worldview of the eternal recurrence of the same are: Heraclitus (frags. 30 and 31 as well as 51, 63, 67, 88); Empedocles (frag. 115); almost all myths of Plato, especially the myth of Eros in the *Phaedrus* as well as the myth of the *Politicus*; Aristotle, *Metaphysics* XII, 8, and Eudemus, the Aristotle pupil, often mentioned in Nietzsche's philological writings, who grasped the eternal recurrence of the same mathematically and astronomically; and the Stoics, e.g., Nemesius, *De nat. hom.* 38, 147.—Cf. on the ancients' view A. Tilgher, *La visione greca della vita,* 2d ed. (Rome, 1926); Zeller, *Philosophie der Griechen*; Gomperz, *Griechische Denker,* esp. I, pp. 112f. and 434; W. Jaeger, *Aristoteles,* pp. 131ff.

28. X, 45f.

29. XIX, 173ff.

30. XV, 65.

31. X, 34f. and XIX, 178ff. Cf. on the other hand Baeumler, pp. 59ff.

32. X, 41.

33. X, 42f.

34. XIX, 188.

35. Songs of Prince Vogelfrei: To Goethe.

# 5. "How One Becomes What One Is" in the Idea of the Eternal Recurrence

1. *Jugendschriften,* Musarion ed., I, pp. 60ff.; cf. Biogr. I, pp. 98ff., and *Der werdende Nietzsche,* pp. 131ff. Cf. on both lectures the essay by Schopenhauer "Transzendente Spekulation über die anscheinende Absichtlichkeit im

Schicksal des Einzelnen" (Reclam ed., IV, 229) and R. W. Emerson's essay on fate, "Das Fatum," which appeared in German translation in 1962. See further H. Heimsoeth, *Metaphysische Voraussetzungen und Antriebe in Nietzsches Immoralismus* (1955), pp. 40ff.—The autobiographical sketch of 1862 was first published in 1936.

2. Cf. *Br.* IV, pp. 186f.

3. Cf. further the simultaneous attempts by Dilthey to derive a philosophy of "reality" from natural science and history. On Dilthey's judgment on Nietzsche see: *Werke* IV, 528; V, 370ff.; VIII, 162, 224; *Briefwechsel mit Yorck von Wartenburg*, p. 238.

4. See above, p. 93.

5. *Jugendschriften* I, pp. 67ff.; cf.—twenty-six years later—"Every individual is still the whole line of development (and not only, as morality conceives him, something that begins at birth)."

6. Cf. XV, 183.

7. Cf. the poem by Francis Thompson "The Hound of Heaven." On Nietzsche's own interpretation of God's status as executioner, see *G.d.M.* II, 22.

8. See also Karl Reinhardt, *Nietzsches Klage der Ariadne* (1936).

9. IX, 302, 318, 408; cf. 300, 357, 377, 417.

10. I, 283f.

11. Frag. 67 of the Dionysus Dithyrambs; cf. the fragment of a prologue of 1887 (XIV, 419), where the state of "deepest reflection" is a state of forgetting.

12. I, 285.

13. I, 292.

14. I, 298.

15. I, 379.

# 6. The Problematic Connection between the Existence of Man and the Being of the World in the History of Modern Philosophy

1. "Now the spirit wills *its* will; he who was lost to the world gains *his* world" (VI, 35).

2. A. Koyré, *Entretiens sur Descartes* (1944).

3. XIII, 55.

4. XVI, 45.

5. XIII, 307 and 308.

6. XIII, 311.

7. XV, 466 and XIII, 9.

8. XVI, 453. (In the text "und" occurs erroneously instead of "aus.")

9. Cf. Nietzsche's criticism, XIV, 4ff.; XVI, 13.

10. VI, 11.

11. XIV, 326; cf. further Kierkegaard's radicalization of Descartes's theoretical doubt into an existential "desperation," in order to come, in the face of

the nothing, to Being. *Werke* VII, 49ff. and *Johannes Climacus; oder, De omnibus dubitandum est,* ed. W. Struve (1948).

12. Cf. XIII, 51ff. and Dilthey's *Briefwechsel mit Yorck von Wartenburg,* p. 178.

13. XIII, 56.

14. XIV, 5.

15. XIV, 7.

16. XIII, 10.

17. See moreover Nietzsche's characterization of Kant in the Prologue to *M.,* par. 3.

18. Ed. Cassirer, Vol. 5, pp. 174ff.

19. Cited below according to the edition of 1825.

20. P. 20.

21. Pp. 23f.; cf. *W.z.M.,* aph. 332.

22. Pp. 25f.

23. Pp. 122f.

24. Pp. 138f.

25. Cf. Dilthey's essay on the reality of the external world.

26. Pp. 162f.

27. P. 251.

28. P. 254.

29. Schelling, *Sämtliche Werke* I, 7.

30. Pp. 108ff.

31. Reclam ed., pp. 15f.

32. Pp. 62, 106, 113.

33. P. 110.

34. P. 215.

35. Pp. 222f.

36. See on this matter and on the following the author's *Von Hegel zu Nietzsche,* 3d ed. (1954).

37. XVI, 47f.

38. See above, p. 97f.

39. The analogies—which even include particular formulations—between Nietzsche and Stirner regarding the destructive impulse are all the more striking because in other respects the two are worlds apart. Cf. A. Lévy, *Stirner et Nietzsche* (Paris, 1904), and Andler, IV, pp. 166ff.

40. Reclam ed., p. 14.

41. P. 23.

42. Pp. 37f.

43. Pp. 50f.

44. P. 111.

45. P. 165.

46. P. 182.

47. P. 201.

48. P. 423.

49. P. 429.

50. *M.A.M.* II, 304.

# 7. The Eternal Recurrence of the Same and the Repetition of the Selfsame

1. Weininger was born in Vienna in 1880 and ended his life voluntarily in 1903, after he had previously attempted, during a trip through Italy, to penetrate into "saved joy." In addition to the precocious work *Geschlecht und Charakter*, 3d ed. (1904) (cited below as *G.u.Ch.*), the genius of which has still hardly been appreciated philosophically, there appeared after his death a selection from his diaries and letters (*Taschenbuch und Briefe an einen Freund* [1920]; cited below as *T.*) as well as a series of essays, *Über die letzten Dinge* (1907) (cited below as *L.D.*). For our purposes, out of that series above all the essay "The Unidirectionality of Time" ("Die Einsinnigkeit der Zeit") comes under consideration and further *G.u.Ch.*, Chapters V to VII, particularly p. 193, on the connection between "logic" and "ethics" and the significance on principle of the memory for the temporal existence of man. Reference should be made further to the thirteenth chapter on Judaism, the self-negation of which, by a Jew who converted to Protestantism, still is unique within the self-criticism of Jewish existence. Weininger admired the same two spiritual powers that also stood in the center of Nietzsche's lifelong confrontations: Christ and . . . Wagner.

2. *L.D.*, p. 81.

3. *G.u.Ch.*, pp. 172f.

4. *L.D.*, p. 55.

5. *L.D.*, p. 60.

6. Cf. p. 54, Weininger's comment on interpreting the robbery and murder in the chapter of *Zarathustra* "On the Pale Criminal."

7. *L.D.*, p. XXIII; on the concept of the "nothing" cf. *T.*, pp. 31, 39, and 48.

8. *L.D.*, p. 59.

9. *L.D.*, pp. 31f.

10. Cf. further, besides VI, pp. 18 and 35 as well as frag. 67 of the Dionysus Dithyrambs, the beginning of the second *Untimely Meditation*.

11. "As is natural, the measure by which men will be in a position to notice differences as well as similarities depends upon men's memory. This capacity will be most developed among those in whose lives the whole past always extends into the present, for whom all individual moments of life flow together into a unity and are compared with one another. Thus these men most especially have the opportunity to use similes, *and in particular with exactly that tertium comparationis on which everything plainly depends* [the *Oxford English Dictionary* defines "tertium comparationis" as "the factor which links or is the common ground between two elements in comparison"]; for these men will always grasp out of the past what shows the strongest agreement with what is present, because both experiences—the new and the older that is recurred to for comparison—are sufficiently *articulated* in them so as not to conceal from their eyes any similarity or any difference; and just for that reason, too, what is

long past can assert itself here against the influence of the years. Not for no reason, therefore, has one for the longest time seen in the poet's abundance of beautiful and perfect similes and pictures a special merit of his genus. . . . Today, because Germany lacks great artists and great thinkers for the first time in 150 years—even though soon no one can be found who has not 'written' something—today the time of similes seems to be past; one does not seek such things, one also would not find anything. An age that sees its essence best expressed in vague, unclearly opalescing moods, an age the philosophy of which has become the unconscious in more than one sense, shows too obviously that not one truly great man lives in it; for greatness is consciousness, before which the fog of the unconscious vanishes as before the beams of the sun. If a single man gave this age a consciousness, how gladly would the age give up all its art of moods, of which it still boasts today!—Only in full consciousness, in which all experiences of the past come into play with great intensity in the experience of the present, does fantasy—the condition of philosophic as well as of artistic creation—find a place" (*G.u.Ch.*, pp. 150f.; cf. pp. 156 and 160ff.).

12. *G.u.Ch.*, pp. 167ff.

13. *G.u.Ch.*, p. 162.

14. *G.u.Ch.*, pp. 173ff.

15. *L.D.*, p. 52; cf. further M. Scheler's essay "Reue und Wiedergeburt," in *Vom Ewigen im Menschen* (1923), Vol. I, pp. 5ff.

16. Cf. *G.u.Ch.*, p. 209.

17. *L.D.*, p. 51.

18. *G.u.Ch.*, pp. 210f.

19. *L.D.*, p. 109.

20. *L.D.*, p. 97.

21. *L.D.*, p. 104.

22. That Nietzsche's "But so I willed it" precisely does *not* will to "change" the past but wills it exactly as it already was, is not conceivable for Weininger's moralistic metaphysics.

23. *L.D.*, pp. 104f.

24. *L.D.*, p. 103.

25. *L.D.*, p. 103 note and p. 64.

26. *L.D.*, p. 108.

27. *L.D.*, pp. 100f.

28. *L.D.*, p. 98 and *T.*, p. 42.

29. *L.D.*, p. 64.

30. The citations refer below to Vol. 3 of the German edition of 1909 (*Furcht und Zittern*; *Wiederholung*).

31. Pp. 196f.

32. P. 144.

33. Pp. 180f.

34. P. 119.

35. Cf. on this matter the author's *Kierkegaard and Nietzsche*, p. 30.

36. P. 136.

37. P. 170.

38. P. 158.

39. P. 159.
40. P. 160.

# 8. The Critical Yardstick
# for Nietzsche's Experiment

1. *A.* 51; cf. Hegel, *Werke* XII, p. 224, and Marx, *Ges. Ausg.* I, 1, p. 133.
2. This formulation by Nietzsche is the title of a presentation by K. J. Obenauer, *Friedrich Nietzsche, der ekstatische Nihilist* (1924).
3. XII, 361.
4. IX, 130.
5. See the chapter "Langbehn" in Podach's *Gestalten um Nietzsche* (1932).
6. XIV, 359.
7. XIV, 419.
8. *W.z.M.*, aph. 749.
9. *Die Weltalter,* p. 141.
10. XV, 186f., and *A.* 54.
11. XII, 366.
12. VI, 291; cf. XIV, 265: "*Principal teaching*: at every level to achieve perfection and a *feeling of well-being*—and *not* to leap to them!"
13. XIV, 263.
14. XV, 51 and XVI, 339f.
15. See further X, 292ff.
16. XVI, 283.
17. XVI, 303, and *A.* 57.
18. *M.A.M.* II, 230.
19. XV, 12f.
20. VI, 426 and *A.* 57.
21. Cf. the Portofino poem, entitled "Sils Maria":

> Here I sat, waiting, waiting—but for nothing,
> beyond good and evil, now enjoying the light,
>
> and now the shadow, all play,
> all lake, all noon, all time without goal.
>
> There, suddenly, lady-friend, One became Two—
> —and Zarathustra passed me by . . .

22. VI, 400ff.; cf. *Br.* IV, p. 305.
23. XII, 361; VI, 15, 18, 24; cf. 334, 421.
24. See the conclusion of the poem "Klage der Ariadne"; cf. on the symbol of lightning the poems: "Wer viel einst zu verkünden hat"; "Pinie und Blitz"; "Ruhm und Ewigkeit."
25. Cf. *G.d.M.* III, par. 13; XII, 3, 360; XIII, 276; XV, 347, 371. Nietzsche's *distinction* of man from beast according to the measure of determinacy (VII, 88, 431; XIII, 276; XIV, 66f.) presupposes that man and beast by nature

have the *same* essence. This biological naturalism would lack philosophic significance if Nietzsche did not, with this comparative distinction between man
and beast, simultaneously ask the decisive question of the whole relationship
of human existence to the Being of the natural world. Conscious of the offensiveness of his assertion that man belongs entirely to the character of the physical world, Nietzsche calls it his "new insight" that man "plainly and without
simile" is one animal species among others (VII, 135), because man altogether
belongs to the one world that, as the whole, also determines all particular
things. Nietzsche's frequent designations of man as a peculiar animal refer not
to the traditional definition of man as a "rational" animal but to the *one* "total character of life" within which man is only a particular instance. Man is a
"more interesting" animal than all other animals; he is "more endangered"
and "more dangerous," a "courageous" and "cruel" animal, but also an animal that "suffers" over itself and is a "failure"; he is a "multifarious, artificial, opaque" animal; a "domesticated" animal, but also a "beast of prey"; a
"laughing" and a "weeping" animal; a "monstrous animal" ["Untier"] and
"super animal" ["Übertier"]. As an organic, living being he has, analogously
to plants and beasts, organized the world as it is accessible to him into his
own world.—This man, abysmally related to the beast, had once been firmly
fixed, namely by means of the faith in a highest divine authority that told
man what he is and commanded him what he is to be. When this authority,
which up to now excessively elevated and defined human nature, ceases to exist, man loses his fixed position between God and beast. He now finds himself,
left to his own will, facing the possibility of an ascent to the superman or a
descent to the herd-animal man. The general and prevailing tendency of present humanity is toward an equalizing definition of man. The act of defining
occurs as an equating. Under the dominion of the "purposiveness of the species," the goal is "to make man just as uniform and fixed as has already happened regarding *most animal species*" (XII, 120). In opposition to that goal,
Nietzsche-Zarathustra wants an "overcoming" of man, who once was defined
in a high and demanding sense, and who is now fixed in an average sense. The
symbol for this path to self-overcoming is Zarathustra's going under, going
over, and crossing over the "bridge" man, or the ropedancer. That man is the
not-yet-determinate animal thus does not mean that Nietzsche wants primarily
to define him by means of a "pre-setting presentation" ["Vorstellen"] in the
figure of Zarathustra (Heidegger, *Was heißt Denken*, pp. 24ff. and 66; cf. *Vorträge und Aufsätze*, p. 106), but that he confronts the solidifying human type
with the experimenting will to overcoming; for this will to overcoming, only
one thing stands firm, namely that man, having got rid of God and therewith
left to his own devices, has to be able to command himself in order to be able
to assume mastery over the earth. He must be able to say to himself whether
he wants to be at all and how he wants to be in the future. It belongs to the
characteristic greatness and danger of the enigmatic and contradictory animal
"man" that he wants and dares more than any beast and therefore is more uncertain and indeterminate than all other animals together. He still has a future
before himself if he launches his goal beyond himself.

26. VI, 386, 415, 417; *J.* 43.

27. *Der Fall Wagner,* 3.

28. *Briefwechsel mit Overbeck,* p. 227.

29. See further H. Weichelt, *Also sprach Zarathustra* (1910), pp. 225ff.; K. Schlechta, p. 54.

30. VI, 435f.; 281.

31. *J.* 247.

32. *Die Weltalter,* p. 103.

33. *F.W.* 380.

34. See further Schelling, *Die Weltalter,* Nachlaß edition (1946), pp. 196 and 254.

35. Schelling, *Vorlesungen über die Methode des akademischen Studiums* (1803), pp. 138f.; cf. above, p. 139ff.

36. The most important source for the ancient theories "of the eternity of the world" is an essay, erroneously ascribed to Philo, with the same title.

36a. In a note from the time of *Zarathustra* (XII, 57), it is said: "He who does not believe in a *circular process of the universe must* believe in the *arbitrary* God—thus my meditation is stipulated in opposition to all theistic meditations so far!"

37. See thereon the author's "Natur und Geschichte," *Neue Rundschau,* 1951, no. 1.

38. VI, 113; 206, 290.

39. XII, 405; XIV, 301.

40. *F.W.* 346.

41. *F.W.* 354; *W.z.M.,* aph. 707. In departing from the modern principle of self-consciousness, the discovery of "unconscious," or of the consciousness as a mere "function," was for Nietzsche *the* means of access to a rediscovery of the one *nature* in all that happens.

42. G. Teichmüller, with whose book *Die wirkliche und die scheinbare Welt* (1882) Nietzsche was familiar, had made an attempt, departing from Greek ontology, to provide a "new foundation for metaphysics" from the viewpoint of modern subjectivity. If Nietzsche had ever been interested in the ontological problems of Being and the things that are; Being and nothing; time, space, and motion, this important work must have provided him the occasion such as no other could have. Instead, he refers to the book only to corroborate with it the merely "fictitious" character of "the basic forms of extreme abstraction" and to abolish with the "true" world the "apparent" world, too (XVI, 66ff.). In Nietzsche's view, all talk of "Being" rests only on the persuasive power of language, which pretends in every sentence that something "is" thus and so (*G.D.,* "'Reason' in Philosophy").

43. *W.z.M.,* aphs. 581 and 582.

44. *F.W.* 370.

45. *W.z.M.,* aph. 112.

46. *W.z.M.,* aphs. 38ff.

47. *G.D.,* "Morality as Antinature," 5; cf. "The Four Great Errors," 8; *F.W.* 1 and 357; *W.z.M.,* aphs. 708 and 711.

48. XIV, 293.

49. XIV, 331; XII, 399, 408; XIII, 73ff.

50. See further R. Pannwitz, *Einführung in Nietzsche* (1920) and *Beiträge zu einer europäischen Kultur* (1954), pp. 216ff.

51. VI, 114f.

52. Cf.—eleven years earlier—in a letter to Gersdorff of 1 April 1874: "My writings are said to be so dark and unintelligible! I thought if one speaks of need that those who are in need will understand one. That is also certainly true: but where are those who are 'in need'?"

# Appendix

1. "Die Entwicklung des Nietzsche-Bildes in Deutschland" (University of Bonn doctoral dissertation, 1933).

2. *Nietzsche in seinen Werken* (Vienna, 1894; new printing, 1911; 3d ed., Dresden, 1924).

3. O. Ewald, *Nietzsches Lehre in ihren Grundbegriffen: Die ewige Wiederkunft des Gleichen und der Sinn des Übermenschen* (Berlin, 1903).

4. E. Horneffer, *Nietzsches Lehre von der ewigen Wiederkunft und deren bisherige Veröffentlichung* (Leipzig, 1900), pp. 22ff. In agreement with A. and E. Horneffer, the editors of Vol. XII, E. Förster-Nietzsche (*Das Leben F. Nietzsches*, Kleine Ausgabe, Vol. II, pp. 137ff.), too, elaborates the teaching of the return primarily as an educational idea. The problem of the inner *connection* between Nietzsche's "physics" and his "ethics" remains wholly unexplained in her writings as in theirs, and is hidden by the editors by the innocuous distinction between a more "theoretical" and a more "poetic" mode of presentation (cf. XII, 424).

5. A. Riehl, *F. Nietzsche: Der Künstler und der Denker*, 3d ed. (1901), pp. 143ff.

6. A. Drews, *Nietzsches Philosophie* (1904), pp. 323ff.

7. R. M. Meyer, *Nietzsche: Sein Leben und sein Werk* (1913), pp. 437ff.

8. R. Richter, *F. Nietzsche*, 3d ed. (1917), pp. 326f. and 334ff.

9. K. Heckel, *Nietzsche: Sein Leben und sein Werk* (1922), pp. 150ff.

10. *Schopenhauer und Nietzsche* (Leipzig, 1907).

11. *Nietzsche: Versuch einer Mythologie* (1918).

12. Cf. also the critical analysis of George's Nietzsche poem in the *Seventh Ring* in R. Thiel, *Die Generation ohne Männer* (1932).

13. Cf. on the other hand H. Landry, *F. Nietzsche* (1931), p. 186.

14. Cf. Andler's judgment of Bertram's book: "Il y a quelque paradoxe à vouloir faire Nietzsche très grand, sans faire état de son œuvre" ["There is some paradox here, wanting to make Nietzsche very great without attaching much significance to his work"] (Vol. VI, p. viii).

15. *Nietzsche: Sa vie et sa pensée*, particularly Vol. IV (1928), pp. 225ff., and Vol. VI (1931), pp. 60ff.

16. Cf. Emmerich's critique, pp. 88ff., where she rightly points out that Andler's attempt to unify the teaching of the eternal recurrence with that of

the superman abandons the eternal recurrence of what is always the *same*; conversely Emmerich himself fits the teaching of the return in one piece into the "essence" of man and in this way eliminates the problem of that teaching.

17. *Die psychologischen Errungenschaften Nietzsches* (1926); cf., on what follows below, the author's "Nietzsche im Lichte der Philosophie von Klages," *Reichls philosophischer Almanach*, vol. 4, ed. Rothacker (1927), pp. 285–348.

18. Cf. on the analysis in "Handschrift und Charakter" also "Nietzsche und seine Handschrift," *Zeitschrift für Menschenkunde*, Vol. 2 (1927), no. 6.

19. Theodor Lessing in *Nietzsche, Wagner, Schopenhauer* already understood the teaching of the return in a similar fashion as "a kind of suicide," in the form of an absolute affirmation of existence.

20. See *M*. 274: "We human beings are the only creatures that, when they fail, can delete themselves like a failed sentence. . . ."

21. *Nietzsche: Der Philosoph und Politiker* (Reclam, 1931); see further Baeumler's introduction to the unpublished writings: *Die Unschuld des Werdens*, Vol. I (Kröner), 1931; cf. also "Nietzsche und der Nationalsozialmus," *Nationalsozialistische Monatshefte*, Vol. 5 (1934), no. 49. The discussion below was "intolerable" and "unwelcome" in Germany in 1935, for which reason this whole Appendix (secs. 1–9) could not appear as a part of the book on Nietzsche but had to be distributed privately. The immediate relevance that the critique had at that time is apparently obsolete today. If this critical discussion nevertheless is subsequently published here, it may exculpate the remarkable brevity of the political memory, which in this way is reminded of the extent to which the mind can become victim of the age.

22. Cf. Emmerich (below, note 25), pp. 73f. Toward establishing on textual grounds the essential connection between *Zarathustra* and *W.z.M.*, see above all XV, 102; XVI, 435f. and 474 as well as the foreword to *A*.

23. *All* love, Nietzsche once says, thinks not of duration but of the moment and of eternity. In the same sense he says of desire that it wants itself because it wants eternity, i.e., eternal recurrence (VI, 469); and as the epigraph to the last chapter of *W.z.M.* Nietzsche noted down from Dante: *Come l'uom s'eterna* [Dante, *Inferno* XV, 85: "How man makes himself eternal"].

24. Cf. Baeumler, *Männerbund und Wissenschaft* (1934), p. 108.

25. *Wahrheit und Wahrhaftigkeit in der Philosophie Nietzsches* (Halle, 1933). The entire work has the merit of taking the teaching of the return seriously without abbreviation and of interpreting that teaching in the horizon of the Greek concepts of Being, being in motion, and being true. But the work is defective in that its author sees Nietzsche through the double lens of Heidegger's ontological question and of O. Becker's idea of a "paraontology," and most naively places Nietzsche between the two (p. 43).

26. F. Giese, in a meditation of 1934 that was opportune for the time [*Nietzsche—die Erfüllung* (Tübingen: Mohr)], more resolutely than Emmerich represented the present—"stated briefly"—as the veritable fulfillment of Nietzsche. To establish his assertion, he took his bearings from the writings of Moeller van den Bruck, Rosenberg, Krieck, Günther, Wirth, Bergmann, and Kynast (on p. 36 a section begins with the lapidary sentence, "If one says with 1933 and Kynast"), but also from "honest converts" who are not yet "seers

born by experience" (Benn, Prinzhorn, Gründel, Diesel, Jünger). According to Giese, what Nietzsche wanted is now fulfilled in real politics (pp. 2, 27, 157, 186f.), for his distinction between Apollonian and Dionysian corresponds to that between the manly-Aryan and the womanly-Semitic. *The Birth of Tragedy* is an anticipation of the modern theory of race (pp. 29ff.). Likewise the concept of the "great health" is to be understood as "Nordicizing" (p. 60), although Nietzsche himself did not quite forge ahead to that "absolute and resolute anti-Semitism" like—his brother-in-law Förster! (pp. 133 and 166). Therefore Nietzsche did not succeed, per Giese, in squaring his opposition to Christianity with the still Semitic formula "Dionysus" (pp. 159ff.). On the basis of Giese's "interpretation" the problem of the teaching of the return, too, can be crudely solved with force. Since it is a petty matter to "switch" the No of nihilism into a Yes (p. 122), and since the Yes of real politics in 1933 is symbolized by the swastika, it emerges with the help of the prehistorian Wirth that "Zarathustra and primeval writing are just as related as the course of the sun to the swastika. . . . The flag of the Third Reich symbolizes in the swastika the teaching of the eternal return of the same" (p. 127). "Somehow the air of the Stone Age surrounds us" (p. 190), one can conclude with Giese himself; but about one thing he is doubtless correct: "If we had had more courageous philosophers, many a surprise would have been avoided for the civil world" (pp. 97f.).

27. *Nietzsche* (Paris, 1933).

28. *Nietzsche: Einführung in das Verständnis seines Philosophierens* (1936).

29. *Nietzsche: Existenzialismus und Wille zur Macht* (1950).

30. "Nietzsches Wort: 'Gott ist tot,'" in *Holzwege* (1950), pp. 193ff.; *Was heißt Denken?* (1954), pp. 19ff.; "Wer ist Nietzsches Zarathustra?" in *Vorträge und Aufsätze* (1954), pp. 101ff. Cf. on this discussion the more fundamental justification of our criticism of Heidegger's interpretation of Nietzsche in the third chapter of the author's *Heidegger: Denker in dürftiger Zeit* (1953).

# Translator's Notes

T1. Löwith "modestly" omits the words, "(or one: it would require a ge-nius for that!)." He takes the motto to this Foreword from Nietzsche's May 1884 letter to Josef Paneth.

T2. "Unrevealed" would be the alternative translation of "*unbewiesen*" here.

T3. *Thus Spoke Zarathustra* (hereafter *Zar.*) II, "On Redemption."

T4. *Zar.* III, "On Virtue That Makes Small," 2.

T5. The translator wishes to express gratitude to Robin Cackett for calling attention to the nineteenth-century nationalist slogan "*Nur am deutschen Wesen, kann die Welt genesen,*" i.e., "Only in Germanness can the world recu-perate." Apparently the reference to Zarathustra's essence, or "Zarathustra-ness," alludes to this slogan.

T6. "'*Wende der Not.*'" This expression is wordplay, for "*Notwendigkeit*" is the German for "necessity." "*Not*" means "distress," "plight," "need," "exi-gency," or "necessity," and will usually be translated as "need" or "distress." "*Notschrei,*" for example, will be rendered in this book as "cry of distress." Cf. note T43.

T7. Löwith alludes to *Beyond Good and Evil*, "Sayings and Interludes," aph. 150.

T8. In this chapter "*Versuch*"—which also means "experiment" or "trial"—is translated as "attempt," and "*versuchend*" as "attempting," in both cases even at some cost in smoothness of style. Otherwise, one of Löwith's and Nietz-sche's points might remain obscure to the reader. The philosophers of the fu-ture are called "*Versucher*" in *Beyond Good and Evil* (hereafter *BGE*), aph. 42. "*Versucher*" can mean either "attempters," "experimenters," or "tempters." The translations "at-tempters" and "at-tempting" preserve this wordplay. "Temp-tation" is "*Versuchung.*"

T9. Latin for "fate." The word has become a part of the German language, so will henceforth be translated into English whenever it is capitalized in Ger-man. Cf. note T14.

T10. "*Notwendiger Zu-fall.*" The English word "accident" derives from the Latin preposition *ad*, "to" or "toward," plus the Latin verb *cadere*, "to fall"; the English "chance" also derives from *cadere*. Like "accident," the German "*Zufall*" literally means "a falling to," and when Löwith inserts a hyphen here, he calls attention to this original meaning.

T11. *Twilight of the Idols*, "Skirmishes of an Untimely Man," 51. This remark immediately follows the passage quoted in the text at Löwith's note 24. The German reads "*in zehn Sätzen zu sagen, was andere in einem Buche—nicht sagen.*" Literally, this boast is "to say in ten sentences what others in a book— do not say." Nietzsche plays on a simple parallel to what others *do* say in a book.

T12. Italian for "slow," often indicating musical tempo.

T13. *BGE*, aph. 70.

T14. Latin for "love of fate." See note T9.

T15. From the Dionysus Dithyrambs, "*Ruhm und Ewigkeit*" ("Glory and Eternity"), 4. The last six words are italicized in the original poem.

T16. *Human, All-Too-Human* II, preface, 6.

T17. "*[Z]wischen Pyrrhon und einem Altem*" can alternatively be translated: "between Pyrrhon and an ancient." Cf. the following aphorism in *The Wanderer*, 214.

T18. This quotation, too, comes from *Zar.* IV, "The Shadow."

T19. "*Schleiermacher,*" the surname of the enormously influential Protestant theologian Friedrich Schleiermacher (1768–1834), literally means "veil-maker." In the fragments of 1884 Nietzsche says, "Fichte, Schelling, Hegel, Schleiermacher, Feuerbach, Strauß—all theologians."

T20. "Nature is such that everywhere she *indicates* a *lost God,* both within man and without man."

T21. *Zar.* IV, "The Ass Festival," 1. The remark about divinity refers to *Zar.* III, "On Apostates," 2 and "On Old and New Tablets," 11.

T22. "*[D]er Gott-losgewordene Mensch*" combines "*der gottlos gewordene Mensch*" or "man who has become godless" and "*der Gott losgewordene Mensch*" or "man who has rid himself of God." Note that for reasons of style this translation follows Kaufmann in generally rendering "*Mensch*" (literally "human being") as "man" in the generic sense. Occasionally "human being" will be used as an explicit reminder of the generic meaning of the term.

T23. *Zar.*, Prologue, 5.

T24. *Zar.* IV, "Retired."

T25. Ibid. The preceding sentence reads: "Some god in you converted you to your godlessness"; Löwith omits "in you."

T26. *Zar.* IV, "The Ugliest Man."

T27. Ibid.

T28. See note T22.

T29. *Zar.* III, "On Virtue That Makes Small," 3.

T30. The German word for "disappointment" is "*Enttäuschung,*" which literally means "disillusionment." Löwith hyphenates the word to make conspicuous the literal meaning, which escapes notice during ordinary use: "*Ent-täuschung,*" "dis-illusionment."

T31. "*[W]er hielte sich*" can also mean "Who would still comply with."

T32. *Zar.* III, "On Old and New Tablets," 8.

T33. *Zar.* I, "The Pale Criminal."

T34. "*Da-Sein.*" "*Dasein*" (without a hyphen) means "existence."

T35. Musical direction in Italian: "from the beginning."

T36. As Walter Kaufmann points out in his translation of *BGE,* this Latin sentence is ambiguous. It can mean: "A vicious circle is made god." Or: "God is a vicious circle." Or: "The circle is a vicious god."

T37. "*Schwer*" can mean "heavy" or "difficult"; "*leicht,*" "light" or "easy." Each of these double meanings is important for Nietzsche and Löwith.

T38. Concluding lines of the final stanza of the "Aftersong" of *BGE.*

T39. "*Voll-endung,*" literally "fully ending." "*Vollendung*" means "completion" or "perfection."

T40. "*Um-willen.*"

T41. Latin for "The tragedy begins."

T42. "Of being there, which has fallen to man like an accident," translates "*des zugefallenen Da-seins.*" See also note T34.

T43. In common parlance, "*Not*" means "need," "distress," "plight," "exigency," or "necessity"; "*Wendigkeit*" means "maneuverability" or "flexibility"; and "*Notwendigkeit*" means "necessity." Here Löwith hyphenates "*Not-wendigkeit.*" "This highest happiness is that flexibility vis-à-vis need which is at the same time necessity" translates "*die Not-wendigkeit*" and the colon that separates this noun from the previous sentence. Cf. note T6.

T44. "[M]y own and my quintessence" in Latin.

T45. The word for "excess courage" is "*Über-mut,*" "*Mut*" means "courage," and "*über,*" "above," "excess," "over," or "super." "*Übermut*" without a hyphen means "cockiness," "high-spiritedness," "insolence," or "prankishness." "*[D]er Übermensch*" is "the superman," and "*übermenschlich*" is "superhuman."

T46. "*Geworfenheit,*" a term made famous by Martin Heidegger, Löwith's great teacher, in *Sein und Zeit* (*Being and Time*). "Plan" or "sketch" is "*Entwurf*" in German, and here the text exploits the common root "*werfen,*" "to throw." See note T51.

T47. "*Hinterwelt*" literally means a "world behind" the world of the senses. The translation "backworld" will be used consistently. Cf. note T152 below.

T48. See note T39.

T49. "*Hinterweltlich.*" See notes T47 and T152.

T50. Alternative translation: "And only then did the ghost of the backworldly sermon retreat from death." This possibility seems to make less sense in the context.

T51. "Plan" is "*Entwerfen,*" and "thrownness" is "*Geworfenheit.*" The wordplay is manifest, here: "*Ent-werfen*" literally means to "un-throw" or "de-throw." The question is, how can man, who is *thrown* into existence, gain such control over himself that his superhuman self-planning, his "*Entwerfen,*" is more decisive for his existence than his accidental origins and circumstances? The supplanting of "thrownness" by "dethrowing," of "*Geworfenheit*" by "*Entwerfen,*" is the overcoming of accident by design.

T52. See note T36.

T53. "The longest repose" translates "*die längste Weile.*" But "*die Lange-weile*" is "boredom," on which Nietzsche is punning, and Kaufmann understandably renders "*die längste Weile*" as "the longest boredom." The term "*Langeweile des Daseins,*" the boredom of existence, does occur later in this paragraph of Löwith's text. Cf. note T54.

T54. "*Die lange Weile*" is translated here as "the long repose." The "long repose" is the obverse of "the meaningless boredom," "*die sinnlose Lange-weile.*" Cf. note T53.

T55. See note T45.

T56. "*Wohlan,*" which might also be translated "now, then," or "all right, then."

T57. *Zar.* III, "Before Sunrise."

T58. "*Übermut.*" See note T45.

T59. "*Ohngefähr.*"

T60. Kaufmann translates "*vor dem Tage*" as "in the presence of the day." Löwith, on the other hand, clearly understands this prepositional phrase to mean "*prior to* the day," and he is probably correct.

T61. "*Lust*": "desire," "pleasure," or "joy."

T62. "*Um-willen.*"

T63. "*Wende der Not.*" See notes T6 and T43.

T64. This sentence translates "nämlich des Zufalls, der das Da-sein als solches ist, *weil es immer schon zufiel und da ist, bevor es sich wollte.*" See notes T10, T34, T42, and T51.

T65. Latin for "the first cause."

T66. "*[J]enes . . . 'Ringes.'*" "[W]restling" is "*Ringen.*"

T67. *Zar.* II, "On Redemption."

T68. "*Unwille.*"

T69. Alternatively, "devaluates the past time."

T70. "*Nicht ringend bezwingt.*" "In this temporal whole of the ring" is "*In diesem zeitlichen Ganzen des Ringes.*" Cf. note T66.

T71. See notes T6, T43, and T63.

T72. "*Voll-endet.*" Cf. note T39.

T73. "Case" is "*Fall,*" "accident" is "*Zufall,*" and "falls upon" is "*zu-fallen.*"

T74. "*Von Ohngefähr.*"

T75. The hunchback asks this question at the conclusion of *Zar.* II, "On Redemption," immediately before the speech "On Human Sagacity."

T76. Latin for "I believe because it is absurd."

T77. "*Gleich-Sein,*" literally "Equal-Being" or "Same-Being."

T78. "*Beisichsein.*"

T79. "*Wesen.*" Cf. note T95.

T80. Italian for "new life."

T81. "*Ver-ewigung.*"

T82. "*Bruch im Gedanken.*" "Dash" in German is "*Gedankenstrich,*" literally a "thought-line" or "thought-stroke." What on the face suggests a continuation of thought, the "*Gedankenstrich,*" in fact turns out to be an interruption of thought: that is the point of Löwith's wordplay here.

T83. The Dog Star.

T84. The word that Löwith omits here is "beloved."

T85. Latin for "God or nature," the first words of Spinoza's *Ethics*.

T86. The word for "light" is italicized in the original Nietzschean text.

T87. See note T86.

T88. Latin for "thinking thing."

T89. Latin for "extended thing."

T90. Ancient Greek for "paradox," "perplexity."

T91. Although the translation follows Löwith in combining the parenthetical remarks with the main sentence in each of the six stages here, Nietzsche separates them in every instance.

T92. French for "good sense."

T93. "*Not-wendig.*" See notes T6 and T43.

T94. "*Verkehrt*" can also mean "perverts" or "inverts."

T95. "*Wesen*" means "essence," "being," or "nature."

T96. "*Auswachen.*" "*Ausschlafen*" means "to sleep one's fill," "to sleep quite long enough," "to sleep off (inebriation, etc.)." Kaufmann translates "*auswachen*" as "to wake it off."

T97. "*Sicherheit,*" which also means "security."

T98. "*Die Sonne Sinkt,*" "The Sun Sinks," of the Dionysus Dithyrambs.

T99. French for "superior force," a force from on high.

T100. "*Leibhaftig.*" The same word is translated as "carnal" in the previous sentence.

T101. Latin for "By this sign [the Cross] you will conquer."

T102. Ancient Greek for "right," especially as dependent on law or custom.

T103. Ancient Greek for "endedness" or "completion." Here the word suggests a natural standard of perfection toward which things strive. The Latin *causae*, "causes," can refer to any of the four Aristotelian causes, including "efficient cause" (see note T104).

T104. Latin for "efficient cause" and "final cause."

T105. "*Sein und Schein,*" which actually means "Being and Appearance." The Kaufmann translation relied on here is otherwise admirably sensitive to both the form and the content of Nietzsche's verses, and in this case a more literal translation would require sacrificing the rhyme scheme.

T106. See John 19:5 in the New Testament.

T107. "*Zu-flucht,*" literally "flight to." "*Zuflucht*" means "refuge." Cf. three sentences earlier, "both seeking him in flight and fleeing him," "*hinfliehend und wegfliehend.*"

T108. "Crush the infamy," Voltaire's anti-ecclesiastical motto.

T109. The chthonian gods ruled the underworld. "*Chthōn*" means "earth" or "ground" in ancient Greek, and can also refer to the goddess Earth.

T110. The maenads were ecstatic women in the cult of Dionysus.

T111. "*Die Modernität hat ihren nächsten Ursprung in der Entstehung der neuzeitlichen Welt.*"

T112. Latin for "Everything is true that is perceived clearly and distinctly."

T113. Latin for "one bewitched."

T114. Latin for "thinking thing."

T115. Latin for "extended thing."

T116. "*Bestimmung.*" "Thoroughly determined" is "*durchgängig bestimmt.*" Fichte exploits several senses of "*Bestimmung*" in his work *The Destiny of Man* (*Die Bestimmung des Menschen*), and Löwith's discussion of Fichte continues the wordplay. See text at notes T117 through T121.

T117. "*Bestimmung.*" See note T116.

T118. "*[B]estimmte Mensch.*" See note T116.

T119. "*[B]estimmt.*" See note T116.

T120. "*Bestimmung des Menschen.*" See note T116.

T121. "*Bestimmung des Menschen.*" See note T116.

T122. Latin for "primary thing."

T123. "Having to do with the origin of the gods or of God."

T124. The text has "*ahnden,*" "punish," which is apparently a typographical error for "*ahnen,*" "suspect."

T125. French for "Supreme Being."

T126. "*Eigenheit.*"

T127. "*Eigene: Eigennutz, Eigensinn, Eigenwillen, Eigenliebe, und Eigentum.*"

T128. "*Die Eigenheit schließt jedes Eigene in sich.*"

T129. "*[D]es—Eigners.*"

T130. "*[S]o ist es 'das Ich,' nicht Ich bin es.*"

T131. "Same" is "*das Gleiche*"; "selfsame," "*das Selbe.*"

T132. "*Entwürfe des Menschen aus seiner Geworfenheit.*" See note T51.

T133. "*Eigensinnigkeit der Zeit.*"

T134. Italian for "gay science" and "serenity."

T135. See note T45.

T136. "The 'I' is detestable." *Pensées* I, 9, "Scattered Moral Thoughts," aph. 23.

T137. "*[D]em Alleinen, All-Einen.*"

T138. The German for "newspaper" is "*die Zeitung,*" and "time" is "*die Zeit.*"

T139. Latin for "metaphysical thing."

T140. "*Sich-wieder-Erinnern.*"

T141. "*Da-sein.*" See note T34.

T142. "Recollection."

T143. The pun is somewhat better in the German: "*auftreten*" literally means "to walk up," "to step up."

T144. "*Übergang,*" literally a going across. The primary meanings of "*kinesis*" are "motion," "change."

T145. The German text actually says "For what is not repeated . . ." "*[N]icht*" ("not") appears to be a typographical error.

T146. The German word inside the quotation marks here is "*Aufhebens.*" The extremely important, technical word for "sublation" in Hegel's philosophy is "*Aufhebung.*" The pun is thus a sharp disparagement of Hegel's whole system as a lot of erudite huffing and puffing that is oblivious of the seriousness of human existence.

T147. "*Wiederholung,*" for which the standard translation in this discussion will be "repetition." Cf. note T148.

T148. "*Repetition*" will be translated as "replication" to distinguish it from "*Wiederholung*." See note T147.

T149. "*[W]iederholt.*"

T150. "*Wiederholend.*"

T151. "*[V]erkehrte.*" See note T94.

T152. "*Hinterweltlich*," which Kaufmann translates as "after-wordly." The word refers to those who believe in or teach about a "backworld" or world behind the world of the senses. The word sounds very similar to the strongly pejorative adjective referring to "backwoodsmen" or "hillbillies," namely "*Hinterwäldlich*." Cf. note T47.

T153. "Superman, superspecies, superhero, excess high-spiritedness (see note T45), superdragon, over-blessed, over-pitying, over-kindness, excess riches, excess time."

T154. From Horace, *Odes* II, 10:

> Better you will live, Licinius, if
> While seaborn steering, never you press too close—
> Bewaring the storm, affrightened—
> To the treacherous shore.

This chapter of the *Odes* teaches the "golden mean."

T155. The fifth line was apparently composed by Strindberg:

> Meanwhile, enjoy insanity! Farewell and Adieu!

T156. French for "wretched, miserable, petty, shabby."

T157. Latin for "the mean [is also] gold." Cf. note T154.

T158. "*[N]icht schon im Über*menschen, sondern über-*menschlich.*"

T159. "*[W]ahr-sagt.*" "*Wahr*" means "truly"; "*wahrsagen*," "to prophesy."

T160. "*[D]ie einmalige Wiedergeburt aus der Umkehr lehrt.*"

T161. Latin for "lamb of God." These words open a liturgical prayer to Jesus Christ as the Savior of mankind.

T162. "*Not-wendigkeit.*" See notes T6 and T43.

T163. "*Wende der Not.*" See notes T6, T43, and T162.

T164. Ancient Greek for "nature."

T165. Ancient Greek for "philosophers of nature," e.g., Democritus, Empedocles. The word literally means "experts on nature."

T166. "*[D]er Mensch ist nicht da durch sich selbst*," literally "man is not there by means of himself."

T167. Löwith's quotation marks.

T168. This Greek term means "cosmic man," "well-ordered man."

T169. "*Nun sind Sie—bist du—.*" Nietzsche shifts from the formal "*Sie*" to the familiar "*du*," as if Burckhardt belonged to Nietzsche's family or closest friends.

T170. See the last sentence of the Foreword to the first edition of this book.

T171. "On the Death of a Destroyer."

T172. Andreas-Salomé's book was reprinted in 1983, but in the meantime it has gone out of print again.

T173. "*Selbstübersteigerung.*"

T174. "Short of" translates "*diesseits*," which is the opposite of "*jenseits*," the first word in the German title of *Beyond Good and Evil: Prelude to a Philosophy of the Future*. The point is that Ewald's failure to get beyond good and evil prevents him from comprehending Nietzsche's teaching.

T175. The German is "*da-zu-sein*."

T176. "Cosmological vision." As mentioned in the Acknowledgments, all translations of French below were generously provided by Robin Cackett, who again deserves most cordial thanks for his generous and crucial contributions to this English edition.

T177. "One did not understand until now that one could accept the Eternal Recurrence and the Superman at the same time. It seemed as if the grand vision of the Regenerated Man would not appear but at the end of a straight and ascending path. But how would such a straight ascent be possible within the eternal recurrence? The answer is that time has a bent ray. In infinity all straight lines turn back upon themselves. The fatality of the eternal recurrence makes possible a pure contingency since all our actions modify their past in view of the future. The decision by which we agree to live our present again is the immensely free action that justifies the worlds, not by its content, but by its freedom.

". . . The Eternal Recurrence is the pledge of our Superhumanity. Superhumanity allows us to accept the Eternal Recurrence. From now on one will not separate these two ideas any more."

T178. "Mysteries."

T179. "A great mystical intuition, the value of which does not depend on its content."

T180. "Physical gravity," "gravity of the past."

T181. "Hence, there are two aspects to the eternal recurrence, and not one of the commentators has noticed them. Physics suffices to demonstrate the eternal recurrence in the material world; Nietzsche, in following the Oriental wisdom, will try to descend to Hades in order to abolish the past where the forgotten dead sleep. One must not confound the two resurrections, but they are simultaneous; and this simultaneity frees us from the burden that is—next to Gravity—the heaviest burden to carry: the Past."

T182. "But this second theory that meshes with the first: how can it be discussed? It translates the profound feelings of Nietzsche before the universe."

T183. "What shall we make of this free eternity? But what else can we make of it than to become supermen?"

T184. "It is a beautiful poem that cannot be communicated. With its help Nietzsche steps out of his solitary and somber refuge and presents himself to us with a clarity that belongs only to himself. We, however, retain nothing thereof but the fascinating emotion that made him feel his union with nature and with humanity."

T185. "Nature," "humanity."

T186. "He pretends to emerge from the abyss of irrationality and to climb the peak of rational liberation. An inexhaustible effort and, without doubt, a contradictory one, but an effort that translates a powerful need of modernity. Nietzsche is not the sole victim of this innermost discord who strives to regain inner integrity. Perhaps he just suffered more than anybody else from it. The present times are not tragic, because their mysticism constantly resorbs heroic affirmation. Therefore, the contemporary tragedies are, at bottom, lyric poems; and it is for that reason that the tragedy that is contained in *Zarathustra* was not able to disentangle itself from the verbal music, on which it floats as its reflex."

T187. The expression translated as "an ambiguous advocate of life" is *"ein zweideutiger Für-*Sprecher *des Lebens."* Löwith implies that Nietzsche not only vocalizes life but also argues on behalf of it.

T188. "In effect the monistic theory of the world out of which Nietzsche made his last philosophy—curiously enough, the German mind, monistic by nature, is unable to arrive at the definition of an irreducible duality without seeking to resolve it by synthesis—this theory induces him to extend and enlarge his humanism to such a degree that it takes account of the whole universe: he is not satisfied with his definition of the hero unless it also explains to him the infusoria and the planets, and only linked and subordinated to some cosmic chain of interconnections does tragic morality acquire all its value. Consequently, the tragic purity no longer is a means to oppose or expose man to fatality; rather it has to discover this fatality in man himself, and the last word of the human ideal would be nothing but the awareness of the universe in oneself. Hence the extreme point of inner purification and the total experience of heroism do not consist in dissociating man as much as possible from nature, but in his becoming equal to nature, his dissolving in it, his feeling it alive in himself. . . . The fundamental duality of man and destiny, of freedom and nature—the principle both of the Christian and of the tragic struggle—is finally resolved; man has been freed for nothing but the Dionysian excess."

T189. "Spirit," "consciousness," "judgment," "reasoning," "will," "elementary instinct."

T190. "Nietzsche's efforts aimed, from the very beginning, at restoring this consciousness in its supreme richness, lucidity, and autonomy; in reality, however, such consciousness has no place any more in the Dionysian universe. Too remote is the contact henceforth, too necessary the cosmic chain of interconnections, no longer are there, between the cosmic fatalities and the human gestures, any fissures in the substance of the world, where human freedom could insert the play of its deliberations or negations."

T191. "Consciousness," "mechanism," "human dignity," "elementary life," "will," "instinct," "human values," "natural phenomena," "determinism," "fatality," "freedom."

T192. "Logical absurdity."

T193. ". . . whether, in annihilating the autonomy of the human will in that profound power of the universe, Nietzsche has not made tragedy impossible while striving to make it purer. For, tragedy precisely assumes a fatality that is alien to man and a will that is irreducible to destiny, since it assumes a conflict between the one and the other. . . . Yet in Nietzschean mysticism the superhuman Moira and the actions of the hero both follow the same inflexible tracks. Fatality is tragic only insofar as man does not consent to it; the fatality of crystals and plants is not at all tragic, the planets are not at all in conflict with their ellipses. One of the greatest attempts to exalt and to shape heroism comes down to putting man on a par with phenomena. Hence everything that has been achieved is not far from being lost."

T194. "Communion."

T195. "We have already noted how German all this is, how German it is to throw out of balance two irreconcilable experiences so as to arrive at their synthesis. Like Goethe, like Hölderlin, like Novalis, Nietzsche founders on the seduction of pantheism. . . . Hence man, whose dignity no doubt lies in the rejection of the universal innocence, has become an instance of the universal innocence. . . . We do not deny the grandeur of this new man, enthusiastic about the universe, chained to a past and to a future both unlimited, necessary in every moment to the world that ceases and to the world that is being born, and equally weighty from a heritage and a posterity of cosmogonies. But this grandeur that arises from the necessity of man within the universe and from the gratitude that acknowledges such necessity, is nothing else but the grandeur of the world itself, reflected in ourselves. This grandeur is certain; but Pascal has defined another one, which the former, for all its being unified, will not be able to crush."

T196. "[A]lmost scandalous in him who has carried the properly human exigencies so high. One regrets that the most painful effort for the liberation of man, for the violence of the soul and the purity of desires, that the most subtle reflections, the longest disciplines, and the hardest chastities have led Nietzsche to nothing but a grand yet simple fervor that is hardly different from the ecstasy of life that a child achieves out of its own spontaneity."

T197. "The prince of liberations," "renaissance of idols."

T198. "Mysticism for a shadow."

T199. "A man who was not Nietzsche any more went to live a clashless life that finally accorded with the rhythm of the world. The illness overtook his mind without attacking the basic organic mechanisms. Nietzsche's assumption that consciousness is not necessary in order to accomplish the actions necessary for life was verified on himself. Consciousness, 'the little light at the surface of life,' had been extinguished; life went on, still ordered, consenting, fully embracing the evolution of the world: the body animated by this life was nothing more than a fragment of the universal mechanism. But the fragile gleam that had been extinguished in Nietzsche had been the sovereign element, which he had failed to recognize as the sole adversary to fatality, superior to it in dignity and, sometimes, in power. The world had reconquered a patch of human freedom."

T200. "Concupiscence of pain."

T201. "The creation of joy," "creation of luck."

T202. "Nietzsche could shout his contempt at Rousseau and . . . speak of 'that wretch' who 'wanted, he too, the return to nature.' In fact, however, he does not reproach Rousseau for having wanted the return to nature. Rather, it is for having believed that nature is equality whereas nature is inequality and war, for having wanted to rediscover morality in nature whereas one has to escape from morality in nature. Thus, in order to judge civilization Nietzsche takes up the principles of Rousseau and reverses them. Like Rousseau he seeks salvation in a return to the virtues of the natural man."

T203. "There is no universe around Nietzsche; in the towns where he strays, he looks for nothing but a climate more suitable to his nerves, a resort more favorable for his work; when he proposes to a girl, it is only after he has recognized in her a disciple; when he falls ill, it is because he has thought too much: when he finds or loses a friend, it is in philosophical discussion; the countryside for him is only solitude; his sky . . . has no clouds and no dreams . . . , it is just the pure and empty arena where his intellectual flight is most direct and least delayed. . . . The most physical of the innocences, sleep, is not granted to him without reservation; he has to buy it with the help of chloral. . . . There is nothing in this body, in this view, in these lips, that is made for ordinary human relationship, gesture, embrace, or discourse: 'He who has lost the world must gain his own world.' There is nothing around Nietzsche: never has a thinker remained so relentlessly enclosed in himself.

". . . This philosopher of life has neglected nothing except living.

". . . Unable to save his solitude across occupations, love affairs, and mundane relations, he has to part from the world."

T204. "[T]o imagine a world more painful, more crushing, more suffocating than the world he resented. . . . It is important, for the creation of joy, that the world abandon man, . . . that it should have no end and meaning, that it not lead us anywhere."

T205. "It is easy and therefore vain to look for the arbitrary and puerile elements in the teaching of the Eternal Recurrence; suffice it to say that it is the normal outcome of the philosophy of solitude and its metaphysical fatality: not the most ingenious, or the most plausible, or the most consoling, but the most terrible explanation of the world. Well, the most terrible that has been sought."

T206. "His lost tragedy," "salvation," "happiness."

T207. "In search of death"; "to live and die in full."

T208. "[T]he creator of the new tragedy wanted to define nothing else for man than a dignified path to death."

T209. "An untiring provocation of fatality."

T210. "'*Rationalistic*' heroism." Löwith italicizes "*rationaliste*."

T211. See note T6.

T212. "[T]he formless cults of the superman, of innocence, of the Eternal Recurrence, that cannot but deform and impoverish him. Even more: deluded by Germanic mysticism from which he mistakenly believes himself emancipated, victim of the romantic heritage that he has forsworn in vain, he does not hesitate to alter the tragic essence itself of his hero whom he wishes to define and purify."

T213. "[I]t is still a Germany that he opposes to Germany, cults to its cults, a drunkenness to its drunkenness, the Eternal Recurrence to Becoming, and the Valhalla of Dionysus to the Valhalla of Wotan" . . .

T214. "In the Greece to which he recurs, it is the Greek Germanism that he discovers: not Greece, but that German colony which the painters, philosophers, and poets of his country have established in Greece, the territory of which, disregarding Athens and Plato, stretches from Delphi to Eleusis and from Orpheus to Empedocles: a Greece of myths, orgies, mysteries, hazardous philosophies, of formulas and initiations, a real Greece, no doubt, but not *the* Greece."

T215. "The sense for the moment is properly Mediterranean, the power to grasp in time an immediate presence, a friendship. . . . For a philosophy of metamorphoses, the present is nothing but an abstraction, a point in time, 'a bridge and a passage' from the past to the future; for us, present is the most real reality. A world untiringly tending to surpass itself does not allow of any existence that has a pure and incomparable value. The Mediterranean wisdom, on the contrary, makes not a passage but an end of every minute, attaches an absolute and irreducible price to it, encloses therein an irrestorably depleted and exhausted pleasure: every moment thus receives . . . a value in itself, a magnificent uselessness. Remarkable example: Mr. André Gide, taking from Nietzsche the main lines of his attitude toward life, in one point completes this attitude, and that is in creating a philosophy of the moment. The whole Latin aestheticism of perfection ultimately derives from a particularly strong and vivid apprehension of the present: all perfection is eternalized moment. It is this divinization that is lacking in Nietzsche. . . . The Nietzschean hero knows the will to power but not the action. Beyond the sense of Being, it is the sense of the moment that Nietzsche is deficient in; and beyond the sense of the moment, it is the sense of action. Every philosophy of becoming ignores action."

T216. "German mind, out of balance by nature."

T217. "[T]o bundle into a unity the hostile forces of destiny and man, magisterially opposed for the tragic struggle. It is necessary, then, that man integrate himself into a monistic theory of the world, that he stop having another reality than that of the moment within the universal movement. He agrees with the world even when he judges it or is being crushed by it. Hence the philosophy of power finds itself driven to the negation of a power properly human and different from the natural forces, to the negation of a freedom of choice, a freedom to weigh and to refuse. Such a philosophy can triumph only in the realization of the most intimate and spontaneous accord of the decisions of the soul with the movements of the world: innocence is now its aim. Thus the image of the great civilized man of the Caesarean type tends, in the last works of Nietzsche, to give way to the image of the instinctive barbarian."

T218. A "Note on the Eternal Recurrence of the Same" concludes the essay on Nietzsche's *Zarathustra* in Heidegger's *Vorträge und Aufsätze*. It reads as follows (translation mine):

Nietzsche himself knew that his "most abysmal idea" remains a riddle. All the less may we suppose that we can solve the riddle. The darkness of this last idea of Western metaphysics must not mislead us into evading it through subterfuges.

At bottom there are only two subterfuges.

Either one says, This idea of Nietzsche's is a kind of "mysticism" and does not belong before [the bar of] thinking;

Or one says: This idea is already quite ancient. It amounts to the long familiar cyclical image of world events. Within Western philosophy, it can first be identified in Heraclitus.

The second piece of information, like each of its kind, says nothing at all. For how should it help us if it is established about an idea that it occurs, e.g., "already" in Leibniz or even "already" in Plato? What is this statement supposed to mean if it leaves what is thought by Leibniz and by Plato lying in the same darkness as the idea that one deems to have been clarified by such historical references?

As concerns the first subterfuge, however, according to which Nietzsche's idea of the eternal recurrence of the same is a fantastic mysticism: well might the current epoch teach us better—supposing, to be sure, that thinking is destined to bring to light the *essence* of modern technology.

What else is the essence of the modern engine than one embodiment of the eternal recurrence of the same? But the essence of this machine is neither something mechanized nor even something mechanical. Just as little does Nietzsche's idea of the eternal recurrence of the same lend itself to be interpreted in a mechanistic sense.

The fact that Nietzsche explained and experienced his most abysmal idea from [the standpoint of] the Dionysian is only testimony that he still had to conceive that idea metaphysically—and only metaphysically. But this fact does not contradict [the observation] that this most abysmal idea conceals something that has not been thought about, something that remains aloof from metaphysics.

Cf. *Was heißt Denken,* W[inter] S[emester] 51/52, which was published as a book in 1954 by Verlag M. Niemeyer, Tübingen.

T219. There is considerable wordplay here. "To turn into" is "*Verkehrung in,*" "overturning" is "*Umkehrung,*" "its opposite, that which has been overturned" is "*das Umgekehrte,*" "reversal" is "*Umkehr,*" and "recurrence" is "*Wiederkehr.*"

T220. "*Unwesen,*" literally, "deplorable state of affairs" or "mischief," depending on the context.

T221. "*[I]m Wesenlosen.*"

T222. "*[M]öglichst gleichförmiges und gleichmäßiges.*"

T223. The passage comes from *Zar.* III, "The Convalescent," 2.

T224. Cf. *BGE,* aph. 280.

T225. Or, more literally, "the sickness of time."

# Index of Names

Braces { } enclosing a page number indicate that the person is referred to but not explicitly named.

When two notes with the same number appear on a single page, they are distinguished in this index by a superscript numeral: e.g., "n. 6$^1$" refers to the first of two note 6's on that page.

Abelard, Peter, 138
Aeschylus, 176
Alexander (the Great), 111
Anaximander, 117
Andler, Charles, 195, 196, 205–207, 240 (nn. 140, 147), 245 (n. 266), 246 (n. 276), 248 (n. 24), 250 (n. 39), 256 (nn. 14, 16)
Andreas-Salomé, Lou, 196–199, 246 (n. 278), 248 (n. 24), 265 (n. T172)
Arion, 205
Aristotle, xxv, xxvi, 8, 119, 248 (n. 27)
Augustine, Saint, 119

Bachofen, J. J., 210
Baeumler, Alfred, xii, xx, xxi, 93, 195, 196, 210–214, 248 (n. 31), 257 (nn. 21, 24)
Bahlsen, Gerhard, xii, xx, 233 (n. 4)
Bahnsen, J. F. A., 49

Bauer, Bruno, 151, 237 (n. 44)
Becker, O., 244 (nn. 255, 259), 257 (n. 25)
Belyi, Andrei, xiii
Benardete, Seth, xix
Benn, Gottfried, xiii, 196, 257 (n. 26)
Bergmann, Ernst, 257 (n. 26)
Bergson, Henri, xiv
Bernoulli, C. A., 231, 234 (n. 6$^1$), 235 (n. 39)
Bertram, Ernst, 195, 196, 204–205, 210, 214, 219, 247 (n. 8)
Binswanger, L., 248 (n. 27)
Bizet, G., 158
Bollnow, O. F., 246 (n. 292)
Boscovich, R. J., 94
Brandes, Georg, xiv, 128, 192, 195, 243 (n. 241)
Bryusov, Valeri, xiii
Buddha, 40, 114
Burckhardt, Jacob, xx (n. 4), 115, 192–193, 204, 234 (n. 5$^1$), 236 (n. 2),

238 (nn. 61, 70), 246 (n. 287), 248 (n. 25), 265 (n. T169)

Caesar, 72, 135
Carrouges, M., 232
Celsus, 119–120
Columbus, C., 4, 11, 100, 115, 123, 135, 174
Confucius, 242 (n. 202a)
Copernicus, N., 11, 52, 163, 188

Dannhauser, Werner, xxvii (n. 25)
D'Annunzio, Gabriele, xiv, 195
Dante, 257 (n. 23)
Deesz, Gisela, 196
Delius, Frederick, xiv
Democritus, 265 (n. T165)
Descartes, René, xxvi, 15, 95, 138–141, 149, 150, 151, 187, 202, 216, 219, 240 (n. 133), 249 (nn. 2², 11²)
Diesel, E., 257 (n. 26)
Dilthey, Wilhelm, xiv, 139, 249 (n. 3¹), 250 (nn. 12, 25)
Diogenes, 169
Dostoyevsky, F. M., 47, 231
Drews, Arthur, 202, 256 (n. 6)
Dühring, K. E., 49, 94, 238 (n. 69)

Eckermann, J. P., 161
Eleatics, 169, 170
Emerson, R. W., 249 (n. 1¹)
Emmerich, Erika, 196, 214–215, 256 (n. 16), 257 (nn. 22, 25, 26)
Empedocles, xxv, 96–97, 119, 175–176, 180, 220, 247 (n. 12), 248 (n. 27), 265 (n. T165)
Epicureans, 135
Eudemus, xxv, 119, 248 (n. 27)
Ewald, Oskar, 196, 199–202, 256 (n. 3), 266 (n. T174)
Exekias, 233

Feuerbach, L., 37, 38, 39, 151, 152, 260 (n. T19)
Fichte, J. G., xxvi, xxvii, 142–146, 149, 153, 203, 260 (n. T19), 264 (n. T116)
Figgis, J. N., 231
Förster, B., 258 (n. 26)
Förster-Nietzsche, Elisabeth, xii, xx, 231, 256 (n. 4)
Frederick, William IV, 80

Gadamer, Hans-Georg, xix (n. 1)
Gast, Peter, 128, 231, 245 (n. 266), 246 (nn. 291, 297)
George, Stefan, xiii, 8, 195, 196, 205, 207, 233 (n. 3), 256 (n. 12)
Gersdorff, Carl von, 99, 256 (n. 52)
Gide, André, xiii, 195, 220, 238 (n. 65)
Giese, F., 257–258 (n. 26)
Giesz, Ludwig, 196, 223–225
Goethe, J. W. von, xxvii, 58, 85, 101, 113, 120, 161, 217
Gomperz, H., 248 (n. 27)
Grau, G.-G., 232
Gründel, Ernst Günther, 257 (n. 26)
Guardini, R., 238 (n. 65)
Günther, J., 257 (n. 26)

Haecker, Theodor, 242 (n. 205)
Hafiz, 58
Hartmann, Eduard von, xxvi, 49, 146
Heckel, Karl, 202, 256 (n. 9)
Hecker, K., 237 (n. 46)
Hegel, G. W. F., xxvii, 8, 37, 38, 39, 40, 49, 82, 95, 149–150, 151, 154, 169, 170, 171, 204, 209, 237 (n. 40), 238 (n. 59), 247 (n. 10), 250 (n. 36), 253 (n. 1), 260 (n. T19)
Heidegger, Martin, xi, xiii, xiv, xv, xvi, xvii, xxi–xxiii, {8}, 196, 225–229, 232, 233 (nn. 1², 3), 237 (n. 52), 242 (n. 201), 254 (n. 25), 258 (n. 30), 261 (n. T46), 264 (n. 146), 270 (n. T218)
Heimsoeth, H., 249 (n. 1¹)
Helmholtz, H. von, 94, 245 (n. 266)
Heraclitus, xv, xxv, xxvii, 115, 116–119, 122, 147, 170, 171, 180, 213, 242 (n. 188), 248 (n. 27)
Hesse, Herman, xiii
Hildebrandt, Kurt, xxvii (n. 25), 195
Hölderlin, F., xxii (n. 11), 8, 211, 217
Horace, 177
Horneffer, August, 256 (n. 4)
Horneffer, Ernst, 202, 256 (n. 4)
Husserl, E., xxvi

Immermann, K., 237 (n. 46)
Ivanov, Vyacheslav, xiii

Jaeger, W., 248 (n. 27)
Jaspers, Karl, xii, xiv, xv, xxiii, 196, 221–223, 225, 231, 233 (n. 1²)

Job, 168, 171
Joel, K., 195
Judas, 205
Jung, C. G., 233 (n. 1²)
Jung, K., 240 (n. 140)
Jünger, Ernst, 196, 236 (n. 13), 258 (n. 26)
Justin Martyr, 119

Kant, Immanuel, xvii (n. 5), xxvi, xxvii, 11, 141–142, 149, 159, 161, 162, 166, 171, 202, 210, 221, 244 (n. 255), 250 (n. 17)
Kaufmann, Walter, xxiv (n. 17), 225, 260 (n. T22), 261 (n. T36), 262 (nn. T53, T60), 263 (nn. T96, T105), 265 (n. T152)
Keller, Gottfried, 158
Kepler, J., 163
Kerner, J., 240 (n. 140)
Kierkegaard, Søren, xx, xxvii, 8, 53, 82, 157, 158, 167–173, 221, 223, 240 (n. 133), 249 (n. 11²), 252 (n. 35)
Klages, Ludwig, xiv, 93, 195, 196, 207–210, 214, 236 (n. 8), 240 (n. 132), 244 (n. 261), 257 (n. 17)
Koyré, A., 249 (n. 2²)
Krieck, E., 257 (n. 26)
Kynast, K., 257 (n. 26)

Labriolle, P., 238 (n. 92)
Lampert, Lawrence, xxvii (n. 25)
Landry, H., 256 (n. 13)
Langbehn, J., 176, 253 (n. 5)
Lawrence, D. H., 195
Lawrence, T. E., 195
Leibniz, G. W., 169, 271 (n. T218)
Leonardo da Vinci, 11
Lessing, Theodor, 257 (n. 19)
Levison, Arnold, xix (n. 1)
Lévy, A., 250 (n. 39)
Lichtenberg, C. G., 238 (n. 92)
Lorrain, Claude, 205
Löwith, Karl, xi–xvii, xix–xxviii, 233 (n. 1²), 237 (nn. 40, 52), 250 (n. 36), 252 (n. 35), 255 (n. 37), 257 (n. 17), 258 (n. 30), 259 (nn. T10, T11, T25, T30), 261 (nn. T37, T43, T46), 262 (nn. T53, T60, T82), 263 (n. T91), 264 (n. T116), 265 (n. T167), 267 (n. T187), 269 (n. T210)
Lubac, H. de, 232

Lucretius, 18
Luther, Martin, 112, 151, 186

Mahler, Gustav, xiv
Mainländer, Philipp, 49
Malesherbes, C.-G. de Lamoignon de, 240 (n. 133)
Mann, Thomas, 196
Marx, Karl, xx, xxvii, 82, 138, 150, 153, 154, 155, 253 (n. 1)
Maulnier, Thierry, 196, 216–221
Mayer, Julius Robert, 94, 245 (n. 266)
Meier, Heinrich, xxii (n. 13)
Meyer, Richard Moritz, 202, 256 (n. 7)
Mittasch, A., 245 (n. 266)
Möbius, P. J., 63, 240 (n. 140), 245 (n. 267)
Moeller van den Bruck, A., 257 (n. 26)
Musil, Robert, xiii, 196

Napoleon, 85, 205, 247 (n. 8)
Natsume, S., 242 (n. 202a)
Naumann, G., 238 (n. 92)
Nemesius, 248 (n. 27)
Nigg, W., 232
Novalis, 217

Obenauer, K. J., 253 (n. 2)
Oehler, R., {8}, 233 (n. 3)
Origen, 119
Otto, W. F., 238 (n. 92), 242 (n. 185), 247 (n. 14)
Overbeck, Franz, 20, 87, 181, 192, 210, 231, 233 (n. 2²), 235 (n. 39), 239 (n. 118), 240 (n. 128), 243 (n. 211), 255 (n. 28)

Paneth, Josef, 259 (n. T1)
Pannwitz, Rudolf, 195, 256 (n. 50)
Parmenides, 18, 248 (n. 27)
Pascal, Blaise, 39, 139, 159, 217, 240 (n. 133)
Paul, Saint, 82, 127
Philo, 255 (n. 36)
Plato, xiv, xxiii, xxv, xxvii, xxviii, 97, 98, 119, 147, 220, 248 (n. 27), 271 (n. T218)
Platonism, Christian, 182, 221, 226
Podach, E. F., 231, 234 (n. 5¹), 246 (n. 287), 253 (n. 5)
Porphyry, 119

Pre-Socratics, xxiii, 95, 110, 115, 119, 187

Prinzhorn, H., 257 (n. 26)

Proclus, 37

Pyrrhon, 13, 33, 260 (n. T17)

Pythagoreans, 135

Reinhardt, Karl, 248 (n. 27), 249 (n. 8[1])

Rey, Abel, 245 (n. 266)

Richter, Raoul, 202, 256 (n. 8)

Riehl, Aloise, 195, 202, 256 (n. 5)

Rilke, Rainer Maria, 195

Rohde, E., 234 (n. 26), 235 (n. 19), 236 (n. 2)

Rosenberg, Alfred, 257 (n. 26)

Rousseau, J.-J., xxvii, 187, 218, 240 (n. 133)

Rubens, P. P., 58

Ruedorffer, J. J., 248 (n. 26)

Ruge, A., 235 (n. 1[2])

Saint-Exupéry, Antoine de, 195

Scheler, M., 252 (n. 15)

Schelling, F. W. J., xxvi, xxvii, 79, 80, 82, 146–149, 176, 186, 243 (n. 210), 247 (n. 14), 250 (n. 29), 255 (nn. 34, 35), 260 (n. T19)

Schestow, L., 231

Schlechta, Karl, xxi (n. 7), 103, 246 (nn. 292–294, 299), 255 (n. 29)

Schleiermacher, Friedrich, 260 (n. T19)

Schmitt, Carl, xxiii (n. 13), 235 (n. 1[2])

Schopenhauer, Arthur, xxvi, 8, 23, 49, 58, 78, 80, 146, 159, 175, 195, 244 (n. 255), 245 (n. 267), 248 (n. 1), 256 (n. 10), 257 (n. 19)

Seillière, E., 240 (n. 140)

Shaw, George Bernard, xiii

Simmel, Georg, xii, xiv, {87}, 195, 196, 202–204, 244 (n. 242)

Socrates, xxiii, xxvii–xxviii, 115

Solovjeff, W., 231

Sophocles, 8

Spengler, Oswald, 195–196, 236 (n. 13)

Spinoza, B., xxvi, 89, 263 (n. T85)

Stirner, M., xxvii, 138, 150–155, 250 (n. 39)

Stoeving, Curt, 176

Stoics, xxv, 15, 119, 135, 248 (n. 27)

Strauss, David Friedrich, 260 (n. T19)

Strauss, Leo, xxiii (n. 14)

Strauss, Richard, xiv

Strindberg, August, xiii, 128, 177, 246 (n. 297), 265 (n. T155)

Teichmuller, G., 246 (n. 276), 255 (n. 42)

Thiel, R., 256 (n. 12)

Thompson, Francis, 249 (n. 7[1])

Tilgher, A., 248 (n. 27)

Tolstoy, L., 165

Tschizewskij, D., 238 (n. 59)

Vaihinger, Hans, xii

Voltaire, F. M. A., 36, 237 (n. 35)

Wagner, Cosima, 22

Wagner, Richard, 22, 27, 58, 80, 104, 110, 111, 136, 158, 159, 176, 184, 186, 195, 245 (n. 267), 247 (nn. 8, 9), 251 (nn. 1, 6), 255 (n. 27), 257 (n. 19)

Weichelt, H., 255 (n. 29)

Weininger, Otto, xxvii, 157–167, 168, 171, 202, 251 (n. 1), 252 (n. 22)

Winckelmann, J., 113, 120

Wirth, W., 257–258 (n. 26)

Würzbach, F., 232

Yeats, William Butler, xiii

Yorck von Wartenburg, P., 249 (n. 3[1]), 250 (n. 12)

Zeller, E., 248 (n. 27)